D1477469

# The Art of Musical Phrasing in the Eighteenth Century

# Eastman Studies in Music

Ralph P. Locke, Senior Editor
Eastman School of Music

## Additional Titles in Music of the Eighteenth and Early Nineteenth Centuries

A complete list of titles in the Eastman studies in Music Series,
in order of publication, may be found at the end of this book.

# The Art of Musical Phrasing in the Eighteenth Century

## Punctuating the Classical "Period"

### STEPHANIE D. VIAL

UNIVERSITY OF ROCHESTER PRESS

First published 2008

University of Rochester Press
668 Mt. Hope Avenue, Rochester, NY 14620, USA
www.urpress.com
and Boydell & Brewer Limited
PO Box 9, Woodbridge, Suffolk IP12 3DF, UK
www.boydellandbrewer.com

ISBN-13: 978-1-58046-034-7
ISBN-10: 1-58046-034-8

ISSN: 1071-9989

**Library of Congress Cataloging-in-Publication Data**

Vial, Stephanie.
  The art of musical phrasing in the eighteenth century : punctuating the classical
period / Stephanie D. Vial.
     p. cm. – (Eastman studies in music, ISSN 1071-9989 ; v. 55)
  Includes bibliographical references and index.
  ISBN-13: 978-1-58046-034-7 (hardcover : alk. paper)
  ISBN-10: 1-58046-034-8
  1.  Performance practice (Music)–History–18th century.  2.  Music–
Interpretation (Phrasing, dynamics, etc.)  3.  Musical notation.  I.  Title.
  ML457.V53 2008
  781.4'309033–dc22

                    2008000925

A catalogue record for this title is available from the British Library.

*In memory of a much-loved father and sister*
*Donald Vial, 1923–2005*
*Diane Krista Vial, 1950–2003*

# Contents

# *Preface*

The idea that eighteenth-century musicians conceived their compositions as comprised of the punctuation marks of language is one that immediately captivated my interest and curiosity as a performer. I could readily imagine a full cadence as the musical expression of a period, a lesser point of repose as analogous to a comma or a colon, a vehement rhythmic pattern as an exclamation point, an upturned melody as suggestive of a question mark, and on and on. The process of further pursuing this very vivid analogy to language not only profoundly impacted my playing, but led me far deeper than I had anticipated into a whole new and rich linguistic world—one inhabited by the likes of Haydn, Mozart, and Beethoven—with its varied and complex rhetorical, philosophical, scientific, social, and political influences.

My particular interest in the subject of musical punctuation lies in what the analogy can teach us about the moment-by-moment inflections and nuances (sometimes subtle, sometimes dramatic) within the single musical *period*. Rather than focusing on larger periodic structures (how individual sentences become the building blocks for movement-length forms), I have directed my attention towards how music's smaller and more discreet rhythmic and tonal gestures can be manipulated to create the diverse effects of punctuation. I want to understand how the rise and fall of melody impacts simple harmonic progressions, half cadences, and full cadences. And I ask: how also might the addition of articulation symbols—a series of two-note slurs, or perhaps a longer slur over the bar line—affect the structure and/or expression among the punctuation points of a musical sentence? To what extent do displaced rhythmic and melodic emphases and accents alter the overall metrical orientation and direction of a phrase? I believe it is the performer's ability to recognize, analyze, and above all, persuasively execute these and similar punctuation-related details, which ultimately brings the musical language of the classical "period" to life, a language that is at once compelling, spontaneous, imaginative, and meaningful.

The present work is organized into three parts. The first, which requires the least technical musical knowledge, explores the details of the role of punctuation in eighteenth-century rhetorical theory. In its chapters, I aim to establish the nature of the analogy as well as the historical basis for punctuation's application to music. This, I feel, is key to using the analogy effectively in modern performance. We cannot expect the application of musical punctuation to lay bare the precise semantic content of a musical composition (where words are lacking). But by our recognizing the spirit in which the analogy was adopted and acknowledging punctuation's crucial role among the rhetorical ideals of the Age of Enlightenment, the study of musical punctuation can indeed provide very specific and significant information about the nature of eighteenth-century musical expression.

Part 2 is the core of the work, its three chapters aimed most directly at the practicality of applying musical punctuation to modern performance. The subjects covered in these chapters are: identifying punctuation's written and unwritten rests embedded in the conventions of eighteenth-century musical notation; appreciating the essential distinction and relationship between the expressive symbols of articulation and those of punctuation; and, most importantly, understanding the role of a composition's character or affect (often subject to frequent and sudden shifts) in determining the length and nature of its pauses. Again an historical perspective is taken with the recognition that while musical notation has changed very little since the eighteenth century, the conventions associated with it have—based on more modern aesthetics of sound production, the physical gestures and venues of performance, and the instruments themselves.

In Part 3 we examine some of the most detailed, case-specific theory on musical punctuation. Its two chapters on the very divergent qualities of *recitative* (representing musical prose) and the *minuet* (representing musical verse) demonstrate the degree of thoroughness with which eighteenth-century musicians were willing to explore the relationship (areas of both confluence and departure) between language and music. The theories discussed encompass complex and intertwining elements of punctuation—including concepts of harmonic and melodic contour, gesture, rhythm, meter, accent, and emphasis—all of them ultimately relevant to and suggestive of performance practices. The work concludes with two appendixes. Appendix A provides a translation of the single most extensive study of musical punctuation as it applies to vocal recitative—F. W. Marpurg's essay from his *Kritische Briefe über die Tonkunst*. Appendix B provides a comprehensive chart of diverse theoretical and practical references to the subject of musical punctuation, its entries presented chronologically and interspersed with contemporary accounts from language.

# *Acknowledgments*

The present work is the result of many years spent garnering insight and information through research and performance experience. I am indebted to a great number of people who have helped and encouraged me along this gradual (and by no means completed) path of discovery. The project could never have been begun had I not been given the opportunity to attend Cornell University and to work with John Hsu, whose understanding of and ability as a performer and conductor to convey the expressive nuances and phrase structures of eighteenth-century music has been a constant source of inspiration. I am forever grateful to him for his warmth and generosity as a teacher, and to the other members of the Cornell community, particularly Malcolm Bilson, James Webster, and Neal Zaslaw, for the wonderful learning environment they helped to foster, and for their introduction to a level of music making where scholarship and performance combine to produce the most creative and exciting results.

I also owe a great deal to the many performers, scholars, and students with whom I have had the privilege of making music: in particular my fellow Cornellians Tom Beghin, Blaise Bryski, Elizabeth Field, and Andrew Willis; the extraordinary flute and keyboard pair, Mary Oleskiewicz and David Schulenberg; Lex Silbiger and the graduate students and community members of the Duke University collegium musicum, with whom it was a great pleasure to work; and my wonderful and supportive colleague Brent Wissick at the University of North Carolina at Chapel Hill. I want to thank Gesa Kordes and Johannes Rudolph for their very willing help and advice with many of my German translations. I would also like to acknowledge my great friend Stacy Moore, who has seen me through this project from the beginning, and who is one of the most eloquent and elegant speakers and writers about music I know.

My work owes much to the previous efforts of others in the fields of musical and historical rhetoric, as is evident in my bibliography. I am particularly grateful to Thomas Conley, who very generously agreed to read and comment on the sections of my manuscript devoted to rhetorical history. I would also like to acknowledge David Beach for his considerable contributions to my translation of Friedrich Wilhelm Marpurg's essay on musical punctuation. His expertise regarding eighteenth-century German theoretical terms and numerous suggestions as to how I might best extract the accuracy and flavor of Marpurg's language has been invaluable. I take full responsibility for any failure on my part to address either's excellent advice. The readers of my drafts have also contributed significantly, particularly Sandra Rosenblum, and a final anonymous reader, whose criticisms, while they forced me to do some rather unwelcome rewriting, in the end helped to make the book a much stronger one. The last stages of the book were greatly enhanced by the very kind and assured guidance of Ralph Locke and the superb editorial work of Katie Hurley and Louise Goldberg.

I have been fortunate to have had access to a number of excellent research libraries and their supportive staff of librarians and research assistants: at Cornell University, the University of California at Berkeley, Stanford University, Duke University, the University of North Carolina at Chapel Hill and Greensboro (cello music collection), the New York Public Library, the Library of Congress, the British Library in London, and the Sibley Music Library at the Eastman School of Music.

Permission to reprint facsimile copies of eighteenth-century parts and scores has greatly enhanced my ability to write about the subtleties of historical notation practices. For this I would like to thank the following:

Bärenreiter Verlag, for permission to use materials from Mattheson, *Der vollkommene Capellmeister* 1739, Kassel: Bärenreiter 1954, and Türk, *Klavierschule* 1789, Kassel: Bärenreiter 1962.

Böhlau Verlag, for permission to use material from Riepel, *Sämtliche Schriften zur Musiktheorie*, Vienna: Böhlau, 1996.

The British Library, for allowing us to reproduce the example from their copy of Thomas Bolton's *A Treatise on Singing*, London, 1812.

Broude Brothers, for permission to use materials from the following publications: C. P. E. Bach, *Sei sonate per cembalo* (PF 2); Couperin, *Quatrième livre de pièces de clavecin*; Telemann, Sonata for viola da gamba and continuo; and Zarlino, *Le istitutione harmoniche*.

Éditions J. M. Fuzeau, for permission to use material from *Méthodes & Traités, Violon, Habendck, France 1800–1860*, Éditions Fuzeau Classique, p. 107.

Georg Olms Verlag, for permission to use materials from the following facsimile editions: Koch, *Versuch einer Anleitung zu Komposition*; Marpurg, *Kritische Briefe über die Tonkunst*; Mattheson, *Kern melodischer Wißenschaft*; and Sulzer, *Allgemeine Theorie der schonen Künste*.

Oxford University Press, for permission to use the table of two common minuet patterns from the article "Minuet" in *Grove Music Online*, edited by L. Macy (2005).

Performers' Editions, for permission to use material from the facsimile edition of C. P. E Bach's Keyboard Sonatas, Wq 48.

Taylor & Francis Group, LLC. Domenico Corri, *A Select Collection of the Most Admired Songs, Duets, &c.*, Copyright ©1993 by Garland Publishing, reproduced by permission of Routledge/Taylor & Francis Group, LLC; and Reinhard Keiser, *La forza della virtù*, Copyright © 1986 by Garland Publishing, reproduced by permission of Routledge/Taylor & Francis Group, LLC.

Finally, I would like to acknowledge my mother, Rosemary, and sisters, Liz and Kate, who have been an enormous support, encouraging me to continue writing during a period of tremendous loss and grief for us all. Another very special group of women, in their various roles as child-care providers, friends, and neighbors, need to be recognized: Roberta Cone, Martha Lefebvre, and Heidi Sobb. I am extremely grateful to my daughter Charlotte, for continuing to take such fantastic afternoon naps, and to my son, Theodore, for being a content and easy infant. Above all, I thank my husband, Paul, for his forbearance and patience, and for his many painstaking hours spent typesetting all of my music examples.

# Notes to the Reader on Sources and Terminology

The chart in appendix B is designed both to present a ready overview of the subject of musical punctuation and to facilitate discussion regarding the various issues surrounding its practical applications. The reader will recognize references in the text to the chart by a number in brackets following the name of the author from whom the quotation is taken. For instance, I refer to no. 17 or no. 42 in appendix B as Mattheson [17] or Grétry [42]. There are a few references in the chart which use vocabulary from language sources—dictionaries, encyclopedias, grammars, and rhetorical treatises—rather than musical sources; these are designated by an [L] after the author's name.

The terminology of punctuation presents a number of difficulties since many of the terms have duplicate meanings. Commas, colons, and semicolons can refer both to the individual signs and to the rhetorical units contained by them. I will indicate the modern signs of punctuation in Roman type and the larger rhetorical units in italics. For example, a *colon* is the rhetorical unit of speech which is indicated by a colon at its conclusion. I will also, as necessary when translating a source, take advantage of the British English term "full stop" as a way of retaining original language usage and differentiating the rhetorical unit of the *period* from its delimiting punctuation point. Many of the references to musical punctuation have required translation, and in cases where I have relied heavily upon or used a published modern translation, I cite both the consulted original and the translated source.

In attempting to recapture fully the spirit of eighteenth-century punctuation, I have presented the references (in both appendices and in the body of the text) much as they appeared in their original publication. Eighteenth-century writers, wishing to enhance understanding and to convey more accurately the nature of the spoken word, employed many typographic methods of emphasis and meaning, including various fonts, capitalizations, and type styles.

In my translation of Marpurg's essay on musical punctuation in appendix A, I have attempted to preserve the basic layout and format of the original. Such visual aids, in addition to the typographic tools described above, play a key role among eighteenth-century punctuation practices. In the same spirit, and to the extent that it is practical, I have also tried to preserve the essence of Marpurg's technical terminology, which, as it corresponds to a very particular eighteenth-century way of thinking about music's melodic, harmonic, and rhythmic elements, does not translate easily into standard modern terminology. For instance, Marpurg describes chords in terms of harmonies built above the bass, not as inversions of triads or seventh chords (units with essentially rearrangeable parts). Thus Marpurg calls what in modern terminology we would refer to as a third inversion seventh chord, a *Secundenaccord*: a *chord of the second*, consisting of the second and fourth above the written bass note. However, for ease and clarity for the reader, I will also employ standard modern terminology in my own discussions and analyses of eighteenth-century harmonic progressions.

German terms like *Einschnitt*, *Cäsur*, *Absatz*, and *Rhythmus*, which are used to describe the interior divisions of the musical *period*, present further difficulties. Not only are they difficult terms to capture in translation, but their usage even among eighteenth-century writers is inconsistent. As Georg Friedrich Wolf [44] explains in 1792, "There is not yet complete agreement regarding the explanation of these and several expressions of the kind; that is why what one calls the Einschnitt, another gives the name Caesura." Modern translators of eighteenth-century treatises have similarly taken different approaches with these terms. Therefore the reader is likely to see in the course of this book, a single term like *Einschnitt* translated as "incise," "division," "caesura," or simply "pause" or "stop." Where these terms appear in quoted passages (translated by myself and by others), I will often include them in brackets following the translated terms. Marpurg's use of these terms is of particular interest in the way that he modifies them in order to categorize the various formulas of musical punctuation. He presents a three-tiered hierarchy of harmonic progressions, ranging from the most incomplete to the most complete: *schwebende Absätze* or "suspended breaks"; *ordentliche Absätze* or *Quasischlüße*, "regular breaks or quasi-closes"; and the *ganze Cadenzen* or "full cadences." And just to make translation of these terms more difficult he also refers to the necessary *Pausen* (pauses) which accompany simple *Einschnitte* (incises) in the melody, and *Cäsuren* (caesuras) which occur in the middle of recitatives. Additional discussion of these terms, and particularly Marpurg's usage of them, can be found in chapter 7 on p. 189 and in the notes of appendix A.

# Introduction

# *The Pledge of Allegiance*

Therefore, the pledge should *not* be spoken this way: ". . . one nation . . . (pause) . . . under God . . ."
Rather this way: ". . . and to the Republic for which it stands (pause), one nation under God (pause), indivisible (pause), with liberty and justice for all."

Most organizations and groups you visit will recite the pledge improperly, and it is doubtful that this habit can be corrected in this generation. But bring these facts to people's attention at every opportunity you can, and certainly, in your Toastmasters club, speak it as it is written.
—South Bay Toastmasters, 2004

In February of 1998, the Miami Dade county school board voted to change the rhythm with which their students recite the Pledge of Allegiance, the words American public-school children have chanted in salute of their country's flag since the late nineteenth century. More specifically, the school board agreed to eliminate the *pause* customarily made between *one nation* and *under God*. The story was broadcast on National Public Radio's Saturday morning weekend edition with Scott Simon, who invited his guest, U.S. poet laureate Robert Pinsky, to comment on the significance of the disappearing pause.[1] Pinsky's first remark was to congratulate the Dade county school board for taking the issue of pauses and rhythm so seriously. (I, too, was impressed—punctuation was in the news!) Nevertheless, he disagreed with their decision, expressing a liking for the comma-sized pause which stresses that America is *one nation*, not one among many nations, invoking God in their oaths and pledges. For Pinsky, the pause signifies that the nation's indivisibility is the responsibility of its own inhabitants, not that of a divine will. In other words, *under God* becomes a kind of parenthetical avowal rather than a direct condition: *one nation, under God, indivisible.* According to Pinsky, the pause serves as a necessary reminder for American citizens of the racial tensions which once threatened to divide the country.

But what neither Simon nor Pinsky considered was the fact that the prepositional phrase *under God* was not part of the original pledge commemorating the four hundredth anniversary of Columbus's arrival in the New World, but a 1954 addition. The Civil Rights Movement, just gaining momentum in the early 1950s, played no role in the political agenda behind the new declaration. It was amidst the anticommunist fervor of the period that Congress, under President Eisenhower, could be persuaded to accept "the inclusion of God in our pledge," which would "serve to deny the atheistic and materialistic concepts of communism with its attendant subservience of the individual."[2] Lawmakers even debated the punctuation for the new pledge. The Library of Congress, solicited by the House Judiciary Committee, was asked to consider three proposals: *one Nation, under God*; *one Nation under God*; and *one Nation indivisible under God*. The second version, excluding the comma, was recommended:

> Under the generally accepted rules of grammar, a modifier should normally be placed as close as possible to the word it modifies. In the present instance, this would indicate that the phrase 'under God,' being intended as a fundamental and basic characterization of our Nation, might well be put immediately following the word "Nation." Further, since the basic idea is a Nation founded on a belief in God, there would seem to be no reason for a comma after Nation; "One Nation under God" thus becomes a single phrase, emphasizing the idea desired by the authors. . . .[3]

One might very well ask, "Why, then, a half century later, are we still debating the presence of such a pause?" The answer lies in the fact that firmly established oral traditions, as suggested by the South Bay Toastmasters (quoted above), are not so easily overturned. Anyone who knew the pledge in its original form naturally tended to speak the words as though they had been merely tacked on (as indeed they had). The delivery style would then have been passed along to subsequent generations as they in turn learned to recite the pledge.

More recently, a politically charged battle has been waged over the constitutionality of the 1954 addition to the pledge. On June 26, 2002, the 9th Circuit Court of Appeals ruled, agreeing with the Rev. Dr. Michael Newdow, who was suing on behalf of his six-year-old daughter, that reciting the Pledge of Allegiance in public schools with the words *under God* was an "unconstitutional endorsement of religion."[4] Reaction to the ruling was immediate and vehement, and that very day the country was witness to the spectacle of more than one hundred House members (mostly Republicans) gathered on the steps outside the Capitol to recite the Pledge of Allegiance.[5] The enthusiastic shout of "under God!" offered the American public yet another possible version of the pledge's punctuation, rhythm, and emphasis. Meanwhile, the constitutional question raised by the pledge remains. The Supreme Court managed to sidestep the issue of the separation of church and state, ruling on June 14, 2004 (Flag Day), that because Newdow was engaged in a custody dispute with his wife, he did not have the right to speak as the legal representative of their third-grade daughter.[6]

This little history recounting the evolution of the Pledge of Allegiance calls attention to some basic issues that arise in all historical discussions of punctuation, including musical ones. One such issue, as we observed with our four-word phrase, *one nation under God*, is that punctuation is a phenomenon of both *written* and *unwritten* conventions. Although no pause is explicitly indicated within the phrase, nevertheless a performance practice has developed whereby everyone of a certain age has learned (correctly or incorrectly) to deliver the words with an implicit comma. Initially, all pauses indicating the oral delivery of a text were similarly left to the discretion of the speaker, a practice we can more readily appreciate when we consider the abiding connection between the development of punctuation and the history of the written word.[7] In antiquity writing was perceived solely as the means of recording spoken language; the modern ability to read rapidly and silently, and to consult numerous texts quickly, was not a goal desired by the ancients. Instead, the act of reading was profoundly rhetorical. Value was placed on a refined understanding of the metrical and accentual patterns of a text, relying on short-term oral recall and long-term memory rather than visual stimuli. Ancient writing habits, reflecting the more deliberate style, led to the practice of *scriptura continua*, the notation of text in one continuous stream without word separation or interpunctuation (a point or symbol placed between words).[8] Gradually, however, as the written word came to be viewed as a more autonomous mode of visual communication, new conventions such as word separation, features of layout, and punctuation were developed and refined, thus enabling readers to extract information from the text with greater ease.[9]

It is particularly with the development of the printing trade in the late fifteenth and early sixteenth centuries that punctuation developed an increasing number of standardized symbols capable of indicating a variety of elements within the text: the rhythm and shape of its rhetorical structure, the grammatical boundaries of sense units, as well as some of the more subtle, logical relationships between its syntactical structures. According to M. B. Parkes, in his 1992 treatise on the history of punctuation, the balance between these various modes—rhetorical, grammatical, and logical—has dominated attitudes towards punctuation practices ever since. The balance, however, has proven to be a precarious one, as shifting attitudes towards discourse tend to favor one mode of punctuation over another.[10] Among eighteenth-century attitudes alone, we find that a more rhetorical, declamatory punctuation serves the demands of pulpit oratory, public lectures, recitations, and even the more intimate art of polite conversation, while the language of scientific discourse requires a stronger logical and grammatical foundation for punctuation. Still yet, developing theories on the psychology behind human communication yield an even greater focus on the basic syntactical structures common to all languages. Contemporary philosophies, cultural, social, and political values—all of these elements impact the relationship between punctuation and the spoken and written word.

Our modern-day Pledge of Allegiance has itself been tossed around, adjusted to suit a rapidly changing population, legislated and fought over at both the local and national level, and generally subjected to the vagaries of the political climate. We can even observe a little of the "balancing act" among the different modes and multiple layers of punctuation (both implicit and explicit) buried within its text. As we delve just a little more into our pledge's century-long history, paving the way for our study of musical texts handed down from the eighteenth century, we will also find that the punctuation reflects not one attitude but several. And although, as Parkes tells us, "this can make it more difficult to disentangle the punctuation of an author where it may be present, such a combination was intended to make the text easier for a reader to comprehend, and can often reflect general patterns of usage contemporary with the synthesis itself."[11]

Here now is Frances Bellamy's original patriotic poem, as it first appeared on September 8, 1892, in the Boston children's magazine, *The Youth's Companion.*[12]

> I pledge allegiance to my Flag and (to) the Republic for which it stands: one Nation indivisible, with Liberty and Justice for all.[13]

Many sources which quote the original version of the pledge, incorporating the *to* (above in parentheses) added in October of the same year, indicate a comma after the words *my Flag.*[14] Logically, the conjunction *and* links the two parts of the first *colon* and therefore no comma is grammatically necessary. Yet while the comma is not required in order for the sense to be understood, it does serve to underline the pledge's rhetorical structure: a *periodus* divided into four nicely balanced parts, two *membra* indicated by a colon, each with two *incisa* divided by commas. The original pledge also came with a set of directions regarding gesture which tended to further emphasize the midpoint of the first *colon*: "At the words, 'to my Flag,' the right hand is extended gracefully, palm upward, towards the Flag, and remains in this gesture till the end of the affirmation; whereupon all hands immediately drop to the side."[15] The motion of the arm and the rhythm of the words would appear to support the presence of a small but anticipatory pause (written or unwritten) at the words *my Flag.*

Most Americans never see their pledge written—I certainly hadn't until I began to study its history. It is something we learn orally as children (perhaps before we can even read) and parrot back accordingly. The rhetorical nature of its original punctuation and performed gesture seems to suit the pledge's public function and recitation style, delineating the rhythmic and structural proportions, and emphasizing the relationship between the written form and its oral delivery. However a number of sources quoting the original pledge also employ a punctuation which seeks to express the logical connection between the two rhetorical parts.[16] Through the replacement of the colon with a semicolon, a sign first introduced in the 1490s to indicate a unit of sense midway between the comma and colon, the Republic becomes more directly amplified as an indivisible Nation where all members carry the rights of Liberty and Justice.[17]

Concern that the act of pledging allegiance to *my* flag could be confusing to a country full of immigrants prompted the modification in 1923 of *the Flag of the United States*. The further specification, *of America*, was added a year later in 1924. With the words *under God* then added in 1954, we end up with the following rather unwieldy mouthful (compared to the original pledge):

> I pledge allegiance to the Flag of the United States of America and to the Republic for which it stands, one Nation under God, indivisible, with liberty and justice for all.[18]

Where did all the punctuation go? The sense of a rhetorically pointed *period* has completely vanished—in part of course because the original rhetorical structure has as well—yet there does not seem to be any attempt in the above punctuation to indicate the rhythm and pacing of the pledge. The colon (or semicolon) that was used to divide the sentence at *stands* remains in most of the 1923–24 versions, and in a few from 1954. Most commonly, however, as seen above, a comma stands in its place. Occasionally one finds a written comma after *America* and only a handful of sources indicate the comma after *Flag*, as we discussed in the original version. Even the performed gesture at the words *to the Flag* disappeared around the beginning of World War II; the face-up direction of the palm had at some point been turned downwards, the style of salute adopted by Hitler and his army of the Third Reich—hence the gesture's sudden unpopularity.[19] Even though it is extremely difficult to recite the entire opening grammatical unit in one breath, without gasping for air after the phrase *for which it stands*, the general consensus among the myriad versions of the pledge is that the rhetorical pauses are, at least visually, unnecessary.

This minimal, grammatically oriented approach to punctuation is also reflected in contemporary attitudes towards the subject. As I read from the basic style manual which sits on my desk: "For practical purposes, it is best to keep in mind that too much punctuation is as confusing as too little. The current trend is towards a minimum of punctuation, just enough to make the writer's meaning clear."[20] Paul Robinson, in his short essay on the subject included in his book written in 2002, adds that punctuation should be unobtrusive and virtually unnoticeable. He believes usage should be limited to the "pure" and "uncomplicated" signs of commas and periods. Semicolons and colons he considers as "pretentious and overactive," used most often as a means of glossing over bad logical connections in writing. On the other hand, he *would* like to see greater use of the highly neglected question mark and exclamation point.[21] Lynne Truss, in her recent best seller on punctuation (*Eats, Shoots and Leaves: The Zero Tolerance Approach to Punctuation*), concedes the prevalence of attitudes like Robinson's: "Nowadays the fashion is against grammatical fussinesss. . . . People who put in all the commas betray themselves as moral weaklings with empty lives and out-of-date reference books."[22]

However, if we wander back to the eighteenth century, we find vastly different attitudes regarding punctuation. Note not only the tenor and force, but also the style (so many punctuation marks!) with which the Elocutionist, Joseph Robertson, introduces his essay on the subject (1785).

> The art of punctuation is of infinite consequence in WRITING; as it contributes to the perspicuity, and consequently to the beauty, of every composition. It is likewise of the utmost importance in READING; as a clear, easy, natural modulation of the voice depends, in a great measure, on the pauses, or the art of dividing compounded sentences in proper places.[23]

Indeed, what a long way we have come from such attitudes repeatedly expressed throughout the eighteenth century that punctuation is a very serious subject, where errors or omissions in pointing result in "invincible difficulties" surrounding issues "of the utmost importance to society."[24]

On the one hand, interest in punctuation appears to be making something of a comeback with works like Lynne Truss's 2003 monograph. In September of 2005, the *Financial Times* ran an article by Trevor Butterworth noting Truss's popular success and the "sudden surge in punctophilia." The article featured the fact that it was a semicolon that saved San Francisco's gay marriage law from recent attack. A conservative group had erred in their written court request for the city to "cease and desist issuing marriage licenses to and/or solemnizing marriages of same-sex couples; to show cause before the court," placing a semicolon where the conjunction *or* should have been. This mistake, according to the San Francisco Superior Court Judge, James Warren, "is a big deal." He told reporters, "I'm not trying to be petty here, . . . That semicolon is a big deal."[25] The increase in electronic methods of communication—email, chat exchanges, and text messaging—has also led to some new and highly creative pointing practices. Although internal punctuation marks and final periods are often absent in "netspeak," yet the more rhetorical marks—questions, exclamations, dashes, and parentheses have taken on a whole new life; *smileys* or *emoticons* like :-) and :-(, as well as ecstatic hug greetings like {{{{{{{{Hi!!!}}}}}}} are common sights. Many perceive such practices with great concern, as symptomatic of the general decline in grammar and the linguistic irresponsibility of the "computerized" generation. But others perceive an attempt to bring the printed word again closer to the nature of spoken discourse, a relationship so esteemed among both ancient and eighteenth-century rhetorical theorists. The immediacy of net interaction, they argue, makes it feel more like speech than traditional forms of writing, creating the greater desire to include these affective elements.[26]

On the other hand, the sense of gravity and consequence of punctuation as a subject is absent. The *New York Times* review of Truss's "unlikely" best seller describes her work as "this year's intellectual stocking-stuffer, the perfect novelty gift for the chronically hard-to-amuse."[27] Truss's genuine distress that punctuation is so currently disregarded is somewhat undermined by her apologetic appeals to fellow "obsessive" sticklers and pedants, and her light, joking style.

And the amusement in Butterworth's account of the semicolon as a "pause cele-bre" is palpable. The titles of other works devoted to punctuation betray similar tendencies: G. V. Carey's 1993 *Mind the Stop*, a take-off on the London Tube directive, "Mind the Gap"; Karen Elizabeth Gordon's 1993 *The New Well-Tempered Sentence: A Punctuation Handbook for the Innocent, the Eager, and the Doomed*; and Eric Partridge's 1953 *You Have a Point There*. I, too, could not refrain from exploiting the double meaning between a *period* of time and the *period* at the end of a sentence. Other scholarly works like Parkes's *Pause and Effect* and John Lennard's 1991 study of parentheses in English verse, *But I Digress*, employ sim-ilarly punning, amusing titles. No matter how seriously we take punctuation, we can't resist poking a little fun at our rather esoteric and arcane subject—calling to mind Victor Borge's outrageous sound effects in his stand-up-comedy routine on "phonetic punctuation."

Now I choose to introduce the subject of eighteenth-century musical punctua-tion in this rather oblique manner, according to the construction and perform-ance history of the century-old Pledge of Allegiance, both to give the subject a contemporary flavor and familiar context, and to stress the many levels at which it is similar to any such historical study. The transmission of the various gram-matical, rhetorical, and logical elements of punctuation in musical texts bears on the whole a remarkable similarity to its transmission in language. Music, too, has *unwritten* as well as *written* pauses. Jacob Schuback explains in 1775 that "musical punctuation concerns the duration of the pauses, or to speak musically, the rests, which a composer makes." But as Baillot notes in 1835: "The slight sep-arations, the very short silences, are not always indicated by the composer; it is necessary then, for the performer to introduce them."[28] And just as there are performance traditions of the *unwritten* rest in the Pledge of Allegiance, so there are in the standard musical repertoire, handed down over generations from teacher to student. Musical practices, like those of language, evolve and change over time, but at any given point exhibit a set of standardized performance prin-ciples. These are, of course, subject to variation according to the different schools of playing, but one finds a certain degree of consistency: among basic aesthetics of sound production, concepts of articulation, ideas about nuance, dynamic inflection, and rhythmic impulse, all of which in some manner con-tribute to a sense of musical punctuation. There are ways of notating these ele-ments of composition and performance, but to a large extent, reliance is placed on a common awareness and knowledge of the conventions associated with a particular notation. As a very generalized and simplified example, a modern musician will tend to assume that a 4/4 measure of straight quarter notes should be played in a legato style with a rhythmic impulse leading from the downbeat of the bar forward into the next measure. That is, unless written rests, staccato markings, accents, or a decrescendo should indicate otherwise. An eighteenth-century musician, however, would have assumed from the very same notation that a detached style was indicated with a rhythmic impulse generated primarily from the downbeat of the bar.[29]

Musicians, too, must sift through the numerous "layers of attitudes" represented in the various editions of any given work. Handwritten copies of a composer's autograph, even those which are contemporaneous with the date of the composition, introduce numerous discrepancies from the original. This we will have to figure into our analysis, for instance, when in chapter 6 we compare Haydn's autograph of his op. 77, no. 1 string quartet (the opening musical period of the Adagio) with both the manuscript of his copyist and secretary, Johann Elssler, and the very different first edition published by Artaria in Vienna, which is based on Elssler's copy. Haydn authority James Webster comments in 1998 that this is the case with the treatment of all Haydn's autographs: "Every other source changes his performance markings, each in its own way: new indications are added, others altered to conform to 'house style' or scribal habits, and variant readings regularized."[30] Successive editions and performers' editions of such works are by nature designed to improve upon previous editions, to make them "easier to read." The "instructive" editions much in vogue in the late nineteenth century particularly took this highly interpretive approach towards reproducing the "classical" works—adding crescendos, decrescendos, ritards, accelerandos, slurs, tenuto signs, dots, wedges, and accents in a combined effort to adapt historical works to contemporary performance styles, and at the same time make explicit the lost notational conventions for modern players. The trend now is to attempt a restoration of the composers' intentions through so-called *Urtext* editions, yet these also must to a certain extent conform to the practical demands of presenting compositions in a user-friendly, modernized, and standardized manner.

The punctuation practices of the eighteenth century present an even greater challenge than does our example of the Pledge of Allegiance, whose history is still, so to speak, within living memory. My parents, who as children recited the pledge without the words *under God* can tell me of their insertion, as well as the removal of the accompanying gesture. I myself have learned the pause, and note with interest the controversy surrounding it. But with both the language and music of the eighteenth century, we have lost that aural counterpart. Schuback would advise a composer who feels his weakness in the matter of punctuation (question marks and exclamation points in particular) to consult the best models for musical imitation and observe those who speak publicly. The composer, he feels, should not be concerned with the business of singing until he himself is able to speak properly.[31] We, however, are not in a position to follow Schuback's sound advice; we can neither go and listen to eighteenth-century people speak (sing, or play), nor, just as importantly, see them—observe their Elocutionary hand, body, and facial gestures. But barring this, even if we should have access to the best available eighteenth-century sources, the Urtext editions, or perhaps even the autograph of a composition, we then have the challenge of interpreting the lost conventions of the notation. Clearly, it is no easy task to simply play, or as the South Bay Toastmasters advise us, to "speak" a text "as it is written."

In using the Pledge of Allegiance to point to the fact that punctuation is still very much a contemporary issue, I also point to the most dangerous and potentially misleading element in our historical study of the subject. While the subject of punctuation is very much a contemporary issue—a fundamental part of a rapidly developing "net-speak," the subject of a New York Times bestseller (as well as two highly scholarly works), and a matter of legislation at both the local and national level—our generally minimalistic, rather anecdotal approach to the subject has little in common with the attitude among eighteenth-century rhetoricians that "punctuation is of infinite consequence." Thus in order truly to grasp the import of eighteenth-century musical punctuation, we must put aside our modern concept of the subject in language as one merely for sticklers and grammatical pedants. We must rediscover the attitudes toward discourse whereby the French opera composer André Grétry could draw the analogy in 1789 that "above all, it is necessary to attend to musical punctuation, from which will result the verity of declamation."[32]

The musical application of punctuation as a tool of composition and performance covers a broad period, roughly a century and a half, corresponding to a parallel linguistic fascination with the subject. But also within this broad period these applications will exhibit all the trends of changing notational conventions which we observed in our discussion of the Pledge of Allegiance, and which must necessarily coincide with the continually changing natures of both language and music. The concept of musical punctuation involves many diverse linguistic and musical cultures, and thus the task at hand—to provide an historical context for its practical modern usage—is an immense one. It will be necessary to limit our goal to that of providing a framework by which we can begin to interpret and organize the subject's many theoretical and practical applications. We will not be able to satisfy or enlighten experts in the field of eighteenth-century linguistics and rhetorical theory; rather we will rely heavily on their work. But we wish to grasp enough of the historical motivation behind the analogous usage to enhance our understanding of its specific manifestations. Our premise must be that as musical performers, composers, historians, and theorists are today influenced by and engaged with contemporary linguistic and philosophical trends in varying degrees, so too were their eighteenth-century counterparts.

Our focus will be mainly that of musical punctuation as it is applied to instrumental music, which devoid of accompanying texts and the punctuation signs of language, poses the greatest challenges and has received the greater share of speculation and scholarly attention. But we will not neglect the highly influential punctuation practices associated with vocal music, which make up a large portion, if not the largest portion of commentary on the subject. We must always keep in mind that a strong basis for the persistence of the linguistic analogy lies in the fact that up until the early nineteenth century, vocal music was generally considered to be an aesthetically superior genre to instrumental music.[33] While the musical examples we discuss will themselves be kept to within the eighteenth century (perhaps crossing over a few years into the nineteenth), we will take advantage, where possible, of subsequent analyses of the same examples. This is a way of bridging the gap between our own understanding of a given composition and the punctuation practices espoused among eighteenth-century treatises. In this way we can begin to peel back the "layers of attitudes," shedding light on our own practices as we attempt to rediscover what Blainville [27] describes in 1767 as "the diverse cadences and vehicles" that are "rests for light, that create play and movement, to make things turn, as one says of figures in a painting."

*Part One*

# Establishing an Historical Perspective

# Chapter One

# *Musical Punctuation, the Analogy*

And whereas I *Treat,* and *Compare,* or *Similize Musick* to *Language,* I would not have *That* thought a *Fantasy,* or *Fiction:* For whosover shall *Experience* It, as I have done, and consider It Rightly, must needs *Conclude* the *Same Thing*; there being no *Passion* in Man, but It will *Excite,* and *Stir up,* (*Effectually*) even as *Language,* or *Discourse It Self* can do. This, very many will acknowledge with me. . . .

   But *Thus much I do affirm,* and shall be ready to *Prove,* by *Demonstration,* (to any Person Intelligible) That *Musick* is as a *Language,* and has Its Significations, as Words have, (if not more strongly) only most people do not understand that *Language* (perfectly).

—Thomas Mace, 1676

Intrinsic to the term *Musical Punctuation* is the analogy between music and language: like language, music expresses ideas through various grammatical and rhetorical units, such as phrases, periods, and paragraphs; these units, according to the extent to which they convey completeness or incompleteness, are more or less separated from each other through the pauses, rests, and inflections of punctuation. Such an analogy is not conceptually difficult. We are accustomed to the exchange of terminology between language and music: music theorists analyze the "sentence" and "paragraph" structure of a composition; performers determine how best to "phrase" a given passage. In fact, much of music's basic terminology is, in its inception, verbal—meter, rhythm, cadence, period, theme, composition—all are either grammatical or rhetorical in their origin.[1]

   For modern musicians, however, these terms have retained only the loosest ties to their original linguistic counterparts. For instance, could one imagine a modern violin instructor thus apostrophizing: "Diastolica (from Διαστολὴ) is one of the most necessary things in melodic composition . . . What can one think of a man who cannot even arrange six clear words of his mother tongue and set them down intelligibly on paper, but nevertheless considers himself a trained composer?"[2] Leopold Mozart, at any event, considered this speech on the theory of *diastolica,* which explains how speech is made intelligible by the modulating influence of punctuation,[3] to be a logical corollary from the subject of bow control in cantilena-styled compositions. For not only did many eighteenth-century musicians (such as Mozart and others cited in appendix B) perceive a fundamental relationship between language and music, but they accorded music, purely instrumental music, recognition as a language in its own right.[4] As Rousseau states, "[Melody] does not only imitate, it speaks; and its language, inarticulate but alive, ardent, and passionate, has a hundred times more energy than speech itself."[5]

Yet while the revival of a musical-rhetorical terminology can stimulate our discussions with an impressive and vivid vocabulary, to what extent does it actually inform our understanding and performance? In other words, can we apply our perception of the close relationship between eighteenth-century language and music, particularly in the case of instrumental music, in a concrete and specific manner? It will be my goal to demonstrate that through analogy to language (musical punctuation in particular) meaningful information regarding the nature of musical expression can indeed be extracted. But first let us play devil's advocate with our subject, questioning its fundamental effectiveness and usefulness in order to establish, at the outset, some important premises by which we can proceed. In thus pointing initially to the analogy's shortcomings, we will sooner be able to focus on its strengths, and to gain an understanding of what it was that made the analogy so compelling to eighteenth-century musicians.

One criticism leveled at contemporary writers on music of the "classic" period is that in the attempt to recognize the historically perceived affinities between language and music, they display "a persistent concern with a shadowy linguistic analogy at all levels, . . . whose meaning and significance are anything but clear."[6] To a certain extent this "shadowiness," referred to by Kofi Agawu in his 1991 study of musical semiotics, is inevitable. Part of the nature of analogy is that comparisons are made in order to explain or enhance unfamiliar ideas through more familiar terms.[7] I felt that the unfamiliar concept of musical punctuation might be more easily understood through reference to our common pool of knowledge regarding the Pledge of Allegiance. Similarly, for Leopold Mozart, an explanation of the way in which a violinist must use his bow in connecting the notes that belong together and separating those that do not, is clarified by the more familiar concept (for eighteenth-century musicians) of *diastolica.* Further, what underlies Mozart's need for the analogy is the sense that music's mode of expression is somehow deficient. The notes on the violin lack the precise semantic meaning that words can provide, just as Rousseau explains that melody, although it is "alive and passionate," is nevertheless "inarticulate."

The music/language punctuation analogy is a reciprocal one; the proponents of each adopt qualities from the other which can then be used to address deficiencies within their own systems. While music (textless music) lacks the specificity of meaning and grammatical content which language can convey, "everything language cannot express with the help of punctuation signs—height and depth of pitch, duration, tempo, dynamics, rhythm, articulation—music is able to bring to expression through its notational system and additional signs . . ."[8] Lynne Truss describes the highly musical quality of the comma, which functions not only to "illuminate the grammar of a sentence," but "to point up—rather in the manner of musical notation—such literary qualities as rhythm, direction, pitch, tone and flow."[9] The Elocutionist Joshua Steele concocts an elaborate notational system in 1779, drawing upon the symbols of music, in order to convey exactly these features: "to explain more precisely the *melody and measure* of speech," its "*accent, emphasis, quantity, pause,* and *force.*"[10] The Italian violinist and composer Giuseppe Cambini concocts dramatic texts in 1795 in order to inspire the appropriate gestures that a violinist must make with his bow arm in declaiming a four-bar and an eight-bar phrase from string quartets by Boccherini and Haydn.[11] Music theorists Mattheson, in 1739, and Koch, in 1793, import the short and long syllables of poetic feet to characterize the musical meter and rhythm of punctuation.[12] Bishop Robert Lowth [23], in his influential *English Grammar* of 1762, equates the length of pauses associated with periods, colons, semicolons, and commas as proportional to the musical semibreve, minim, crotchet, and quaver (whole note, half note, quarter note, and eighth note). And Kirnberger [29], espousing his harmonic theories in 1771, compares these same units to the musical paragraph of perfect cadences, half cadences, and interrupted cadences.

Yet as the scholar of rhetoric Brian Vickers asks in 1984: "How far can one aesthetic system, a linguistic one, be adapted to another, non-linguistic?"[13] The question is a valid one, and in the spirit of our reciprocal analogy we might also ask: How far can a non-linguistic analogy be adapted to a linguistic one? The English actor and Elocutionist John Walker, while recognizing the importance of using musical concepts to describe speech, nevertheless questions its practicality in his 1781 response to Steele's *Essay*:

> I never so much deplored my total want of knowledge in music, as I did in the perusal of this work; for though I could conceive the truth of this system in speculation, I had no means of understanding how it could be reduced to practice: I understood enough to find, that the author was a very ingenious and philosophical grammarian, but could go no farther; my ignorance of music made me incapable of entering into particulars and deriving that benefit which so ingenious a performance might have afforded me.[14]

Steele's notational system, sampled in figure 1.1, consists of a complex mixture of both musical and linguistic symbols: durational symbols which resemble noteheads (some of them dotted); quarter-, half-, and whole-note rests borrowed directly from music; bar lines accompanied by symbols to help further convey a sense of meter (Δ heavy, .. light, ∴ lightest); the acute ( / ) and grave ( \ ) symbols of language, and their combination in a variety of circumflexes ( ^ ); the suggestion of melodic contour through the vertical placement of the symbols relative to the text; and last but not least, a musical *fermata* at the sentence's conclusion. As Steele maintains, "And whoever would pronounce our heroic lines of ten syllables with propriety, must allow at least six cadences, by the assistance of proper rests, to each line, and frequently eight."[15]

Koch faces a similar dilemma concerning the student musician's level of understanding in the areas of grammar and logic. In part II, section III of his

Oh, happinefs ʳ our being's end and aim!

Oh, happinefs! our being's end and aim!

Figure 1.1. A heroic line of ten syllables. From Joshua Steele, *Prosodia rationalis, or An Essay towards Establishing the Melody and Measure of Speech*, p. 26.

*Versuch einer Anleitung zur Composition* (1787), he sets out to elucidate the very subject of this book: how the divisions of speech, delineated through the ending formulas of punctuation, can be applied to musical utterances. He begins by describing the more or less noticeable "resting points of the spirit" (*Ruhepuncte des Geistes*) in melody, in terms of what he calls "melodic punctuation" (*melodische Interpunction*). He embarks on a detailed analogy between music and language, centered on the parsing of a four-bar musical sentence which contains both a subject and a predicate (ex. 1.1).

Example 1.1. A complete basic phrase consisting of a subject and predicate. From Heinrich Christoph Koch, *Versuch einer Anleitung zur Composition*, vol. 2, p. 352.

Koch then proceeds to illustrate how the same subject and predicate, through various manipulations (some of which are shown in ex. 1.2), can become more or less defined. For instance, through the changing of the predicate in examples 1.2a and b, the subject acquires another meaning, or another turn of thought. I would imagine that the dotted rhythm of example 1.2b lends a rather grand, stately quality to the subject, while the repeated sixteenth-note gestures of example 1.2a might give the sentence a more excited and impetuous character, the sense of which is further enhanced by a quick descent to the tonic (rather than the third) at its conclusion. The predicate in example 1.2c also descends to the tonic through a two-bar extension and elaboration, which as Koch explains, gives a "more precise definition of the subject." In example 1.2d, Koch's seventh permutation of the sentence, both subject and predicate are in this way "more completely defined."

Example 1.2. Subject and predicate manipulated. From Heinrich Christoph Koch, *Versuch einer Anleitung zur Composition*, vol. 2, pp. 353–55.

But at this point, Koch feels he must abandon his project:

In the first draft of this and the following sections, I was indeed willing to compare further the similarities which are manifested between the phrases of speech and the way in which they are connected with the melodic phrases and the way in which they are joined (not only with regard to the matter already pointed out, but generally). I believed I would be able to give more clarity and precision to the melodic structure of periods. I abandoned this plan, however, as the single aim of this treatise is to be useful to developing musicians who wish to learn composition. These seldom have either grammatical knowledge of speech or familiarity with that part of logic which explains the different types of phrases and their closures. Without knowledge of these matters, both of these sections would remain very obscure to beginners.[16]

The implication is that Koch would have continued his close analogy between musical phraseology and the punctuation of language were he writing for a more advanced audience. The analogy is workable in theory, but as in Walker's case, Koch finds the practicality of a detailed application questionable due to the requirement of a relatively sophisticated knowledge of the analogous art. Thus, while an elite few are in a position to profit fully from the linguistic analogy, the rest must glean only a "shadowy" relationship.

Vickers, however, not only calls our attention to the "irredeemably vague analogies between the two arts," but questions the analogy's basic efficacy; since it is ultimately impossible for a purely musical language to convey the precise semantic messages of verbal language, how can music's "terminology" be applied in any meaningful context? He remarks, for instance, on how little has been achieved by Johann Mattheson's learned discourse on punctuation theory. He particularly criticizes Hans-Heinrich Unger's adaptations (1969) of the principles from Mattheson's often-cited example from 1737 of a punctuated minuet.[17] We will be examining the many elements of this minuet by Mattheson in chapter 8, but for now I include it here in example 1.3 as Unger presents it: Mattheson's punctuation symbols are included, but not his additional signs indicating rhythm (poetic feet), accent, and emphasis.

Example 1.3. Johann Mattheson's punctuated minuet. From *Kern melodischer Wißenschafft* (1737), pp. 109–10, and Mattheson's *Der vollkommene Capellmeister* (1739), p. 224; punctuated by Hans-Heinrich Unger in *Die Beziehungen zwischen Music und Rhetorik im 16.–18. Jahrhundert* (1969), p. 56.

For Unger, the mere presentation of Mattheson's minuet settles all questions regarding the importance of punctuation in instrumental music. He therefore feels no need to further explain the example: i.e., pointing out the minuet's cheerful affect and homophonic texture; its clearly delineated and symmetrical phrase units; or its compositional basis in the six-beat, two-bar unit of the very popular minuet dance-step. Neither does Unger explain his own choice of a punctuation exercise: the first four bars of the solo flute part from the Affettuoso of J. S. Bach's fifth Brandenburg Concerto. This I have given in example 1.4, along with Bach's full scoring of the passage.[18]

Example 1.4. J. S. Bach, Brandenburg Concerto No. 5, 2nd movement, bars 1–4. The solo flute part is shown as punctuated by Hans-Heinrich Unger in *Die Beziehungen zwischen Music und Rhetorik im 16.–18. Jahrhundert* (1969), p. 56.

To a certain extent I agree with Vickers that not a great deal is gained here by the addition of a few commas, a semicolon, and a period. In fact much is lost through Unger's punctuation of the flute part alone, which fails to take into account the highly imitative and conversational style of the movement's trio-sonata texture, as well as its very tender and flowing *affettuoso* character. For instance, the comma placed after the downbeat eighth-note a♯$^1$ makes little sense to me for two reasons: it interrupts both the melodic direction and the harmonic rhythm. Not only has the flute barely begun its answering phrase to the violin, but the comma appears in the middle of a dominant harmony, part of a half cadence in B minor, which spans the entire beat. I can imagine a slight breath or inflection at this point in the violin part, before the F♯ octave leap, but the sense of moving forward through the harmony is quite strong. I think Unger must have had in mind a very slow tempo for this movement, hearing it in eighth notes rather than its written quarter-note pulse. This is also evident in the two commas he places in bar 4. The first comma after the d$^2$ downbeat completely undermines Bach's effect of a false ending, where instead of coming to rest on the tonic, the flute immediately interrupts itself. If anywhere, the comma should occur *before* the anticipated downbeat of bar 4, which, rather than breaking up the momentum of the phrase, would create a longer line by allowing the flute to move forward in anticipation of the expressive highpoint g$^2$ on beat three— the dissonant seventh of the diminished-seventh chord.[19] Here again is not a point of punctuation, but a kind of rhetorical emphasis—a rhythmic and melodic focal point—after which follows a gradual release of tension as the period's conclusion unfolds through a i$\overset{6}{4}$–V–i cadence. Unger's semicolon at the midpoint of the sentence in bar 3, after the V–I cadence in D major, is more appropriate. We do have the sense of a new gesture in the flute part (beginning with the same interval and rhythm of the opening), which, as Koch would say, comments on and adds definition to the previous statement. The violin, however, has already begun its new phrase, the d$^2$ downbeat in bar 3 serving as both an ending and a beginning from which it can continue, weaving its ideas in and out of the flute's expressions. Perhaps a comma, rather than a semicolon, might better express the size of this pause. Even the period in bar 5 (which I agree with) is also a beginning; the keyboard continues immediately from the impetus of the downbeat with a new statement of the opening theme, while the flute embellishes, filling in the space before beginning its answer on the pickup to the fourth beat.

My criticisms of Unger's efforts are therefore that he has not properly considered the overlapping and intertwining style and *affettuoso* nature of the trio-sonata movement, which by comparison (his own) to the well-defined, highly stylized structure of the *cheerful* minuet, simply does not exhibit the same kind of punctuated clarity. But Vickers's criticism is based not on the specifics of Unger's punctuation, but on the understanding that any such effort is necessarily doomed from the outset.[20] Vickers goes so far as to say that "music cannot use the idea of a sense unit," asserting that in music one cannot break off a sentence with the sense incomplete, and therefore all that can be achieved is a general pause.[21] Many musicians (including myself) might argue that Vickers does not fully understand the musical half of his analogy; an unresolved cadence can indeed convey a very incomplete sense. Consider for instance, the dramatic pause which Mozart creates towards the end of the Adagio from his F-major Oboe Quartet, K. 370 (368b); see example 1.5.[22] This is the familiar technique, often used in concertos and other solo works, of an anticipatory tonic 6/4 chord followed by a solo cadenza on the dominant, which then leads the ensemble (usually with an anticipatory trill) to a full cadence on the tonic. Beginning in bar 28, the oboe and strings urge and prod each other forward with repeated, interrupted dotted-rhythm and half-step gestures. The dynamic increases to *forte* in bar 30, the texture also thickening as the viola begins repeated sixteenth notes and the violin and cello, moving in eighth notes, zero in on the expectant D-minor 6/4 chord of bar 31. Imagine simply stopping at this point with so much yet remaining for the sense to be completed! Not only the V–I progression from the oboe's cadenza to the tutti entrance, but also the calming and gentle repetitions of the cadence during the remaining six bars, the same dotted rhythms and half-step intervals now allowing the movement to draw to its restful close.

Handel employs a similar effect in the Adagio of his A-minor Recorder Sonata, HWV 362 (see ex. 1.6), through a pause on an E 6/5 dominant chord in bar 15.[23] Our expectation of a resolution to A minor is realized in bar 16. But here, the final bars rather than achieving a sense of full closure, turn suddenly upward and "conclude" again on an E dominant. Anyone paying attention knows that more must follow, and many, I would argue, could even sing the "A" downbeat of the following Allegro movement.

But again, Vickers's attitude is not without eighteenth-century precedent. The music historian Charles Burney complains in 1782 that "music has never had the power, without vocal articulation, to narrate, or instruct; it can excite, paint, and soothe our passions; but it is utterly incapable of reasoning, or conversing, to any reasonable purpose."[24] Even Koch, a true believer in the musical "sense unit," describes the inherent difficulty in determining the incompleteness or completeness of melodic phrases, explaining that if one could "distinguish subject and predicate in melody as definitely as in speech, . . . then an incomplete phrase or an incise [*Einschnitt*] would be a melodic segment which lacked either a subject or a predicate." But this is not possible in music, and furthermore:

The number of measures generally cannot determine where in the melody resting points of the spirit must be which divide the whole into sections in order to let it be felt distinctly. The ending formulas of these sections are so various and can be formed in such manifold ways that it would be very questionable to decide, by means of these figures, where resting points of the spirit are present in the melody; not to mention that such figures in the melody also can be used where there is no resting point of the spirit. In short, nothing concrete can determine the places where they are in melody.[25]

Example 1.5. W. A. Mozart, Quartet for Oboe and Strings, K.370 (368b), 2nd movement, bars 28–37.

Example 1.6. G. F. Händel, Sonata for Recorder and Basso Continuo in A Minor, HWV 362, 3rd movement, bars 13–17.

At very detailed levels then, the analogy begins to show signs of breaking down. With regard to concepts of rhythm and meter—defined according to classical rhetoric as the combination and arrangement of syllabic feet into *commas*, *colons*, and *periods*—if anything, language seems to gain more from analogy to music than the other way around. For instance, many of language's verse-like structures, the types of text most suitable for dances and songs, exhibit in their regularity of accentual and rhythmic patterns many properties that are felt to be primarily musical. As Mattheson proposes (and demonstrates), the relationship between the two is very close. Not only can dance music be created solely by the direct setting of nothing but the syllabic feet of church songs, or "sound-feet" (*Klang-Füsse*) as he calls them, but those same *Iambs*, *Trochees*, *Dactyls*, *Anapaests*, etc., can then be turned back again from dance music into pure chorales. In this process of taking the meters from prosody (the study of poetical forms) and presenting them in musical notes, Mattheson draws the conclusion that in fact poetry is derived from music since the latter has many more rhythms than the former. And here he is not above poking a little fun at his subject, embarking on a calculation of how many times 24 sound-feet can be permuted, the answer being 62, 044, 840, 173, 323, 943, 936, 030. If one were to then calculate the degrees of various longs and shorts in each rhythm as they combine among the various types of meters, one would be amazed to find oneself "admiring infinity in a mirror, and asking: **Who can grasp or calculate it**?"[26]

The frequent attempt to relate the long and short syllables of poetic feet to the respectively strong and weak, or accented and unaccented beats of meter, begins to lose its practicability with the acknowledgment that instrumental music creates many "feet" which do not exist in poetry. As Koch explains, when the divisions or subdivisions of the measure which define the meter are decorated with different types of melodic figures, some of the external similarity between poetry and music with regard to meter is lost: "In this case, the meter in music possesses something exclusively its own—something which is not known in poetry."[27] It is further noted by Mattheson and others that very often such decorations and embellishments exceed the technical and physical boundaries of the voice. Instruments, in their compositions, are capable of much more "fire" and freedom" than the voice which must always consider the nature of breathing. Mattheson particularly compares what a keyboard player can do (especially an organist with ten fingers and two feet) to what can be done with "the single, narrow little tube of the throat." Vocal melody, Mattheson concludes, "**does not permit such an impetuous, punctuated nature**." These words of Mattheson's immediately call to my mind J. S. Bach's famous Toccata and Fugue in D Minor, BWV 565, whose opening flamboyant gestures seem specifically designed to test the compass and range of the organ while dazzling the listener with the technical feats of both the instrument and its player. The necessarily short excerpt in example 1.7 doesn't even begin to demonstrate the very impetuous, nonvocal nature of this work.[28]

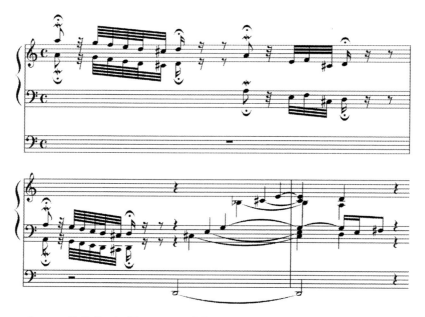

Example 1.7. J. S. Bach, Toccata and Fugue in D Minor, BWV 565, bars 1–3.

It is not then surprising that the most detailed sources of musical punctuation tend to deal exclusively with texted music. Friedrich Wilhelm Marpurg, in the one-hundred-odd pages from his *Kritische Briefe über die Tonkunst* (1762), explains punctuation primarily in reference to the vocal arts—mainly recitative with occasional remarks on aria practice.[29] Yet in his keyboard manual, *Anleitung zum Clavierspielen* (1755), the specific terminology of colons, commas, periods, question and quotation marks, exclamations, dashes, and parentheses—so prevalent in the later work—are markedly absent. Mattheson, in 1739, uses entirely texted examples to explain the different modes of semicolons, colons, commas, etc. in his chapter "On the Sections and Caesuras of Musical Rhetoric," and then defensively insists that punctuation exists in instrumental music just as it does in texted music, presenting his punctuated minuet as proof of this:

> It is most amazing that everyone persists in the opinion that instrumental music does not require such marks: however, it shall be proven below, lucidly and clearly, that all instrumental melodies, long as well as short, must have their proper **Commata**, **Cola**, Full Stops, etc., no differently than does the human voice in song: because it would be otherwise impossible to find **clarity** in such melodies.[30]

This espoused relationship between vocal and instrumental music is confusing and often contradictory. In one sense, the leap from texted music to instrumental music does not appear to be so very great. Many eighteenth-century instrumental compositions in some way carry extramusical associations—a poetic text, program, narrative, descriptive title, or stylistic label—either as part of the original compositional design, or applied after the fact (with or without the composer's knowledge).[31] Works like Johann Kuhnau's six *Biblical Sonatas* (1700), Vivaldi's *Four Seasons* (ca. 1725), C. P. E. Bach's *Sanguineus and Melancholichus* (1749), Haydn's *Farewell* Symphony (1772), Beethoven's *Eroica* Symphony (1803), or the Adagio of his Piano Sonata, Op. 2, no. 1 (1793–95), to which Franz Wegeler's "Die Klage" was underlaid (presumably with Beethoven's permission) represent only a tiny tip of the iceberg.[32] Such efforts, however, made for a variety of reasons—in response to contemporary events, intellectual interests, social activities, popular taste, even marketing ploys—were not always viewed as either positive or effective. The application of musical punctuation intersected the aesthetics of musical practice at a pivotal point in its history. Late eighteenth-century instrumental music was undergoing a shift from that of a mimetic art, necessarily inferior to vocal music in its inability to arouse precise and specific sentiments, to the art form it would become in the nineteenth century, valued as an expressive medium in its own right and independent from any programmatic intent. Such a fundamental aesthetic shift, as Mary Sue Morrow explains in her 1997 discussion of late eighteenth-century attitudes towards instrumental music, could not have happened overnight, but would have been prepared and shaped gradually by a number of disparate social and cultural factors.[33]

The diverse claims concerning musical punctuation's applicability must therefore be regarded within this context, as part of the ongoing quest to define and account for the overwhelming quantity and variety of eighteenth-century instrumental works. These are the numerous symphonies, sonatas, concertos, quartets, trios, and duos—some destined for public performance in salons, masonic lodges, and newly built concert halls, and others designed solely as domestic entertainment to be used, enjoyed, and ultimately discarded. We are today still grappling with how to interpret music's many expressive abilities: Which linguistic analogies best describe our understanding and experience of music? To what extent must we even rely on analogy? Can music in fact be explained in purely musical terms?[34] Bernard Fontenelle's famous and perplexed question from the early eighteenth century, regarding the expressive nature of instrumental music, resounds still: "Sonate, que me veux-tu?" ("Sonata, what do you want of me?")

Consider for a moment, some of the modern analytical models for music. Agawu proposes *semiotics* as the means of overcoming the "shadowiness" of analogy in order to look within that which is "purely musical" for an interpretive framework. Semiotics and semiology, considered to be the most significant semantic theories of the early twentieth century, were developed from a combination of several intellectual traditions at the turn of the twentieth century, including those of the American philosopher Charles Sanders Peirce and the Swiss linguist Ferdinand de Saussure. The study of signs derives its modern usage from seventeenth- and eighteenth-century philosophers and linguists like John Locke, Wilhelm Leibniz, Étienne Bonnot de Condillac, to name a few, but also has ancient roots in the works of Plato, Aristotle, and St. Augustine.[35] Agawu finds that not only do many contemporary writers on music exhibit a "semiotic awareness" (the awareness of music as a sign system), but so do eighteenth-century theorists like Mattheson and Koch. I do not wish to dispute this claim, but I must ask: What is semiotics other than a linguistic and semantic theory or system, much like punctuation? Agawu himself explains: "The present attempt to engage literary-critical discourse forms part of the contemporary history of music theory (whose antecedents, in any case, include borrowings of concepts as well as terminology from grammar, rhetoric, logic, and other areas)." He further adds, "any attempt to suppress this affinityy . . . should be construed as a-historical."[36] In the last century, we have evidence of many such borrowings. Leonard Bernstein's *The Unanswered Question* (1976) was inspired by the work of Noam Chomsky, considered by many to be the most important figure in modern linguistics after Saussure (of semiology). Chomsky's radical "new" view of the nature and analysis of language, propounded in his *Syntactic Structures* (1957) and *Aspects of the Theory of Syntax* (1965), proposed a "generative grammar" and "deep structure," to bring linguistic analysis closer to mental operations.[37] Bernstein sought to adapt Chomsky's concept of "innate grammatical competence" to define a universal *musical* grammar.[38] Musical analyses are also based on deconstructionist models, gender-based models—I am participating in

a trend to revive the eighteenth-century rhetorical model, and may even be participating in the beginning of a renewed interest in punctuation. No doubt I also
display a "semiotic awareness." In other words, whatever the prevailing trends
are in language, music (along with other disciplines) adopts them. And as we
discussed earlier, the benefit to be gained is not just one-sided, but reciprocal.

I think we can conclude from such trends that one model—musical punctuation, semiotics, deconstruction, etc.—is neither the sole means to understanding nor inherently better than another, but is merely a product of its time.
Shifting attitudes are a necessary result of the continual attempt to improve
understanding. For instance, Chomsky's work, after being highly influential for
many years, has since been seriously questioned (Chomsky himself has even dis-
avowed some of his own work). We expect each new theory to claim a greater
efficacy and we recognize that the dissenting voices in its applications (Charles
Burney in the eighteenth century, Brian Vickers more recently) are a vital part
of this process. At the same time, we must not devalue a theory simply because
it does not seem to be as expressive, meaningful, or precise as we think it should
be. So while we are duly cautioned from making overzealous claims that musical
punctuation functions as a literal equivalent to its linguistic counterpart, I think
we would also be mistaken in insisting that its value exists primarily through such
a function. It is unlikely, regardless of whether or not we (as modern interpreters) find the analogy to be "shadowy" and "vague," that these highly articulate, erudite theorists of the eighteenth century adopted the analytic model
lightly. To do so we would have to accept that somehow they were not quite thorough in their applications—this is difficult to credit in light of Marpurg's
exhaustive study of German language punctuation in 1762 as a preparation for
its precise musical setting in recitative. Indeed, I think it is safe to assume (and
arrogant and patronizing not to) that eighteenth-century theorists were probably no less exacting in the use of their analytic models than modern theorists are
today.

Before we judge, we must first discover as much as we can about the particular model historically and try to enter into the sense that it was felt to be meaningful and powerful. We show our own biases and limit our understanding of the
analogy if we dictate the ways in which it must "measure up." For instance, pre-
conceived notions about the subject of musical punctuation can influence our
interpretation of Koch's decision to abandon his close comparison between the
phrases of music and speech (due to a lack of linguistic knowledge on the part
of musicians) and also his statement that nothing concrete can determine the
manifold resting points in music. We can perhaps ascribe his failure to elucidate
musical structure through grammar and logic as a basic flaw in the music/lan-
guage analogy. We might also choose to find a kind of higher order in his resulting explanation of musical structures through primarily musical terms (rather
than "shadowy linguistic analogy").[39] At the same time, we might also, given the
prominent role of punctuation in eighteenth-century rhetoric and the level of

complexity which the subject had attained, find that Koch's "failure" is at least in part a reflection of similar difficulties encountered in language. The diverse eighteenth-century cultural, social, philosophical, and scientific demands placed on a punctuation system which had to convey each implicit and explicit pause of both written and spoken language resulted in an explosion of handbooks and manuals on the subject which ultimately only a limited circle of theoreticians and printers could lay any claim to understanding.[40]

An historical perspective of musical punctuation also warns us against being too tendentious in our applications of the analogy. It forces us to ask the questions: Are certain concepts valid for a particular type of music? Or the corollary, are they not valid for a particular type of music? If punctuation were going through radical development and reform today, would we find a way to talk about how our own contemporary music ought to be punctuated? In other words, does music adopt a linguistic analogy because it particularly suits the music, or because it is in the air, in the mind of the theorists, composers and performers? Similarly, is an analogy dropped because the music ceases to fit the analogy, or because that analogy has become passé?[41]

Let us explore these possibilities for a moment. Johann Philipp Kirnberger implies in *Die Kunst des reinen Satzes in der Musik* (1776–79) that it is music which adjusts to the trends of language. He explains that some time previously a literary style which was in vogue in France, the so-called *stile coupé*, characterized by a succession of short periods, had on occasion crept into music. However the style had mostly gone out of fashion, and Kirnberger never thought much of it anyway. He explains that if the expression of the text demands a cadence every other measure or even every measure, a practice in which some find beauty, then such is justifiable. But if one is not so restricted, the style soon becomes flat and boring and one is much better off writing longer periods.[42]

The fugue represents a type of composition that appears both to adjust to linguistic trends and to be adjusted by them. Gregory Butler, writing in 1977, explains that in the late sixteenth century, the fugue was the most frequent and conspicuous recipient of the application of rhetorical figures to its musical structures. Butler offers a number of reasons why the genre was so singled out for attention, among them its highly expressive and learned qualities, making it a logical choice for the very learned and intellectual field of rhetoric.[43] Yet is the analogy of rhetorical figures adopted because the fugue is highly expressive, or is the fugue highly expressive because it is thought of in terms of rhetorical figures, the primary focus of rhetorical theory at the time?

By the eighteenth century a new focus had emerged, demanding that attention be paid to the final branch of classical rhetoric's five-partite division, *Delivery* (or *Elocution* as it was renamed), and away from the focus on *Style*, the third branch of rhetoric, which concerned the appropriate and effective means of expressing ideas. A mistrust had developed regarding the manipulative power of "specious tropes and figures," and the new quest was instead for correctness and precision in speech, punctuation playing a vital role. Musical punctuation may not seem the obvious analogy for describing the intertwining, contrapuntal textures of the fugue, but as the "hot" topic of the day, it had somehow to be made to do so. Mattheson, recognizing the fugue as the "clever device wherein the *Mimesis, Expositio, Distibutio,* and other little flowers which seldom ripen to fruit find their residence, as in a green house," states in 1739 that the concept of punctuation really does not apply. As he claims, "resting places are not at all appropriate in fugues and counterpoints."[44] Nevertheless, he manages, in the fugue from J. S. Bach's C-major Solo Violin Sonata, BWV 1005 (ex. 1.8), to show where a point of punctuation might occur. But in doing so, he is forced to adjust the theory to the form, admitting that in other circumstances what would function as a period must, in the case of the fugue, be treated merely as a comma. "We want to explain the matter with an example as regards full, or evaded cadences: for, where the asterisk stands over the note there is indeed a little pause, perhaps like a comma; but it is actually nothing less than a full stop, a formal and actual cadence."[45]

Fugal Phrase without a Full Cadence

Example 1.8. The role of punctuation in the Fugue from J. S. Bach's Sonata in C Major for Violin Solo, BWV 1005. From Johann Mattheson, *Kern melodischer Wißenschafft* (1737), p. 146.

For Mattheson, punctuation in the highly imitative, contrapuntal fugue is still present, only disguised and minimized. We might apply the same principle to our discussion of example 1.4, the Affettuoso movement from Bach's fifth Brandenburg Concerto. What one might consider a semicolon at the midpoint of the phrase and a period at the sentence's conclusion, would receive in performance pauses which are much smaller. In other words the concept of a clearly delineated punctuation, derived from the minuet model, needs also to be adjusted to suit the imitative, overlapping phrases of a trio-sonata movement.

In the early nineteenth century, Antoine Reicha takes a very different approach to the fugue and adapts the form to the theory. In doing so, he not only embraces the new rhetorical ideology, but utterly rejects the old. The fugue, which he claims was invented at a time when music was in its infancy and when one had no idea of its real nature or true language, is flawed and must therefore be adjusted: "The fugue, as one has practiced it for centuries, has A DRASTIC FAULT; it is NEITHER PHRASED NOR PUNCTUATED. Genuine music is a language which follows and must follow the principles of a well made discourse. It must, therefore, proceed by phrases and periods, else all is vague or confusing."[46] As Leonard Ratner explains in 1980, Reicha deliberately "punctuates" the fugue with full cadences preceding each new exposition in the effort to adapt newer concepts of periodicity to traditional procedures.[47] Reicha does not attempt to adjust the very characteristic cadence which occurs between subject entries within the fugue exposition, as described above by Mattheson. But note the frequent cadences, punctuated by rests, in what Reicha describes as "a well-regulated and well-phrased episode of a fugue" (ex. 1.9).[48]

Example 1.9. A well-regulated and well-phrased episode of a fugue. From Antoine Reicha, *Traité de haute composition musicale*, vol. 2, pp. 222–24.

We shall find, as we have just encountered with the fugue, that the application of musical punctuation encompasses a very broad period which witnesses enormous stylistic change. Musical punctuation was adapted to many aspects of composition, performance and pedagogy, and by many different proponents with divergent interests, biases, backgrounds, and even languages. We must therefore allow for the analogy's flexibility and breadth of usage, but at the same time always make sure that we understand the context in which it was adopted. The appropriation of linguistic theories as analytical musical models is an enduring phenomenon, and eighteenth-century musical punctuation is only one of its many manifestations. Its real strength, as in any such analogy, lies in the status punctuation maintained as a highly influential and prominent element of contemporary rhetorical theory. In order to understand the *musical* in musical punctuation, we must first understand *punctuation*, and as modern interpreters of an historical practice, we cannot simply rely on our own attitudes towards the analogous art, but must attempt to recreate its eighteenth-century environment: the social and political, scientific, and philosophical forces affecting styles of discourse, and particularly the important Elocutionary focus on the voice and gesture of delivery—all of which is translated to a music whose aesthetic value relies heavily on its vocal models. We must understand what the attitudes were that made punctuation so compelling (and if we can, how it came to be so), and ultimately the specifics of the theory itself. Then we can begin to effectively put the eighteenth-century *Art of Musical Punctuation* into practice. This, I believe, is our ultimate responsibility as performers. To quote Giuseppe Cambini, "I have always thought that he who said, Sonata, what do you want of me? had reason only because the musician who produced and executed the sonata was at fault . . . had it been otherwise, that man of wit would not have had the time to have said this; he would instead have cried out, sonata, you touch me . . . you move me!"[49]

# Chapter Two

# *A Surprisingly Complex and Lively Picture of Pointing Theory*

The title for this chapter is inspired by an observation made by Park Honan in 1960 concerning the nature of English punctuation practices (pointing theory) in the eighteenth and nineteenth centuries.[1] I find the remark particularly apropos, in light of our discussion thus far, because it embraces not only the very vibrant nature of the subject, but also the sense of amazement we tend to have today that punctuation could be anything other than a rather tedious if necessary element of language, most effective when barely noticeable.

The concept of punctuation as a significant, fascinating, and vital element of spoken and written discourse is one we must recapture if we are to enter into the true spirit of the musical punctuation analogy. In order to do so, however, we must work forward by stages, establishing first (in as summary a fashion as possible), how the diverse social, political, and intellectual developments of the eighteenth century influenced attitudes towards discourse; second, how these attitudes in turn made demands upon and impacted punctuation practices; and third (which we will undertake in chapter 3), how these punctuation practices were then incorporated into musical theory. The route is confusing and circuitous, and, like all histories, the history of punctuation follows no single straightforward path leading to a set of universal principles, but instead chases after a jumble of diverse prospects, revealing in the end a very multifaceted subject. In addition, the sources for our research are to be found not only among the traditional formal studies of grammar, rhetoric, and logic (the classical *trivium*), but also among the numerous textbooks, handbooks, and other less-scholarly forms of discourse regarding social behavior and etiquette, polite conversation, and fictional writing. All of these contribute to a very complex and constantly shifting rhetorical theory, or what we will broadly call the *Art of Communication*.[2]

## Classical Precepts

Eighteenth-century philosophies and attitudes towards "the art of communica-tion" reveal an abiding connection to the precepts of classical rhetoric. Countless editions of the rhetorical works of Cicero, edited and abridged versions of Quintilian's *De institutione oratoria*, and numerous copies and translations of Longinus's *On the Sublime* were widely available, influencing both the teaching and practice of rhetoric. The rhetorical curriculum, based on the classical five-partite conception of the art (listed below), remained largely unchanged throughout the seventeenth and much of the eighteenth century.[3] This legacy was aggressively defended, to the virtual exclusion of all modern ideas by some, while it was absorbed and incorporated into contemporary rhetorical practice by others. John Ward's *System of Oratory* (1759) falls easily into the first camp. Similarly, Giambattista Vico, in his *Institutiones oratoriae* of 1711, strongly defends classical rhetoric against the Cartesian denial of the important function language plays in producing knowledge.[4] Johann Christoph Gottsched [21] (*Ausfürliche Redekunst,* 1736) and Charles Rollin (*Traité des études,* 1726–28), while they were thoroughly modern in their promotion of vernacular languages and literature alongside that of Latin, nevertheless drew heavily from the works of Cicero and Quintilian.[5] It is essential, therefore, that we establish at least a few of the basic principles of the great ancient orators (particularly with regard to punctuation) before we can proceed to their eighteenth-century adaptations.

Quintilian, whose sole surviving work provides one of the most impressive syn-theses of the classical oratorical tradition ever written,[6] and who was also a par-ticular favorite among eighteenth-century musicians, shall serve as our spokesman.[7] Quintilian defines rhetoric as "the art of speaking well," using the word "well" in a two-fold manner to mean not only persuasively and effectively, but also virtuously. In other words, he insists, "a great orator must be a good man." In fact, Quintilian claims, it is of more estimation and importance that the orator is a good man than that he is skilled in speaking, since "should the power of speaking be a support to evil, nothing would be more pernicious than elo-quence alike to public concerns and private."[8] This concept of the "good man skilled in speaking," thus defining the orator's positive role in society, is an important contribution to rhetoric, one which we will encounter again among the ideals of eighteenth-century social discourse.[9]

Within Quintilian's "art of speaking well," punctuation plays a key role both in the final presentation of the completed oration and as a function of the com-positional process itself, stages three and five of classical rhetoric's five-partite division:[10]

1. Invention (*inventio*), the discovery or finding of ideas
2. Arrangement (*dispositio*), the proper ordering or distribution of ideas to ensure that all means of persuasion are present and properly disposed

3.  Style (*elocutio*), the use of correct, appropriate, and striking language throughout the oration
4.  Memory (*memoria*), the retention in the mind of the ideas' arrangement and words
5.  Delivery (*pronuntiatio* or *actio*), the presentation of the oration through vocal modulation and effective gesture

In his discussion of *Delivery*, Quintilian emphasizes how important "distinct phrases" are towards achieving clarity in pronunciation. Using the first *period* from the *Æneid* as an example, he points out precisely where the words "are to be reined in, as it were and suspended, and where they are to be altogether brought to a stand."[11] In addition, since "*Delivery* is by most writers called *action*," deriving "one name from the voice, and the other from the gesture," the eloquence of the body must also come to the aid of the voice in executing the necessary breaks, suspensions, and imperceptible pauses of speech.[12] Quintilian describes a kind of hand alternation that accompanies the slight percussions or feet in language. But he warns against the overuse of this rhythmic gesture, which should instead conform to the breath and larger units of sense:

> It is therefore a better method, as there are in every period short phrases, at the close of each of which we may, if we please, take breath, to regulate our gesture in conformity with them; for example, the words *Novum crimen, C. Cæsar*, have a kind of complete sense in themselves, as a conjunction follows; and the succeeding phrase, *et ante hanc diem non auditum*, is sufficiently complete; and to these phrases the movement of the hand should conform, especially at the commencement, when the manner is calm. But when increasing warmth has given it animation, the gesture will become more spirited in proportion to the ardour of the language.[13]

While Quintilian pays the greatest attention to the movement and position of the hands (and the fingers), no part of the body is neglected—the head, the face (eyes, nose, and lips), the shoulders, neck, arm, breast, stomach, legs, feet—all are addressed: "How much power gesture has in a speaker, is sufficiently evident from the consideration that it can signify most things even without the aid of words. Not only a movement of the hand, but even a nod, may express our meaning; and such gestures are to the dumb instead of speech. Dancing, too, unaccompanied by the voice, often conveys a meaning, and touches the feelings."[14]

However Quintilian's most detailed descriptions of the *incisum, membrum*, and *periodus* (*comma, colon,* and *period*) emerge from his discussion of Style or *elocutio.*

> A *comma* according to my notion, is a certain portion of thought put into words, but not completely expressed; by most writers it is called a part of a *member*. The following

examples of it Cicero affords us: *Domus tibi deerat? At hab bas. Pecunia superabat? At egebas.* "Was a house wanting to you? But you had one. Was money superabundant with you? But you were in want."

A *member* is a portion of thought completely expressed, but detached from the body of the sentence, and establishing nothing by itself. Thus, *O callidos homines!* "O crafty men!" is a complete member, but, abstracted from the rest of the period, has no force, any more than the hand, or foot, or head, separated from the human body.

To the *period* Cicero gives several names, *ambitus, circuitus, comprehensio, continuatio, circumscriptio.* There are two kinds of it; one simple, when a single thought is expressed in a rather full compass of words; the other consisting of members and commas, which may contain several thoughts.. . . A period must have at least two members; the average number appears to be four; but it frequently admits of more. Its proper length is limited by Cicero to that of about four iambic trimeters, or the space between the times of taking breath. It ought fairly to terminate the sense; it should be clear, that it may be easily understood; and it should be of moderate length that it may be readily retained in the memory.[15]

The above definitions of punctuation units, with their focus on the rhythmical and structural patterns of the text, are geared towards the needs of the orator. We must remember that in Quintilian's day, writing was regarded solely as the means of recording the spoken word. As Paul Saenger explains in 1997 concerning the origins of silent reading, "The ancient world did not possess the desire, characteristic of the modern age, to make reading easier and swifter because the advantages that modern readers perceive as accruing from ease of reading were seldom viewed as advantages by the ancients."[16] The decision as to how to phrase a given text when reading out loud, where the pauses should occur and how long they should be, was left almost entirely up to the discretion of the educated reader. Scribes, most of them slaves or freedmen, would painstakingly reproduce the text exactly as it appeared on the written page, without any word separation or other interpretive aids, according to the practice of *scriptura continua.*[17] This attitude towards the merits of spoken language over written also reemerges in the late eighteenth century at the height of the Elocutionary Movement; writers like Hugh Blair and particularly Thomas Sheridan would bemoan the loss of that special relationship between reader and book which ancient writing practices achieved, a relationship requiring a close study of a text's meaning as well as a careful, lingering attention to its metrical and accentual patterns.

Of course the punctuation practices of antiquity are not summed up quite so easily. Writing developed parallel conventions of a separated consonantal script (languages without vowels adopting word separation), and the opposite, unseparated vocalic script (languages with vowels but no word separation). The Romans were employing an interpunct between words, which were sometimes accompanied by a small space, at the same time that the Greeks were not. However, by AD 65, the *scriptura continua* convention of the Greeks was also adopted by the Romans. Since scribes in one language were aware of the other's graphic traditions, the reason for the discrepancy remains something of a mystery. Why the Romans gave up their very practical convention of word spacing is something we as modern readers find particularly perplexing, although in light of the ancient reading habits described above, the stylistic preference becomes more understandable.[18] Parkes claims that class differences between readers and scribes would also have contributed to the perseverance of *scriptura continua*; it would have been insubordinate for a scribe to impose his personal interpretation on a text through the use of either word space or punctuation.[19]

Saenger observes that when written Latin was still separated by interpuncts, some visual signs were also being used by the reader to indicate units of sense and their related rhetorical pauses. However, after the shift to *scriptura continua*, the signs for punctuation of sense completely disappeared and new Greek marks of punctuation were introduced. These were used solely for pedagogical purposes and were based on a system of elevated points corresponding primarily to the rhetorical phrasing. Saenger adds that in the early Middle Ages, as the written medium became a more direct means of communication to a wider reading public, interword space was reintroduced into texts at the same time that scribal punctuation increased. The result was a more rigorous effort to relate punctuation to units of sense.[20]

The above account reveals what Parkes describes as the two different modes of analysis on which theoretical discussions of punctuation have been based throughout history: the grammatical, which divides according to content (the production of complete and incomplete sense); and the rhetorical, which divides according to form (the rhythm and shape of discourse).

> The grammatical analysis of punctuation has been concerned with the boundaries of *sententiae* (later, "sentences") and the units of *sensus* or grammatical constituents within them. Rhetorical analysis has been concerned with the ways in which punctuation reflects the periodic structure of a discourse and indicates the *periodus* and its parts (*commata* or *incisa, cola* or *membra*). With its emphasis on pauses for breath this mode of analysis has been preoccupied with bringing out correspondences between the written medium and the spoken word. A rhetoricians' *periodus* should not be confused with a grammarians' *sententia* (the length of a *periodus* was a matter of opinion), and *cola* and *commata* should not be confused with such grammatical units as clauses.[21]

But as Parkes explains, "There is usually some agreement between grammarians and rhetoricians as to what constitutes complete and incomplete sense." In the case of Quintilian's definitions of the punctuation units, Parkes observes a great deal of interdependence between form and content, where a *sententia* is a semantic unit which overlaps with the rhetorical *period* and the grammatical sentence.[22]

The interdependence between grammar and rhetoric functions on a larger level as well. Although Quintilian is careful to assign each profession "its due limits," he also argues that the two "should in some degree be united." In order that one may speak well, one must first, according to the *Art of Grammar*, "speak correctly." And while a boy begins his studies with the grammarian, as soon he "produces his little exercises in praising and blaming," then the attention of the rhetorician is required. As Quintilian asserts, "He who shall suppose that these matters do not concern the orator, will think that a statue is not begun when its limbs are cast."[23]

The definition and application of punctuation according to either grammatical or rhetorical principles, the various *modes* of punctuation which we discussed earlier in reference to The Pledge of Alligiance, also play an important role in the eighteenth century. Yet as we pursue our history of these different approaches to punctuation, we do not want to present them as conflicting principles, but, like Quintilian, as complementary and crucial elements of the theory. David Cram, in his 1989 article on seventeenth-century punctuation, relates the questionable but often-told story of how rhetorical and grammatical punctuation vie with each other for dominance—the one based on the requirements of breathing, the other on syntactic boundaries and functioning as an aid to comprehension.[24] Then, following a period of uncertainty, at which time punctuation practices were in a considerable state of chaos (i.e., the explosion of punctuation manuals and handbooks in the late eighteenth century), the syntactic principle (the basis of our own contemporary practices) ultimately won the day. But as Cram states, this supposed conflict is "either spurious or has been blown up out of all proportion."[25] Parkes supports this conclusion, describing the different modes of punctuation employed in the eighteenth century as supportive practices, a "disciplined flexibility of usage" resulting from the extraordinary demands placed on both spoken and written discourse.[26]

Quintilian's discussion of punctuation (within the context of style or *elecutio*) emerges from his efforts to define the terms *rhythm* and *meter*, both of which are used to describe the lengths of time by which individual words and groups of words are combined, arranged, and connected to create *commas, colons, and periods. Meter* according to Quintilian, corresponds to the specific feet and their arrangement. For instance, the *iamb*, which is formed by a short syllable followed by a long syllable, is very different from and cannot be exchanged with a *trochee* (Quintilian calls it a *choreus*), which is a long syllable followed by a short one. *Rhythm*, on the other hand, measures the length of time the meter takes to run its course; the internal organization, whether *iamb* or *trochee*, does not matter.[27] He then proceeds to describe the attention which must be paid to the management of these feet, according to the principles of rhythm, among all parts of a *period*. Although the beginnings and endings of *periods* are most important, since that is where the sense commences and concludes, he also describes stresses or emphases that can occur within the middle parts, causing slight, almost imperceptible pauses. His example (from Cicero) is quoted repeatedly throughout the eighteenth century as further evidence of the superiority of spoken language over written.

> Who can doubt, for example, that there is but one thought in the following words, and that they ought to be pronounced without respiration, *Animadverti iudices omnen accusatoris oralionem in duas divisam esse partes* (I observe members of the jury that the whole of the speech for the prosecution is divided into two parts): yet the first two words, the next three, the two following, and the last three, have respectively, as it were, their own numbers, which allow relief to the breath; at least so it is thought by those who are studious of rhythm.[28]

There are two types of rhythm, Quintilian concludes: one dictates the flow of the feet themselves, the character they produce—a gentle flow, speed, pugnacity, ornateness, simplicity, etc.; the other describes the general rhythm of the period produced by the combination of the feet, its *commas* and *colons* as defined above. Ideally of course, the structure of the phrases should correspond to the characters produced by the rhythms.[29] As we shall find in chapter 3, the adaptation of these important elements of punctuation to modern English, German, French, and Italian exercised eighteenth-century writers (on both language and music) considerably.

## The Impact of Printing

Punctuation practices developed by stages according to changing attitudes regarding the relationship between reading and the written word. Nothing had a more profound impact on this development than the advent of the printing press, leading to the regularization of the marks themselves as well as their functions.[30] As Lynn Truss proclaims, "Our system of punctuation was produced in the age of printing. . . . The good news for punctuation is that the age of printing has been glorious and has held sway for more than half a millennium."[31] Punctuation is essentially a visual phenomenon and is effective because readers have been trained to appreciate the nuances of its printed conventions. Linguistic study has proven that skilled modern readers, whose decoding is more visual than aural, are best able to extract meaning from the symbols of punctuation—no wonder the readers of antiquity had little need for them![32]

The development of the printing trade in the late fifteenth and early sixteenth centuries made it possible for the first time not only to distribute multiple copies of a single text among a much wider geographic region, but to do it more quickly than ever before. The number of Greek and Latin works suddenly available, including the complete texts of Quintilian's *Institutes* and Cicero's *De oratore*, sparked the humanist enthusiasm for all things classical as well as a new appreciation for the art of eloquence.[33] The Humanists rejected what they perceived as the dry expressions of their predecessors, the Scholastics, who sought to understand the precise and logical formulation of thoughts by adapting the syntactic rules and semantic functions of Latin to that of ordinary language. Yet they also profited from these same contributions, incorporating a new awareness and understanding of the formal laws of logic into their concept of language. Arguments, the Humanists felt, as well as being persuasive and demonstrative, should proceed elegantly and gracefully.[34]

Prior to the advent of printing, there could be no guarantee that any text would be copied the same way twice. As a result no system of punctuation developed that could consistently indicate both the grammatical and rhetorical structure of a text, while at the same time discriminating among its different possible emphases. Parkes describes two widely different approaches to punctuation taken by medieval scribes: at one end of the scale, a scribe might adopt a kind of selective approach, favoring certain interpretations or emphases over others; or instead, he might employ a more neutral and extensive punctuation which gives equal value to all possible emphases within a text. Meanwhile scholastic contributions to punctuation had been minimal at best, based on the concept that a logically constructed discourse required no further clarification. As an example, take the first clause of the original Pledge of Allegiance: "I pledge allegiance to my Flag and the Republic for which it stands." The scholastic attitude would have been that the conjunction *and* obviates the need for a comma because the word itself is sufficient.

Thus the Humanists were left frustrated by the inadequate number of marks available to convey the various rhetorical, grammatical, and logical aspects of a text. The *punctus exclamativus* (equivalent to the modern exclamation point), parentheses, and the semicolon were all introduced by the Humanists in response to this recognized need for signs with distinctive graphic properties and specific functions. The Humanists pursued, as Parkes explains, "a more exact disambiguation of the constituent elements of a sentence." Rather than a system of coinciding rhetorical and grammatical units, they sought to expand the capabilities of punctuation while at the same time maintaining a balance between outlining the rhetorical structure of a period and pointing to its logical and syntactical structures—a balance which has been an essential element of punctuation ever since.[35]

The sixteenth-century reformer Petrus Ramus (or Pierre de la Ramée) set about an upheaval of this balance, as he set about the upheaval of rhetoric in general, attacking the classical trio of Aristotle, Cicero, and Quintilian.[36] In his revision of classical rhetoric's five-partite division, Ramus draws a sharp distinction between the formulation of ideas and their expression: *Reason*, which deals with certainties and makes its aim that of truth, and *Speech*. Ramus essentially reduces *Rhetoric* to the embellishment (or *Style*) of speech through tropes and figures, and its dignified *Delivery*. *Invention*, *Arrangement*, and *Memory* all belong to *Dialectic*, which requires *Logic* and therefore belongs to *Reason*.[37]

In his *Arguments in Rhetoric against Quintilian*, Ramus particularly criticizes the inclusion in rhetoric of that which belongs to the subject of grammar, i.e., the division of speech into the *comma, colon,* and *period.* "All of this," he claims, "deserves the consideration of grammar, since in grammar a pupil must be taught how he should divide a speech with punctuation and how he should mark off the clauses."[38] Ramus also removes the rhythmic and rhetorical element from Quintilian's definitions of the punctuation units: "Quintilian defines a comma as the expression of a thought lacking rhythmical completeness, as if indeed the rule for the comma were to depend on rhythm, so that whether a rhythm were completed or not there would either have to be or not be a comma, and as if in commas a full rhythm could not exist without commas ceasing to exist." He adds that one can understand nothing about the nature of colons and periods from Quintilian's discussion. But he says, since Quintilian does not, "that a comma (*incisum*) is an incomplete expression of a thought (*imperfecta sententia*); that a colon (*membrum*) is a completed expression of a thought (*perfecta sententia*), yet related to some other part: a period (*periodus*) is absolutely complete and independent."[39]

Parkes explains that the Ramist distinction between the thought process and expression meant that although logic would be required to guarantee the validity of a statement, the statement could be rendered more effective by being distanced from the language of everyday speech. This was reflected in punctuation practices by the application of only a select range of marks for a very specific function. For instance, Parkes describes a kind of pure rhetorical punctuation which delineates the division of a *period* into its constituent *colons* and carefully balanced *commas*. No use, however, is made of semicolons (although the signs were widely employed at the time) to distinguish among the *colons* and point to the logical analysis of the text.[40] Ramus's separation of invention, arrangement, and memory from rhetoric would have important repercussions in the decades and centuries to come, yet his reforms never quite achieved the revolutionary effect intended, continuing to exist side by side in the sixteenth century with competing rhetorics which sought Quintilian's notion of the art as all-inclusive and part of the dialectic/logical process.[41]

## The Language of Science

By the end of the seventeenth century, a general mistrust of rhetoric had developed with the increasing perception that the ancient "art of speaking well" had come to be an art of obfuscation rather than one of elucidation.[42] Adverse reaction to the painstaking and laborious efforts of the Scholastics had contributed to the development of a copious, highly ornate speech.[43] In addition, a rhetoric based on persuasion through emotional appeal, using vivid and extravagant language, had been sanctioned by the church so long as it was employed for the proper purposes. But the practice had spread outwards to affect the language of the royal courts, leading eventually to a deep-seated suspicion regarding rhetoric's power to shape and manipulate language.[44] Rhetoric's apparent divorce from logic and the foundations of knowledge was also in part a result of Ramist reforms, which by reducing rhetoric to the study of "specious tropes and figures," brought so many "mists" and "uncertainties" to knowledge.[45] But such indignation regarding rhetorical practices, expressed in 1667 by Thomas Sprat on behalf of the British Royal Society, and additional demands for a plainer and more direct language—like Dominique Bouhours's (1687) assertion in his *La manière de bien penser* of 1687 that "good thinking and expression should be unadorned, clear, and intelligible"—were largely a response to revolutionary ideas concerning the study of knowledge and the psychology of human behavior.[46] The reign of the scientific method over *dialectic* as the method of inquiry, combined with radical reconceptions regarding the nature of the physical universe, led philosophers to reexamine the ways in which human beings acquire knowledge and to try to bring communication closer to the ideal of scientific discourse.[47] Punctuation would play a key role in the unfolding process of fixing this hitherto untrustworthy language.

Francis Bacon believed that only scientific experiment could result in a true knowledge of nature. His mistrust of rhetoric, although he was himself a consummate master of the art, is expressed in his claim that the first "distemper of learning" is "when men studie words, and not matter." By no means rejecting the necessity for eloquence, Bacon believed that "wordes are but the Images of Matter, and except they haue life of reason and inuention: to fall in loue with them, is allone, as to fall in loue with a Picture."[48] The use of overblown and flowery language in scientific discourse was naturally one of the worst offenses and in 1662, the British Royal Society was founded in order to promote the acquisition and communication of knowledge according to scientific values. Rhetoric would be banished and a plain, unencumbered language would describe things as they really are.[49]

Belief that a plain style could be a more effective means of communication was also held outside science: in the theater this resulted in "improved," streamlined versions of Shakespeare; among preachers, the call was for a more natural sermonizing which would display not artifice, but *real* understanding of the subject matter with *real* conviction.[50] Thomas M. Conley argues in his 1990 history of rhetoric that the plain style was not in all cases a retreat from the use of highly affective prose, but an improved "rhetoric of emotion." He explains that "the plain style can be more effective because it is more concrete (therefore impressing the imagination more deeply), easier to follow (hence more directly affective), more precise in its diction, and better fitted as they thought, to the way the mind, appetites, and will of man work psychologically."[51]

It is difficult to overestimate the impact of Cartesian philosophy on this "new rhetoric." In the search for a totally secure foundation for knowledge, René

Descartes insisted that proof, not argument, was the sole method of distinguishing between that which is true and that which is false. The communication of knowledge then requires a clear and distinct language which persuades without being disguised through the use of rhetoric.[52] Descartes's ideas were systematized and popularized by the French Port-Royalists in the early 1660s. According to Port-Royal logic, the discovery process, modeled on the Cartesian method of rigorous geometric proof, is communicated through the process of presentation, where the act of persuasion and emotional appeal is founded on a strong understanding of basic human psychology.[53] Language, too, falls under the rubric of human behavior; as a direct manifestation of the thought process, the diverse syntactical features among different languages are mere variants of one underlying universal language.[54]

The role of punctuation within the context of an affective and "emotional," yet also plain and scientific language, becomes once again both logical and rhetorical. For instance in the writings of Bacon and Sprat, Parkes observes an overlap and two-fold function of punctuation points to indicate the rhetorical structure as well as the logical relationships within that structure. Even more importantly for the role of punctuation, such usage enables the reader "to accept both logical and rhetorical structure, and to see the relationship between them as a desirable quality of discourse." The activities of the Port-Royalists further encouraged the use of punctuation in both its logical and rhetorical functions, as well as promoting an increased interest in the grammatical analysis of punctuation.[55]

So that we understand the concept of this logical/rhetorical punctuation and also that we keep in mind what a so-called "plain" style of writing looked like in the seventeenth century, I include a passage from Thomas Sprat's *The History of the Royal-Society of London,* as provided by Parkes. The colons, semicolons, and commas are used not only according to their rhetorical hierarchy, but also logically, according to the immediate context. For instance, the colon after *extravagance* not only serves to indicate a pause which is greater than that of the semicolon and less than a period, but also points to the explanation or answer which follows. Similarly the semicolons which divide *positive expressions, clear senses,* and *a native easiness,* give more weight to these itemized features of natural speaking than would commas in their place.

> They have therefore been most rigorous in putting in execution, the only Remedy, that can be found for this *extravagance*: and that has been, a constant Resolution, to reject all the amplifications, digressions, and swellings of style: to return back to the primitive purity, and shortness, when men deliver'd so many *things*, almost in an equal number of *words*. They have exacted from all their members, a close, naked, natural way of speaking; positive expressions; clear senses; a native easiness: bringing all things as near the Mathematical plainness, as they can: and preferring the language of Artizans, Countrymen, and Merchants, before that, of Wits, and Scholars.[56]

Although Sprat's subject is that of the Royal Society's effort to clean up the excesses in the language of Natural Philosophy, it is important to remember that not all use of tropes and figures immediately fled before the new strictures dictated by science. The degree of ornateness or plainness of style became a subject of much debate. For instance, Bacon had reservations about the Senecan style, which was characterized by a loose structure and relatively brief sentences of short phrases and jerky rhythms, yet which seemed to be concerned more about avoiding stylistic display for its own sake than with the nature of the thoughts actually being expressed.[57] The Cartesian proponent of Port-Royal logic, Bernard Lamy, argued a very different point of view from the Senecans in his *Art de parler* of 1675: "No Language is rich enough to supply us with the terms capable of expressing all the different Faces upon which the same thing may be represented: We must have recourse to certain manners of speaking called Tropes." Lamy then proceeds to describe in great detail these tropes and their appropriate uses.[58] Style, too, was a matter of changing tastes and fashions. By 1731 John Constable, in his *Reflections upon the Accuracy of Style*, is far from complimentary regarding the "masterpieces" of the Port-Royal gentlemen, though they once held a "mighty vogue":

> [The World] grew weary of their frequent *Parentheses*, which clog a discourse and make it languid and unintelligible. Their long *Periods* grew tedious, and were found to be, not so much the effects of an abundance of sense, as a want of that exactness of thought, that just dimension and extent of parts, which makes the lasting beauty of Styles.[59]

Attitudes towards language were also strongly influenced by the philosophical works of John Locke, whose 1690 *Essay Concerning Human Understanding* helped consolidate ideas at the turn of the century about how the human mind works. Locke believed that there is a delicate balance between words and ideas which can be easily upset by either incomplete knowledge or unclear communication. Words are all too human and fallible, carrying cultural and personal connotations which complicate the relationship between an idea and its expression. Locke was extremely intolerant of a rhetoric which interfered with understanding, and argued that language needed to be highly regulated in order to achieve correctness and precision.[60] A large number of philosophers (French, German, and Italian) attempted to follow Locke in this desire to purify language and ensure that words were used consistently and bore a simple relationship to their ideas.[61] The result was a proliferation of prescriptive grammars, responding to the need to reduce practices to a clearly formulated set of rules. Within this context, punctuation, too, came under much closer scrutiny.[62]

## Elocution and the *Honnête Homme*

Social and political factors affected eighteenth-century attitudes towards language and communication in a manner very different from the essentially "anti-rhetorical" influences of science and philosophy. All over Western Europe, the expansion of trade and colonization had created a much larger, wealthy urban class which threatened the old social order and shifted the centers of power. One method of establishing some kind of stability amidst this cultural upheaval was through attention to higher education. An increased enrollment among students from the new middle class helped foster a sense of national cultural identity through a common pool of knowledge about language, history, poetry, literature, and all the *belles lettres*. In addition, nonaristocrats were able to acquire the necessary skills for administrative positions, royal posts, and parliamentary seats which had been previously denied to them. Thus, regardless of the class to which one was born, one could still aspire to attain the qualities—the knowledge, accomplishments, manner, address, etiquette, and above all the ability to speak well—necessary for membership in the highest echelons of society. As a means of such social mobility, the study of rhetoric was accorded a prominent position.[63]

Charles Rollin (1661–1741), dedicated to the reform of rhetoric in the Parisian education system and advocating the study of French alongside Latin, was among the first to articulate the new social order: theoretically, any child, through the development of his natural reason, could become a member of polite society, what Rollin termed an *honnête homme*. In his *Traité des études: De la manière d'enseigner et d'étudier les belles-lettres* (1726–28), Rollin recommends the study of literature, history, and poetry, and a development of the ability to speak and write in a simple, yet elegant style (absence of ornament did not in itself guarantee eloquence). Such a study would enable one "to pass a right judgment upon other men's labors, to enter into society with men of understanding, to keep the best company, to have a share in the discourses of the most learned, to furnish out matter for conversation, without which we must be silent, to render it more agreeable by intermixing facts with reflections, and setting off the one by the other."[64] Rollin borrowed an important part of his definition of the *honnête homme* from Quintilian (Rollin himself translated and published an abridged version of *De institutes oratoria* in 1715), admonishing that the skilled orator must be a "good man." Rollin quotes, "In a word, the most necessary qualification, not only in the art of speaking and in the sciences, but in the whole conduct of our life, is that taste, prudence, and discretion, which upon all subjects and on every occasion teaches us what it is we should do, and how it is we should do it."[65] This concept of the *honnête homme* or ideal orator skilled in the speaking of his national tongue would be adapted and rearticulated by rhetoricians all over Europe.[66]

In Britain, a new movement in rhetoric was also underway, focusing on the *Delivery* of an oration, or its *Elocution*, as the primary skill of the *honnête homme* and the means to his social advancement.[67] Eighteenth-century Elocutionists understood that only through the proper use of voice and gesture could one hope to gain favor at court, appointment at the university, preferment in the church, or success on the stage. Among the Irish and Scottish, the cultural disadvantages of a dialect considered rustic and comical, or worse, completely incomprehensible to polite English speakers, were particularly manifest.[68] A key element of the elocutionist argument concerned the vast superiority of spoken language over written. In his *Lectures on Rhetoric and Belles Lettres*, published in 1783, the Scottish Elocutionist Hugh Blair maintains that "the voice of the living Speaker, makes an impression on the mind, much stronger than can be made by the perusal of any Writing. . . . Hence, though Writing may answer the purposes of mere instruction, yet all the great and high efforts of eloquence must be made by means of spoken, not of written language."[69] In the fifth of his *Lectures on Elocution* of 1762, the famous Irish actor and educational reformer Thomas Sheridan argues more specifically for the superiority of punctuation as it is spoken rather than written.

> The art of punctuation is of modern invention, and probably was not known, previous to the discovery of printing, at least we are sure that the Ancients made not any use of stops in their writing. A plain proof of what I asserted in my first lecture, that the art of writing amongst the Ancients, was not calculated for the use we put it to, of reading works aloud to auditors, but only to enable the speaker to get the words by rote, in order that he might recite them from memory. And happy had it been for the state of modern elocution, that the art had still remained unknown; for then every one who had anything to deliver in public, must, like the Ancients, have been obliged either to recite it without book, or apply himself closely to study the meaning of what he had to read, so as to be able to deliver it properly . . . every one, having no rules to misguide him, would of course follow the obvious one, that of reading words as he would speak them.[70]

Diderot [26], in 1765, also gives a decided emphasis to the spoken element of punctuation in his *Dictionnaire*. He even feels the need to repeat his point, coming back to the very same statement with which he begins his definition of the term: "Everyone feels the justice there is in defining *punctuation*, as I have done from the beginning; the art of indicating in writing, through the accepted signs, the proportion of the pauses that one should make in speaking."[71]

A kind of declamatory punctuation above and beyond any logical or rhetorical function was developed to better reflect the oral delivery of a text. Rollin quotes Quintilian's sentence, *Animadverti judices, . . . omnen accusatoris orationem . . . in duas . . . divisam esse partes* ("I observe members of the jury . . . that the whole of the speech for the prosecution . . . is divided . . . into two parts") to describe the rests and pauses required for correct pronunciation beyond those of grammar alone.

> This short period contains but one sense, which is not to be distinguished by any comma, except at the word *judices*, which is an apostrophe; and yet the cadence, the ear, and even the breath require different rests, which make up all the chain of pronunciation. By accustoming the scholars to make these pauses, as they read, even where there are no commas, they will be taught at the same time to pronounce well.[72]

Sheridan, too, describes "continual instances occurring, where the voice ought to be suspended, without any comma appearing," adding that there are also "instances as frequent, where commas are put down in places, where there ought to be no suspension of the voice."[73] In addition to pauses which mark the distinctions of sense, Blair describes the "Emphatical Pause": it is made "after something has been said of peculiar moment, and on which we want to fix the hearer's attention. Sometimes, before such a thing is said, we usher it in with a pause of this nature."[74]

Parkes provides a passage from Laurence Sterne's *The Sentimental Journey* (1768) as an example of "elocutionary" punctuation. Sterne draws the reader directly into the experience of the character Yorrick, "fixing" attention on the words *I thought* through the use of commas.

> The impression returned, upon my encounter with her in the street; a guarded frank-ness with which she gave me her hand, shewed, I thought, her good education and her good sense; and as I led her on, I felt a pleasurable ductility about her, which spread a calmness over all my spirits—
> —Good God! how a man might lead such a creature as this round the world with him.

The two semicolons serve to link the interior phrase logically to the surround-ing action, and at the same time enhance the moment of intimacy shared between Yorrick and the reader. Parkes adds that the dashes and exclamation marks emphasize the conversational quality of the prose.[75]

John Lennard also points to Sterne's effective use of dashes in *The Life and Opinions of Tristram Shandy, Gentleman,* noting the use of variable lengths in the dashes (often standardized in modern editions), which reflect "a highly per-sonal and humanly inconstant voice."[76] Such an effective and creative means of mimicking the pace and cadence of spoken language would have been admired by Sheridan, who argued that there was much more to observing the pauses of punctuation than their exact proportion of time. This is the concept, reiterated throughout the chart in appendix B, that the semicolon is double that of the comma, the colon double that of the semicolon, and the period double that of the colon. Sheridan explains that the pitch and tone of the voice, not the exact duration of the pause, will inform the mind "whether the sense is still to be con-tinued in the same sentence; whether the succeeding one is to be the last mem-ber of the sentence; whether more are to ensue; or whether the sentence be closed, and a new one is to begin." In addition, according to the nature of the speech, sometimes the speaker may choose to continue on in a sentence sud-denly, overriding a rest, and at other times may choose to delay longer than nec-essary.[77] The Elocutionist John Walker makes the distinction in 1785 between grammatical punctuation, "punctuation of the eye," and rhetorical punctuation, "punctuation of the ear."

> In order . . . to have as clear an idea of punctuation as possible, it will be necessary to consider it as related to grammar and rhetoric distinctly. A system of punctuation may be sufficient for the purposes of grammar; or, in other words, it may be sufficient to clear and preserve the sense of an author, and at the same time be but a very imperfect guide to the pronunciation of it. The art of speaking, though founded on grammar, has principles of its own: principles that arise from the nature of the living voice, from the perception of harmony in the ear, and from a certain superaddition to the sense of language, of which grammar takes no account.[78]

The elocutionary high regard for the spoken, performed langauge naturally led to a strong focus on the *actio* element of delivery, the essential counterpart of gesture to the voice (or *pronunciatio*) as described by Quintilian. Michel Le Faucher, often considered to be the Continental authority behind the English Elocutionary movement, explains the crucial relationship in his treatise *The Art of Speaking in Publick* (first translated into English in 1727):

> Tis *Time* now to come to *Gesture*, which is of no little Importance and Advantage to a Man that *speaks in Publick*; for it qualifies the *Orator* to convey the *Thoughts* and the *Passions* of his Mind to his *Auditors* with greater Force and Delight; their Senses being far more effectually wrought upon by *Pronunciation* and *Gesture* TOGETHER, than by *Pronunciation* ALONE."[79]

As a key element of *pronunciation*, gesture also plays a key role in *punctuation*. Lennard boldly argues that "all punctuation may be considered as an equivalent of gesture in written language." He makes particular reference to an orator's waggling fingers in indication of quotation marks and the raising of a hand to one side of the mouth for words enclosed in parentheses. However, he acknowledges that in texts that are read either meditatively or silently, the gesture associated with punctuation, while comparable, is of an entirely different order.[80] The subject matter of speech, public or private, must dictate the degree to which gesture is employed as well as the degree of theatricality appropriate to each gesture. As Gilbert Austin observes in *Chironomia* (1806), a system of gesture should take into account its suitability for "the licentiousness of the theatre, the gravity of the law, the dignity of parliament, or the modesty of the pulpit."[81] In general, Austin adds, gesture should not be used on every word, but "to such words and passages only as admit, or rather require, such illustration or enforcement"[82]

Unearthing a system of gesture specifically associated with punctuation practices in the eighteenth century is a difficult task, as gesture is a primarily *unwritten* convention. With few exceptions, texts do not come with a set of written-out gestural instructions, let alone a set of understood gestural symbols.[83] Our perusal of the important relationship between gesture and punctuation, as described among the many eighteenth-century acting manuals and elocutionary handbooks, will be necessarily brief. Yet we will try to establish at least a basic sense of how the pauses of speech can be enhanced and made more meaningful through stance, countenance, and particularly the motion of the arms and hands.

Like a sentence or *period* of words, there is also what is called a *period of gesture.* John Walker, in prescribing the elements of gesture for school boys in 1796, emphasizes that great care must be taken to end one sentence completely before beginning another. He describes a total cessation of movement in the body between sentences (very much like the gestural directions accompanying the original Pledge of Allegiance):

> When the pupil has pronounced one sentence in the position thus described, the hand, as if lifeless, must drop down to the side, the very moment the last accented word is pronounced; and the body, without altering the place of the feet, poize itself on the left leg, while the left hand raises itself into exactly the same position as the right was before, and continues in this position till the end of the next sentence, when it drops down on the side as if dead; and the body, poizing itself on the right leg as before, continues with the right arm extended, till the end of the succeeding sentence and so on from right to left, and from left to right alternately, till the speech is ended.[84]

Writing in 1753, the French professor of rhetoric Charles Batteux describes gesture associated not only with the beginnings and endings of periods, but within periods of up to "six members and more": "Now every one of these requires a certain tone of voice and manner of gesture, which accompanies them from the beginning to the end, terminates the members by means of some inflection, marks the divisions, prepares the way for the next member, and at last marks the full stop or place of resting."[85]

Gilbert Austin provides the most detailed description of the gestural period, which he considers to be the "epitome of a complete composition," consisting of a "commencing gesture," followed by a "suspended gesture," and concluding with a "terminating gesture." This he illustrates through a "moral sentence of narrow compass," according to his own notation system marked for the gesture of the right hand (see fig. 2.1).[86] The commencing gesture consists of a supine palm (*s*), rising horizontally (*h*), forward and across the body (*f*). The suspended gesture begins at the word *wise*, with the palm and fingers falling inward in a "natural" position (*n*) while the arm is elevated (*e*) forward and across the body (*f*). For the terminating gesture, the palm and arm return to their former

shf——    nef—— shf st——    R
No man is wise at all times.
com.        susp.        emph. ter.

Figure 2.1. Gestures for a moral sentence of narrow compass. From Gilbert Austin, *Chironomia*, p. 394.

positions (*shf*) with a striking motion (*st*) at the word *all*, and falling to a rest (*R*) at the end of the sentence. The final gesture, with its force of motion, is also what Austin terms an "emphatical" gesture. Walker describes a similar kind of movement where the arm is suddenly jerked into a straightened position in front of the body to accompany an emphatic word. "This coincidence of the hand and voice," he explains, "will greatly enforce the pronunciation."[87] The emphatic words are often the modifying words, the adjectives describing the quality of the nouns. In the sentence shown in figure 2.1, it is not the grammatically important subject *man*, nor the prepositional object *times*, that is emphasized, but instead the adjective *all*.[88]

Lesser points of emphasis require only small gestures. Austin explains that when new ideas or modifications are introduced, then separate clauses or members of a sentence may admit a distinct gesture on the principal word: "But for this purpose, unless the word be important or emphatical, a turn of the hand, a small motion in the transverse direction or in the elevation of the arm, or a small inclination of the head, are sufficient."[89] Johann Gottfried Pfannenberg describes in 1796 this kind of discriminatory gesture between alternating members of a sentence: "For the semi-colon it is especially to be noted, that, if two opposites are separated from each other, it is often appropriate, depending on the nature of the matter, to use the hands alternately; e.g.: wild animals are often exposed to want and hunger; however, those which man protects, find through his care shelter and food."[90]

Gestures do not necessarily coincide with the very points of *commas*, *colons*, or *periods*, at either their beginnings or ends, but instead accompany the force of the idea introduced in each new phrase, enhancing the rhythm and flow of the overall periodic structure.[91] According to Quintilian, gesture should begin and rest with the sense. "Otherwise the gesture will either precede the sense, or will fall behind it; and propriety is violated in either case."[92] Austin (quoting from Rollin, quoting from Quintilian) agrees that gesture should neither precede nor follow the words, especially in calmer discourse. But if the speaker is warmed or excited, "some difference of time, however small, will take place between the gesture and the language." In a rather amusing footnote, Austin adds, "Only intoxicated or insane persons gesticulate after they have concluded speaking."[93] The German scholar and teacher Karl Böttiger observes in 1796: "Among the fine French actors who have certainly reached high perfection in ordered gesture-language, there is general acceptance of the rule; as often as possible, the gesture precedes the speech. It is here, however, more the preparation of the gesture or the first faint tremor, than the gesture itself, which always falls together with the speech itself."[94]

In the expanded and more complex version of Austin's moral sentence shown in figure 2.2, we can observe the introduction of these discriminating gestures as they correspond to each new idea (again the sentence is notated for the gesture of the right hand). The first phrase, a simple statement, consists of one

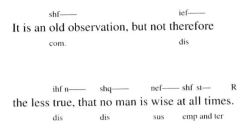

Figure 2.2. Discriminating gestures added to the moral sentence. From Gilbert Austin, *Chironomia*, p. 394.

commencing gesture, which according to Böttiger, would precede the words with the stroke of the gesture falling on the adjective *old*.[95] The position is held during the pause of a comma. However the following modifying phrase, treated to two discriminating gestures, contains a little more momentum and interest. At the adverb *therefore*, the hand changes from a supine position to one of pointing with the index finger (*i*), with the arm elevated in the forward, transverse position for additional emphasis (*ef*). At the adjective *true*, the arm is lowered to its original position (*hf*), still pointing (*i*) and with a noting motion (*n*) that continues through the point of the comma. The comma is one of expectation, the index finger warning, wait until you hear what I have to say next—no man is wise at *all* times. In other words, "though the sound is to be interrupted . . ., the gesture and countenance must express that something further is to be expected." Austin adds that rhetorical pauses in particular, where the sense is suspended unexpectedly and in an unusual manner, serve to arrest the attention. In such pauses, a gesture of expectation helps the speaker convey sincerity and appear to take time for reflection, to exercise thought, to doubt, to resolve, to be alarmed, i.e., to "speak as nature dictates."[96]

The proper use of voice and gesture, the key ingredients of effective oral delivery or *Elocution*, immediately betoken membership in polite society. Correct pronunciation and accent, decorous stance and countenance, graceful arm and hand gestures, and particularly the appropriate use of punctuation, were all desirable attributes for the aspiring *honnête homme*. According to Conley, as much as eighteenth-century rhetoric was influenced by intellectual ideas regarding the acquisition and communication of knowledge, its central concerns were social rather than philosophical. The philosopher's aversion to rhetorical practices seemed to be at cross-purposes to the "classical" curriculum persistent in education. Thus rhetoric, rising to meet the needs of a larger and wealthy, nonaristocratic class, became a system of "managing appearances" and "looking good."[97] The compass of rhetorical practice within this realm of polite society therefore became much broader, embracing not only the formal elements of public oratory, but also those of ordinary, everyday speech.

## The Art of Conversation

Conversational skill, the nature, purpose, function, and management of everyday talk in eighteenth-century society, was a subject of extraordinary interest and attention among works from a great variety of sources: full length manuals, conduct books, essays, rhetorics and logic books, sermons and religious tracts, as well as poetry, novels and plays.[98] Many of these works, a significant number of them written by women, belong to fields outside those of traditional rhetorical study, reflecting the diverse philosophical, scientific, political and social influences on the eighteenth-century *Art of Communication*. As Kevin L. Cope states in his introduction to the collection of essays *Compendious Conversations* (1992), Enlightenment culture is abundantly eccentric and resistant to systematization. Dialogue in particular is "spontaneous and wide ranging, didactical and deceiving, functional and free, informative and asystematic."[99] Conversational practices blur the boundaries between public and private speech. The distinction between the two is often difficult to perceive, occurring somewhere between the intimacy of the family and the public stage—in academies, salons, coffee houses, public assemblies, clubs, dinner parties, etc.[100] Conversational styles, too, are often less formal than the highly mannered and studied language of the public speaking model. Yet the by-now-familiar values of eighteenth-century discourse—the recognized superiority of spoken language over written, the ideal of the *honnête homme* as the good man (or woman) speaking well, the adept management of voice and gesture, and the ability to communicate knowledge plainly and precisely—are all essential to the exchange of elegant conversation in polite company.

Conversation is by definition social, an activity considered in the eighteenth century as fundamental not only to all methods of discourse, but the very means to character ennoblement (at least in appearance if not in actual essence). Henry Fielding maintains in his 1743 *Essay on Conversation* that the pleasure and advantage obtained from the society of conversation is what sets man apart from beast. He describes the admirable conversationalist as essentially an *honnête homme*, defining the "Art of Conversation" as "Good Breeding," or "doing Good to one another." Conversation is the means by which truth is examined, the "only accurate Guide to Knowledge," and Fielding is amazed that "this grand business of our Lives, the foundation of every Thing, either useful or pleasant, should have been so slightly treated of. . . ."[101] In 1762 Sheridan considers silent reading to be a selfish habit and an enemy to the "facility of utterance." The solitary act prevents both the need and the development of communicative skills, preventing the transmission of either knowledge or emotional response. On the other hand, the sociable activity of conversation gives vigor to the noble quality of benevolence, "the source of every Christian virtue." Sheridan argues that conversation should be the primary focus in the education of youth: only then will we "make the living language, as it ought to be, our first object of attention; and consider the written one, as it should be, only in a secondary light."[102]

Taking a more pragmatic approach, Maria Edgeworth, a successful novelist and coauthor of the 1798 textbook *Practical Education*, also emphasizes the scholastic attention due to conversation: young men, no matter how well tutored in public speaking, are likely to become nervous and agitated when confronted with a large assembly, reverting naturally to the vulgar and ungrammatical language they are accustomed to at home. However, Edgeworth counters, "example, and constant attention to their manner of speaking in common conversation, we apprehend to be the most certain methods of preparing young men for public speakers."[103] Adolf Knigge also presents a practical philosophy to the art of conversation, laying down the rules for achieving a peaceful, happy, and useful life in his *Über den Umgang mit Menschen* of 1788. He addresses every conceivable conversational situation, including conjugal conversation, conversation among friends, relations between benefactors and the objects of their kindness, conversation with people of fashion, conversation with men of letters and artists, and so on.[104]

Eighteenth-century literary genres were strongly influenced by the public fascination with conversation, revealing attempts to recreate the impression of actual spoken dialogue through the written medium.[105] The philosophical or oratorical dialogue of antiquity continued to hold a place as a valued method of instruction. The works of Plato were particularly admired, "as a true philosopher only wants to strengthen his arguments and uses no other language than that of an ordinary conversation; everything is clear, simple, and informal."[106] John Constable, in his 1731 *Reflections upon the Accuracy of Style*, explains that he employs the method of dialogues because the reader imagines himself to share in the conversation.

> He takes up with one side or other, and is glad to meet the answers he had already given in his own thoughts, and to find them approv'd by the *Author*: Or where he is in a different opinion from him, he is either willing to be civilly disabused by one who seems rather to converse with him, than to pretend to teach him: Or he is pleased to look upon himself as judge between two contending parties.[107]

Hugh Blair adds that one can both "instruct and please" through the "natural and spirited representation of real conversation."[108]

But it is in the novel that the desire to produce more informal and realistic dialogue is particularly felt.[109] In order to create the effect of spoken discourse for the reader, novelists experimented with new conventions of layout and punctuation, resulting in an explosion of graphic devices used to indicate dialogue.[110] Techniques like the continual repetitions of "he said" and "she said" were felt, in the words of the critic, dramatist, and short-story writer Jean-François Marmontel in 1754, "to retard the vivacity of dialogue and make the style listless where it should be more animated."[111] As Vivienne Mylne explains in 1979, the authors and printers of French and English fiction explored various alternate methods (often in combination) of more realistically presenting dialogue: italics, dashes, *points de suspension* ( . . . ), *guillemets* (« »), or quotation marks, new lines for each change of speaker, and name-headings of the kind found in printed plays.[112] As in the case of French works of fiction from the period 1775 to 1800, one might witness three or more dialogue markers "used so indiscriminately" that none appear predominant. Mylne also notes the "terribly bedashed" style of midcentury English fiction, of the sort already observed in Sterne's clever depiction of the "humanly inconstant voice"—its hesitations, interruptions, moments of drama and tension, and sudden changes of thought so characteristic of conversation.[113]

The following passage from Fanny Burney's *Evelina* of 1779 demonstrates not only the kind of punctuation which had developed to convey a sense of real conversation in a dramatic context, but also the important role conversation had come to play in society as a measure of one's good breeding and manners.[114] The wicked character of the rake, Sir Clement Willoughby is revealed through the impropriety of his conversational style, as is the virtue of Evelina through her proper objections to his undue familiarities.

> "And will you,—can you command my absence?—When may I speak to you, if not now?—does the Captain suffer me to breathe a moment out of his sight? —and are not a thousand impertinent people for ever at your elbow."
> "Indeed, Sir Clement, you must change your style, or I will not hear you. The *impertinent people* you mean, are among my best friends, and you would not, if you really wished me well, speak of them so disrespectfully."
> . . .
> "And when may I speak to you again?"
> "No matter when,—I don't know,—perhaps—"
> "Perhaps what, my angel?"
> "Perhaps *never*, Sir,—if you torment me thus."[115]

All "he saids" and "she saids" are avoided in these passages, although they often appear elsewhere in the novel in less fraught situations. Instead, the use of quotation marks and new lines clarify the changes between speakers.[116] Notice the use of dashes to convey both Sir Clement's undue familiarity and rush at Evelina, as well as Evelina's increasing discomfort in her responses. Her first response is quite composed and no dashes are indicated. But later in the conversation, the three dashes in *No matter when,—I don't know,—perhaps*—seem to indicate her hesitation and dislike at being forced into the rude reply of "never."

The style and character of dialogue naturally varied considerably. The French novelist, essayist, and philosopher, Madame de Staël-Holstein, in her chapter "The Spirit of Conversation" from *Germany* (1810), describes an amiable and entertaining manner that is less about communicating ideas and knowledge than in "giving mutual and instantaneous delight, of speaking the moment one thinks, of acquiring immediate self-enjoyment, of receiving applause without labor, of displaying the understanding in all its shades by accent, gesture, and look."[117] The dramatic dialogue, on the other hand, as described in Diderot and d'Alembert's *Encyclopédie* (1751), needs to be more direct and precise in its objectives, "to the extent that the movements of the heart are faster than those of the mind."[118] Cultural attitudes and taste also played a role.[119] For instance, de Staël maintains that the German language cannot (and should not, else it lose all its grace and dignity) be adapted to suit the precision and rapidity of French conversation. Because of its grammatical construction, the sense of a German sentence is not understood until the very end, thereby eliminating the pleasure of interrupting, which in France, gives so much animation to discussion.[120] De Staël also claims that conversation in Germany easily becomes too metaphysical: "There is not enough intermediate space between the vulgar and the sublime; and yet it is in that intermediate space that the art of conversation finds exercise."[121]

Another way of looking at the supple and malleable qualities of spoken dialogue (and the resulting developments in punctuation) is to regard them as essentially feminine ideals and attributes. Burke notes that what stands out from his compilation of nearly three centuries worth of conversation manuals is "what might be called the 'feminization' of conversational standards in seventeenth-century France, and the rise of informality (or more exactly, of less formal forms) in eighteenth-century England."[122] Women's exclusion from many of the public places frequented by men—the work place, coffee houses, Masonic lodges, and the university with its formal rhetorical training—led to the use of a less academic, more conversational style. As Jane Donawerth observes in her 2002 book *The Art of Conversation*, since women did not have the rights to preach, make political speeches, or defend themselves in law courts, their rhetoric did not fit the public speaking model. Instead she finds that women's theory often takes conversation as a model for public discourse in ways never found in the classical men's tradition of rhetoric.[123] Hannah More, in the chapter entitled "Thoughts on Conversation" from her 1777 *Essays on Various Subjects*, makes this distinction between men's and women's speech abundantly plain:

> That species of knowledge, which appears to be the result of reflection rather than of science, sits peculiarly well on women. It is not uncommon to find a lady, who, though she does not know a rule of Syntax, scarcely ever violates one; and who constructs every sentence she utters, with more propriety than many a learned dunce, who has every rule of Aristotle by heart, and who can lace his own thread-bare discourse with the golden shreds of Cicero and Virgil.[124]

This alternative, "less-studied," and feminine rhetorical style has been credited with having a great deal to do with the success and rise of the novel.[125] Judith Mattson Bean, writing in 1997, also observes that in the nineteenth century, women were continuing to be "praised for writing spontaneous, 'artless' prose and poetry, while men were lauded for their control of language." Bean describes the types of informal strategies expected of the female gender in her analysis of Margaret Fuller's 1845 extended essay, *Woman in the Nineteenth Century*. Fuller inserts comments by means of parentheses or dashes; employs question and answer pairs; and rather than moving from one topic to another in a linear manner, according to the principles of classical rhetoric, she simulates the effect of conversation or extemporaneous discussion through an informal movement back and forth among subtopics.[126]

One important way in which women gained entry into the masculine world of learning was through the role of literary hostess or *salonnière*. France in particular was the center of activity for the salon, a truly elite gathering of men and women of letters with a common purpose to "engage in the new and developing art of conversation."[127] The purity of language, and conversation itself, was a topic of great concern at these gatherings.[128] The role of the hostess as arbiter of taste was to ensure that in the pursuit of truth, the conversational language used—among the celebrated artists, musicians, scientists, philosophers, novelists, and journalists attending—remained clear, void of specialized jargon or unnecessary Latin, polite, and unheated.[129] This required serious application on the part of the *salonnière*, first in her preparation, through reading and by writing about her reflections and reactions, and then in the great attention paid to her own words, as well as those of others, in order to guide the conversational exchanges effectively. In Dena Goodman's often-quoted words, written in 1988, "eighteenth-century salon women transformed a noble, leisure form of social gathering into a serious working space."[130] Burke adds, "Given the importance of the salons and their concern with the art of conversation, it is possible that historians of the French language have overestimated the importance of Vaugelas and Bouhours [male grammarians widely published throughout the eighteenth century] and underestimated the role of women in the development of new standards of polite speech."[131]

The feminine influence on conversation has not always been viewed as positive—another phase in the centuries old debate (known as the *querelle des femmes*) over female virtue and achievement. Rousseau is famous for his disapproval of the salon women who neglect the duties of their "natural calling" in order to preside over the society of men.[132] However, the Scottish philosopher David Hume expresses his approval in 1742 of the manner in which French ladies are "the Sovereigns of the *learned* World, as well as of the *conversible*." Hume is of the opinion that "Women of Sense and Education . . . are much better Judges of all polite Writing than Men of the same Degree of Understanding."[133] Adolf Knigge credits women only so far. On the one hand, he avows in 1784: "NOTHING is more adapted to give the last polish to the education of a young man than the conversation with virtuous and accomplished women. Their society serves to smoothe the rough edges of our character and to mellow our temper." But he goes on to describe domestic affairs thrown into disorder—the victuals brought to the table cold or half-raw and the poor husband forced to go about with torn stockings—while the women attempt to rival men in pursuits for which they are unequal.[134]

Positive or negative, the tremendous impact of women on the rise of the new art of conversation is undeniable. Jennifer Georgia, in her article "The Joys of Social Intercourse," goes so far as to suggest that "perhaps the eighteenth century, the golden age of conversation, was the one age in which women's communicative style prevailed"—a communicative style which is artless, serious, spontaneous, delightful, attentive, reflective, natural—adding a whole new layer of demands to an already well-taxed system of punctuation.[135]

## The Eighteenth-Century Fetish for Correctness

We have described an eighteenth-century punctuation, which on the one hand must be able to convey all the vital elements of language in its highest form, as it is spoken and conversed: the "humanly inconstant voice" of the living speaker with its various gestures, points of emphasis, and "pauses of the ear" above and beyond those which are written. But on the other hand, the logical and rhetorical rules of punctuation must be pinned down and subject to precise prescription, in order to regulate an all-too-fallible language, which according to the strictures of science and effective communication, must be plain, clear, and direct. The Elocutionist Robert Lowth states the dilemma plainly in 1762: by elocutionary standards, the doctrine of punctuation, as it applies to a "just pronunciation," leaves much to be desired:

> The several pauses, which are used in a just pronunciation of discourse, are very imperfectly expressed by Points. For the different degrees of connexion between the several parts of sentences, and the different pauses in a just pronunciation, which express those degrees of connexion according to their proper value, admit of great variety; but the whole number of Points, which we have to express this variety, amounts only to Four [comma, semicolon, colon, period].
>
> Hence it is that we are under a necessity of expressing pauses of the same quantity, on different occasions, by different points; and more frequently of expressing pauses of different quantity by the same points.
>
> So that the doctrine of Punctuation must needs be very imperfect: few precise rules can be given, which will hold without exception in all cases; but must be left to the judgment and taste of the writer.[136]

Nevertheless, Lowth continues, we will have to be content to lay down the rules of punctuation with as much exactness as possible. This he does according to the rules established by grammarians and rhetoricians. He lists the traditional rhetorical proportions of the pauses (see appendix B, entry 23), but adds that in order to apply the points properly, one must consider the construction of a sentence. Here the rules of grammar dominate, as in his definition of the comma:

> Simple members of Sentences closely connected together in one Compound member or sentence, are distinguished or separated by a Comma. . . . So likewise the Case Absolute; Nouns in Apposition, when consisting of many terms; the Participle with something depending on it; are to be distinguished by the comma: for they may be resolved into simple members.[137]

Lowth's efforts are evidence of what Bizzell and Herzberg describe as "the eighteenth-century fetish of correctness in language," referring to the period as an "era obsessed with correctness."[138] Similarly, John Lennard titles his chapter on eighteenth-century uses of parentheses "The Dislike of Dubiety," drawing a comparison between cleanliness and a refinement of manners. The popular phrase "Cleanliness is next to Godliness," dating from John Wesley's 1791 sermon, symbolizes for Lennard the culture of the elite, particularly with regard to their language; voice and gesture, as immediately recognizable external behavior traits, are what distinguish the upper classes and set them apart from the provincial and uneducated.[139]

The practical effects on punctuation in the eighteenth century result in what Parkes describes as a "disciplined flexibility" of usage. Influential writers such as Dr. Johnson and Laurence Sterne might in one sentence use punctuation to indicate the logical structure and then in the next sentence use it to indicate the rhetorical. Or perhaps they might adopt a kind of elocutionary punctuation beyond any logical or rhetorical function, to enhance either the sentimental, conversational, or dramatic style of the prose. As Parkes states, "In the second half of the eighteenth century such authors analyzed their discourse and applied punctuation according to the nature of the style employed in particular contexts much more obviously than before."[140] Honan remarks, regarding his "surprisingly complex and lively picture of pointing theory," that what is arresting is not the lingering infatuation with elocutionary pointing, or a system that would designate "time for breathing," nor is it surprising to find the clear syntactical element present: "What is striking is to find these two contrasting theories of punctuation voiced at the same time."[141]

Yet the results of this "complex and lively pointing theory" are not entirely positive. Elocutionists such as John Walker [34] and Joseph Robertson [40], in attempting to establish a new pointing theory that would fully accommodate all the necessary elements, were ascribing some forty uses for the comma alone. For Honan, the year 1800 represents a kind of nadir in punctuation theory, where the points were sprinkling the written and printed page with feverish and often fanciful liberality. Laments over the lack of principle were voiced frequently.[142] Noah Webster vouches in 1807: "I have never examined any author, whose use of the points is either accurate or uniform."[143] The French philosopher, historian, philologist, and educator Claude Buffier [15] similarly admits, "It must be allowed indeed to be exceeding difficult, if not impossible, to form an exact system of pointing, which all the world shall agree to."[144] And as noted by the Irish writer Trevor Butterworth, in his September 2005 article "Pause Celebre" for the *Financial Times*, American and British writers are still very much at odds over the use of the semicolon. The latter, he claims, embrace its subtlety and mystique, while the former regard it with a deep-seated hatred and suspicion.[145]

Part of the story of punctuation is that in its role of controlling a far-too-fallible language, it must do so through a written medium, a medium far less flexible than that of spoken language. Truss reminds us that our punctuation system is very limited and we are obliged "to wring the utmost effect from a tiny range of marks."[146] The danger is always that having too many signs, and too many varying uses of the same signs, results not in the desired clarity, but in confusion. Throughout the history of punctuation, new signs and combinations of signs have been introduced and then either replaced by more effective signs or discarded as unnecessary. For instance, Nicolson Baker remarks, in his short essay "The History of Punctuation," on the disappearance in the twentieth-century of the great dash-hybrids which were so important in Victorian prose, what he calls the *commash* ,— , the *semi-colash* ;— , and the *colash* :— .[147] We of course have our new net-speak hybrids: [:-) (user is wearing a walkman), 0:-) (user is an angel at heart), :-o (user is shocked and amazed).[148] Other signs also went in and out of fashion. We have already witnessed the terribly "be-dashed" style of eighteenth-century English fiction, and in the sixteenth and seventeenth centuries (again, especially in England) parentheses were employed much more freely than at any other time: to indicate grammatically independent clauses as well as to enclose exclamations, attributions of direct speech in dialogue, *lemmata* in commentaries, sententious statements, invocations, and even to enclose page numbers.[149] It is only when the practice of punctuation becomes standardized that it is able to flourish. As Honan states, "Given some generally recognized norm of use, the points may be adapted artistically, but there must be the norm."[150]

Were we to pursue our history, probing the issues behind why, over the course of the nineteenth century, punctuation ceased to be such a hot and hotly contested topic, and how we ended up with our current rather minimalist and primarily grammatical approach to usage, we would easily stray too far afield from our subject of eighteenth-century musical punctuation. We have already spent enough time on rhetorical history in a book which claims to be about music and for musicians. But hopefully we have managed to create something of the exciting linguistic environment in which eighteenth-century musicians themselves— composers, theorists, and performers (dilettantes as well as professionals)— would have been immersed, both consciously and subconsciously. Before we proceed directly to these musical applications of punctuation theory, let us be reminded that as the subject of rhetoric is ever-changing and ever-evolving, so there were already underway, in the eighteenth century, diverse intellectual, philosophical, social, and political movements that would continue to alter the course of attitudes regarding the *Art of Communication.*

# Chapter Three

# Musical "Resting Points of the Spirit"

Heinrich Christoph Koch begins his chapter "The Nature of Melodic Sections" from Part II of his *Versuch einer Anleitung zur Composition* (1787), with the following statement:

> Certain more or less noticeable *resting points of the spirit* [*Ruhepunkte des Geistes*] are generally necessary in speech and thus also in the products of those fine arts which attain their goal through speech, namely poetry and rhetoric, if the subject that they present is to be comprehensible. Such *resting points of the spirit* are just as necessary in melody if it is to affect our feelings. This is a fact which has never yet been called into question and therefore requires no further proof.[1]

Aside from his remarkable assertion regarding the *unquestionable* relationship between music and the punctuation points of speech, Koch's choice of terminology is in itself fascinating. The long and unwieldy designation of *Ruhepunkte des Geistes*, which Koch repeats throughout his *Versuch*, is a difficult one to translate. The German concept of *Geist* is capable of conveying so many meanings: not only the *spirit* (my term of convenience), but that which animates and brings beauty to an object; it refers to the capacities of the mind and the intellect, even the genius that an artist brings to his or her art.[2] Koch's use of the term in characterizing musical punctuation conjures up for the reader that of a living, breathing art, one which is supple and adaptable, embodying the very nature of human communication itself.[3] This is the essence of the musical punctuation analogy we are working to reclaim—to recognize, understand, and put into practice.

Music making permeated eighteenth-century life, through the increasing number of publicly held performances in opera houses, salons, and concert halls, and as a popular form of domestic amusement among upper- and middle-class households. It became a kind of magnet for Enlightenment ideals, resonating the intellectual, social, cultural, and philosophical concerns of the age.[4] All the complex and diverse influences on the punctuation of discourse, described in the preceding chapter, were absorbed and digested by a musical community that continued to regard the vocal arts as the idealized form of musical expression. Critical reviews of performances, musical journals discussing aesthetics and theory, and performance and composition manuals all reveal an abiding interest in the principles of "classical rhetoric," alongside contemporary concerns for the science and psychology behind musical sentiments. As in language, eighteenth-century punctuation in its musical guise was both dynamic and complex, recognized as an important and powerful tool of rhetoric which sought to reconfirm the relationship between *sense* and its *expression*. Eighteenth-century musicians faced the same dilemma as did the rhetoricians, grammarians, and Elocutionists: how punctuation could be made to convey the all-important elements of language as it is spoken (or sung and played)—in a variety of styles from the very public and theatrical to the more intimate and conversational—and at the same time conform precisely to a prescribed set of rules regarding rhetorical structure and grammatical sense.

In the following sections, we will explore first how eighteenth-century musicians, employing typical Enlightenment strategies of meticulously detailed lists, diagrams, and categories, attempted to exert control over the many overlapping and intertwining elements from discourse which they incorporated into their theories. Second, we will examine the way in which eighteenth-century concepts of musical punctuation embraced the new vogue for polite conversation. And lastly, before proceeding to Part 2 and the specific practical applications of musical punctuation, we will review how as modern interpreters, once we have established an historical and linguistic perspective, we can best approach the very large body of references to what Koch so aptly terms the *Ruhepunkte des Geistes*.

## Organizing a Complex Subject: Categories, Lists, and Rules

The four characteristics of melody, according to Johann Mattheson in his *Der vollkommene Capellmeister* of 1739, are that it be "facile, clear, flowing, and lovely." In laying down the rules by which these qualities are achieved, and thereby the moving or stirring nature wherein true melodic beauty exists, Mattheson espouses many of the eighteenth-century linguistic values which we encountered in the previous chapter: the call for a plain and direct language; the avoidance of any artifice that might obscure the sense; proper attention to issues of grammatical clarity, rhetorical rhythm, and meter; and logical relationships among ideas. Here is a mere smattering from among the thirty-three rules Mattheson lists:

- One should avoid great artifice, or hide it well.
- The caesuras and divisions [*Ein- und Abschnitte*] should be observed precisely: not just in vocal but also in instrumental pieces.
- One must very carefully avoid embellishment [or use it with great discretion].
- One must aim at noble simplicity in expression.
- One must not base the aim on words, but on their sense and meaning: not look to sparkling notes, but expressive sounds.

- In the course of melody, the little intervening resting places must have a certain connection with that which follows.
- Observe well the relationship between all parts, members and limbs.[5]

The need to control truth's all-too-fallible expressions—to classify and systematize (as in Mattheson's list above), and reduce musical punctuation to a science—is very much in evidence. Daniel Gottlob Türk voices the general "dislike of dubiety" particularly well, addressing the importance of "clarity in execution" in the chapter "Von der Deutlichkeit in der Ausführung" from his *Klavierschule* (1789):

> Just as the words: **He lost his life not only his fortune** can have an entirely different meaning according to the way they are punctuated: **He lost his life, not only his fortune** or: **He lost his life not, only his fortune**: in the same way the execution of a musical thought can be made unclear or just wrong through incorrect punctuation.[6]

The resulting attempts to pin down and define musical punctuation reveal a "liveliness" and "liberality" parallel to that of language. Marpurg, in his attempt to lay down the rules in 1762, details nineteen examples relating to the use of the colon, nine for the semicolon, and fourteen for the comma.[7] Mattheson, writing in 1739, is slightly less wild in his punctuation practices; he ascribes eight modes for the colon, four for the semicolon, and three for the comma (although each of these can be treated to a number of variations).[8] But at the center of these lists and rules lies the important role punctuation plays in language as it is spoken, in the performer's ability—through an effective use of voice (or instrument) and gesture—to persuade, impress, and stir the emotions of the listener.

## Voice and Gesture

Musical punctuation, as in Quintilian's "art of speaking well," is fundamental both to the compositional organization of ideas as well as to the final delivery of the completed song, sonata, fantasia, symphony, etc. As we learned from Leopold Mozart [22], a knowledge of *diastolica* is necessary not only for a "good violinist," but also for a "sound composer." Schuback explains in 1775 that he writes on the subject of punctuation in musical declamation "mainly for composers,"[9] and Rousseau [28] addresses punctuation when "speaking of composition" in 1768. Yet musical punctuation's primary focus, as in Türk's example above, is ultimately geared towards ensuring the correct and persuasive execution (or performance) of a composition, what in German is termed *Vortrag*. This musical equivalent of Elocution flourished as a new category and technical term among eighteenth-century musical dictionaries and encyclopedias, and as chapter headings in vocal and instrumental method books.[10] Many composers and publishers were anxious to cash in on the increasing demand for both compositions and "how-to" manuals from the large number of amateur musicians—new members of the middle class, with the leisure for private musical entertainments, and the desire to acquire the accomplishments suitable to their new position in society.[11] Couperin [10] prefaces his introduction of the comma-figure (,) in his 1722 *Troisième livre de pièces de clavecin* as an aid "for marking the end of melodies or harmonic phrases," with the following appeal to the amateur consumer: "I hope that the amateurs of my works perceive, in this third book, that I try twice as hard to please them; and I dare to flatter myself that they will like it, at least, as much as the two preceding volumes."[12]

While this demonstrated concern over proper musical "elocution" is often directed at the amateur, one might imagine that the "professional" or more seasoned musician could also profit from some of the subtleties in performance often conveyed. For instance, in the excerpt from Couperin in example 3.1, the commas appear at first merely to mark out the very typical, regular phrase structure of a lively, straightforward dance movement.[13] Couperin's subject, however, is quite specific, that of the foppish, young men of fashion (*Les jeunes seigneurs cy-devant les petits maîtres*). Their foolish behavior is characterized by sudden octave transpositions, wide leaps, and repetitious patterns.[14] Notice that Couperin charts the progress of their short and rather banal expressions by sometimes placing commas in both the right and left hands and sometimes only

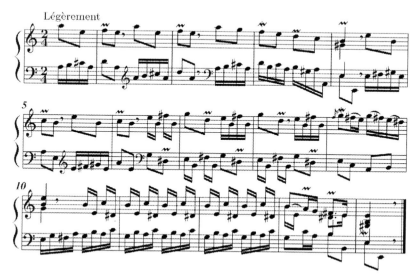

Example 3.1. François Couperin, *Les jeunes seigneurs cy-devant les petits maîtres*, bars 1–14.

in one, providing a kind of weighted rhetorical hierarchy among the punctuation points. In the first four-bar phrase, containing a standard interior structure of 1+1+2 bars, bars 2 and 4 receive commas in both parts. However the repetition of the statement on the dominant in bar 5 is expanded to a 1+1+2+2 structure. Then in bar 10, rather than a two-handed pause, the left hand, joined midbar by the right, carries on its absurd ostinato through an undivided four-bar phase to a full cadence in the dominant key of E major in bar 14. Without commas as guides, there are no other explicit indications for this interpretation of the phrase structure.

Türk, in his discussion of musical punctuation (*musikalische Interpunktion*), explains that when the *periods, colons, semicolons,* and *commas* of music conclude with visible rests, as in figure 3.1 below, then they "should be perceptible to even the dullest senses," in which case the use of more signs would be superfluous.

In the examples marked a) the close of a musical segment [*musikalishe Teil*] or a complete period is expressed; in the examples marked b) the end of a Rhythmus is made perceptible; c) gives examples of phrase members [*Einschnitte*], and the rests in d), which do not permit actual repose, may be regarded as caesuras.[15]

Figure 3.1. Members of a phrase separated by rests.

But he goes on to explain that when such phrase segments, particularly the smallest members, are not separated from one another by any visible rest, then "a much more refined perception" (i.e., a more experienced musical ear) is required in order to find them quickly. This he demonstrates in figure 3.2.[16]

Figure 3.2. Members of a phrase not separated by rests.

The needs of the beginner aside, Domenico Corri [35] feels that musical notation (even when accompanied by words) very imperfectly conveys the style in which it should be executed, "the signs expressive of manner, graces, etc. being so few, that the performer can derive but little (if any) assistance from them." Corri hopes that the introduction of his new signs (ca. 1782), indicating the proper divisions of the *periods*, will prove advantageous to the science itself.[17] In example 3.2, from Paisiello's "Ah che nel petto io sento" ("Hope told a flattering tale"), Corri inserts an asterisk to enable the performer "to distinguish at sight the musical periods where a pause is always necessary."[18] Notice that the first two pauses are accompanied by a decrescendo, emphasizing the downward (restful) melodic inflection. The pause after *tormento*, however, is of an entirely different nature.

Koch expresses a very different attitude from Corri regarding the "discrimination of the sections of melody." Although he writes for the developing musician, he is forced to admit that ultimately one's "feeling" and "familiarity" with musical phraseology is the only reliable way of determining "both the places where resting points occur in the melody and also the nature of these resting points."[19] In other words, from an elocutionary standpoint, the rules of punctuation ultimately leave much to be desired. Too few of them are ever precise enough to hold true in all cases.

Even once these resting points are known and understood (by whatever means—rests, additional notational aids, compositional knowledge, judgment, taste, feeling), their observance through the nuances of the voice alone are

Example 3.2. Proper divisions of the *period* in Paisiello's "Ah che nel petto io sento," with an accompaniment for the harp. From Domenico Corri, *A Select Collection of the Most Admired Songs, Duetts, etc.*, vol. 4, p. 36.

not enough to convey to an audience the structure, character, and sense of a composition. Gesture, too, must come to the musician's aid. Mattheson devotes an entire chapter to the subject, justifying his efforts with a quote from among the "wise writings" of the French rhetorician Charles Rollin:

> The art of gesticulation also belongs to music, it illustrates and teaches the steps and postures of dance as well as of the common walk, together with the postures which one uses in a public oration. In short, music comprehends all the art of composing and writing public utterances that have nothing to do with singing, through which annotations the sound of the voice in speech as well as the tempo and movement of the gestures would be ordered: which was a very useful art to the ancients but is completely unknown to us. So says **Rollin**.[20]

Dance in particular, Mattheson adds, must be carefully constructed according to the character of the actions it accompanies: the various steps, turns, and leaps that give rise to either funny or serious gestures.[21] This most integral union between music and gesture finds its roots in the ancient *Art of Pantomime*, or theatrical dance. C. F. D. Schubart, in his *Ideen zu einer Ästhetik der Tonkunst* of 1784–85 (published in 1806), describes the minuet, or French dance (along with the English, Dutch, Polish, Hungarian, and German dances), as belonging to the *Pantomimischer Styl*, imitating the great ancient mimes. Schubart avows that the composer of the dance must faithfully interpret "each twitch of the sole of the foot, each movement of the hands, each expression of the face, and each position of the body."[22] The Italian choreographer, dancer, and composer

Gaspero Angiolini describes in 1765 the ancient art as a kind of speaking without words: "These movements, these gestures had to constitute, so to speak, a running discourse; this was a kind of declamation created for the eyes, which was made more understandable for the spectators by means of music."[23] As the Italian castrato Giambattista Mancini states in 1774: "The comedians, the *buffi*, with their actions, the ballerinas with their pantomimes, are today the only ones which treat and express good comedy, and are in consequence the only ones who receive the greatest effects of applause and esteem."[24]

Mattheson's discussion of the skills necessary for the composition of dance is prefaced by the acknowledgment that it is the singing stage in the opera which is "the true place and real college for all sorts of gesticulations."[25] Charles Burney agrees, quoting from the essayist and playwright Richard Steele, in his account of the Italian singer Niccolini, who made his debut in London in 1708: "[He] sets off the character he bears in an opera by his action, as much as he does the words of it by his voice. Every limb and every finger contributes to the part he acts, insomuch that a deaf man may go along with him in the sense of it."[26] Mancini adds his opinion to this account: "Let Niccola Grimaldi, called the *Cavalier Niccolino*, be testimony to this; this virtuoso possessed the comic with such perfection that this alone, had he been poor in other talents and not furnished with a beautiful voice, would have been able to acquire for him the singular merit which he held in the profession."[27]

The degree to which the grand gestures of the theater were appropriate to musical performance, as we observed in the section "Elocution and the *Honnête Homme*" in chapter 2, p. 47, was a matter of both taste and venue. Mattheson, for instance, complains of serious and sacred pieces performed in church that "are sung and played in such a manner, chattering, smirking, trifling, so that devout listeners are very annoyed," and similarly, the "quite marvelous and unseemly poses at *Concerten* which sometimes do not have anything in common with either the subject or words."[28] Robert Toft, in his book on expressive singing in England from 1780 to 1830, gives us an example from the English music teacher and singer Thomas Bolton, which suggests some rudimentary gestures appropriate in less theatrical settings (i.e., the drawing room). In his 1812 *Treatise on Singing*, Bolton inserts gestural instructions above the words and music in various practice songs. In addition to directions like "right hand exalted," "full inspiration," and hands alternately "clasp'd" and then "spread," he adds a plus symbol (+) to indicate where breaths should be taken, corresponding primarily to the points of punctuation. In Toft's example from Bolton, most of the gestures occur at the end of the song, with the repeated refrain of "For Love is Heav'n and Heav'n is Love" (ex. 3.3). Initially, a new gesture accompanies each part of the phrase (separated by a breath), but with repetition the gestures become more frequent and emphatic.[29]

It is easy to imagine much of what we learned in the section "Elocution and the *Honnête Homme*" about *periods of gesture* (and their constituent *members—colons* and

Example 3.3. Singing gestures designed for the drawing room. From Thomas Bolton, *A Treatise on Singing*, pp. 14–15.

*commas*) applied to singing. But even when one is seated at a keyboard, with a flute at one's lips, or a violin and bow in one's arms, many of these gestures can (and should) be approximated: the total cessation and relaxation of breath and body at the end of a *period*, the abrupt movements which accompany emphatic moments, or the sense of anticipation through a suspended pause created by an expectant countenance and an arm poised to strike. C. P. E. Bach makes this very point in his 1753 claim that the keyboardist must be able to invoke for his audience the various affects of a composition, asserting: "Those who maintain that all of this can be accomplished without gesture will retract their words when, owing to their own insensibility, they find themselves obliged to sit like a statue before their instrument."[30] Similarly, Baillot, in describing how a violinist can be most advantageously positioned in a quartet in 1835, explains that "in general the sense of sight seems to come to the aid of the sense of hearing in conveying to the listener more completely the expression of the *accent* through that of the physical motions."[31]

Giuseppe Cambini, in his *Nouvelle méthode théoretique et pratique pour le violon* (ca. 1795), demonstrates how very eloquent and persuasive a violinist's bow arm can be in performing a phrase from the first movement of Boccherini's String Quartet, Op. 2, no. 1, shown in figure 3.3:

> Electrify your arm with the fire of this thought . . . so that your bow becomes your tongue and your facial countenance; so that it tells me: (What! You know that I am innocent, you see me as unhappy! And you will not deign to console me!) Then, strongly moved yourself by the energy of this expressive interpolation, declaim the phrase as I have written it for you.[32]

Figure 3.3. The expression of a phrase by Luigi Boccherini in his String Quartet, Op. 2, no. 1, 1st movement, bars 1–4. From Giuseppe Cambini, *Nouvelle méthode théorique et pratique pour le violon*, p. 20.

The execution depicted in figure 3.3 is arrived at by a three-fold process beginning with Boccherini's unadorned notes (stripped bare of nearly all articulation and dynamic information), which Cambini then gradually annotates: adding first sensible fingerings which enable the violinist to negotiate the passage with ease; slurs and wedges to indicate bow strokes, and lastly the crescendos and decrescendos which indicate the speed and flourish of the bow arm in creating the necessary nuances and inflections.

What I find fascinating about this passage is the way that the physical mechanics of playing are completely integrated with the phrase's expressive interpretation (and a very theatrical one at that!). If I were to punctuate this phrase, I would place only a very slight comma at the end of the second bar. Boccherini has already obscured the sense of this midpoint division through the embellishment of the E♭ resting point, creating a kind of connective tissue between the two phrase segments on the third and fourth beats. Cambini's gestural directions only enhance this effect. The phrase began with the urgency of the two opening half-step intervals (connected and intensified by slurs and dynamics), followed by a slight relaxation in the first half of the second bar. But the violinist is not to be consoled, and where he might have paused (with a more restful E♭ gesture), he instead rebounds off of the third beat $e♭^2$, throwing up his arms as it were, before beginning the second phrase of accented, syncopated motions and their abrupt subsidence in the third and fourth bars. Cambini argues that by following the process he has laid out, the above passage is transformed from one of "a uniform and constantly loud sound" which produces only "an insignificant and harsh noise," to one which "begins to carry some intention, albeit vague," and ultimately to a delivery which gives the performer "the pleasure of seeing the spectator moved, immobile, and ready to forget everything in order to hear you." As Cambini avows, "The dramatic art has always inspired these great masters [Haydn and Boccherini among them], even in works which are not presented upon the stage."[33]

An effective use of musical gesture also depended upon a becoming attitude at the instrument. The concern was how to execute difficult passages without disfiguring contortions and manipulations of the face and body. Türk maintains that the countenance of the keyboard player should approximate the character of the composition in a decorous manner. He does "not hold that such a pantomimic play in music contributes very much to expression as was formerly maintained."[34] As C. P. E. Bach also explains, "Ugly grimaces are, of course, inappropriate and harmful; but fitting expressions help the listener to understand our meaning."[35] Leopold Mozart specifically addresses the manner of holding the violin, depicting two possible methods. The first, where the violin is held chest-high in an unconstrained manner, he describes as "natural and pleasant to the eyes of the onlookers." But at the same time, it is "somewhat difficult and inconvenient for the player." The second method, with the violin placed at the neck, "whereby the violin remains unmoved in its place even during the strongest movements of the ascending and descending hand," is more "comfortable" for the player.[36] Baillot, in his *Méthode de violoncelle* of 1804, describes the careful attention required in holding the head and body upright when playing, so as to avoid "all that could have the air of negligence or of affectation." As Baillot explains, grace and skill go hand in hand: "It is extremely rare and almost impossible to see a virtuoso charm the ears who offends the eyes at the same time."[37] The *virtuoso* instrumentalist or singer is the musical *honnête homme*, having perfected the elocutionary arts of voice and gesture in the highest degree.

Some instruments were felt to be more naturally becoming than others. Mattheson claimed that the viola da gamba and lute produced the most refined postures, whereas wind instruments like the flute, easily contorted and inflated the lips.[38] For women, outward physical bearing became a key component in determining which instruments were deemed appropriate for study. The harp, keyboard, lute, and voice were considered most decorous and likely to display the female form to best advantage.[39] The gracefulness of gesture, one's deportment at the instrument, will also become an important part of our discussion in the section below on music's conversational qualities, "Dialoguing a Melody," and again later in chapter 6, when we examine the nature of punctuation according to the affect and character of the topic being expressed.

Amidst a rhetoric of "managing appearances," eighteenth-century instrumental (and vocal) method books were thus preoccupied with the physical mechanics of playing. Elisabeth Le Guin describes this physical and mechanistic attentiveness in 2002 as one more manifestation of the general Enlightenment desire to control and permanently fix all aspects of communication. She describes a "fundamental hopefulness" and belief that the nature of human beings could ultimately be so completely understood that "dancers and instrumentalists would be able to achieve vivid expression merely by recourse to movements that felt right; *thus the most cherished human communications would at long last become infallible.*"[40]

## *Modes of Punctuation*

Like gesture, which finds its roots in the precepts of classical rhetoric, so do the characterizations of musical punctuation. This includes basic concepts of the ancient arts of grammar and rhetoric, where grammar is preparatory yet essential to the art of speaking well. Bonds, writing in 1991 and quoting authors such as Marpurg, Koch, Hiller, and Kollman, summarizes, in his chapter entitled "Musical Grammar and Musical Rhetoric," the distinctions between the two elements of music; grammar is able to ensure the technical correctness of a work, yet a work can be considered rhetorically "correct" only to the extent that it is aesthetically persuasive. The aesthetic value of a work then falls under the domain of rhetoric. But one must not underestimate grammar's foundational basis for all rhetorical arts: "A work must be correct before it can be eloquent."[41]

Rousseau captures the relationship within the concept of punctuation itself.

> A composer, who punctuates and phrases well, is a clever fellow; a singer who feels, marks well his phrases and their accent is a man of taste: but he who can only see, and render the notes, the tones, times, and intervals, without entering into the sense of the phrases, however sure, however exact he may be, in every other respect, he is no more than a sapscull.[42]

In other words a man may know his grammar, but he must remain only a "sapscull" or a third-rate musician unless he can enter into the sense of the whole and do it well.

Mattheson turns to classical sources (those he deems worthy of respect) for his initial definitions of the punctuation marks: Quintilian teaches him that the period or sentence should be structured so that it concludes the rhetorical meaning clearly and perceptibly, and not be immoderately long, lest one be unable to remember it; Isidor tells him that the comma is a small part of a sentence (*particula sententiae*), the colon a *membrum*, but the period and *ambitum*, is a compass, *sive circuitum*, or a range.[43] As Mattheson proceeds with his chapter on punctuation, he also tries to express where form (rhetoric) and content (grammar), as Parkes explains, overlap. Listen to his definition of the semicolon:

> The semicolon has yet its own characteristic, namely this, that it often occurs even before the grammatical sequence of words is completed; which however does not occur with the *Colo* [sic] since that actually requires a formal grammatical sense. At which point nonetheless the complete meaning of the whole rhetorical presentation is as yet undetermined.[44]

Marpurg distinguishes between the grammatical and rhetorical elements of punctuation according to the different signs. The regular signs (*ordentlichen Abtheilungszeichen*)—the period, colon, semicolon, and comma—fall under the first category, and the extraordinary or exceptional (*außerordentlich*) signs—the question mark, exclamation point, parenthesis, and dash—fall under the second.[45] Marpurg only wishes there were more of these latter rhetorical signs in order to better observe the many small pauses of speech and accents of declamation. He is nevertheless forced to admit that "we have no more [rhetorical signs], and one is bound, based on general observation, to leave the rhetorical pronunciation of individual words and phrases to one's own feeling and judgement."[46] Like the Elocutionist John Walker, Marpurg seems to be making a distinction between a grammatical "punctuation of the eye" and a rhetorical "punctuation of the ear," where the latter must remain largely unwritten in order to preserve that crucial relationship between reader and text, performer and composition.

The various types of metrical and rhythmic accents and emphases, which define the character and content of the commas, colons, and periods, also came under scrutiny according to concepts of grammar, logic, and rhetoric. For instance, Koch refers to the "good" and "bad" beats of the bar, the stresses within the measures which correspond to the meter of the poetic feet, as receiving "grammatical accents." He contrasts the grammatical accents from the rhetorical accents, which not only receive a more striking execution, but also are restricted to no fixed part of the measure. The dramatic (*pathetische*) accent, he describes as even more striking than the rhetorical.[47] Writing in 1780, Hiller also describes the grammatical accents as corresponding to the long and short syllables of speech. He portrays the *oratorische* accent as having the role of fixing the expression and marking the sense of a certain concept. The nature of these accents approaches that of the stronger *pathetische* accent, which has the same source.[48] Matteson however refers to such nongrammatical accents, which appear in his punctuated minuet, as *emphases.*

Coming from the French-language perspective, Rousseau acknowledges that "there are as many different Accents as there are methods of modulating the voice thereunto, and there are as many various kinds of Accents as there are general causes for such modulations." He organizes them into three basic kinds, the study of which should be the main business of the musician: first, the grammatical accent which is based on whether the sound of the syllables is grave or acute and whether the quantity of each syllable is short or long; second (and often confused with the former), the logical or rational accent which denotes the degree of connection between propositions and ideas, and is indicated primarily through punctuation; and finally, the Pathetic or Oratorical accent, expressing the sentiments which agitate the speaker and communicates them to the audience.[49]

In an attempt to make sense of these complex relationships, Forkel proposes in 1788 that the line between grammar and rhetoric is a hierarchical one: "The precepts for joining individual notes and chords into individual phrases are contained in musical **grammar**, just as the precepts for joining several individual phrases are contained in musical **rhetoric**."[50] Yet the distinction between the two is not so very great. Forkel admits that "in many respects, musical rhetoric is different from musical grammar only in that it teaches on a large scale what grammar teaches on a small scale." The ordering of several thoughts, from the standpoint of logic and rhythm, observes the same relationships as the ordering within a single thought. This is the basis of what Forkel calls *Periodologie*, how the phrases of grammar are joined to create the periods of rhetoric.[51]

Bonds notes that the concept of *Periodologie*, or periodicity, appears repeatedly throughout the eighteenth century as part of almost all contemporary accounts of movement-length form. And while the theorists may disagree on details and terminology, there is consensus on several basic points, one of which is an almost universal reference to the conventions of verbal punctuation:

> The full, authentic cadence is the equivalent of a period; the half cadence is like a colon or semicolon; and weaker points of articulation are analogous to commas. There

is, moreover, a consistent emphasis on the underlying need for such points of articulation. Without them, individual phrases would be indistinguishable from one another; a movement consisting of unintelligible phrases would be unintelligible as a whole.[52]

This is the essence of the manner in which writers like Riepel, Kirnberger [29], Koch [41], Grétry [42], Reicha [47], and Sechter [55] compare the concept of rhetorical punctuation—how the points of rest delineate the periodic structure of discourse—to the hierarchy of cadences or resting points in music. Mattheson's minuet (ex. 1.3) is a perfect example of a basic periodic structure with its rhetorical hierarchy of cadences and punctuation points: two-bar *commas* combine to create four-bar *colons*, which in turn result in the two eight-bar *periods* of the basic binary dance form.

The trend in musicology in reference to punctuation has been to focus on this element of periodicity to explain form, the results of which have been invaluable.[53] Bonds recognizes:

This concept of periodicity—small-scale units concatenated into increasingly larger ones—provides a key link between the grammar and rhetoric of both language and music. On the smallest scale, periodicity falls within the realm of syntax, for it is concerned with the construction of brief and relatively discrete units. On the largest scale, it merges into the broader idea of rhetoric, for it addresses the totality of an oration or movement, that is, the ordering and disposition of all the periods that together constitute the whole.[54]

It will not, however, be our goal to consider "the largest scale," the complete musical oration, but rather to focus on the *period* or sentence, what Gilbert Austin describes in 1806 as the "epitome of a complete composition," and wherein we find the details of our "surprisingly lively and complex picture" of punctuation. We must remind ourselves that efforts to determine which elements of punctuation belong to grammar and which to rhetoric was only part of the quest to adapt concepts of language to musical expression. The importance, as we have learned, lies not so much in the distinction between the approaches, but the complimentary nature of the various logical, rhetorical and declamatory applications.

## Rhythm and Meter

The belief that language (including musical language) could be minutely dissected and scientifically understood, coupled with the overwhelming desire to organize and prescribe its usage, resulted in the numerous, highly complex definitions (touched on above) of the metrical, rhythmic, and accentual nature of musical punctuation. The adaptation of classical Greek and Latin concepts to modern (eighteenth-century) German, French, Italian, and English, makes the further analogy to music even more abstruse. We will explore a little of this, both to show the level of detail to which the analogy was pursued, and with the hope that in Parts 2 and 3, we may be better able to untangle some of the layers of information embedded in its practical application.

Koch's 1793 concepts of meter and rhythm are very similar to Quintilian's: meter encompassing the specific nature of feet according to short and long syllables, and rhythm occupying the length of time the meter takes to run its course. Koch asserts, "It is well known that the technical term for *meter* is borrowed from poetry, where it defines the flow and the length of the line by help of feet."[55] Koch contrasts meter from rhythm by explaining that as meter describes the subdivisions of the bar (maintaining according to his sense of aesthetics a certain likeness in their movement), the relationship of their length compared with one another is called their rhythmical nature (*rythmische Beschaffenheit*).[56] But what seems to best define the concept of musical meter, is the correspondence of short syllables to weak beats (also called "bad" beats) of the bar, and long syllables to strong beats (or the "good" beats) of the bar. In other words, an *iamb*, consisting of a short syllable followed by a long syllable, must begin on a weak beat so that the second syllable then falls on a point of metrical stress. On the other hand a *trochee*, consisting of a long syllable followed by a short syllable, must begin on a strong beat and conclude on a weak beat. Koch claims that meter (poetic feet) and metrical stress are so similar to each other that one clarifies the other.[57] Thus examples 3.4a and b are both trochaic, while 3.4c and d are iambic.

Example 3.4. The relationship between poetic feet and metrical stress. From Heinrich Christoph Koch, *Versuch einer Anleitung zur Composition*, vol. 3, p. 13.

Mattheson, however, while acknowledging the "accentual" quality of what he calls the *rhythmus*, also stresses its purely quantitative element:[58]

> What a **rhythmus** is, is taught to us by prosody, or that instruction in the art of speaking by means of which it is ascertained how one should properly place the accent, and whether one should utter a long or a short. The meaning of the word **rhythmus** however is merely **quantitative**, namely, a certain measuring or counting out, there the syllables, here the sounds, not only with regard to their multiplicity; but also with regard to their brevity and length.[59]

Mattheson calls rhythms in music "sound-feet" (*Klang-Füsse*) since "song as it were walks along with them." Notice how different from Koch's are his demonstrations of the manner in which the meters from prosody "can be presented in tones or notes." The only distinction Mattheson makes between the setting of the iamb in example 3.5a and the trochee in example 3.5b is the addition of accentual trills. The uniting and manipulating of these feet, the power of which he demonstrates through the production of the various dances—minuet, gavotte, bourée, sarabande, polonaise—he terms *rhythmopöia*. It is later on that he speaks of *meter*, the daughter of *rhythm*. Meter he defines as the "**orderly combination of different or even similar syllabic feet, by means of which they are enclosed within certain limits and are measured.**"[60] And here, demonstrating the meters appropriate for melody, he is careful to set iambic types of meter so that the short syllables fall on weak parts of the beat, and long syllables on strong beats.[61] For instance, figure 3.4 illustrates four possible ways of setting an iambic type of German meter of three syllables mixed with other species (mixed because otherwise it might sound too trifling and childish).

Example 3.5. The quantitative nature of poetic feet. From Mattheson, *Der vollkommene Capellmeister*, p. 164.

Figure 3.4. An iambic type of German meter. From Johann Mattheson, *Der vollkommene Capellmeister*, p. 198.

The problem here, according to Joshua Steele, is that we confound our whole concept of both modern and ancient prosody by not distinguishing between *emphatic poize* and *accent*: "I leave accent entirely out of the question, as it has nothing to do with rhythmus or metre.—And here I must repeat, that it is emphasis, cadence, or the poize of heavy and light (by the Greeks called *thesis* and *arsis*), which alone governs, by its periodical pulsation, that part of music and poetry (as well as of dancing) properly called rhythmus." It does not matter whether a bar of music, which begins a cadence, starts with a short or a long syllable, but that first syllable, or note, or even rest, must carry with it a "heavy poize, or *thesis*."[62] Rousseau also is careful, in 1768, to differentiate ancient and modern languages, drawing rather unfavorable conclusions about the latter. He derives his definitions of meter and rhythm from Aristides Quintilianus, the Greek author of the musical treatise *On Music* (ca. 3rd century).

> The metric measure, according to Aristides Quintilian, is the part of music, in general, which has, as its object, the letters, syllables, feet, verses, and the poem; And there is this difference between the metric and rhymic, that the first is used only in the form of the verses, and the second in that of the feet which compose them, which can be applied even to the prose. From whence it follows, that modern languages may even have a metric music, since they have a poesy, but not a rhymic music, because their poesy has no direction by feet."[63]

As Forkel stresses in 1788, in the context of his discussion regarding the rhythmical connection of tones to musical words and phrases, all of this can become extremely complicated:

The use of rhythm is very diverse, far more so than in poetry. Rhythm is used for the definition of accents, musical feet, measures, and relationships of so-called phrases made up of musical feet. These different uses are divided into as many subdivisions, about which so many things could be said.[64]

It is not really surprising that these highly interrelated and interdependent concepts from classical rhetoric—rhythm, meter, accent, quantity, cadence, and measure—were neither uniformly interpreted nor understood by eighteenth-century theorists. First, the works of the great Roman rhetoricians Cicero and Quintilian were originally based on the ancient Greek rhetorics, which were then regrafted, particularly the work of Aristotle, onto the Latin tradition during the explosion of Greek studies during the Renaissance.[65] The principles of these ancient languages then had to be adapted to the rules and practices of modern languages. Joshua Steele acknowledges the difficulties in his Essay of 1775, noting "the puzzling obscurity relative to the *melody and measure* of speech, which has hitherto existed between modern critics and ancient grammarians." Steele maintains that at least part of the fault lies with the ancient grammarians themselves, "chiefly owing to a want of terms and characters, sufficient to distinguish clearly the several properties or accidents belonging to language." He complains that only *accent* and *quantity* were discussed, with some loose hints concerning *pauses*, "so that the definitions required for distinguishing between the expression of *force* (or loudness) and *emphasis*, with their several degrees, were worse than lost."[66]

Efforts to absorb and digest the rhythmical and metrical patterns of ancient Greek and Latin sparked a great deal of conversation and intellectual exchange among the community of scholars devoted to the subject. A significant part of Steele's *Essay* was written in response to the number of doubts, queries, objections, and observations he received from "learned correspondents" regarding whether or not his choice of terminology and examples of accentuation agreed with those of the "ancient writers and their commentators."[67] The *Essay* itself was written as a rejoinder to the chapters on music from Lord James Burnet Monboddo's work, *The Origin and Progress of Language* (1774), particularly addressing his question as to whether the English language has either the *melody of modulation* or the *rhythms of quantity*.[68] The two maintained an amiable exchange of ideas, the latter proposing to make use of Steele's treatise in the republication of his own work.[69]

The work of the eminent Dutch scholar Isaac Vossius, particularly his *De viribus rythmi, et cantu poëmatum* of 1673 (On the Singing of Poems and the Strength of Rhythm), is often central to the discussion. For instance, discrepancies regarding the quantitative and/or accentual properties of verse by Koch, Mattheson, and others, as described above, arise, according to Monboddo, from the improper use of the word *prosody*, the degrees of acuteness or gravity in language. Its application to quantity and not to accent, "has made Isaac Vossius, among others, believe, that quantity and accent were the same, or at least that the long syllable always was accented."[70] John Foster, in his *Essay on the Different Nature of Accent and Quantity* (1762), criticizes the manner in which Vossius readjusted the accents of the ancients. According to Foster (also quoted by Monboddo), Vossius felt that the acute accent was inconsistent with short syllables and so placed it on the long. This coincided with the laws of Roman accents, but ignored Greek practices, which even Quintilian maintained were more diversified and harmonious than the Latin manner of accentuation.[71] Forkel also denies Vossius's assertion (in *De viribus rythmi*) that the rhythms in the music of the Greeks were far more diverse than they are today (in the eighteenth century). According to Forkel, it only appeared that way since their music lacked the internal structure and tonal language of more modern practice.[72] Mattheson, on the other hand, praises Vossius for his useful work on the "power of rhythm" which in composition is "uncommonly great," and for having taken the trouble of looking rather more deeply into the subject of poetry than other scholars.[73] Similarly, Rousseau's condemnation of modern *rhyme*, without which melody is nothing, is based on Vossius's claim that "language and modern poetry are little suitable to music; and that we shall never have good vocal music till we make verses favourable to the air; that is, till we confine our language, and give it, after the example of the ancients, the quantity and measured feet."[74]

In addition to the complex relationship between Greek, Latin, and eighteenth-century concepts of prosody, and their applications to music, we have also to consider the differences among the individual languages: German and English are both stress-timed and built around the concepts of Latin and Greek syllabic feet; French, on the other hand is a syllable-timed language, where the syllables are uttered at a fairly even rate and the lines of poetry are divided according to the numbers of their syllables; Italian, too, is syllable-timed, though with greater structural stresses.[75] We must always keep in mind these complicating factors surrounding eighteenth-century applications of musical punctuation. For instance, as we will observe in chapter 8 regarding Mattheson's punctuated minuet, variant readings of the metrical orientation and character of its rhythms or "sound-feet," as well as the important emphases within its *colons* and *commas*, give rise to a number of divergent interpretations. And as we will find in chapter 7, the rhythmic pacing and structural pauses of French recitative are very different from the "Italianate" German style. We do not wish to become lost amidst the formidable details of our subject, but we do want to take away at least a basic sense of the issues at stake, as well as the degree of seriousness and gravity with which our erudite musical theorists approached their subject.

## Dialoguing a Melody

Private music making among family, friends, and close acquaintances became a favorite pastime in the middle- and upper-class households of the eighteenth century. This very social form of musical entertainment—a violinist (or perhaps a flutist or oboist) and a cellist gathered around the keyboard to play together a newly published composition, or perhaps an arrangement of a favorite tune— paralleled the contemporary public fascination with polite conversation. Musicians, too, in their compositions and writings about music, became eager to produce works that would incorporate into their art the new and fashionable taste for skillful repartee.

For theorist and composer Charles Henri Blainville [27], in his *Histoire générale, critique et philologique de la musique* of 1767, the style is fundamental to composition and the concept of musical punctuation; all melody must be so "conversed" (*dialogué*) through the use of full stops and commas, which impart a sense of completion, repose, and suspension. Antoine Reicha, however, is far more specific, prescribing four individual punctuation techniques for writing instrumental melody in the form of a dialogue.

> Writing a melody in the form of a dialogue involves the distribution of the phrases, members, ideas, and periods among two or more voices or instruments, or even between an instrument and a voice. In practicing this, one first makes a succession of well-connected periods, while observing the following.
>
> There are only four ways to write a melody in the form of a dialogue: (1) by alternately performing entire periods, (2) by distributing the phrases, or members of periods, between the different voices which must perform the melody, (3) by creating a dialogue with the figures [*dessins*], that is, through small imitations, (4) by beginning a phrase in one voice, and concluding it in another.[76]

The first method, according to Reicha, is the easiest (although one should be careful to create only short periods or else the dialogue will become sluggish). The second method, as shown in example 3.6a, he describes as more intense and more interesting, consisting of a series of opening and responsive phrases. The responses may take a variety of forms: simply repeating the opening phrase, providing a slight variation, or creating a complete contrast through a totally different character and movement. This latter manner, though not for a single voice (one person could not so constantly change from one mood to another), can be particularly "exciting, natural and impressive." Reicha provides an example of this in which the opening phrases appear in a major key marked Allegro, while the responsive phrases are minor and marked Andante. The two voices can also be interwoven, as in example 3.6b, the responsive voice subsumed under the final note of the preceding phrase. This can create considerable intensity and is the means by which dialogue is achieved through small figures and imitations, as in method 3. Reicha describes method 4 as appropriate only for dramatic music when the words absolutely require it. The effect, as seen in example 3.6, can be quite impressive. But, Reicha argues, the interest of true melody suffers.[77]

Example 3.6. Melody in the form of a dialogue. From Antoine Reicha, *Traité de mélodie*, vol. 2, pp. 61–64.

Similar concepts of a conversational/dialogic musical punctuation (some general, others quite specific) were attributed to a wide array of eighteenth-century compositions, from solo keyboard works, sonatas, trios, and quartets to vocal and instrumental works of orchestral forces.[78] For instance, Mattheson and Marpurg focus specifically on how quotations in vocal music should be represented according to the rules of the musical colon. Mattheson explains that "when a **quotation** or otherwise **thoughtful saying** occurs in excerpt form, then not only must the melody be interrupted, but the key must also be altered."[79] Marpurg, too, emphasizes the necessary contrast which must be felt with the introduction of the new voice, offering a number of examples for the setting of quotations in recitative. He claims that in music one has far more means than one does in language of distinguishing between passages which are quoted (one's own words or the words of another) and those which follow or precede them.[80] In general, they are accompanied by what he terms a "quasi-close" (Quasischluß) in addition to a small pause. The voice should rise in expectation, and, as Mattheson dictates, the quoted words should begin in a new key. Marpurg also illustrates how the dash, created through the dissonance of an ellipse or sudden stop, can be used to indicate dialogue in both the recitative and arioso styles.[81]

As one might expect regarding the *solo*, Koch maintains that it functions as a kind of monologue: "The expression of feeling by the solo player is like a monologue in passionate tones, in which the solo player is, as it were, communing with himself; nothing external has the slightest influence on the expression of his feeling."[82] Yet *dialogue* is also one of the solo's possible features. Koch states that in a sonata (including the *two-voice sonata* or the *solo*), "the composer can aim at expressing either a monologue in tones of sadness, of lamentation, or affection, or of pleasure and of cheerfulness; or he can try to sustain in sentiment-laden tones a dialogue among similar or contrasting characters; or he may merely depict passionate, violent, contradictory, or mild and placid emotions, pleasantly flowing on."[83] Koch borrows much of his material on the sonata from J. A. P. Schulz's article on the subject for Johann Georg Sulzer's encyclopedic *Allgemeine Theorie der schönen Künste* (*General Theory of the Fine Arts*), first published in two large volumes in 1771 and 1774. Schulz claims that only the sonata is capable of assuming any and all characters and expressions. He adds that the sonatas of C. P. E. Bach are "so eloquent that one almost believes to be hearing not a series of musical tones, but a comprehensible speech that moves and engages our imagination and emotions."[84] Schubart is similarly impressed by the sonata's all-inclusive nature. He defines the "intimate and social" sonata as so many friends talking amongst each other in an intimate group: "The sonata is therefore a musical conversation, or an imitation of human speech with inanimate instruments. The arioso, cantabile, recitative and all kinds of singing and instrumental music, consequently lie in the sphere of the sonata."[85]

But it was the string quartet which was particularly singled out as embodying eighteenth-century sociability. Baillot describes the quartet in 1835 as a type of composition "whose appealing dialogue seems to be a conversation among friends sharing their sensations, feelings, and mutual affections. Sometimes their different opinions bring about an animated discussion in which each develops his ideas."[86] Goethe's famous remark to C. F. Zelter on November 9, 1829, also supports this view of the quartet: "If I were in Berlin, I would rarely miss the quartet evening of Moser. This exhibition of art has always been to me the most comprehensible type of instrumental music: one hears four reasonable people engaged in conversation with one another, believes one might gain something from their discourse, and become acquainted with the unique qualities of their instruments."[87] Barbara Hanning, writing in 1989, describes the *quatuors concertants*, published in France in the latter half of the century, as cultivating what composers and theorists termed the *style dialogué* —a simple, elegant, and pleasant style with short phrases, rapid changes of affect, textural play and reciprocity among parts—essentially the musical language of the *galant style* which catered to the Parisian taste for witty and lively discourse.[88] Hanning describes the musical style as a kind of "cultural self-image" imitating the pleasure to be had through animated conversation, which Madame de Staël so aptly describes as "an instrument on which [the French] are fond of playing, and which animates the spirits, like music among some people, and strong liquors among others."[89]

The prestige attached to a piece which claimed to be in a conversational style was so great that it became a way for publishers to attract prospective buyers.[90] In his 1998 article Simon Keefe attributes this motive to Koch's use of the term "passionate dialogue" (*leidenschaftliche Gespräch*) to describe the nature of the relationship between the concerto player and the accompanying orchestra: "He expresses his feelings to the orchestra, and it signals him through short interspersed phrases sometimes approval, sometimes acceptance of his expression, as it were. Now in the allegro it tries to stimulate his noble feelings still more; now it commiserates, now it comforts him in the adagio." Keefe claims that the term and description was useful to Koch both commercially and as a kind of a general defense of the genre, which had been criticized in the past by the likes of Schulz and Kirnberger as a vehicle designed only for the virtuosic display of the soloist.[91] Not only did composers try to infuse their compositions with the sense of a dialogue style, but some musical theorists—like Fux, Riepel, and Bemetzrieder—chose to present their teachings in the form of a philosophical dialogue, expounding their theories of melody and harmony through staged conversations between teacher and pupil along the Platonic model.

But the attribution of conversational qualities in a composition could also be perceived as negative. Mary Sue Morrow presents in 1997 a rather devastating remark from a provincial newspaper published in Flensburg in 1792. The writer admits that a beautifully performed Haydn sonata can do a lot, but "such things . . . are like an agreeable, entertaining conversation that one hears with relish, but without interest. They are more sleight-of-hand than nourishment for the heart."[92] She also quotes from Forkel (who quotes Sulzer): "[Instrumental pieces] generally represent no more than a lively and not unpleasant noise, or a pleasant, entertaining conversation which does not, however, engage the

heart."[93] Such criticisms are generally expressive of the eighteenth-century preference for vocal music over instrumental; the latter might be entertaining and
diverting, but without the ability to convey the precise semantic content of vocal
music, it could never achieve the same status. In a similar light, the attempt to
attach a program or narrative to a purely instrumental work was often viewed as
serving merely to call attention to its shortcomings. For instance, in reference to
C. P. E. Bach's 1749 trio *Sanguineus und Melancholicus*, subtitled "A Conversation
between a Cheerful Man and a Melancholy Man," Charles Burney complains in
1789 that despite the composer's powers of invention, melody and modulation,
his attempt to depict two disputants of different principles remains "as obscure
and unintelligible, as the warbling of larks and linnets."[94]

It is important to note that while for the most part our descriptions of musical
conversation have reflected the style of give and take which mirrors the French taste
for lively, pleasant, and amusing discourse, yet a very different graver and more
imposing vocabulary associated with dialogue is also in evidence, particularly in the
context of the concerto.[95] Mattheson, in his description of the *concerto grosso*, presents the image of a battle among participants: "One can easily guess that in such a
contest, from which all concertos get their name, there is no lack of jealousy and
vengeance, or envy and hate, as well as other such passions."[96] Friederich Erhardt
Niedt similarly conveys the element of a dispute, defining the concerto in 1721 as
"a skillfully composed piece in which the voices argue and alternate with one
another."[97] Koch describes the concerto (at great length), not so much in terms of
a contest, but yet as a highly impassioned and theatrical work. The more dramatic
means of "dialoguing a melody" (as described by Reicha) are present: short phrases
which do not always wait for the conclusion of the incise or phrase in the principle
part, but are heard alternately in brief imitations. "In short," Koch concludes, "by a
concerto I imagine something similar to the tragedy of the ancients."[98]

Schulz describes the trio or *sonata a tré* in similar tones, very likely referring
to C. P. E. Bach's sonata for two concerted instruments accompanied by a
bass, *Sanguineus und Melancholicus*: "Good trios . . . are rare and would be still rarer
if the composer portrayed, in tones, a complete passionate dialogue between similar
or opposing characters."[99] These highly dramatic conversations, the contest of the
concerto and the confrontation between two opposing characters in C. P. E. Bach's
trio, are very different from the idealized, decorous conversations of polite society.
As Keefe points out in 1998, equality in participation among all present was a
highly valued component of conversation which the concerto could never hope to
achieve.[100] Similarly, the confrontational dialogues, which Richard Will describes in
1997 as occurring in various eighteenth-century instrumental compositions, bear
more resemblance to an argument between philosophers, each trying to prove the
folly of the other's position, than the amiable exchange of a multiplicity of ideas,
characteristic of Goethe's "Conversation among friends."[101]

The English curate, composer, and writer William Jones [37] delightfully captures the often capricious and bantering quality of this latter conversational style in
his 1784 comparison between the contemporary works of Haydn and Boccherini

and those of the elder Handel. (Note the same vocabulary of wild "warbling" used by Charles Burney, quoted above, but without the degree of negativity.)

> As for *Haydn* and *Boccherini*, who merit a first place among the Moderns for *invention*, they are sometimes so desultory and unaccountable in their way of treating a Subject, that they may be reckoned among the wild warblers of the wood: And they seem to differ from some pieces of *Handel*, as the Talk and the Laughter of the Tea-table (where perhaps, neither Wit nor Invention are wanting) differs from the Oratory of the Bar and Pulpit.[102]

Perhaps Jones had in mind passages like those shown in examples 3.7 and 3.8 from the opening movement of Boccherini's String Quartet, in E-flat Major, Op. 32, no. 1, lavishly titled Allegretto lentarello e affettuoso.[103] In example 3.7 note Boccherini's "unaccountable" way of treating his subject. After a *forte* deceptive cadence in bar 24, the "conversationalists" suddenly put their heads together and begin a murmur which repeats just a few times too many (four full bars), and then just as suddenly in the middle of bar 28, they seem to shake themselves apart for their appointed task of closing the movement's exposition in the dominant key of B flat (four bars later). In example 3.8, from the development section of the same movement, Boccherini gives us the kind of dialogue Reicha describes as achieved through small figures and imitations, in this case a gentle exchange and banter among the four players.

Example 3.7. Luigi Boccherini, String Quartet in E-flat Major, Op. 32, no. 1, 1st movement, bars 23–28.

Example 3.8. Boccherini, String Quartet in E-flat Major, Op. 32, no. 1, 1st movement, bars 52–55.

Jones's words and these examples from Bocherini are also suggestive of the way that dramatic dialogue departs from the *feminine* ideal of conversation we discussed in the section "The Art of Conversation" in chapter 2, pp. 54–55: where all is pleasant, easy, natural, and unstudied; where one moves from one subject and affect to another with ease (rather than through methodical reasoning and argument); where the language used is understood by all present; and where no single voice either dominates or is left out; in essence the French cultural self image described so well by Barbara Hanning above. Mattheson sums up these ideals (although without labeling them as "feminine") with astonishing clarity when describing the first characteristic of true melodic beauty, a **facile** quality.[104] He begins by explaining, "**We cannot have pleasure in a thing in which we do not participate,**" from which he derives the following seven rules:

1. There must be something in all melodies with which almost everyone is familiar.
2. Everything of a forced, far-fetched, and difficult nature must be avoided.

3. One must follow nature for the most part, practice to some degree.
4. One should avoid great artifice, or hide it well.
5. In this the French are more to be imitated than the Italians.
6. Melody must have certain limits which everyone can attain.
7. Brevity is preferred to prolixity.[105]

In the chapter "Of Good Execution in General in Singing and Playing" in his *Versuch einer Anweisung die Flöte traversiere zu spielen* of 1789, Johann Joachim Quantz makes some of the same points, also applicable to the feminine ideal of conversational etiquette. He warns against crowding an adagio with so many graces in the effort to appear learned that they serve only to ruin a composition's agreeable character; for there is more art in saying much with little, than little with much. In speaking, too, he explains, we must use expressions that others understand. What use is it if we execute ideas in an obscene and bizarre manner which is incomprehensible and arouses no emotion? Further, we should not demand that all of our listeners be connoisseurs and professionals, but should seek to play distinctly so that each piece is intelligible to the learned and unlearned alike.[106]

As we examined women's role in the development of a spoken and written conversational style (and its impact on punctuation), it is also worthwhile to examine briefly the broader music-making activities of women to observe their role in the mapping out of a parallel musical conversational style. Excluded from the more formal, Latin-centered rhetorical training of the University, music assumed a prominent role in a woman's education (as she was given little opportunity to learn much else).[107] Proficiency on the keyboard in particular became practically mandatory for women among families aspiring to the social mobility that educated daughters represented. The harp, lute, or voice were other options since brass, woodwind, and bowed instruments were considered to be unbecoming to the female form. Maria Edgeworth gives a particularly amusing account in 1798 of the high social value attached to a young lady's musical accomplishment. She poses a question to the mother of the young lady:

> But would not you, as a good mother, consent to have your daughter turned into an automaton for eight hours in every day for fifteen years, for the promise of hearing her . . . pronounced the first private performer at the most fashionable, and most crowded concert in London?

Although concerned at such a cost to her daughter, the mother replies:

> What a distinction! She would be immediately taken notice of in all companies! She might get into the first circles in London! She would want neither beauty nor fortune to recommend her! She would be a match for any man, who has any taste for music! And music is universally admired, even by those who have the misfortune to have no taste for it. Besides, it is such an elegant accomplishment in itself! Such a constant source of innocent amusement! . . . I should wish my daughter to have every possible

accomplishment; because accomplishments are such charming *resources* for young women, they keep them out of harm's way, they make a vast deal of their idle time pass so pleasantly to themselves and others![108]

Many classical sonatas, and particularly the accompanied sonata, were targeted for women. The latter were especially popular, with the woman at the keyboard, flanked by men on a violin and cello, doubling respectively her right and left hands. The accompanying parts were often optional and it became a popular commercial practice to arrange solo sonatas (with or without the composer's permission) in order to improve their entertainment value. C. P. E. Bach admitted to Forkel (1775) that he finally had to bow to fashion and write sonatas for keyboard that are easy, and that one can play either with a violin and violoncello, or alone without missing anything.[109] Matthew Head (1999) describes a stream of songs and keyboard pieces from European presses dedicated to the ladies. These works included polonaises, minuets, rondos—in other words all the natural, songful, and easy, galant-styled melodies. But Head makes the point, quoting Hiller in review of Johann Friedrich Wilhelm Wenkel's *Clavierstücke für Frauenzimmer* (1768), that as many men as women shared the preference for such *galanterie*. The dedication to "the fair sex" serves also to define and brand the fashionable taste, described so well by Mattheson and in such demand from the new bourgeois class of amateur players, as feminine.[110]

Not surprisingly, such a branding was not always deemed positive. In Morrow's collection of instrumental music reviews from the late eighteenth century, the labeling of a piece as feminine, easy, or light was often a kind of criticism. For instance, the *Berlinische musikalische Zeitung* dismissed some serenades by Anton Groene as "tinkly little pieces for women and effeminate men." A reviewer of C. P. E. Bach's *Sonates à l'usage des dammes* in the *Frankfurter gelehrte Anzeigen* implies that the works are so good, he doubts if women can really play them. And Türk, in the *Allgemeine deutsche Bibliothek* compares the *Kleine Sonaten* of Caspar Daniel Krohn to food served on plates that is very easy and light: "You won't have to worry about getting a stomach ache from them . . . but you won't get any healthy nourishment either."[111] Perhaps, too, derogatory references to a piece as "conversational," like those we discussed earlier, are as much reflective of this attitude as a general disparagement of instrumental music's semantic capabilities.

But the boundaries of women's participation in music, between the amateur and domestic and professional and public spheres, are often blurred. Maria Edgeworth's "good mother" sends out very contradictory messages, applauding on the one hand great accomplishment with its necessary repetitive and demanding physical training, and the distinction of performing in a very crowded concert. At the same time, she refers to the "private" domestic sphere of "innocent amusement," and a daughter's "charming resources" with which to pass "idle time pleasantly." As Head explains, the discourse of easy music, with little or no physical effort involved, exits side by side with contrary discourse surrounding professional female music making.[112] We discussed, too, with regard to musical gesture, that there was a more general desire (among male performers as well as female) for a graceful and becoming attitude regardless of the technical demands or difficulties in singing and playing. Haydn dedicated some of his most difficult sonatas to women musicians, including his six sonatas H. XVI:35–39 and 20 to Marianna and Katherina von Auenbrugger, stating in a letter to his publisher Artaria in 1780: "The approval of the Demoiselles von Auenbrugger is most important to me, for their way of playing and genuine insight into music equals those of the greatest masters: Both deserve to be known through public newspapers in all of Europe."[113] Female singers could more easily gain fame than their fellow instrumentalists through highly public performances in operas and oratorios, genres which allowed equal participation from both men and women. And musical salons, like those of Marie Emmanuelle Bayon Louis (credited with bringing the fortepiano into vogue in France) and Anne Louise Brillon de Jouy in the 1770s, and later, those of Fanny Hensel in the 1830s, offered women as wide a variety of musical activities as the professional in the public arena—a venue for subscription concerts, teaching, and selling compositions.[114]

My purpose for this apparent diversion into the realm of women and music, via the subject of conversation, is that although we have been observing feminine labelings weaving their way in and out of our discussions—regarding physical gesture, virtuosity and accomplishment, and in defining the various affects and compositional styles of the sonata, concerto, fugue, minuet, polonaise, etc.—yet in this monograph on musical punctuation, women's voices, their own words regarding the practice of music, are virtually absent. The extant manuals and teaching methods by women date primarily from the latter half of the nineteenth century. Also women's involvement in the higher intellectual debates over the science and philosophy of music and the details of their activities in the salons remains largely unrecorded.[115] But is it not possible that the theory Jennifer Georgia proposes, regarding the eighteenth century (the golden age of conversation) as the one age in which women's communicative style prevailed, could also be true for music? Women as models, dedicatees, consumers, students, performers, teachers, and composers of eighteenth-century music were always present, even at the root of activities, helping to define what we have come to understand of the very rich, complex, and wide-ranging elements of the "classical style." Conversational techniques seem to embody the musical language of the galant style, with its frequent and easy changes of affect and topics of discourse. In addition, the boundaries of this purportedly feminine style, like the diverse sphere of women's music-making activities itself, easily merges into more traditional masculine contexts. Witness the quintessentially galant minuet, deprecated as frivolous and feminine, yet at the same time touted as the perfect compositional model for the ways in which individual phrases could be combined, varied, and manipulated into complex, symphony-length movements.

Such deeply rooted questions naturally exceed the scope of our study on musical punctuation, but hopefully we have given some food for thought regarding women's role in the development of eighteenth-century communicative styles, and by extension, concepts of musical punctuation. Let us then conclude for now with a statement by Joshua Steele, who professed great faith in women's power of influence. He maintained that although it was in the province and power of the (masculine) universities to bring the important study of music and language together, should they fail to do so, he could comfort himself with the hope that the notation system proposed in his *Essay* would be patronized by the ladies.

> The study of music being almost universally thought a necessary part of their education, they will find no difficulty in understanding the subject of this treatise; and if they should make the care of their nursery their principal amusement, as all the best of them do, may we not expect to see the rising generation instructed by their fair mothers in the joint knowledge of letters and music, and our typical marks of ACCENT, QUANTITY, EMPHASIS, PAUSE, AND FORCE, as added to their spelling book (which will then be a compleat *Gradus ad Parnassum*), and as familiarly known as the alphabet."[116]

## The Currency of Musical Punctuation

Having established the spirit in which the punctuation analogy is adopted, and explored its diverse, intertwining components—"classical," rhetorical, grammatical, logical, scientific, affective, elocutionary, gestural, and conversational—let us now consider how best to approach the body of information on the subject. In order to achieve an overall historical perspective, I have attempted to cover the gamut of references on musical punctuation. The result is a remarkable number of accounts in many languages—English, French, German, Latin, and Italian—from a wide variety of sources—grammars, dictionaries, elocutionary handbooks, singing manuals, instrumental handbooks, and compositional methods—and covering an enormous time span. I have compiled a chart (in appendix B) of this fairly comprehensive list of musical punctuation references, interspersed with accounts of corresponding language usage (designated by an [L]) and presented in chronological order.[117]

The chart serves as a point of departure. Its purpose is both to present a ready overview of what is an overwhelming body of information on the subject, and to facilitate further discussion of the issues at stake. I debated trying to provide some kind of categorical sense for the punctuation entries—i.e., a grammatical focus vs. a rhetorical one, composition vs. performance, harmonic vs. melodic— but there is so much overlap and crossover among such categorizations that in the end I abandoned the idea. I also feel that a chronological presentation of the entries is both more accurate and more interesting; the degree of diversity and complexity among the applications (as well as the similarities) dramatically parallels the diverse compositional, performative, grammatical, rhetorical, logical, scientific, philosophical, and social elements (to name a few) to be found within the analogy's linguistic origins.

The entries include, for the most part, only those authors who specifically incorporate the terminology of verbal punctuation, and the selected passages are direct quotes which reflect the manner in which the authors introduce and define the subject. The categories are mainly confined to those of the four standard punctuation signs (comma, semicolon, colon, and period) for the reason that the larger, smaller, and more "rhetorical" signs do not receive the same systematic treatment in the treatises. The primary focus of the chart is the 150 year period after 1700, reflecting the tendency on the part of music to adopt the latest and most fashionable trends of linguistic thought. The chart begins with Quintilian representing the classical preceptor of the others. The following earliest entries, such as Zarlino [2] (1558), Morley [3] (1597), Butler [4] (1636), and Simpson [5] (1667), demonstrate the initial association with purely vocal music—the use of the musical rest to indicate the punctuation points of the text. At the other end of the chart, with Lussy [56] (1873), Riemann [58] (1882), and Fischer [61] (1926) we have some of the analogy's final advocates and the initial historical overviews of the subject—although Callcott [46] (1810) should probably be credited with the first history of the subject, quoting passages from the likes of Koch [41], Riepel, Kirnberger [29], Rousseau [28], and Jones [37]. The two entries by Hofmann [59] (1908) and Alexanian [60] (1922) reveal the lingering impact of the analogy's terminology on musical discourse.

Perhaps the most remarkable aspect of the punctuation chart, aside from the enormous time span it encompasses, is that the tenor of the analogy remains relatively constant throughout. Rousseau's [28] (1768) definition of punctuation is included with Momigny's [48] extensive essay on *ponctuation* in N. É. Framery's musical *Encyclopédie méthodique* of 1791 (edited with P. L. Ginguené), and appears again in Riemann's *Vademecum der Phrasierung* of 1900 with an exclamation point to emphasize that punctuation is being spoken of compositionally: *Ponctuer, v. a. c'est en terme de composition (!)*.[118] Is Sechter's [55] concept of hierarchical cadences in 1853 so very different from Kirnberger's [29] in 1771, or even from Butler's [4] in 1636? The fundamental proportional relationship between the signs, each progressively doubling the value of the previous sign in the order of comma, semicolon, colon, and period, remains the same for Walker [34] in 1781, Marpurg [24] and Lowth [23] in 1762, and the anonymous English author [7] in 1680. Parkes offers an explanation for this phenomenon, and adds a note of caution:

> Most writers on punctuation are aware that they are writing in a scholarly tradition which began at a time when education was dominated by the ideal of the orator. Like all literary traditions this one produced its own *topoi*: the analogy between hesitations in the reading process and pauses in spoken discourse; the assignation of arbitrary time values to these pauses, graded in relation to each other; and the relationship conceived between punctuation and accentuation. Such *topoi* owe as much to the influence of a

literary tradition which begins with the ancient grammarians, as to empirical observation of usage. The principal value of the theorists lies in what they reveal about attitudes to language in general rather than the prevailing uses of punctuation in particular.[119]

Indeed it would be ludicrous to claim the continuing interest (and sameness of application) in the punctuation analogy as evidence of static performance practices and compositional styles. Consider the changes in instruments between 1700 and the mid-nineteenth century: the developments from the plucked strings of the harpsichord to the cast-iron frame and overstrung bass of the Steinway Grand: the natural tapering stoke of the arched baroque bow versus the sustaining stroke of the Tourte bow; the movement away from intimate venues to a public arena of large halls and auditoriums. Witness also the stylistic changes in composition, for instance the treatment of the fugue by J. S. Bach and later, Antoine Reicha. Robert Toft notes in 1994 that although the practices associated with punctuation, rests, and breathing remained relatively stable throughout the period under consideration (and Toft refers to a mere eighty-year period between 1770 and 1850), the style of music to which the expressive pause was applied changed dramatically.[120] So how do we cope with this enormous time span of two centuries?

Scholars tend, and not without reason, to consider the latter half of the eighteenth century as a kind of "heyday" for musical punctuation (although we might consider the explosion of pointing manuals and handbooks, and the resulting "utter confusion" as something less positive). It is during this period that the linguistic analogy really takes root among musicians. In 1768 the subject makes its way into dictionaries for the first time with Rousseau's [28] entry, *ponctuer*, and the term "to punctuate" becomes the accepted synonym for "to phrase."[121] This would have greatly pleased Mattheson, who in 1739 bemoaned the fact that diastolica is so neglected that "one does not even find it in the most recent musical dictionaries."[122] Koch (1787–93) also falls subject to the trend. In spite of the fact that he is not entirely happy with the term, cadences and phrase endings are throughout his *Essay on Composition*, continually referred to as the "punctuation formulas" (*interpunctischen Formeln*) of music.[123] But perhaps the best example of the extent to which punctuation had invaded the vocabulary of musicians is found in a letter from W. A. Mozart (1778) to his father. Mozart describes how the veteran singer, Raaff, helped his younger colleague, Hartig, sing the role of Admet in Schweitzer's *Alceste.* "The best part . . . is the beginning of the recitative O Jugendzeit! —and it was Raaff's contribution which made this a success; for he *punctuated* [*punkirt*] it for Hartig . . . and by so doing introduced the true expression into the aria."[124]

Musical theorists of the late nineteenth century also tended to consider the latter half of the eighteenth century as the era of well-defined phrase structure, often expressing condescension towards the efforts of earlier eighteenth-century theorists. In Riemann's judgment in 1900, Schulz's 1774 article on *Vortrag* (execution) is the first German critical work truly to understand the importance and problematic nature of phrase boundaries (*Phrasengrenzen*). Riemann copies the entire middle section of Schulz's article on Vortrag, and explains that while Mattheson (1739), Riepel (1752), and Leopold Mozart (1756) laid the groundwork for such studies by Schulz, Kirnberger (1771–79), Koch (1782–93), and Türk (1789), it was the latter group which really understood the complicated relationship between meter (*Taktweise*), emphasis (*Betonungswiese*), and phrasing (*Phrasierung*).[125] Writing in the late nineteenth century, Lussy is similarly condescending towards Mattheson's analysis of a minuet. He refers to it as a "curious specimen of musical punctuation," copies it, and states: "We need add nothing to this analysis, so strange and remarkable, especially for the time in which it was made."[126]

But if we pursue such categorizations, we run the risk, as James Webster maintains in 1991, of denying "both the strong continuity of late eighteenth-century music with earlier musical cultures of the century, and its very different continuity with that of the nineteenth."[127] As Bonds recognizes, it is by no means that the kinds of phrase constructions which lend themselves to the concept of periodicity were new in the second half of the eighteenth century. Rather it is that they achieved "unprecedented prominence at this time."[128] Further, the trend towards judging the unity of a work according to the ordering and proper connection of individual phrases, what Morrow claims distinguishes the nineteenth-century approach to formal structure from that of the eighteenth century, began in the 1780s and 1790s and is observable particularly in the writings of Koch, Forkel, and Türk.[129]

Thus we must take care to use our chart intelligently. Sometimes it will be appropriate to apply the punctuation practices of a late eighteenth-century theorist to a piece written in the early part of the century. This is acceptable, for instance, in the case of the baroque dance structures from which the well-defined phrase structures of "classic" music were drawn. The "topic" at hand and its accompanying *affect* must guide us; punctuation practices associated with the moderately gay, well-defined structures of the minuet are not appropriate for the subject of the serious and learned, contrapuntal fugue, nor are they appropriate for the recitative-like and impassioned expressions we find in many sonatas and symphonies. And while there may seem to be no language barriers—French definitions of the signs are much the same as the German—we must keep in mind that as the analogy becomes more closely tied to language, these differences will surface with greater frequency.[130] It will be acceptable in our discussion of minuets to use examples from Couperin, Lully, and the dancing master Pierre Dupont as models for German dances (which are in fact modeled on the French dances), but comparisons between punctuation practices in French and German recitative, i.e., Marpurg's resetting of selections from Rameau's *Zoroastre*, are of an entirely different nature.

We must also remember that notational practices, and the conventions associated with them change. While Leopold Mozart [22] (1756) and Westphal [57] (1880) may appear to advocate the same practice (that no break in the sound should be made from one note to the next unless rests or the division of the phrase requires it) we must remember their very different musical aesthetics. The sense of punctuation between phrases can not have been felt in the same way in Westphal's day (and ours) of continuous legato as it would have been in Mozart's where the typical articulation was a detached one. By the time Alexanian [60] (1922) uses the term *musical punctuation*, no mention of pauses or rests is even made, only the necessity of adding dynamic fluctuations to cello bowing in the legato style. Consider also that the basic direction of phrases has changed. As Riemann explains in the third edition of his *Musik-Lexikon* (1887), all figurations within the phrase division have the sense of leading from one point of stress to the next in an upbeat formation.[131] This is extraordinarily different from Türk's concept of the way in which the beginning notes of phrases must be emphasized with a lessening of stress until the next phrase beginning.[132] Also, as our eighteenth-century rhetoricians have warned us, language can be fallible and we must be careful to define our terminology. We must make sure that we do not use language that has either contradictory or imprecise meanings which can lead to misunderstanding. Do we mean the same thing when we speak of "articulating" a phrase as we do when we "articulate" a note or slur? If not then perhaps we should not use the same terminology, or at least we ought to be sure of the context in which we use it.

It is not our goal to trace the development of how musical punctuation reflects changing musical styles, but to find the points of continuity in its eighteenth-century application. If we are to use the body of information on the subject effectively, establish some normative practices from this complex, flexible, and *living* theory, we must constantly maintain the kind of historical perspective suggested in this chapter on both a large and small scale. For if the learned Heinrich Christoph Koch found the subject difficult to take hold of, how else are we to accomplish it more than two centuries later?!

*Part Two*

# The Art of Interpreting Rests

# Chapter Four

# *Written and Unwritten Rests*

*Concerning the Stops, Points, or Pauses*
*Observe,*
That you must endeavor perfectly to know each of them, by their Figures
or Shapes, by their several Names, *but especially* the *time*, you are to Stop
at each of them.

—Anonymous, 1680

Stop, Breathe, Pause, Suspend, Take Time, Rest, Divide, Separate. . . . Such injunctions dominate eighteenth-century (and nineteenth-century) discourse on the Art of Punctuation. As we established in Part 1, the manner in which phrases are formed and differentiated (our "complex and lively picture of pointing theory") encompasses a broad array of subjects: syllabic feet, metrical stress, accent, emphasis, dynamics, inflection, as well as considerations of gesture, affect, compositional type and style, etc. But a quick glance through the chart in appendix B reveals punctuation's defining role as the delineation of phrase structure through pauses, or musically speaking, *rests*. The three chapters here in Part 2 explore the interwoven parameters by which we can begin to grasp this intricate *Art of Interpreting Rests*: the methods of notating the pauses of punctuation, differentiating these symbols from those of articulation, and always taking into consideration the prevailing character or *affect* of the expression at hand.

As performers, students, or teachers, we have all very likely said, or had said to us, something along the lines of "be faithful to the score," or "play only what is *written*." We observed, with regard to the punctuation of the Pledge of Allegiance, that the South Bay Toastmasters similarly advised their members to "speak it as it is written." But as we have also learned, such a request is not as straightforward as it might seem. We must remind ourselves that punctuation is an essentially visual phenomenon with a history inseparable from that of written language. Writing served initially as a visual record of the spoken word, but gradually grew from the sixth century onwards to convey information directly to the mind's eye (silent reading for example), bypassing any oral (or aural) expression. As the practice of disseminating information solely through a written medium developed, notational tools like punctuation, which could promote comprehension, became increasingly important. In Part 1 we discussed the prominent role that punctuation plays in the expression of correct and persuasive discourse (controlling an all-too-fallible language), and now we must consider its ability (and inability) to do so through primarily visual means. Punctuation symbols, which by the close of the eighteenth century "were sprinkling the written and printed page with feverish and often very fanciful liberality," had to be constantly developed, scrutinized, and refined in order to fulfill their diverse rhetorical, grammatical, and elocutionary functions.

In the same way, eighteenth-century music theorists (and performers and pedagogues) were equally concerned that the developing notation of musical punctuation, and specifically that of the rest, continue effectively to convey its very vital and instructive information. The concern, as in language, was based on the inherent imprecision of notation—the difficulty, expressed so well by eighteenth-century Elocutionists, of conveying every nuance of an oral phenomenon. In addition, the conventions associated with any particular musical symbol were (and continue to be) in a constant state of flux; changing compositional styles, larger and more public performing venues, and the evolution of instruments—increasingly larger pianos, heavier bows, the addition of new keys on wind instruments—all contributed to forging new relationships between sound production and its notation.[1] Opinions espoused as to how the musical rest ought to be notated are often contradictory, but it is from these very contradictions, as we examine the many sides and the diverse elements related to the issue, that a great deal of interpretive insight can be gained.

At the heart of these divergent views is the notion that the pauses and rests of punctuation, as we observed in our historical discussion of the Pledge of Allegiance, are often implied rather than explicit. Similarly, some rests of musical notation are *written*, others are *unwritten*. In his chapter "The Nature of Melodic Sections," Koch explains that the "resting points of the spirit" within phrases, or the still incomplete segments of a melody (*Einschnitte*), may not be revealed by anything external, or they may contain an outward sign of a short rest, as seen in figure 4.1.[2]

Figure 4.1. The resting points of incomplete phrase segments. From H. C. Koch, *Versuch einer Anleitung zur Composition*, vol. 2, pp. 361–62.

Note that I have chosen to use facsimile copies of the examples in figure 4.1 from Koch's 1787 edition rather than a modern edition. This is so that the reader may examine for himself or herself Koch's individual placement of the punctuation symbols—the △s which delineate the *Einschnitte* of the phrases. While the placement of the pauses is made very clear in the versions punctuated by rests, such is not the case in the initial examples where the symbols fall more generally over the concluding notes and beats of the phrase. Perhaps this is because the sense and nuance of punctuation pertains not just to the final note of the phrase and its pause, but to the full rhythmic gesture, the overall inflection through which the phrase segments are made distinct. Riepel employs similar symbols for much the same purpose, which also are not assigned specifically to final notes, but seem to apply to entire concluding measures.[3] This apparent lack of clarity and accuracy in the placement of punctuation signs is also part and parcel of the inherent imprecision of notation discussed above and which will feature again in the course of our study.[4]

It is in the same chapter, "The Nature of Melodic Sections" that Koch presents his logical melodic construction in example 1.1, whose main idea or subject, contained in the first two bars, receives a certain direction or definition through its predicate in the following two bars.[5] I include this "complete basic phrase" again in example 4.1, juxtaposed with one of Koch's subsequent variations in which the primary difference is the introduction of a *written* rest. As Koch explains, "if the phrase were formed as in [ex. 4.1b], then the first segment, which is separated from the second by a resting point in the second bar, would not form a phrase or a complete thought. It would contain only the subject, whose predicate first appears in the following bars."[6] In other words, the quarter-note rest cannot on its own create a sense of closure, and the addition of the neighbor-tone embellishment to the subject's caesura note only gives additional character to the nature of the pause; harmonically and melodically, we know that more must follow. Perhaps Koch could have told his story conversely; two phrase segments formed as in example 4.1b, such that the first is separated from the second by a resting point, do not cohere to a greater extent when written as in example 4.1a. Koch explains that while it is true that in some complete phrases, melody may cohere so closely that no noticeable resting points are observable, yet in others these resting points may occur and divide the melody into incomplete segments (as in the present case).[7]

Example 4.1. Subject and predicate with and without a *rest*. From Koch, *Versuch einer Anleitung zur Composition*, vol. 2, pp. 352–53.

Now while Koch implies that the presence or absence of a written rest need not affect the above musical sentence, neither diminishing nor increasing the sense of separation between its subject and predicate, a misunderstanding of the notational convention most certainly can. If the composer fails to indicate the rests between phrases (as is often the case), then the performer must introduce them. Musical ideas that belong together must not be separated, but on the other hand, as Quantz [20] explains, "[one] must separate those ideas in which one musical thought ends and a new idea begins, even if there is no rest or caesura [*Einschnitt*]." As Baillot [50] also notes, "The slight separations, the very short silences, are not always indicated by the composer; it is therefore necessary for the performer to introduce them, when he sees that they are needed, by letting the final note of a phrase member, or of the entire period, die away. In certain cases, he can even cut off the full value of these notes." This is the message reiterated throughout the treatises and aimed in particular (as we discussed in the section "Voice and Gesture" in chapter 3, p. 63), at the amateur market and the student musician.[8]

Thus an interpreter of Koch's sentence must not only perceive the pause of punctuation between the subject and its concluding predicate, but must understand where the pause belongs, the nature of its function, and how it should be executed. Donington, writing in 1974, explains the complexity of this undertaking:

> Phrases are moulded by various means, which may include a dynamic rise and fall, a suggestion of rallentando, *etc.* They are separated by a silence of phrasing which ranges from scarcely perceptible to very conspicuous. The silence may be taken out of the time of the note before, or if the separation in the music is sufficient to justify it, added to the time in the shape of a momentary pause."[9]

In the case of Koch's comma-sized silence, we might, as Frisch [11] (1723) and Mizler [18] (1742) advise, "leave off a little" or allow a "certain natural fall of the voice." At the same time, we want, as Schuback [31] (1775) says, to "express clearly whether the end is expected or something further." Perhaps the sound should swell with the rising melody of the subject creating a sense of expectation, even surprise, through the implied subdominant harmony. A relaxation of the dynamic intensity could then occur through the falling inflexion of the predicate. Rhythmically, perhaps this is an example where as C. P. E. Bach (1753) states, certain notes and rests should be extended beyond their written length for affective reasons.[10] Or alternatively, as Couperin [10] (1722) states, "the silence should be nearly imperceptible and felt without altering the bar." We must also decide as Domenico Corri [35] states in about 1782, whether the time should be deducted from the $d^2$ half note of bar 2 or the following $e^2$ quarter note on the final beat.

But in fact, none of these punctuation elements is *written*. Keller comments on the phenomenon in 1955, noting that although music is able to provide language with so much of what it cannot express through punctuation signs (height and depth of pitch, duration, tempo, dynamics, rhythm, articulation), "in most curious fashion, music has refused to create for itself a system of punctuation marks similar to that of language."[11] On the one hand, perhaps it is not so surprising that music does not create its own set of punctuation symbols. If this were easily achieved, there would really be no need for the analogy. It is the reciprocal nature between the notational systems of music and language that they are beneficial to each other precisely because one enhances concepts which the other cannot fully express. Thus the most rigorous efforts literally to insert commas, colons, question marks, etc., into instrumental music, like Mattheson's (1739) and Löhlein's (1765) minuets (which we will discuss in chapter 6), and Fischer's [61] (1926) "punctuated edition" of classical works, or efforts like Steele's (1775) to create an elaborate musical system for language, will always remain in the realm of handbooks, treatises, and theory. As Keller states, in response to Fischer's work (sampled below in fig. 4.2): "It would be a strange thing indeed to find question marks, exclamation points, and colons in a sonata of Beethoven!"[12]

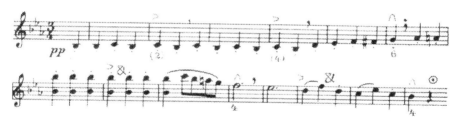

"What boldness, novelty, and clarity in this typical Beethovenesque conception!"

Figure 4.2. The punctuation of the Scherzo from Beethoven, Symphony No. 3 in E-flat Major, Op. 55, 3rd movement, bars 1–14. From Jacob Fischer, *Erläuterungen zur Interpunktions-Ausgabe*, p. 17.

On the other hand, it *is* rather curious that many elements of punctuation, and most particularly the defining symbol of the pause or rest, are often left unspecified. Momigny, in his article on *ponctuation* for Framery's *Encyclopédie méthodique* of 1818, feels that rests do not really work as the material signs of punctuation, since their main function is to mark the amount of time a given musical voice should remain silent. In fact, Momigny begins his discussion with the statement that "musical *punctuation* is devoid of the particular signs" that we find in language. "But," he adds, "the metaphysical signs, which form the real

punctuation, are sufficient in number to separate, one from another, the different units of sense which compose a period. These signs are the diverse cadences
or downward melodic or harmonic contours by which the different sense units
are terminated and rendered more or less complete."[13] Similarly, Koch's apparent ambivalence regarding the *written* and *unwritten* rest stems from the fact that
he is not entirely satisfied with the term *melodic punctuation*. While he is indeed
willing to pursue the similarity between the punctuation of language and the
resting points in music (and does so for volumes), he also notes an important
disparity between the two subjects:

> In the first [speech], the distinctive signs in their visible presentation are nothing more
> than an aid to discover more quickly the more or less noticeable resting points (which
> even without punctuation marks would still be there). In melody, there is no need of
> this aid, because its resting points affect our feeling enough that there is no need to use
> special signs to indicate them.[14]

However, the Elocutionists Lowth and Steele seem to suggest that the musical
rest is in many ways far more explicit than the punctuation signs of language. In
1762 Lowth [23] very specifically equates the eight note, quarter note, half
note, and whole note to respectively the comma, semicolon, colon, and period.
And Steele assigns no symbols in 1775, other than musical rests, to indicate the
various pauses necessary to the *melody and measure of speech*.[15]

Yet while some theorists (like Koch and Momigny) felt that music's notation
was as explicit as it need or could be (it is up to composers and performers to
become aware of conventions—some rests are *written* and others are *unwritten*),
others declared more vehemently that rests were not only unnecessary but could
even be a hindrance.[16] Still others, expressing the need to further control their
"fallible" musical language, pursued various means of enhancing its notation,
either by extramusical devices or by existing ones (i.e., rests and note beams).
The subject of eighteenth-century musical punctuation is very much about this
balance between acknowledging the naturally occurring resting points in music,
while at the same time attempting as language does to ensure the proper execution of each grammatical, rhetorical, and elocutionary pause.

In grappling with this issue of the musical rest, we must first recognize that the
symbol is one with a variety of different functions. Momigny gave us his view of
the rest's primary role in indicating where individual voices should remain
silent, and Leopold Mozart [22] (1756) tells us that there are three uses for the
rest, only one of which belongs to the subject of punctuation. Similarly, as we
have learned from Koch, the figures used to indicate the resting points in
melody can also be used where there is no resting point. Some of these "nonpunctuating" rests we will encounter in the following chapter on articulation,
but take for instance example 4.2 from the opening of Mozart's A-Major
Symphony, K.201 (1774).[17]

Allegro moderato

Example 4.2. W. A. Mozart, Symphony No. 29 in A Major, K.201, 1st movement, bars 1–8.

This case is particularly revealing because we have explicit (written) rests which do not apply to punctuation, and implicit (unwritten) rests which do. The eighth-note rests on the third quarter notes of bars 1, 3, 5, and 7 do not indicate a phrase division but simply a rhythmic pattern. An absence of sound is required, but without the sense of punctuation. The phrase is continuous. However at the end of bars 2, 4, and 6, a very slight shortening of the final eighths (at the most by as much as a thirty-second-note rest) is required in combination with a clear emphasis of the following downbeats, in order to mark the two-bar sequences of the melody. Through this slight anticipatory breath, a sense of punctuation must be felt. Instead, what one often hears is very similar to what had become the practice in the late nineteenth century, where, as stated by Riemann: "All figuration has, first and foremost, the sense of leading from one point of stress (of each order) to the next (of the same order), i.e., gives rise to new beginnings, upbeat formations."[18] A pause of punctuation occurs after the initial octave leap, giving it a very emphatic quality. The next bar and a half then leads to another emphatic downbeat octave leap a whole step higher, which is again followed by the eighth-note rest pause of punctuation. The next bar and a half leads to the C♯ octave leap, rest. . . . Finally we reach the D octave leap, rest. . . . And after all of this resting, we arrive at the A-major cadence which concludes the eight-bar sentence. Now this style of punctuation, where the pauses are quite conspicuous and always occur after an arrival on the strong beat of the bar, chops up the phrases far more than does the former style, which uses much smaller pauses to create energy, expectation, and a sense of forward motion. However, the notational awkwardness of expressing this we see in example 4.3.

Example 4.3. Notating the punctuation of example 4.2.

Such a notation is surely inappropriate and fails, I believe, to answer Türk's first important question (1789) regarding punctuation: "How can one execute a musical thought with suitable continuity and separate two periods from one another, without doing injury to the progress of the meter?"[19] The very small phrase divisions of passages like the one shown in example 4.2 should be created as much out of the sense of rising urgency and expectation with which the even-numbered bars are concluded and the beginnings of the odd-numbered bars are stressed, as out of any implicit rests. In example 4.4, we see Türk's similar demonstration of how visually complicated musical notation can become when each small phrase division is thus explicitly indicated. The use of what Türk calls "the usual sign for a detached tone" ['] as a means of indicating phrase divisions often leads to the mistaken idea that the tone should be accompanied with a "certain violence." At the same time, the use of rests to indicate the shortened final notes of phrases (as we showed in example 4.3) "may lead some beginners into making mistakes in counting."[20]

Example 4.4. The difficulty in explicitly indicating small phrase divisions. From Türk, *Klavierschule*, p. 346.

Of course in the case of texted music, where words (and their punctuation) and music are combined, there would seem to be no need for the use of additional signs to aid the discovery of phrase divisions. As Schulz explains in 1774: "Unlike the player, the singer does this with no difficulty, . . . because the divisions of the words, which he sings and which direct him, must fit precisely together with the divisions of the melody."[21] Kitchiner [49], on the other hand, feels in 1821 that musical notation can and should do much more. Composers must first attend to the accurate punctuation of the words, but they should also place rests over the punctuation points. This will go a long way towards preventing the singer and accompanist from "playing at cross-purposes," which "is inevitable from the musical technicals,—*ad libita*—marks for pauses, &c. being so indefinite that no two persons estimate them exactly alike."

In 1762 Marpurg expresses himself in favor of indicating the smallest of phrase divisions with written rests, what he calls a half comma (*halbe Comma*), even when such caesuras do not coincide with a written punctuation mark (which he calls an unwritten or *ungeschriebne* half comma). He points to the phrase "Non vide il sole più numerosa strage" in a recitative from Hasse's and Metastasio's opera *Ezio*. The phrase is that of the conventional *verso piano* of eleven syllables (*vide* and *il* would be elided), the accent falling on the penultimate syllable. A typical caesura on the fifth syllable appears at *sole*, as seen below in example 4.5.[22] The punctuation formula at *sole* is what Marpurg calls a suspended break (*schwebende Absatz*), a very minor pause due to the dissonance of its progression. A movement from E minor in bar 8 to a vii° chord in B minor, with the interval of a tritone between melody and bass, stresses the break. Marpurg claims that in singing, this break, which expresses a special emphasis through its rising notes, would be accompanied by a pause. The pause is an expectant one, anticipating the resolution to i⁶ in bar 10. "It is basically the same," Marpurg says, "whether the pause is written or not, but because the inexperienced singer is likely to do away with the pauses, . . . the style of specifically indicating the small sectional pauses [*Einschnittspausen*] is preferred, so much more because it is written as one sings, namely with a small stop."[23] Thus while Hasse was content to accompany the text as in example 4.5, Marpurg feels that the rendition in example 4.6 is the more accurate one.[24] Schulz would probably have preferred Hasse's version: "Pauses should be set nowhere other than where true caesuras or phrase members of the sentences appear in the text."[25]

Example 4.5. A recitative passage from Hasse's opera *Ezio*. From Marpurg, *Kritische Briefe*, vol. 2, pp. 385–86.

Example 4.6. The preferred *written* version of example 4.5 with explicit rests. From Marpurg, *Kritische Briefe*, vol. 2, p. 391.

But while such efforts are designed to be instructive and helpful, they may also serve to inhibit the singer from using his own discretion. The debated issue over whether a *written* rest is necessary in vocal music is a long-standing one. Keller explains that Scheidt, in the *Görlitz Tablature Book* of 1650, which contains 100 simple chorale settings, separates the lines of text through "written-out rests." Schütz, on the other hand, writes in the forward to his chorale setting of the Cornelius Becker Psalter in 1628: "Furthermore, I have indicated the pauses with a little stroke at the end of every verse instead of with rests, because in compositions of this character the rests are of course not really observed, indeed

such arias or melodies without measure are also very charming when sung
according to the instructions of the words."[26] Schütz chooses the less rhythmically specific symbol of the comma (*Strichlein*, or little stroke) in preference to
the musical rest. According to Keller, this demonstrates that Schütz "wished to
leave to the performer larger or smaller separations of the line according to the
sense and expression," something perhaps which a punctuation symbol encour-
ages and a musical rest does not.[27]

    Mattheson, writing in 1739, also prefers to use rests in very few places, "since
everything can quite reasonably can be expressed through certain natural vocal
alterations; and this is much better than always setting down little signs at each
articulation."

> One will encounter five perfect articulations in the following [ex. 4.7], though there
> is not the slightest rest in any of them, and yet there is opportunity enough given
> for breathing; also a full cadence is made in a related key at the end of the sentence."[28]

Mattheson explains that in example 4.7, the comma after the word *getrost* is actually imperfect, and indicates with brackets and the word *bis* that one should follow through until the comma at *Hertz*. He claims (as does the famous Irish
Elocutionist Thomas Sheridan a few decades later) that commas, virtually
unnecessary in speech though necessary in writing, and many others of the kind,
must be jumped over in melody.[29]

Example 4.7. Five perfect articulations. From Mattheson, *Der vollkommene
Capellmeister*, p. 185.

    Part of Mattheson's agenda is to stress the primacy of melody over harmony. He
offers an alternative to example 4.7, setting three caesuras or *commata* in the
accompanying lower voice with their corresponding cadences and rests. However,
while Mattheson admits this to be a viable option, he nevertheless disdains its practice. He launches into something of a tirade as to why the "lower" voice must be
governed by the "higher" melody, since were it otherwise, "the melody might

become more wretched and more miserable with so many bass cadences, and since it would sound more mangled, because it would indeed of course have to be adjusted and constrained according to them."[30] In this, Mattheson participates in an ongoing controversy surrounding a statement made in 1722 by Rameau to the effect that harmony serves as the source of melody and not the other way around.[31] Today this may appear as something of a false dichotomy—surely the two work together. Even by the end of the eighteenth century, some of the heated argument over the primacy of either harmony or melody had died down, such that Koch could claim that the best melody was "melody conceived harmonically."[32] Yet at the same time, we do not want to dismiss what was in its day a hotly contested topic. After all, punctuation was itself heavily debated, and the controversy and disagreement as to its manifestation—the degree to which it should be *written* or *unwritten,* or whether it should be expressed musically through the melody or the harmony— helped to fuel a continued interest in the subject. The fact that a composer and theorist like Kirnberger [29] struck a very different pose in 1771 from Mattheson, claiming that "the great variety of smaller resting points are achieved only by the harmonic progression" (although Kirnberger went on to explain how melody and rhythm can also serve to modify or weaken cadential formulas), only adds further insight into the nature and application of the musical punctuation analogy.[33]

The need for explicit symbols of musical punctuation also depended to a large degree on the character and strength of emotion being expressed, which we will take up in chapter 6 on *affective* punctuation. But the primary difficulty, and Mattheson's main objection to indicating the various *commata* with *written* rests, is that such notation could never be precise enough. Schulz adds an important footnote to this effect in his discussion of the *Einschnitte, Abschnitte,* and *Perioden* in melody. He explains that "in execution, all of these divisions are brought out in a similar manner; and if a great instrumentalist or singer observes only the shading underneath them, the result is so subtle and lengthy to describe that we must satisfy ourselves with a simple sketch."[34] Consider also Marpurg's claim (see appendix A, §§97–99) that an improper full stop, as well as a colon, semicolon, and full comma, can all be described within the same category of harmonic progression. Koch, like Schulz, throws up his hands over the fact that nothing concrete, only feeling, can determine the manifold resting points in melody, but he nevertheless proceeds to discuss their very nature at great length. Johann Joseph Fux [12] also, after listing in 1725 the manner in which each punctuation sign ought to be expressed, admits that "knowing how to use all these punctuations is learned more by use and by observing the works of good composers than by rules."

Thus in instrumental compositions, without the text for guidance and without explicit symbols of punctuation, we must simply look to the cues embedded in the implicit conventions of the notation. One time-proven method of determining the rests of musical punctuation is observing the long note. Mace [6] advises in 1676, "and forget not . . . to make your *Pauses . . .* at the *End* of such *Sentences,* where there is a *Long Note.*" Reicha [47], more than a century later, also claims that one of the means of distinguishing the points of repose in melody is by means of "a note which is longer than the preceding one." One would imagine that this is the stuff, as Türk might say, which even the "dullest senses" should be able to perceive. Mathis Lussy, however, feels that the mere recognition of the long note is not enough; rests should also be explicitly indicated. He writes:

For example, the following rhythms are badly written:

Example 4.8

The F♯ of the second bar and the G of the fourth ought to be quarter notes, or dotted quarter notes, followed by a rest instead of half notes, as follows:

Example 4.9

This simple fact, the regular recurrence of a long note or a rest, in the absence of feeling for rhythm or knowledge of it, is a great help towards correct phrasing.[35]

It should be noted that Lussy, writing in 1873, has yet another agenda (which we will address shortly), that of updating notation to conform to new performance practices. Still, his statement reinforces the point being made: the degree to which the ends of phrases exhibit either rhythmic stasis or motion is very much a part of the way in which the larger, and also the smaller divisions of punctuation are effected, a fact which is sometimes overlooked. Riepel, for instance, takes great pains in his multivolume *Anfangsgründe zur musikalischen Setzkunst*, begun in 1752, over the proper distribution and combination among the different types of rhythmic motion which are used to create the two- and four-bar phrase members of the minuet. He describes two main categories of movement: the dead (*todt*), and the living (*lebendig*). A dead figure is a note that lasts for the entire length of a measure (i.e., ¾ 𝅗𝅥.), while a living figure is either imperfectly moving (*unvollkommen*) or perfectly moving (*vollkommen*). A perfectly moving figure has activity on every beat (i.e., ¾ ♩♩♩ or ¾ ♫♫♫) and an imperfectly moving figure contains only partial rhythmic activity (i.e., ¾ ♩♩ or ¾ ♩♩). Riepel proceeds to describe a number of rigid compositional rules regarding the minuet: dead measures should be used only at the end of sentences (just as Mace describes), and two imperfectly moving measures should never appear in succession, but should be effectively interspersed among perfectly moving measures. Riepel himself, however, admits that "rules alone do not make the difference," referring in particular to lively minuets whose melodic organization (using consistently perfectly moving measures) is not as clear.[36]

Looking for the "long note" is manifestly not a reliable way of discovering phrase divisions, but it is interesting to consider the way rhythmic motion, as described by Riepel and combined with melodic and harmonic contour, can give shape and character to punctuation units. Consider example 4.10, the opening eight-bar *period* of the Menuetto from Beethoven's First Symphony in C Major (1799–1800).[37] The movement takes off at once with a rapidly rising melody and a brisk Allegro molto e vivace. And while the bass is "perfectly moving" throughout, still the rhythm of the melody helps provide a definite structure to the overall punctuation (even at such a quick pace). The *period* divides nicely on a "long note" (the half note $g^2$ in bar 4), with a cadence on the dominant. The rhythms of this first phrase, in *piano*, also create an interior two-bar nuance of punctuation (typical of the minuet form based on a two-bar dance step-pattern). The first two bars are both imperfectly moving (breaking Riepel's rule), all over a C pedal. There is an ever-so-slight lilt to the half note $c^2$ in the second bar, that in its length seems to say, "come catch me." The perfectly moving third bar (beginning with the pickup), accompanied by a more rapid harmonic rhythm, responds with an excitement that then gives the half-note "resting point" in bar 4 an extra spark of anticipation. The imperfectly moving rhythm then reappears to begin the second half of the period, this time accompanied by a crescendo and a more active harmony which cadences back on the tonic. The second half of this phrase is answered even more emphatically with a *forte*, perfectly moving exclamation in G—the strings joined by the flutes, oboes, clarinets, bassoons, horns, trumpets, and, on the very last note, which Beethoven has already shortened for us, the timpani. All of these subtle inflections of punctuation, created from a unique set of rhythmic, melodic, and harmonic elements, in no way impede the pace of the *period*. But to my ear, it is the observance of these distinct moment-by-moment gestures that give structure to the *period* and engage the listener with the sense of rising excitement and exuberance.

Example 4.10. Beethoven, Symphony no. 1 in C Major, Op. 21, 3rd movement, bars 1–8.

Another important notational convention in identifying the various rests of musical punctuation is one which incorporates the complex notions of meter and rhythm we encountered in chapter 3: the relationship between the long and short, strong and weak syllables of poetic feet and the grammatical and rhetorical rules of accent and emphasis. The convention at hand is what I term *the melodic rule*, and is introduced within the context of defining the strong (good) and weak (bad) grammatical beats of the bar—the way in which a succession of equal pulses is divided into either duple (and quadruple) or triple meter. As Türk indicates in example 4.11, the first beat in quadruple meter is the strongest, the second relatively weak, the third beat somewhat less strong than the first, and the fourth again weak—all "without regard for their longer or shorter values."[38] Even an eighth note will receive a stronger accent than the dotted quarter note which follows it, if it begins on a strong beat. As Türk explains, these dynamics or "degrees of strength" are implicit in the notation, and if the composer does not wish this kind of realization, he must then specify otherwise.[39] The scale of this relationship remains constant regardless of the style of performance. According to the composer Ernst Wilhelm Wolf, from the instructions for his keyboard works published in 1785, "In a strong manner of performance, even the weak notes stay within the bounds of what is strong, and in a weak manner of performance the strong notes do not exceed the limits of what is weak." These are what Wolf calls "internal accents" (*innerliche Accente*).[40]

Example 4.11. Strong and weak beats. From Türk, *Klavierschule*, p. 335.

However, other factors—*unwritten* conventions embedded in the notation—can come into play; these require variations of the above "good beat" and "bad beat" rule—what Wolf labels "external accents" (*ausserliche Accente*). As Schulz explains, employing the sentence, "He is my master; I am his slave," a sentence can become incomprehensible and the phrase torn if only the accents of the measure are marked and the proper phrase divisions not observed:

[A proper observance of the phrase divisions] is most frequently missed in pieces where the phrases begin in the middle of the bar, in particular on a bad [weak] beat; because everyone becomes accustomed, at first, to mark only the good [strong] beats of the bar, where the different accents of the melody lie, and simply pass over the bad beats. In such cases, the phrases become torn and a part of that phrase is tacked onto the one preceding or following, which is as nonsensical as if in a speech one wanted to place a pause before or after the comma. In the following example, if the phrase division [*Einschnitt*] is so marked, the melody is thus affected; if only the accents of the measure are marked, the song becomes utterly flat, and the effect is as if instead of saying: "He is my master; I am his slave," one were to say: "He is my master I; am his slave."[41]

Example 4.12. A torn phrase. From Sulzer, *Allgemeine Theorie der schönen Künste*, s.v. "Vortrag" (Schulz), vol. 4, pp. 705–6.

In the above examples from Schulz, the signs [o] and [+] indicate where one phrase ends and a new one begins. The "torn" phrase of example 4.12a should instead be expressed as in 4.12b. Türk perhaps states the melodic rule most succinctly:

> One of the best ways of learning how to find phrase divisions is by making oneself aware of whether a composition begins with a full measure or with two, three, or more eighth notes, or other note values (within an upbeat), because for the most part the phrase divisions [*Einschnitte*] fall on the same beat throughout. When the composition begins with an eighth note as an upbeat, then all the following phrase members will commonly begin with the last eighth note of a measure, etc.[42]

If for instance, as Schulz suggests, one were to simply mark the good beats and bad beats of example 4.12, then the first and third beats would be accented, but the second and fourth unaccented. Of the accented beats, the first would in turn be stressed more than the third.[43] However, the sentence's bourée-like rhythm of iambic feet requires that the phrases begin on the "weak" upbeat. Now while these upbeats will always remain weaker than their following downbeats, they will still be stronger than the preceding "good" third beats, which as phrase endings have thus been further weakened.[44]

The melodic rule also has hierarchical implications and is very much a part of the eighteenth-century concept of *periodicity*, the way in which small phrases are linked together and combined to create increasingly larger phrases. Example 4.12 falls into the category of what Koch describes as a typical four-bar phrase containing incomplete incises (an incomplete incise being that which fills only a single measure). In such circumstances, usually two incomplete incises (*unvollkommene Einschnitte*) follow one another and form a complete incise (*vollkommen Einschnitt*) of two measures, resulting in a 1+1+2 pattern.[45] We add to this Türk's description of the periodic stress or accent required at the beginning tones of phrases. These tones are then "emphasized to a greater or lesser degree according to whether they begin a larger or smaller part of the whole, that is, after a full cadence, the beginning tone must be more strongly marked than after a half cadence, or merely after a phrase division, etc."[46] Türk explains that in figure 4.3, "The a marked with an *o* in the sixth measure should therefore not be struck as loudly as the following b, although that section as a whole should be played more strongly than the preceding one."[47]

Figure 4.3. The beginning tones of phrases. From D. G. Türk, *Klavierschule*, p. 336.

These very basic concepts of composition encompassed by the melodic rule are either stated explicitly (as by Türk and Schulz above) or expressed implicitly through practice (as in Koch's exs. 4.1a and b of a subject and predicate) by nearly every music theorist we have encountered thus far—even by late nineteenth-century theorists, in spite of dramatic changes to music, instruments, and their performing venues.[48] The melodic rule can be applied to most of the examples we have already illustrated and will continue to figure prominently as we proceed.[49] However, as with most convenient rules, there are always exceptions, to which the case of *the melodic rule* is indeed no exception. The metrical orientation of melody, as detailed above, does not necessarily remain constant throughout a composition. As Türk explains, a very important caveat must be duly acknowledged: "Nevertheless, this criterion is not always reliable, for in order to bring more variety into the whole, composers are accustomed *often* to place phrase divisions on other parts of the measure in longer compositions."[50] Türk refers all those who need convincing of this matter to the first of the sonatas with varied reprises of C. P. E. Bach, among others. This he extracts, as he does much of his own chapter on *Execution* (*Vortrag*), from Schulz's article on the same. Schulz explains that given the nature of the melody in such large pieces of the fantasia character, one is especially likely to encounter various kinds of phrases and diverse phrase divisions.[51] In example 4.13, from C. P. E. Bach's Keyboard Sonata, Wq 50/3, Schulz again employs o's and +'s to mark respectively the ends and beginnings of the phrases. The rests in the first two bars serve as obvious indicators of phrase divisions and therefore require no additional signs. In the first ten bars of the sonata, the metrical orientation of the melody changes three times, from the downbeat to the second eighth, to the second quarter, and moving from two, two-bar phrases to a 1+1+2 pattern, which is then interrupted by a return of two-bar phrases.

Example 4.13. Diversity among the phrase divisions in C. P. E. Bach's Keyboard Sonata, Wq 50/3, 1st movement, bars 1–10. From Sulzer, *Allgemeine Theorie der schönen Künste*, s.v. "Vortrag" (Schulz), vol. 4, p. 705.

With this level of complexity, it is not surprising that many musicians still felt the need to provide notational devices that could help highlight the conventions of the unwritten rests and emphases implied by the melodic rule and its variations. The result is a wide array of alternate symbols for the written rest. Schulz in example 4.14 suggests the manipulation of the beams which bind notes together.

> If the phrase division [*Einschnitt*] falls between eighth or sixteenth notes [as in the following example], which it would otherwise be stylistically characteristic to link, the composer should mark the division more clearly by writing the notes which belong in the preceding phrase differently from those which begin the new phrase. . . . This style of notation marks the phrase divisions very clearly and deserves at least to be used in doubtful cases.[52]

Türk explains that the more painstaking composers express the notation this way. But both he and Schulz admit that its application is not possible in the case of quarter and half notes. One then uses the sign ['] over the last note of the phrase. However, as we have already noted, Türk objects to this sign for the reason that it already functions as the symbol for a detached tone and tends to be overly accented in performance. Türk's preferred method to either the rests or the ['] of example 4.4, seems to be the double stroke over the caesura note [″].[53]

Many symbols proposed by theorists and composers are also designed to convey the hierarchical or proportional nature of punctuation. As we observed in chapter 3, Couperin [10] seeks in 1722 to help the performer of his *Pièces de clavecin* with a symbol which resembles a comma. This sign appears on either the top or bottom staff or both, according to the strength of the cadence or sense of repose. In 1732 Blavet [14] similarly adds an **h** to indicate breathing, although the sign conveys no hierarchical information regarding the length of the breath or its placement. Riepel explains that for efficiency's sake, he will indicate final and internal basic phrases or tonic phrases (*Grundabsätze*), together with their variations, with the sign ■. Final and internal modulating phrases (*Aenderungsabsätze*), together with their variations, he will indicate with the sign □.[54] Koch, while he avows in 1787 that the distinctive signs are nothing more than an unnecessary visual aid, nevertheless for didactic purposes inserts a △ to represent phrase segments (*Einschnitte*), and a □ to represent the more complete phrases (*Absätze*).[55] In 1793 Gunn [45] places an [*] over the caesura note to designate both segments and complete phrases. Corri [35] (1780–1810) attempts not only to indicate where the pauses occur, but where the time should come from. He uses a ✳ to indicate a comma length pause with the time to be deducted from the note to which the mark is nearest. For instance, if the sign is placed just *before* a quarter note, one would sing something akin to an eighth-note rest followed by an eighth note. But if the sign is placed just *after* a quarter note, one would sing something akin to an eighth note followed by an eighth-note rest. He uses another mark ✶ to indicate the most imperceptible pauses which are technically necessary but not related to punctuation.[56] In 1847 Garcia [53] distinguishes between the breath (*respiro*), which he literally writes diagonally above the notes, and the half breath (*mezzo respiro*) indicated by the label ½R. In 1840 Habeneck employs the familiar symbol of the slur to designate the figures (*dessins*), phrases (*phrases*), and periods (*périodes*) in his examples.[57]

When we come to assess the longevity of the musical punctuation signs discussed above, we find that for the most part, as one would expect, they were used primarily for didactic purposes and never quite achieved wide acceptance as notational devices. However it is possible that some of the very familiar signs of musical notation, although no longer recognized as such, actually originated as marks of punctuation. For instance, Zarlino's [2] signs to indicate the breaths singers must take at the ends of *clausule* and *punti* resemble what we commonly recognize as bar lines and double bar lines (see fig. 4.4).[58] Leo Treitler, writing in 1989, goes so far as to propose, although cautiously, that in the earliest epoch of music writing, notation itself functioned as a system of punctuation from which language developed. Thus the punctuation signs of language are actually a product of musical notation! Treitler compares the Carolingian system of punctuation (ca. 780), which consisted of various combinations of the punctum [.], virgula [/], comma [,], and assorted question mark symbols, to the figures and shapes of neumes: "Virtually all of these signs also came into use as neumes in one or another notational script of the early period of music writing. Since the oldest surviving neumes are at least a half century younger than the oldest texts with full punctuation, we might think that the former are derived from the latter."[59] The fermata also originated as a punctuation sign dating back to the middle ages. Keller explains that towards the end of the seventeenth century, the fermata was used to indicate ends of lines in the Lutheran chorale.[60]

Figure 4.4. Breaths singers must take at the ends of *clausule* and *punti*. From Gioseffo Zarlino, *Le istitutione harmoniche*, p. 212.

The virgula or commas (*virgule* and *virgole* being respectively the French and Italian words for comma) appear to be some of the more successful additions to notation. What Parkes calls the *virgula plana*, a single diagonal stroke, we recognize as the German *strichlein* or comma from Schütz's *Becker Psalter*. Schütz also uses what Parkes calls a *virgula suspensiva*, a diagonal double stroke, in his *Exequien* (1636) to indicate where the chorus should stop singing. As Parkes explains, the double form // was used to indicate a disjunction greater than that indicated by /, which was used to mark the briefest pause or hesitation in a text (usually a comma).[61] Couperin, as we have noted, also used a comma-like sign, as do many composers and editors today. One will find that most music-writing software programs include the comma symbol.

However, it is probably the nineteenth-century development of the slur that has resulted in the most explicit punctuation mark ever created by musical notation. We mentioned that Habeneck used the slur as a guide for punctuation, but Riemann at the end of the century was one of the "phrasing" slur's greatest champions. Although he argues in 1882, in the first edition of his *Musik-Lexikon* (see appendix B [58]), that the legato curve (*Legatobogen*) is too easily confused with the slur symbol to be a useful phrasing guide, by 1890, in his *Practical Guide to the Art of Phrasing* (written with Carl Fuchs), he has developed a different attitude. Riemann explains that since "the employment of the slur as a sign for *legato* playing is quite abandoned, in as much, at least, as its presence neither necessitates *legato* nor precludes *staccato*," there is now a "*new* office" for the slur.[62] In addition to the simple slur, indicating the articulation of a musical thought into its natural divisions, Riemann adds: the cross-slur (what is often called a slur elision), describing how one or more notes can form both the end of one phrase and the beginning of another ✕; interrupted slurs, indicating thoughts broken off abruptly, sometimes to be begun afresh or to give way to a new idea ⌒⌒; and underslurs, a second set of slurs under a larger slur, indicating the inner articulation of any phrase bounded by great slurs.[63] In 1887, in the third edition of his *Musik-Lexikon*, he also describes the Stuttgart Comma, indicating a break before the last note of a slur ⌒'⌒.

This development of the slur and its consequences for modern interpretations of eighteenth-century punctuation practices (i.e., interpreting all slurs as phrase divisions), we will pursue in greater detail in the following chapter on articulation. Riemann's efforts, however, are important to our present discussion simply for their sheer quantity. Riemann was a great champion not only of the slur, but of phrasing signs in general, praising the efforts of writers like Schulz, Kirnberger, Türk, and Koch, who he felt correctly understood the importance of improving notation in order to prevent misunderstanding in concepts of phrasing.[64] And he is not the only one to take this attitude. In the latter half of the nineteenth century, writers like Sechter in 1853 and Lussy in 1873 produced far more literally punctuated examples of instrumental music than Mattheson, Schulz, Kirnberger, Türk, or Koch ever did. In addition to Riemann's efforts of the late nineteenth century, Theodor Wiehmayer produced instructive editions of Classical piano works in which he employed a large stroke as the sign for a semicolon and a smaller stroke for the comma.[65] Also Jacob Fischer's "punctuated editions" appear in 1926 amidst a growing trend for such "instructive" performer's editions. In fact these theorists took the spirit of the late eighteenth-century punctuation craze to an extreme. Perhaps it is this period, ca. 1900, which is musical punctuation's heyday (or nadir, depending on how you look at it). Phrasing indications were certainly "sprinkling the printed page with feverish and fanciful liberality." But what is patently missing from such efforts is the eighteenth-century high regard for language in its oral form (over that of the written). The level of inscribed detail seems to contradict the very notion of punctuation as a living, breathing art, and denies the personal, spontaneous expressions of the "humanly inconstant voice."[66]

Ultimately, it is the very overabundance of symbols and their potential meanings that strips punctuation of its power. It is a part of musical punctuation's history (and that of punctuation in language) that the proliferation of too many signs serves only to confuse and obscure. Marpurg, while he might wish that language had more signs to indicate the smaller rhetorical pauses of speech, is forced in 1762 to accept the fact that these matters are generally left to one's own feeling and judgment.[67] As stated by Francesco Algarotti in his treatise on opera (1755) and later paraphrased by Isaac Nathan, student of Domenico Corri, "There are certain suspensions of the voice, certain short pauses, and a certain insisting on one place more than another, that cannot be communicated [in the score]."[68] Cambini, in his avowal circa 1795 that the violinist's bow arm is capable of expressing "the affections of the soul," also acknowledges: "but besides there being no signs that indicate them, such signs, even were one to invent them, would become so numerous that the music, already too full of indications, would become a formless mass to the eyes, almost impossible to decipher."[69]

Therefore, we should not be surprised to find that the response to efforts like Riemann's and his contemporaries was that of "too complicated!" As Keller states:

> Since the massive confusion raised fifty years ago by Riemann's *Phrasierungslehre* (Grammar of phrasing), this subject had become a hot issue that no one would take hold of, with the result that our conceptions in the whole area of phrasing remained almost no further advanced than they were in Riemann's time."[70]

But at the same time, we would be doing Riemann and others an injustice to simply label their efforts as misguided (or worse, revisionist). Riemann's insistence on visual phrasing indications did in fact have a valid purpose. Far from apologetic that his system of signs was received as "too complicated," he admits that this was in a sense his intention:

> to prove that neither Beethoven nor Mozart, nor Bach and Händel for that matter, thought and felt in that colorless and thread-bare fashion which people now-a-days are so fond of calling classic repose and simplicity; that the diversity and inexhaustibility of rhythm was present to and intuitively seized by them, and that they in truth drank deeply from this well-spring.[71]

What had happened was that all of the highly expressive elements, the pauses, accents, emphases, and rhythms implicit in eighteenth-century notation, were no longer understood in Riemann's day. His efforts, along with Fischer's and Wiehmayer's, were historical in nature, largely aimed at a body of century-old works. As good scholars, they attempted to keep alive the tradition of musical punctuation, but in doing so had to cope with a deceptively familiar notation whose unwritten conventions had nevertheless changed drastically over time. Thus in order to reinvigorate the music of Beethoven, Mozart, Bach, and Handel, they felt the necessity of rewriting the works in order to suit the conventions of

1890s notation (of course with quite a bit of reinterpretation according to changing aesthetics as well).

It is important for us to note that this need to update notation is not only a nineteenth-century phenomenon but an ongoing one. We might include Lussy's insistence on the *written rest* in example 4.8 and 4.9 as symptomatic of the same issue, a reaction to prevailing usage where the practice of tapering or shortening the final note of a phrase had begun to disappear. Perhaps some performers in Lussy's day might even have made a crescendo at the end of the slur in bar 2, creating a pickup into bar 3. In 1847 Garcia describes a passage from Donizetti's *Anna Bolena* which treats the phrases in just this way (ex. 4.15). And while the effect is presented as an exception to the rule rather than the normative practice, it nevertheless foreshadows the upbeat formation of phrases which then become the norm in Riemann's day.

> In certain cases, in order to increase the effect of a phrase, it is allowable to unite its different parts by suppressing pauses which separate them; Example:[72]

del mio pri-mi - e-ro a-mo - re    ah non a - ves - se il pet - - to

a- mo - re   ah

Example 4.15. Suppressing a Pause.

In this passage *Anna* sings, "[The embers] of my first love [smolder still]." And then, "Ah, had I not [opened] my heart [to another love]."[73] The crescendo occurs at the end of *amore* moving to the interrupting expletive *ah* on the downbeat of third bar, creating an exceptional effect expressive of the intensity of the moment.

Corri, too, sounds suspiciously like Riemann in the way he explains that the notation of vocal music needs to be updated, since "the manner of noting it, which remains nearly the same as it was in the infancy of the art, is quite insufficient to express the meaning, spirit, and peculiar delicacy of the composition."

> The want of such signs as would afford adequate direction to the performer in such refinements, must have been long felt; yet, strange as it may appear, no attempt till the present has been made to supply this want . . . for want of such signs, the music of half a century back is in a great measure lost to the present time . . . it is evidently necessary, in the first place to increase the number of signs made use of in writing music.[74]

Five decades earlier, Rousseau expresses very similar sentiments in his proposal for a "Plan Regarding New Signs for Music," published in 1743 as part of his *Dissertation on Modern Music*.[75] He begins by explaining the great need for a new notational system:

> Since Musical signs have for so long remained in the state of imperfection in which we still see them today, it seems astonishing that . . . no one has deigned to remedy it. . . . Music has suffered the fate of the Arts that are perfected only successively. The inventors of its characters considered only the condition in which it was found in their time without foreseeing that to which it might later attain. . . . As it advanced, rules were established to remedy present inconveniences and to multiply a too limited expression which could not suffice for the new combinations with which it was burdened everyday.[76]

Nearly a century later, Baillot takes a more historical perspective regarding the developments of musical notation;

> Toward the end of the last century [the eighteenth], *Haydn, Mozart,* and later *Beethoven* indicated their intentions by notating melodies as they wanted them played, at least with respect to the notes, and, in general leaving almost nothing in this regard to the choice of the performer. Little by little, this usage has spread, and for the past few years, composers have sought to omit nothing that can render their thought more precisely. They have notated not only *ornamentation*, but *nuances, fingerings, bow strokes,* and *character*—all the principal elements of *accent*.
>
> It is up to the performer to recognize what type of notation is used in the music he is playing, so that he can comply with its requirements. This is not as easy to discern as one might believe, if we consider that the manner of writing everything clearly came about only gradually.[77]

It has now been the efforts of scholars for decades to systematically clean up the nineteenth-century "phrased" editions, to peel away the layers of punctuation added through the years and replace them with the modern Urtext editions. But we will not be any better off with these more or less "pure" texts unless we can become the "elite readers of yore," understanding fully the nature of the implicit punctuation points. In our scrupulous efforts to play only what we see on the page, we must be equally aware of notation's ever-changing implicit conventions. What were the conventions of notation in the 1830s when Baillot claimed that modern composers now wrote everything clearly? What are our conventions when we attempt to play only what is *written* on the page? There will always be an element of *scriptura continua* left in both language and music; no visual representation of any auditory phenomenon can hope to convey each and every nuance of expression, no matter what the medium. And thus it is that punctuation, a visual phenomenon, must continually strive to achieve in its notational system a balance between that which is *written* and that which is *unwritten*. As Parkes explains:

The extension of the general repertory of punctuation provided over the centuries an increasing number of symbols, which have helped to resolve further potential uncertainties in a text, or to signal more subtle nuances of semantic significance. Nevertheless, however many symbols were available at the time, it has always been the adroit use of them which has sustained that cooperation between writer and reader (aided and abetted by others involved in the transmission of texts), which constitutes effective communication in the written medium.[78]

# Chapter Five

# *Punctuation vs. Articulation*

> These two areas, so closely related yet so sharply differentiated from one
> another, illuminate one another.
>
> —*Hermann Keller, 1955*

*Articulation* in the daily discourse of the modern musician has acquired such
broad usage that its significance is often obscured. We speak of "articulating"
this or that passage in a kind of catch-all manner with any variety of meanings
and on any number of levels, many of which easily merge into the realm of
punctuation. Take for instance the following two definitions of articulation from
*The New Harvard Dictionary*:

> (1) In performance, the characteristics of attack and decay of single tones or groups of
> tones and the means by which these characteristics are produced. Thus, for example,
> staccato and legato are types of articulation. In the playing of stringed instruments, this
> is largely a function of bowing; in wind instruments, of tonguing. Groups of tones may
> be articulated (i.e., "phrased") so as to be perceived as constituting phrases. . . . (2) In
> the analysis of musical form, a boundary or point of demarcation between formal seg-
> ments, e.g., that produced by a cadence or rest. As a compositional process, articula-
> tion is comparable to punctuation in language.[1]

Writers on the performance practice of early music (anything from the seventeenth to the mid-nineteenth century) interpret articulation with much the
same breadth: Sandra Rosenblum explains in 1988: "Articulation in performance is the delineation of motives or musical ideas by the grouping, separating,
and related accenting of notes. . . . Through this clarification music gains shape
and meaning analogous to that provided for language by punctuation and
accentuation."[2] Donington comments in 1974 on "how extremely *articulate* early
phrasing needs to be."[3] Ratner, writing in 1980, builds a definition of articulation which, in addition to slur and staccato indications, above all stresses clarity
in performance, defining this as does Türk (in 1789) to include "the proper
connection and separation of musical periods."[4] In 1985 Robin Stowell praises
the efforts of the violinist Habeneck (in 1840) for his comprehensive illustration
of the various techniques of "phrase articulation."[5]

Yet is such a comprehensive term a practical one? Can the single designator,
*articulation*, adequately encompass the nature of both detached and slurred

notes as well as phrase divisions?[6] Articulation, like many other musical terms
which have been borrowed and appropriated from rhetoric, has become largely
disconnected from its original linguistic associations. We want to rediscover
these associations, establishing eighteenth-century usage in the process, in order
to determine whether applications of *articulation* are suitable in all their present
musical contexts.

The term *articulation* derives from the Latin *articulus*, the diminutive of *artus*
or "joint." Articulation is then the "the action or process of jointing," with particular reference to the animal body. Mr. Venus, **Articulator** of human bones, in
Dickens's *Our Mutual Friend* (1864–65) brags to his customer, Mr. Wegg: "If you
was brought here loose in a bag to be **articulated**, I'd name your smallest bones
blindfold equally with your largest as fast as I could pick 'em out, and I'd sort
'em all, and sort your wertebrae, in a manner that would equally surprise and
charm you."[7] That which is articulate is "distinctly jointed or marked; having the
parts distinctly recognizable," and an articulate voice thus becomes, "the utterance of distinct elements in speech."[8] Literally, this is the language of musical
punctuation. Listen to Mattheson [17] (1739):

> Now since a Comma in speech represents that which in the human body is the
> Articulus or the joint [Gelencke]: thus by comparison the *Colon* indicates a membrum,
> and **whole member**, as the Greek name implies; but the semicolon (;) indicates only
> **half** of one.

Mattheson is very precise in his usage; the *articulus* represents specifically the
"little joints," or the commas.[9] However Meude-Monpas, in his *Dictionnaire de
musique* (1787), demonstrates a more practical and general application, stating:
"Musical articulation is that which consists of delineating the phrases."[10]

Vickers offers further insight in 1988 into the nature of this punctuating
rhetorical figure, *articulus*. He explains that the author of *Rhetorica ad Herennium*
(ca. 84 BC) differentiates between the *colon*, a brief clause which needs another
to complete its sense, and the *articulus*, where the discourse is cut up by the force
of expression—"You have destroyed your enemies by jealousy, injuries, influence, perfidy." The description is a very visual, gestural one:

> The former moves upon its object more slowly and less often, the latter strikes more
> quickly and frequently. Accordingly in the first figure it seems that the arm draws back
> and the hand whirls about to bring the sword to the adversary's body, while in the sec-
> ond his body is as it were pierced with quick and repeated thrusts.[11]

Is it this same concept of articulation that is applied to individual notes?
Perhaps the image of quick, repeated thrusts of a sword is what the violinist Piani
had in mind in 1712 when he described the execution of eighth notes with dots
over them as "equal notes articulated and a little detached" (*nottes égales articulées
et un peu détachées*). A fairly deft handling of the sword produces such notes

depicted under a slur and played with one sweep of the bow with a kind of up-bow or down-bow staccato effect (*nottes égales et articulées d'un même coup d'Archet*).[12] Mondonville, in his 1735 set of sonatas for violin solo, lists among his ornaments *articulation*, which he depicts as eighth notes with dots over them.[13] This he distinguishes from the *detatché*, a quarter note with a stroke over it.[14] Baillot, while he describes no fewer than nine types of *détaché* in 1835, uses the vocabulary of articulation only in the context of *staccato*, depicted under one bow and termed *détaché articulé*.[15]

The difficulty with this analogy is in perceiving each of these "articulated" notes as units equivalent to that of a comma. More likely *articulation* is employed in the violin treatises above as a synonym for precise vocal pronunciation, where the style of execution demands that each syllable and word be uttered distinctly and separately.[16] In 1720 Hotteterre uses *articulation* in a manner similar to the string treatises, distinguishing between the articulated tongue and the slurred tongue (*Langue articulez, & coulez*). Yet as a wind player, he also uses the term in a way that mimics vocal practice, labeling the two syllables which the flutist must pronounce, *tu* and *ru*, as *articulations*.[17] Meude-Monpas claims in 1787 that this kind of articulation, "articulation of the words" or their "clean and exact pronunciation," extends greater superiority to the voice over instruments, which are capable only of musical articulation, or phrasing.[18]

From these eighteenth- and early nineteenth-century applications of the term, articulation, we see *glimmerings* of the wide scope evident in modern usage: its primary relationship to punctuation and additional function in the labeling of distinctive signs (such as staccato dots) which appear over individual notes. But note that I stress the word *glimmerings*. The term *articulation* appears minimally in eighteenth-century treatises and is not even used to describe all kinds of disconnected notes; as we saw above, very often *articulé* is distinguished from *détaché*. And while the leap from articulating phrases to the *staccato* of individual notes is not a difficult one, nowhere does the terminology become mixed up with concepts of legato or with the slur; articulation is not used in the eighteenth century, as Diran Alexanian [60] uses it in 1922 to describe the bow divisions and dynamic fluctuations of "the legato." We mentioned in the previous chapter that the slur came to be regarded as a symbol of punctuation, and perhaps this is related to the fact that it also came to be described as a type of *articulation*. Although articulation (and its Italian, German, and French cognates) may serve as the standard categorization for staccato and legato in today's dictionaries, encyclopedias, and method books, in this broad and ubiquitous use it is virtually absent from corresponding sources in the eighteenth and early nineteenth century.[19] One will not find for instance, a definition of *articulation* in Rousseau's *Dictionnaire de musique*, or of *Artikulation* in Koch's *Lexicon*.[20] Quantz, in his chapter "Of the Use of the Tongue in Blowing upon the Flute" in his 1752 *Versuch einer Anweisung die Flöte traversiere zu spielen* (analogous to Hotteterre's flute treatise), uses an entirely different term to describe the execution of not only short, but also sustained notes, which he claims *"ist zur musicalischen Aussprache hoechst noethig."*[21] Reilly (1985) translates this as that which "is indispensable for musical articulation."[22] However, if one considers the same passage in the French translation (issued simultaneously with the original German edition of 1752), it reads *Elle est indispensablement nécessaire pour l'espression musicale.*[23] The more obvious translation is then: "It is indispensable for musical expression."[24]

How then are we to categorize that which concerns staccato, legato, slurs, and the like and distinguish this kind of articulation from the articulation that is punctuation? Türk is particularly helpful in this regard. In his sixth chapter, "Concerning Execution (*Von dem Vortrage*)," he places all that we have discussed as belonging to *punctuation* into one section—Part II, "Concerning the Clarity (*Deutlichkeit*) of Execution"—and what has come to be called *articulation*, "the detaching, sustaining, and slurring of tones," into another—Part III, "Concerning the Expression (*Ausdruck*) of the Prevailing Character." Here we have the basis of distinguishing between punctuation and our newly defined "articulation": clarity on one side and expression (also Quantz's category) on the other. Keller, without having gone into the etymology of the term, articulation, comes up with much the same differentiation:

> Phrasing and "articulation" have basically different meanings: *phrasing* is much like the subdivision of thought; its function is to link together subdivisions of musical thought (phrases) and to set them off from one another; it has thus the same function as punctuation marks in language. . . . The function of musical *articulation*, on the other hand, is the binding together or the separation of the individual notes; it leaves the intellectual content of a melody line inviolable, *but it determines its expression.* There is, therefore, as a rule only one possible, thoughtful phrasing, but there are several possibilities of articulation.[25]

Now if the result of our lengthy foregoing discussion has been to simply exchange one broad category, *articulation*, for yet another if not more all-encompassing category, *expression*, our efforts will have been far from satisfactory. For if articulation is too generalized a term, *expression* covers just about every aspect of musical . . . well, expression. Yet the argument over semantics is not without purpose. Admittedly, articulation is so much a part of our modern musical vocabulary that we could scarcely do without it, yet still we want to redefine it (or rename it, perhaps as an element of expression) if only to understand the capacity in which we use it. As was fully appreciated by our eighteenth-century predecessors, we must maintain a vigilant control over our potentially "fallible" language. It is my contention that in labeling all degrees of staccato and legato, and particularly slurs, as kinds of "articulation" (a term which is very often a secondary guise for phrasing and punctuation) we predispose how we interpret them. We want, if we can, to find terminology not thus encumbered and establish another context (preferably an eighteenth-century context) in which to define such musical devices. This will help us shed light on the nature of both "articulation" and punctuation, which (as shall become apparent) is crucial to the *Art of Interpreting Rests.*

Rests play as important a role in the understanding and execution of "articulation" as they do in punctuation. Tartini (ca. 1752–56) introduces both types of silence, or absence of sound (*vacuo*), in his discussion of the "Rules for Bowing."

> In playing, we must distinguish between the cantabile and the instrumental; that is, when we play in a cantabile style we must perform one note after another with such perfect union that no interval of silence can be heard. On the contrary, the instrumental style must be performed with some sort of detachment between one note and another. . . . Moreover, as there are appropriate ideas when we play, we must be careful not to confuse them with one another. Therefore, in order to avoid such confusion, it is necessary to make an audible break in the sound even though we play in a cantabile style.[26]

Tartini literally contrasts that which is singable from that which is playable. The distinction is a widely understood notion, often expressed in terms of *adagio* vs. *allegro*, contrasting that which is more serious and solemn from that which is lively or playful, the basis for determining either a smooth and legato expression of the notes or one which is crisp and detached.[27] The above passage should also be considered in conjunction with Leopold Mozart's [22] (1756) appropriation of Tartini's ideas.[28] "The human voice glides quite easily from one note to another; and a sensible singer will never make a break [Absatz] unless some special kind of expression [Ausdrückung], or the **divisions or rests of the phrase [Abschnitte und Einschnitte]** demand one."

The two amplify each other. Mozart, enlarging on Tartini's notion that music conveys sentiments which should not become confused, appends a footnote at the conclusion of the above passage extolling the importance of *Diastolica*: the theory which explains how speech is made intelligible through the modulating influence of punctuation. Tartini, on the other hand, makes the more explicit distinction between the two styles of playing—"singing" or legato and "instrumental" or detached—allowing us to interpret Mozart's "special kind of expression" (notice the use of the word *expression*) within the context of singing as a non-legato or detached "articulation."

We also want to consider a nearly identical passage from Peter Westphal [57] written in 1880, over a hundred years after Tartini's and Mozart's treatises, which again refers to two types of silences. Like Mozart, Westphal stresses the necessity of maintaining a legato delivery as long as no rests (indications of detached "articulation") occur, except for the essential lifting of the legato at the caesura points (points of punctuation). Really the sole difference among these passages comes from our knowledge that in Westphal's day, a legato execution was considered the ordinary or customary expression, where in Mozart's and Tartini's day it was more the exception.[29]

Türk describes the customary eighteenth-century touch, which is somewhat shortened:

> For tones which are to be played in customary fashion (that is neither detached nor slurred) the finger is lifted a little earlier from the key than is required by the duration of the note. Consequently, the notes in a) [in ex. 5.1] are to be played approximately as in b) or c), depending on the circumstances. If there are some notes intermingled which should be held out for their full value, then *ten.* or *tenuto* is written over them (d).[30]

Example 5.1. The customary eighteenth-century touch.

C. P. E. Bach goes so far as to say that these "customary" notes should receive half their value.[31] However Türk's response to this is that then the note (expressed in [e] above) would be too short and the distinction between it and the truly detached notes unnoticeable.[32]

Thus, as we found in the previous chapter, a notational convention of *unwritten rests* appears to be as much a part of "articulation" as it is for punctuation. Yet how do we recognize and distinguish among them? What is the difference between the silences of Mozart's "special expression," Tartini's "instrumental style," Westphal's "rests," and those which belong to the phrase divisions?[33] Written or unwritten, sometimes rests may serve only to indicate a short "articulation," and may convey no meaning with regard to the pauses and rests associated with punctuation. We want to define "articulation" separately from punctuation in order to differentiate their treatment.

For instance, what are we to make of all the rests in example 5.2 from Mozart's C-major Piano Trio, K.548 (1788)?[34] I maintain that in this example we have the *written* version of two very different kinds of rests. The majority of the eighth-note rests are nonpunctuating, serving to establish the affect of the phrase and calling for what keyboard manuals often refer to as a "light" rather than a "heavy" execution, another angle on describing the degree to which notes should be either detached or sustained. As Türk explains, whether a heavy or light execution should be used is determined, 1) from the character and purpose of the composition, 2) from the designated tempo, 3) from the meter, 4) from the note values used, and 5) from the manner in which the notes progress.[35] The rather jaunty character of the trio's opening, combined with notated rests akin to Türk's example 5.1e, seems then to be calling for a detached "expression" beyond the customary eighteenth-century touch. However, the eighth-note rest which follows the tonic C major cadence in bar 6, while indicative of the general "light" execution, also marks an interior punctuation point, a small one with a playful anticipation of what is to come. A corresponding punctuation point would seem to occur in bar 8 with the deceptive cadence in the left hand, yet the melodic and rhythmic contour of the right hand prevents the sense of this before it can happen, tumbling us forward to the quarter- and half-note rests which follow the period in bar 10.

Example 5.2. W. A. Mozart, Piano Trio in C Major, K.548, 1st movement, bars 5–10.

Koch presents another kind of nonpunctuating rest in example 5.3 below. He explains:

> There are phrases whose figures are combined with short rests which often have the appearance of an incise [*Einschnitt*]. For instance, when the phrase found in [figure 4.1c] is formed as in [example 5.3], it seems that two incises are found in the first measure.

Example 5.3

> Only in this and the following section, we are not concerned with such incises, if one even wishes to call them that. They arise merely through the different variations of the main notes of the melody. Here we shall consider only such incises which are perceptible resting points.[36]

The two sixteenth-note rests in Koch's example are similar in kind to the written rests we encountered in Mozart's A-major Symphony (ex. 4.2), as figurations which require simply an absence of sound.

But notice what happens when the multifaceted word *articulation* becomes an ingredient in such examples. Lussy states at the conclusion of his 1873 discussion on the treatment of long notes which mark the ends of slurs and phrases: "It is understood, of course, that if the phrase is *staccato* the rests everywhere indicate incises."[37] *Incise,* a term which we have come to recognize as belonging to the language of punctuation and referring to a kind of comma or small pause, Lussy defines as "nothing more than an *articulated* note followed by a small silence, or several slurred notes followed by a short rest." *Incises* can indicate anything from a monosyllable or vowel to a polysyllabic word.[38] Lussy is on slippery ground, the consequences of which become apparent in example 5.4.

Example 5.4. How great composers make use of *incises* in their music, demonstrated in Mozart, Piano Sonata in F Major, K.332, 1st movement, bars 1–12, from Lussy, *Traité de l'expression musicale*, p. 59.

According to Lussy, this example from Mozart's Keyboard Sonata in F Major, K.332, demonstrates the manner in which "great composers make use of *incises* in music."[39] Observe that each slurred *incise*, indicating perhaps a syllable or word, is also designated by a point of punctuation. We begin to perceive confused and intertwining notions of articulation, pronunciation, and punctuation. If we apply the same practices to Mozart's trio above (ex. 5.2), each eighth note in bars 5 and 7 and each slurred sixteenth-note pair in bars 8 and 9, then becomes a unit of punctuation. Lussy attempts to justify such departures from recognizable forms in language by explaining that composers of instrumental music are given complete latitude, where as in vocal music they must conform to the sense of the words and the length of the verses.[40]

In Lussy's defense we must applaud his basic intentions. He wants to ensure the proper execution of the slur (to update notation according to changing conventions as we discussed in chapter 4). He illustrates this first vocally and then explains the effect as it would be produced on instruments:

Example 5.5

To produce the desired effect on the piano, the first note must be firmly struck, and held down until the second is softly touched, the two fingers being removed at the same time, by gliding gently off the second key. On the violin they would be played by one stroke of the bow, and on wind instruments by one emission of the breath, giving force to the first note and softness to the second.[41]

This eighteenth-century concept of the slur, so fundamental a part of contemporary "articulation" and performance style, had begun to disappear by Lussy's day.

The implied convention of an accent or stress on the first note, followed by a softer, gentle release, simply ceased to be aesthetically desirable amidst the more powerful, sustaining ability of instruments, combined with the tendency for phrases to lean forward towards the middle of the measure and away from downbeats. In addition, such an execution became more and more physically difficult to reproduce. For instance, the performance technique described below by E. W. Wolf would have been far easier and more idiomatic to a 1785 fortepiano with its naturally quick decay of sound, than on a heavy, iron-framed, and overstrung grand piano.

> One holds the finger down on the note where the slur begins until after the next note has been struck, and only then releases it gently. With several notes slurred together each finger does likewise. Where the slur ends, however, and a new one begins, the finger leaves the key on the last note of the slur before striking the next. A dot or a small dash above the second, third, etc. note of a slur indicates that these notes are to be detached, while those beginning the slur still receive the stronger accent.

(The + here indicates the stronger accent, the letters *a*, *b*, *c*, and *d* the weaker.)[42]

Example 5.6. Slur execution according to E. W. Wolf.

In 1756 Leopold Mozart describes a similar style of slur execution, also very natural to an eighteenth-century, gut-strung violin, played with a more tapered bow and held resting easily against the body without the securing aid of a shoulder rest, which was designed (in part) to aid the production of a more continuously sustained sound.[43]

> Now if in a musical composition two, three, four, and even more notes be bound together by the half circle, so that one recognizes therefrom that the composer wishes the notes not to be separated but played singingly in one slur, the first of such united notes must be somewhat more strongly stressed, but the remainder slurred on to it quite smoothly and more and more quietly.[44]

These stated conventions associated with the slur provide some very useful guidelines for its execution in eighteenth-century compositions. Yet the notational device is still a very imprecise indicator (as is all notation) for the infinite variety of expressions in which it is employed: among lively passages, impetuous gestures, plaintive sighs and laments, etc. The treatment of the slur is not only subject to a great many subtle nuances in its execution—variations in the degree of diminuendo within its compass, the nature of the initial accent or stress, and the amount of separation between groups of slurs—but also directly contrasting applications. As E. W. Wolf remarks, every rule has its exception (as we also encountered with the melodic rule) and the present case cannot be without exception either: "In some cases, with notes of a longer duration, or in a serious **Adagio**, the note beginning a slur can have a milder accent without disturbing the seriousness of the performance." As depicted in example 5.7, "this has the effect of someone taking a deep breath and releasing it with a loud sigh."[45]

Example 5.7. Exceptions to the rule of the slur. From E. W. Wolf, *Anleitung zum guten Vortrag*, viii.

As we return to Lussy's interpretation of Mozart's keyboard sonata (ex. 5.4), thus while his basic concept appears to be correct, still his notation of the passage's punctuation is poor. Mozart's *period* consists of only "complete" incises and not "incomplete" incises, which, according to Koch, fill only a single measure.[46] Lussy's commas are therefore inappropriate, failing to indicate accurately the subtle, nonpunctuating nuances of expression implied by the slurs. And while I agree with his division of the opening sentence into three four-bar phrases concluded by a period, his semicolon divisions are also too large, as we can see more clearly through Mozart's full scoring in example 5.8.[47]

Example 5.8. W. A. Mozart, Piano Sonata in F Major, K.332, 1st movement, bars 1–12.

The concluding measures of both interior phrase units consist of unresolved harmonies (leading to tonic downbeats in the following measures) and continual rhythmic and melodic material in at least one hand. Koch describes just the kind of effect achieved by the left hand in bar 4 as the "connecting of two phrases by filling in the space between the caesura note of the preceding phrase and the first tone of the following." However, he takes care to explain, this effect "should not be mistaken for the compounding of two phrases (where the caesura note of the first and the initial tone of the second phrase are one and the same degree of the scale)."[48] Now in order to interpret this statement of Koch's properly, it is necessary to understand an important aspect of eighteenth-century phrasing which is different from our modern concept of phrasing. This is the placement of the pause on the leading-tone structures (the dominant or diminished seventh), before the termination of the cadence; in other words, the pause does not always have to follow the resolution from V to I, but can in fact very often precede it. Thus the bass eighth notes in bar 4 need not be felt as an upbeat to the tonic in bar 5, but can tolerate a very slight pause, or at least a tapering inflection (nothing remotely as large as a semicolon) before beginning anew with the melodic line. "Pausing" in this anticipatory manner (which we have already encountered in Mozart's A-major symphony, ex. 4.2) allows for a continuing sense of forward motion and expectation, and prevents the sentences from becoming too chopped-up. In bar 8, we have not only an embellished leading-tone trill "filling the space" between the phrases, but also imitation (or conversation) between hands, which further diminishes the weight of this second division by a "compounding" of the phrase in the left hand.

All of Lussy's musical incises in example 5.4, while not entirely incorrect, have therefore been scaled up as the result of applying punctuation marks at the level of articulation. Neither is it difficult to see how such confusion might have arisen. For instance, the following passage from Türk might appear at first glance to be about the incorrect execution of slurs:

> If a keyboard player also does not join the tones together well and consequently divides a thought where it should not be divided, other than at the end of a musical period, then he makes the same mistake that an orator would if the latter would pause in the middle of a word and take a breath. I have indicated these incorrect separations through rests in the following examples [ex. 5.9].[49]

Example 5.9

A little later on, Türk adds;

> A musical thought which has not been completed may never be divided by lifting the fingers from the keys at the wrong time (or by rests). Therefore, the first examples [ex. 5.9] must be executed as follows [ex. 5.10]:[50]

Example 5.10

Now these examples of Türk's are often cited as evidence for what Bernard Harrison describes in 1997 as "the interpretation of patterns of short slurs as a conventional way of notating continuous legato." According to Harrison, writers such as Robin Stowell (1991), Hermann Keller (1955), and Paul and Eva Badura-Skoda (1957) consider that "short slurs should be treated in a cumulative manner" and "elided into a long legato line." Harrison, however, maintains that this would ignore "one of the most characteristic features of eighteenth-century notation on the basis of later concepts of articulation." In defense of his opinion (and I agree with him entirely), he makes the point that Türk's subject is not how slurs should be executed, but the *Einschnitte* in composition.[51] Türk's examples are given to elaborate how the sentence, "He lost his life, not only his fortune," or "He lost his life not, only his fortune," can have an entirely different meaning according to the way in which it is *punctuated.* In other words, example 5.9 is not meant to demonstrate the incorrect slur *articulations* of example 5.10, but rather the inappropriate use of rests associated with musical *punctuation.* In fact, Türk even appends a footnote to example 5.9 to the effect that articulation is not his subject at all: "The tones which the composer, for other reasons, wishes to be played in a detached manner or clearly separate from one another are not under consideration here."[52]

As we mentioned earlier, Türk discusses such "expressive" devices, including slurs, in Part III of his chapter on *Execution.* Here he explains that in executing slurs, the finger remains on the key (without the slightest rest) for the entire duration of the notes which are to be slurred. He does not specifically explain how the last note of the slur is to be treated, but he does add that "the first note on which the curved line begins should be very gently (and almost imperceptibly) accented," even if this gentle emphasis falls on weak beats. He provides examples with groups of slurs very much like example 5.10.[53] Now if there is what Harrison calls a *silence d'articulation,* or what Wolf describes as a "gentle release" at the end of each slur (depicted by Lussy through a sixteenth-note rest in example 5.5), then it is a very slight one—just the right amount, as Rosenblum suggests, to provide a "fresh impulse" or "an appropriate distinctness" without impeding the flow of the line.[54] The sense of note grouping will be unavoidable with the proper execution of the slurs in Türk's example [5.10], but this need not contradict his statement that no *rests of punctuation* may occur until the entire thought has been completed. In fact his description of slurs in Part III really has nothing to do with his description of punctuation in Part II. The only relevant conclusion about slurs we might draw from the above examples, is, as Harrison notes, that sixteenth- and eighth-note rests are far too big to indicate the *silence d'articulation* at the ends of the slurs.

This issue of the implied rest as part of the slur gesture was also a point of discussion between Brahms and his friend, the virtuoso violinist Joseph Joachim. In a letter dated May 20, 1879, Joachim argues that the rest, depicted below in example 5.12, is entirely a pianistic effect, and is something violinists have to be made aware of.

Example 5.11

[The above example, 5.11] can sound just as connected when played [on the violin] with different strokes, while on the piano it should in all circumstances be played like this:

Example 5.12

I always draw my students' attention to this difference in works by composers who are piano players. Think about it also.[55]

In his reply, dated May 30, 1879, Brahms admits that such a rest is generally appropriate, particularly in the case of two-note slurs. But really each note under the slur receives its true, full value.

It is my intention that the curve over many notes does not diminish the value of any of them. It means **legato**, and one draws it according to group, period, or as the mood takes one. When over only two notes, time is taken from the last note:

Example 5.13

For larger groups of notes:

Example 5.14

that would be a creative freedom and subtlety in the execution, which is mostly generally appropriate. With me, such considerations are unnecessary, but you have the broom in hand, and there is much to sweep.[56]

Now I involve myself in this sticky issue because I think that at the crux of Brahms and Joachim's debate over notation (above and beyond any technical issues specific to either the violin or piano), and the difficulty encountered in both Türk's examples and Lussy's, is essentially a confusion over semantics—the conflation of punctuation and articulation. For instance, Brahms gives the symbol quite a wide scope: describing the expressive "refinement" with which it can be treated, its role in delineating groups and periods of notes, as well as the plain arbitrariness of its use according to one's mood. For Joachim, this is the difficulty with the slur—knowing whether it merely indicates a bow stroke or whether it distinguishes a unit of sense: "In the legato it is awkward to distinguish in the curve ⌢ where it simply means: so and so many notes in the same stroke, or else, where it signifies: division of the note groups according to sense."[57] Clearly, the role of the slur in the mid- to late nineteenth century is in a state of great flux and very difficult to interpret: Does the slur demand the nuanced effect described by eighteenth-century theorists, perhaps including the *silence d'articulation* at its conclusion? Is it merely a symbol of the *legato* and a guide to bowing/breathing? Or is it in fact a symbol of punctuation? I believe it is just this confusion regarding its application that has resulted in, on the one hand, Lussy's overemphasis of the implied rests and gestures of Mozart's slurs, and on the other, the more modern tendency to completely remove any sense of note grouping from Türk's similar slurs. Thus the result of labeling slurs as articulations and potential phrase designators is that a very vital and subtle *expressive* device is lost.

I would not like to have to choose between the above two extreme interpretations, but given Lussy's application of the slur, a rebellion against such a disjointed performance practice in favor of a long continuous legato line, seems quite natural. The nuances of slurs which are already more difficult to execute on modern instruments, appear both nonsensical and unmusical when presented as in example 5.4. However if we take "articulation" out of the slur, we can have our cake and eat it too—long lines *and* expressive interior note groupings. As we have already found in our discussion of examples 4.2 and 5.8, to advocate the "punctuated" style of eighteenth-century music need not necessarily promote short, disjoint expressions. Like Türk in examples 5.9 and 5.10, many music theorists were anxious to express the principles of punctuation in terms of the greater connection within periods.[58] Thus, while the primary definition of punctuation is still that of dividing and separating, the concept of combining and connecting plays no insignificant role (a concept also emphasized by eighteenth-century Elocutionists, as we found in the section "Elocution and the *Honnête Homme*" in chapter 2, p. 46).

Thus far we have been looking at relatively short slurs, but to pursue the evolution of the phrasing slur a little further, note that above and beyond Mozart's notation, Lussy introduces long four-bar slurs to indicate the larger structures in example 5.4. The effect is what Hugo Riemann would have called in 1890 "underslurs" bounded by "great slurs," a layered use of slurs not without precedence in the eighteenth century. Türk explains how such an *expression* of the legato would be executed:

Example 5.15

The sign [in ex. 5.15] signifies that all the notes are to be slurred; nevertheless, the first, third, fifth and seventh tones are to be very softly marked.[59]

Habeneck introduces these long, "great" slurs in 1840, but for the purpose of delineating phrase structure. Yet he is so far from sure his readers will understand his usage, that he adds a footnote to his example shown in figure 5.1: "In the whole of this section, the slur ⌒ is in no way to be applied to the bowing; it is used merely to separate the figures [*dessins*], phrases, and periods."[60] Thus in 1840 it would appear that the concept of the slur as a phrase mark is at least not typical. But perhaps the use of the familiar sign for this purpose is another practice which with repetition over time has lent credibility to the interpretation of slurs, particularly long slurs, as phrase marks. As pianist Joseph Hofmann states in 1908, "Find out the start, the end, and the culminating point of your phrase. The last-named is usually to be found upon the highest note of the phrase, while the former are usually indicated by *phrasing slurs*."[61]

Figure 5.1. An example of musical punctuation. From François Antoine Habeneck, *Méthode théorique et pratique de violon*, p. 115. From the facsimile edition, in *Méthodes & Traités, Violon, France 1800–1860*, Courlay: Éditions Fuzeau Classique, p. 107.

Hugo Riemann, as we discussed in the previous chapter, became a great champion of the phrasing slur. In his argument, he explains that the employment of the slur as simply a sign for *legato* playing has been mostly abandoned for the reasons that first of all, legato has become the customary means of connecting tones and secondly, the slur does not necessarily exclude staccato marks that may appear

beneath it. Riemann reasons therefore, "Now, the *new* office of the slur is, to indicate the articulation of the musical thought (themes, periods, movements) into its
natural divisions (phrases)."[62] Heinrich Schenker entirely disagrees with
Riemann's efforts, claiming that the phrasing slur "falsifies both the legato slur
and the musical form." He goes on to say that editors, in their attempt to update
notation, destroy all the subtle "articulative" devices for the sake of structural
unity.[63] But in spite of Schenker's attempt to "abolish the phrasing slur" and even
after the emergence of Urtext editions to clean up the excesses of efforts like
Riemann's, the concept of the phrasing slur remains.

With this history of the slur in mind, combined with our understanding of
legato vs. detached playing (the adagio vs. allegro and sung vs. spoken styles), let
us continue our efforts to untangle the notational practices of punctuation and
articulation. Consider the intricately notated eight-bar *period* which begins the
Adagio from Haydn's 1799 String Quartet, Op. 77, no. 1—replete with a full
scale of dynamics, sforzandi, accents, staccato strokes, and overlapping slurs.
Figure 5.2 is a reproduction from Haydn's autograph manuscript, made available in facsimile, with commentary by László Somfai, by Editio Musica Budapest,
courtesy of the city's Nationalbibliothek Széchényi. The autograph is, I admit,
somewhat difficult to read. But as we are placing notation, particularly Haydn's
notation, under such close scrutiny, I felt it would be worth the trouble to the
reader. We will also be looking at subsequent editions of the same passage, which
should help in deciphering the autograph (including the 1802 Artaria edition
of figure 5.3, also provided by Somfai, whose interest in this passage sparked my
own).[64]

Figure 5.2. Haydn, String Quartet, Op. 77, no. 1, 2nd movement, bars 1–9;
Haydn's manuscript.

In bars 3 and 7 we have "articulated" notes, eighth notes with a staccato
stroke, followed by small silences, eighth-note rests. Yet in bar 3 a long slur is

indicated above the measure, where there is none in bar 7. The question is then, what is the function of the slur? Is it a phrasing device, used to identify a more cohesive unit in bar 3 than in bar 7?[65] If so, is the rather ludicrous corollary then true, that the eighth-note rests in bar 7 stand for small punctuation units because there is no slur? Or alternatively, perhaps the slur has a different function altogether.

First, let us try considering the question in terms of what would happen were we to take away the slur. I observe one eight-bar period ending on the tonic $E\flat$, clearly separated from the second period by rests, except in the case of the first violin, which surges onward in advance of the other parts. The period is divided into two, four-bar phrases, again separated by rests with the cello part "filling in the space" between the $B\flat$ half cadence and the tonic downbeat of bar 5. Each four-bar phrase is further divided into two, two-bar phrases ending on vii° and divided uniformly by rests in all four parts. Neither the addition nor the absence of the slur over the second two-bar phrase can alter the above period structure. However, the slur can affect the sentence's *expression*. As we learned from Keller, there may be only one possible thoughtful phrasing, but several possible articulations.

One result of the slur, as we have mentioned, is an alteration of the beats in the bar. The convention of giving stress to the first note of the slur and connecting the remainder smoothly and successively more quietly, allows accents to fall on unexpected or even weak beats of the bar. While the harmonic rhythm of figure 5.2 is equally active in both bars ($I^6$–$V^6$–$I$–$ii^6$–$V$ beginning in bar 3 and $I^6$–$ii$–$I^6_4$–$V^7$–$I$ beginning in bar 7), the slur in bar 3 tells us not to make so much of the "good beats" of the bar, beats one and two (in cut time), which we would otherwise do. Haydn also tells us by the crescendo in the middle of the bar that he wishes us to avoid any diminuendo implied by the slur, and indicates by the *sforzando* in bar 4 that the effect of the downbeat should not be diminished. This might also be a place where, as we learned from Wolf, "the note beginning a slur can have a milder accent without disturbing the seriousness of the performance."

The *piano* gesture in bar 3 then begins with the initial sixteenth note, although one might also place a slight emphasis or rhythmic impulse on the downbeat eighth note (within a *piano* range) just to maintain a sense of meter. The eighths continue, "articulated" under one bow, but bypassing a rhythmic accent on the (strong) third quarter beat of the bar. We then crescendo, with an additional emphasis on the otherwise weak quarter-note fourth beat created by the secondary "underslur" and $b\flat^1$ grace note in the first violin part. All of this creates a long upbeat enhancing our expectation and arrival at the half cadence with its accented and suspended dissonance. In contrast, when the same gesture returns in bars 7 and 8, we are reassured by the regular metrical accents of the short, lightly executed eighth notes, and their natural downward inflection and release at the concluding cadence—only to be surprised and swept along by the violin's surge upwards to the following sentence.

We might also, like Cambini in figure 3.3 with Boccherini's String Quartet, Op. 2, no. 1, consider the notation from a specifically violinistic standpoint, regarding the player's bow arm as his "tongue" and "countenance" (gesture as well as voice) in expressing the sentiment of the phrase. The slur as a bowing in bar 3 would convey a very different effect, visually as well as aurally, than would the separate bows of bar 7. I imagine a long up-bow, requiring a full sweep of the arm and engaging the entire upper body as it reaches out for the *sforzando* down-bow on the downbeat of bar 4. The violinst must then immediately retake the bow, another large gesture, to prepare the repetition of the opening *forte*, bar-length slur which begins the second phrase. This manner of arriving at and departing from the half cadence and midpoint of the *period* imparts a very different character and sense to the punctuation point than do the more simply executed and circumscribed movements of the separate bows as they lead to the tonic close. Thus we observe, from both a compositional and elocutionary stand-point, that Haydn's "articulation" clearly comments on his punctuation. But as we attempt to perceive the two as operating within separate domains, the results are, I feel, far more descriptive; both the slur and the detached notes become much more informative than the mere clarification of an already abundantly clear phrase structure.[66]

Johann Elssler, Haydn's personal copyist, is very faithful to the autograph in his own manuscript copy of the quartet. However, the first edition published by Artaria in 1802 (fig. 5.3) omits many of Haydn's expressive details: the accents in bars 2 and 6, the staccato strokes on beats 3 of the same measures, and, most particularly, the long slur in bar 3.[67] Perhaps it was felt that such detailed infor-mation crowding the printed page was not necessary, or worse, even harmful. Remember that throughout the history of punctuation and its related symbols, there has always been a balancing act between that which is *written* and that which is *unwritten*; too many signs can easily result not in the desired clarity, but in confusion. It could be that the slur in bar 3 of Haydn's Adagio was deemed unnecessary—indicating what was already evident in the notation—a long, ris-ing gesture with a crescendo into the *sforzando* downbeat. Or perhaps the removal of the slur was an effort to "normalize" the notation—to make both halves of the *period* conform to each other. Note that a staccato stroke has also been added to the pickup sixteenth-note of bar 7, making it identical to its coun-terpart at the end of bar 2. But in fairness to Artaria, not even the best of edi-tions can reproduce all the information embedded in an autograph: where exactly a slur begins and ends; and how the various indications for detached and slurred notes, dynamics, and accents are distributed throughout a piece and among the different part books. As James Webster explains in 1998, the diffi-culty facing editors is that ultimately they must make decisions for performers regarding these points of "ambiguity," "incompleteness," and "inconsistency"— with the added responsibility that the original source of uncertainty is then com-pletely removed from the performer's view.[68]

Figure 5.3. Haydn, String Quartet, Op. 77, no. 1, 2nd movement, bars 1–8; 1802 Artaria edition.

Sometimes such decisions are fairly minor. For instance, the modern Urtext edition of the Op. 77, no. 1 Adagio adds the "missing" staccato strokes on the downbeats of bar 7 in the viola and cello parts (placing them in parentheses to indicate their omission in the autograph).[69] But other decisions, like Artaria's removal of the long slur, begin to have larger consequences. The level of complexity can become immense when dealing with works of many parts (like quartets which are often not written in score form) and with works for diverse instruments. Do the slurs, as Joachim suggests, mean something quite different for the pianist than the violinist? How closely should the cellist's part mimic the bowings of the violinist's, or even the wind player's articulated syllables?

For instance, the slurs in the bassoon part (doubled at the octave by oboe and basset horn) from Trio II of Mozart's Wind Serenade in B-flat Major (ca. 1783–84) are rewritten when adapted for cello (and also violin and viola) by the pianist and composer C. F. G. Schwencke, in his 1818 arrangement of the piece as *Grande quintetto pour le piano forte, hautbois, violon, viola et violoncelle* (ex. 5.16).[70] We can never know how Mozart himself would have arranged these wind passages for strings, but the shorter slurs of example 5.16b are certainly more idiomatic for the cellist than those of the bassoon part in example 5.16a (one rarely encounters such long slurs in eighteenth-century string parts). Further, their context—the rolling, unison momentum of the trio—would likely suggest to the player an overall legato "expression" beyond that which is indicated by one-bar slurs. This would have posed no difficulty to eighteenth-century string players, who (as Joachim claims of violinists in his day) would have been able to execute the smaller slurs with the same cascading effect of the longer, wind instrument slurs.[71] Strong accents and diminuendos accompanying each slur (according to the "rules" of slur execution) would give more swing to the movement, but would perhaps better suit a livelier, jauntier character than the one here. Coinciding with the beginnings of slurs, the hierarchy of downbeats need only be observed: strong on the downbeat of the first bar, weak on the downbeat of the second bar, somewhat strong on the third bar, and weak again on the fourth. Even in example 5.16a, the new slur beginning on the downbeat of bar 3 indicates less of a break in the legato, than a little nudge marking the bottom of the phrase as it swings back upward to its resting point at the half cadence in bar 4. In these examples then, the particular expressive note grouping appears to be based, at least in part, on the technical nature (bowing vs. breathing) of the instrument being played. The nuances of their execution (the degree of stress, diminuendo, and separation between the slurs) are subject to the governing character or *affect* of the expression.

a) Bassoon

b) Cello

Example 5.16. Wind slurs adapted for string instruments. W. A. Mozart, Wind Serenade in B-flat Major, K.361, 4th movement, Trio II, bars 1–8, arranged by C. F. G. Schwencke.

Changes in articulation symbols are also often introduced, as we discussed in the previous chapter, in order to clarify the execution of a passage for the performer. Returning to the Adagio from Haydn's String Quartet, Op. 77, no. 1, we note that in the first violin part from the 1918 Peters edition (ex. 5.17), the editor suggests an additional up-bow in the middle of the opening bar.[72] Here a decision has also been made that the meter should be felt in 4 rather than 2. This allows for a slower tempo, which perhaps was felt to accommodate better the more powerful instruments and larger quartet performing venues of the twentieth century. The additional bow then becomes a natural way to sustain and project the sound through the opening *forte* gesture. The 1972 International edition goes so far as to remove all evidence of the opening slur, moving it over the second two quarter notes, as seen in example 5.18.[73] Certainly the opening bars of Haydn's *period* demand that a level of intensity be maintained. But this can be achieved while still preserving the nuances of Haydn's expressive markings, stated in unison by all members of the quartet. The one-bar opening slur dictates a strong downbeat and that no break should occur between the first and second strong beats of the cut-time meter. The gesture of the slur, the desired degree of tapering, should be executed within the dynamic of *forte* and without disrupting the sense of expectation as one moves forward into the second bar. The *written* accent on the downbeat of bar 2 also indicates that this measure should not receive the typical weaker emphasis within the hierarchy of the phrase segment. This weightiness of the second bar (the accent need not be harsh, but serious according to the affect required by an Adagio) then falls away with a gentle release on the eighth note of the second (large) beat.

Example 5.17. Haydn, String Quartet, Op. 77, no. 1, 2nd movement, bars 1–8; 1918 Peters edition.

Example 5.18. 1972 International edition of example 5.17.

Since we just described the case of a well-meaning, but nevertheless misleading effort to direct the performer, so it is only fair to also present a case where the notational additions are indeed helpful. In example 5.18 from the 1972 International edition, cited above, I think the direction to the cellist to make a diminuendo in bar 4 is a very appropriate and much-needed reminder of an important lost notational convention. This is an example of what we described earlier as Koch's concept of "filling in the space" between phrases. After the initial *sforzando* downbeat in bar 4, all voices pause with the exception of the cello. And as in example 5.8, this should be executed with an anticipation of what is to come (V does resolve to I), but still with a clear separation between the phrases. A slight diminuendo with the falling gesture and a "gentle release" of the bow at the end of the slur and before the second half of the phrase begins, would facilitate this effect (the slur in Haydn's autograph is difficult to read, but very likely encompasses the entire bar).[74] In bar 8, by contrast, the violin really does function in the sense of a "pickup" to the bar, rising to meet the new higher range of the second (cello-less) period.

The synthesis of expressive elements we have been talking about—between dynamics, slurs and short notes, visual gesture, and the mechanics of playing—brings me to Cambini's second example (following the Boccherini passage discussed in chapter 3), in which he illustrates the different expressions a performer can bring to a single phrase of music. The phrase here is taken from "the celebrated Haydn," the Andante of his Symphony no. 53 (ca.1778–79), later dubbed "L'Impériale."[75] The fact that Cambini presents the work as a string quartet (very likely having played it himself on viola with Manfredini, Boccherini, and Nardini) is due to the work's considerable reknown through its frequent arrangements—for string quartet, keyboard (two and four hands), two flutes, violin and keyboard, harp, etc.[76] As with figure 3.3, Cambini's process is a three-fold one, getting the student to hear the difference between bad and mediocre, mediocre and good, and good and excellent. The latter Cambini feels can be achieved through the notation depicted in figure 5.4: "Here I am sure that this is what the author wanted: to engage, to move, to affect the spectator."[77]

Figure 5.4. The expression of a phrase by Haydn, from his Symphony No. 53, 2nd movement, bars 1–8. From Giuseppe Cambini, *Nouvelle méthode théorique et pratique pour le violon*, p. 22.

I must confess that when I first came accross this example, I found it absolutely astounding. To me, as a performer engaged in historical performance practice and attempting to faithfully interpret the composer's intention, the degree to which Cambini felt at liberty to alter the articulation seemed shocking (one might easily have mistaken it for a late nineteenth-century "instructive" edition).[78] If I were playing in a string quartet, or conducting an orchestra where the first violinist proposed this execution, I would very likely ask the player to please stick to Haydn's "original" notation, and play it "as it is written." I would interpret, from the notation in the *Urtext* Haydn edition (ex. 5.19), a moderate pace, "light" execution, with a simple, sweet, and straightforward expression.[79] The phrases are grouped in regularly accented two- and four-bar units, with the divisions recuring on the same beat throughout. The first comma falls on the second beat of bar 2 after a simple I–V–I progression, the second with a greater sense of expectation in bar 4 after a I–IV–V half cadence. Then in the four-bar progression which completes the sentence (vii°6–I–ii6–I⁶₄–V–I), there is again another very slight caesura in bar 6.

Cambini similarly describes the phrase as expressive of "naivety" and "candor." But he digs a little deeper, painting the picture of a pretty and innocent (virgin) village girl reproaching her lover for his infidelity (which she so little deserves). Cambini calls upon the theatrical arts, asking the violinist to endow the shepherdess with a character yet more naive than that of Colette in *Le devin du village* (J. J. Rousseau's opera of 1752). Nothing about the passage, as Cambini describes it, is executed in the ordinary way. He even warns the violinist that "it

Example 5.19. Haydn's full scoring of figure 5.4.

may be some time before you are able to execute what I am telling you here, but at any rate your teacher should be able to give you some idea of it." The sound called for is "sweeter and more gracious" than for the Boccherini phrase (fig. 3.3). The fingerings, rather than sensible, avoid open strings and particularly the brighter sound of the E and A strings where possible. But most extraordinary are the bowing/slurs which cross bar lines and connect the detached notes with a kind of carress as it glides over them. In this way, the bow arm aquires a special lilt and swing, as does the left hand as it shifts up the strings into the downbeats with the accompanying dynamic swells. Assuming the violinist begins down-bow, with each consecutive slur marking a bow change (with no retakes), then each phrase would begin with an alternate gesture—a bit like the orator gesturing first with the right arm and then with the left, or perhaps shifting his weight between the left and right legs. In addition, a very appropriate up-bow falls on the dotted quarter note b$^1$ of bar 4 at the expectant half cadence in the middle of the phrase. Thus while nothing contradicts the simplicity of the phrasing or the regularity of the down beats, still the content within and the connection between the phrases, both aurally and visually, aquires a different expression than would simple slurs and separate short notes (executed in first position). The degree of theatricality proposed by Cambini may be a matter of taste, as we discussed in the section "Voice and Gesture" in chapter 3, p. 67, but the example highlights the role of articulative slurs and short notes in dictating expression, and at the same time presents some exciting and creative interpretive possibilities to the modern interpreter of eighteenth-century music.

Thus far, we have been working primarily with the expressive function of articulation marks within phrase boundaries, but what happens when these indications overlap with points of punctuation? For instance, if the slurs in figure 5.2 tell us not to treat the beats of the bar in their ordinary manner, what happens when a slur is placed over notes on either side of a punctuation point? Consider first the case of the tie, which like a slur indicates that the two notes should be smoothly connected, not broken or detached. For instance, in example 5.20, from Mattheson's punctuated minuet of 1737, the tie between bars 6 and 7 would appear to indicate that the b¹s should be held and not restruck. As Türk explains: "When two or more (consecutive) notes of the same pitch and name . . . are joined together by a curved line, then only the first tone is struck and the finger remains on the key during the duration of the remaining notes."[80] A natural amount of decay would be allowed to occur over the tied b¹s of example 5.20 (particularly on a keyboard instrument) and the downbeat of bar 7 would not receive its customary degree of stress. The effect here is also what could be described as a *hemiola*, a well-known feature in the current analysis and performance of dance music (and particularly the minuet) in which two measures of 3/4 are combined into one large 3/2 measure (the metrical accents falling on 1, 3, and 5 of the new measure of six quarter notes). Channan Willner, writing in 1991, describes the hemiola as "one of the most characteristic hallmarks of Baroque style."[81] And Meredith Little and Natalie Jenne, in their 1991 discussion of the minuet in the music of J. S. Bach, maintain that "the regularity and balance in the phrase structure would quickly become tedious were it not for the syncopations, hemiolas, and other rhythmic nuances in the style."[82] But note that in the middle of the *combined* hemiola measure, within the boundaries of the tie, Mattheson places the *pause* of a comma. Thus we have two concepts seemingly at odds with one another: on the one hand, the connective articulation mark and the resulting metrical orientation; and on the other, the disjunct of a punctuation mark. Furthermore, the tie and comma coincide with the important structural division of the minuet dance into two-bar step-units.

Example 5.20. The tie in Mattheson's punctuated minuet. From *Der vollkommene Capellmeister*, p. 224.

Let us see if we can't somehow reconcile these two ideas. First of all, perhaps our understanding of the hemiola and its application needs to be reexamined. In 1999 Tilden A. Russell claims, based on his study of minuet form and phraseology in eighteenth-century dance collections and manuscript tunebooks, that the hemiola causes "problems at the sub-phrase level" far less than is warranted by the amount that has been written about hemiola and the minuet step: "In fact the minuet step with hemiola is unequivocally described in only a small minority of the contemporary printed dance manuals, books about dance, lexica and so on that discuss the minuet."[83] It is certainly notable that Mattheson himself makes no mention of the hemiola in his highly detailed analysis of the minuet cited in example 5.20. Patricia M. Ranum claims in 1993 that it is even an exaggeration to say that theorists of the seventeenth and eighteenth century speak only rarely of the hemiola: "practically never or even never would be more exact."[84] Ranum also argues that when she looks at French lyrics set to supposed hemiolas in seventeenth- and eighteenth-century minuets, virtually none of the measures is accentuated in a way that fits the standard model described above. She explains that the phrasings are borrowed from rhetoric, suggesting that the hemiola rhythm was not accentuated according to a rigid formula, but that it was instead a flexible and expressive rhetorical clausula or "closing." As such, its use was restricted to the final measures of selected poetic lines, and more often than not the lines that close an important statement or a section of the song.[85]

In addition to the above ramifications for a less rigid observance of the hemiola, let us also look more closely at the performance conventions associated with the tie. The direction to eliminate the otherwise customary metrical stress in the primary melodic voice does not necessarily affect the metrical behavior of the other voices. As Koch explains, "The accompanying voices must reinforce the metrical stress when accented metrical or sub-metrical divisions of the measure are tied to unstressed ones immediately preceding. In the case of tied units, the rule rarely permits an exception."[86] Leopold Mozart also emphasizes the importance of maintaining an overall sense of meter. He explains that when quarter notes are tied over the bar line, the second of the two must be at first differentiated and made apparent by an after-pressure of the bow, but without lifting the latter, which procedure merely ensures that strict time be kept. He points out, however, that once the time is secured, the second note which is tied to the first must no longer be accented but only held on.[87] Sometimes even a crescendo into the downbeat can be appropriate. Quantz writes: "In ligatures or tied notes that consist of quarter notes or half notes, the volume of the tone may be allowed to swell, since the other parts have dissonances either above or below the latter half of such notes. Dissonances in general, in whatever part they are found, always require special emphasis."[88] While example 5.20 may not be a place for the "swell" described by Quantz or the "after-pressure" described by Mozart, nevertheless the above discussion does allow for some independence and flexibility of expression among the different voices. In other words, not all parts, including the tied melodic voice, need accentuate a rigid hemiola which overrides the division of the phrase into two, two-bar phrases.

Neither is Mattheson's example of a tied-note/phrase-division combination a complete rarity. Couperin, in 1730, also juxtaposes the two symbols in the opening phrase of a gavotte from his *Quatrième livre de pièces de clavecin* (fig. 5.5). As in example 5.20, from Mattheson's minuet, the tie occurs in the upper voice, here in bar 2 on a c#². All of the other voices, however, reinforce the half-bar phrase divisions typical in gavottes and which Couperin indicates with his comma breathing mark. In bar 2, the bass outlines a clear dominant harmony in F-sharp minor, after which a new phrase segment is begun on the dominant of B minor and which will produce an even stronger half cadence in the middle of bar 4, as indicated by Couperin with commas in both the upper and lower voices.

Figure 5.5. François Couperin, *Quatrième livre de pièces de clavecin*, Vingt-sixième ordre, Gavotte, bars 1–4.

In example 5.20, we have only the melody and cannot know either the specific harmony or rhythmic motion of the other voices. But perhaps Mattheson imagined something like example 5.21, which creates a fairly weak vii°$^{4}_{3}$–i⁶ cadence at the point of the comma (a very slight one) before the subdominant-dominant-tonic cadence in the final two bars of the minuet. One at least has the option of expressing the phrase division in the bass part—a slight relaxation in bar 6 accompanied by a new attack on the e in bar 7. Of course, even if one does insist on this downbeat emphasis in bar 7, there might still be that suggestion to the ear of other possibilities. Different harmonies, different types of rhythmic motion would no doubt produce different subtle relationships between the two voices, each lending a different nuance to the phrase structure.[89]

Example 5.21. Possible harmonization of example 5.20.

Thus the hemiola (or perhaps we should call it a rhetorical clausula or closing formula) is a flexible, expressive device—an accentuation and articulation of syllables—which is added to the underlying phrase structure, but does not dictate it. Here punctuation and articulation are closely intertwined, one commenting on the nature of the other. The feeling of two-bar phrases in both the Couperin and Mattheson examples is strong enough that a lack of metrical emphasis in one of the voices, even on a very important downbeat, does not prevent the sense of a *comma*. Still, were the ties to be removed, the nature of the phrasing, even though the division remains, would no doubt be felt differently. Such devices are indeed what prevent seemingly rigid dance structures from becoming what Little and Jenne describe as "tedious," but it would also be a mistake, I think, to allot the tie on its own the power of punctuation.[90]

If a little tie can wreak so much havoc, consider what a much more extended binding of notes across phrase boundaries can do. Staying with the two-bar phrase structure of dance movements for a moment longer, look again at the lengthy slurs of Mozart's Wind Serenade (ex. 5.16a). What is the role of the slurs in this example versus those of the trio's B section (ex. 5.22), which isolate the dance's characteristic eighth-note pickups within the shorter, two-bar gesture? I feel that in both of these examples, the articulation and phrasing seem to reenforce each other—the expression naturally suits the form. While the long slurs support the cascading momentum of the melody and bass, and the division of the opening *period* into two, four-bar phrases, the shorter slurs and detached eighths of the second phrase are equally suited to the melody's subsequent upturned and questioning gestures of two bars, accompanied by punctuating rests in the bass. That said, each element is still performing its very distinct function. At no point, in either example 5.16 or example 5.22 do the slurs outline the structure of the phrases, or even the phrase segments.

Example 5.22. Mozart, Wind Serenade in B-flat Major, K.361, 4th movement, Trio II, bars 9–16.

We find an even lengthier slur in example 5.23, from the opening Allegro of Beethoven's Piano Sonata in D Major, Op. 28 (1801).[91] Without the long slur in the above example, one would naturally divide the sentence into two four-bar phrases; bars 63 through 66 move cadentially in F-sharp minor ($V^7$–i–$V^7$–i), and bars 67 through 70 move cadentially in A major ($V^9$/ii–ii–I–$V^7$–I), and the sentence repeats in bar 71 (after a filling in of bar 70). The slur outlines neither the four-bar phrases nor the larger eight, but an unlikely 5⅔-bar group. What the slur does tell us is not to give the downbeat of bar 67 its natural emphasis. One will feel the cadential motion in the left with the very low FF♯ and the subsequent two-octave jump in bar 5, but above this, the right hand floats up and up, oblivious to the harmonic phrase division—only to tumble down a few measures later and then rise again. While the slur is not itself a phrasing mark, the comment it makes on phrasing is huge. The implication seems to be that while the phrase division exists, the expression demands that it not be felt in the customary manner.

Example 5.23. Beethoven, Piano Sonata in D Major, Op. 28, 1st movement, bars 63–71.

In the end, of course, it is impossible to discuss any single element of music in complete isolation. The expression or "articulation" with which one executes a passage will naturally affect the pacing and nature of its pauses, and must conform like punctuation to the character or *affect* of the compositional topic at hand (the subject for our next chapter). I come back to Keller's insightful quote at the beginning of this chapter and agree with him that articulation and phrasing indeed illuminate one another. I feel, however, that it has been useful to separate the two as much as possible in order to understand the full scope of each. If we treat articulation as simply a kind of subcategory of punctuation, we imply a difference in degree rather than in kind, where articulation operates in the same manner as phrasing but only at a smaller level. Then we not only limit the expressive power of articulation, but at the same time diminish the effectiveness of punctuation. If, on the other hand, we give each its separate domain, the notion of eighteenth-century music as highly "punctuated" need not be incompatible with long, continuous lines. We learn to distinguish between the rests (written and unwritten) which are detached "articulations" and those belonging to punctuation, and we reinstate slurs from their status as "extras" or mere clarifications of phrase groupings.

In this chapter I have made a big fuss over semantics in an effort to disentangle varied and complex notions of *musical articulation*, of which we have only barely tapped the surface and which were by no means clear-cut even in the eighteenth century; articulation practices varied considerably from instrument to instrument (or voice), from composer to composer, and even over the course of a single composer's stylistic development. From early applications to specific kinds of short notes, we perhaps see the origins of labeling all such signs (wedges, tenuto marks, slurs, etc.) as articulations. In addition we understand articulation's modern function as a synonym for punctuation. It is unclear at what point in time *articulation* becomes the broad categorization that it is today. There may not be any obvious defining point in history but rather a more gradual growth from the use of articulation to define very specific expressive devices and vocal/wind playing techniques to encompassing all such devices amidst changing aesthetics of sound production and their accompanying notational conventions.

# Chapter Six

# *Affective Punctuation*

On examination of greater and more imposing instrumental pieces, uncommon diversity in the expression of the affects [*Affecten*] as well as the observation of all divisions [*Einschnitte*] of musical rhetoric can be perceived even more clearly if the composers are of the right sort: where for example an Adagio indicates distress; a Lamento lamentation; a Lento relief; an Andante hope; an Affetuoso love; an Allegro comfort; a Presto eagerness; etc.

—Matheson, 1739

Thus far in our efforts to *interpret rests*, we have established that music is far more "pause-ridden" than might otherwise meet the eye; its notation expresses rests that are both written and unwritten. However, many of these rests do not always express pauses which are directly related to punctuation, and furthermore, their notation, explicit or implicit, must necessarily remain somewhat imprecise. This concerns where the pauses fall, how regularly or irregularly they occur, and where they lie on the scale from scarcely perceptible (including those that admit of no repose at all) to highly conspicuous. But if we demand too much specificity from our visual aids, we achieve the opposite, creating confusion and limiting their effectiveness. And while there are some standard rules by which one can learn to discriminate among the various rests and locate those that are "hidden," one can also expect deviations and exceptions to the rules according to any given situation—among the highly diverse array of compositions to which the concept of musical punctuation is applied. But among those compositions, which (as Matheson implies above) are particularly well crafted, the "uncommon diversity" of their expressions and corresponding punctuation marks will be all the more perceptible. It all comes down to the correct and persuasive portrayal of *affect*, the style and character of the musical sentiments being expressed.

Crucial to the expression of the affects (and also identifying them) is an understanding and recognition of the various possible subjects of discourse. This is also the case in language. As Parkes explains in 1993, "A number of treatises are concerned only with usage in particular situations, and relate only to special kinds of texts." He cautions that misinterpretations can occur if this is not taken into account. For instance, "A scribe who regularly copied philosophical treatises might well miss nuances of meaning in a devotional text."[1] In other words, our readings of the treatises as sources on punctuation usage must depend on our familiarity with these "particular situations," which as it happens are rather numerous. In 1988 Brian Vickers lists the "taxonomania" rhetoricians create "to take account of every possible eventuality, in language or life":

> . . . hymns to the gods (subdivided into eight different types); celebrations of countries, cities (including harbors, citadels; the city's origins, accomplishments, virtues), . . . an "imperial oration," or encomium of the emperor; a speech of arrival at a city; a "talk" or more casual form of encomium, less bound by rules; a "propemptic talk," or speech "which speeds its subject on his journey with commendation"; an epithalamium or wedding speech, with its more specialized appendage, the bedroom speech; birthday, consolatory, and funeral speeches, speeches of invitation, leavetaking, lament, and many more.[2]

It has similarly become standard to describe the various "taxonomania" of eighteenth-century music in terms of subject matter or "topics of discourse." Leonard Ratner lays the groundwork in *Classic Music* (1980) which enables us to define and identify the various topics, and their accompanying *affects*, present in both instrumental and vocal compositions.[3] These, as in language, exhibit a similarly limitless and equally daunting range of possibilities. Each topic, divided into two groups of "types" and "styles," is governed by a set of standardized or understood musical characteristics that trigger its recognition. The topic of a musical discourse may be a "dance," or a "fantasia"; it may represent the "singing style," or the "brilliant style." In addition, the distinction between these types and styles may be flexible. A dance, say a gavotte, may be a type of composition but gavotte can also be a style for another composition.

For instance the opening of the Allegro sonata-form movement of Mozart's G-major Piano Trio (1788), seen in example 6.1, with its gay and pleasant *affect*, a phrase structure of four and eight bars with perceptible two-bar incises, and an anapestic rhythm of two short syllables followed by a long one, ⌣ ⌣ —, instantly proclaims itself a gavotte.[4] The pianist is immediately alerted to the regular, mid-bar phrase divisions and the accompanying hierarchy of strong and weak beats. The string players, too, when they take up their part of the dialogue with a repetition of the gavotte theme (beginning in bar 9), should also feel a strong urge to mimic the gestures of the dance, coordinating the light upbeats of the gavotte rhythm with up-bows, and the subsequent strong downbeats with down-bows.

On a basic level then, the performer must be attuned to the nature of the composition as a *pleasing* dance. But at the same time, he or she must be aware that this regularly structured form is also woven into a species of the freer, more *impassioned* sonata, in this case the keyboard trio.[5] We observed in C. P. E. Bach's Keyboard Sonata of a fantasia nature (ex. 4.13) many freedoms in its phrase structure, but perhaps because the *topic* and *affect* of Mozart's trio is that of the "gay" and strictly defined gavotte-dance, we observe in general a greater degree of uniformity. But even in the seemingly formulaic opening of example 6.1, the

Example 6.1. Mozart, Piano Trio in G Major, K.564, 1st movement, bars 1–9.

gavotte makes concessions to the sonata. The Allegro begins with a *forte* gesture on a G-major chord—a kind of call to attention and resonant announcement of the key. When the reverberations die away, which might require a slightly longer silence than the *written* quarter-note rest, the gavotte can begin with its characteristic two-beat pickup to the following bar. The result is that the incises and phrase divisions fall on odd-numbered measures, and yield a nine-bar opening *period*.

The G-major chord is sounded again in bar 9, this time accompanied by an extravagant flourish from the violin before a sudden drop to *piano* with the resumption of the regular gavotte rhythm. This violin gesture, I believe, "fills in the space," as Koch would say, without "compounding" the phrase. One could experiment here with the degree of connection between the *forte* and *piano*, and also the degree to which the transition is a *subito* one. I think the violin gesture should arise precipitately out of the downbeat *forte* chord. The four-note slur embellishing the $g^1$, while it conveys no real diminuendo, still receives its primary impulse from the first note. It should be played with a quick down-bow, with the slightest sense of falling away as the violinist abruptly reins himself in to be ready with an up-bow when the cellist and pianist join him for the second *piano* statement of the gavotte. This second statement led by the strings makes up for the "extra bar" of the first *period*, consisting only of seven bars in a 2+2+3 formation. Then in example 6.2, when it becomes the pianist turn again to lead, beginning with a repetition of the violin's flourish from bar 9, the character of the conversation also begins to shift. This time no sudden change in dynamic accompanies the reappearance of the gavotte rhythm in bar 16, and the melody itself becomes more purposeful, beginning with the insistent falling minor-sixth interval, and continuing with the sequence of running sixteenth-notes. With regard to our discussion in the previous chapter, we might also consider the absence of the "articulative" slur in bar 16 as contributing to the sense of the new expression which this time is not reigned in. Elements such as theses are perhaps the kind of "intemperances" Mattheson, in 1739, associates with instrumental gavottes (gavottes for playing rather than singing or dancing). The true nature of the gavotte, according to Mattheson, is one of skipping, not running as one often finds in gavottes composed for the keyboard, and even more so among those for the violin.[6]

Example 6.2. Mozart, Piano Trio in G Major, K.564, 1st movement, bars 16–21.

When we come to the movement's development section, the seat of the sonata form's drama, the gavotte's "gay and pleasant" anapestic orientation of the bar is virtually absent. In the passage shown in example 6.3, the conversational exchange has taken on an entirely different character. Rather than the alternation of completed ideas, as observed in the opening *periods* by first the pianist and then the strings, we witness a series of rapid-fire exchanges between the two parties. If we wish to incorporate Reicha's principles on "dialoguing a melody," the contrast in style would be roughly analogous to the two effects achieved in examples 3.6a and b. As Ratner explains in 1980, "Periods begin as dances but often move to the fantasia by means of digression and extensions, to return to the dance at the beginning of the next period." It is these two poles, the one rigorously regular and the other free, which complement each other so well in sonata form.[7]

Example 6.3. Mozart, Piano Trio in G Major, K.564, 1st movement, bars 49–53.

It is useful at this point to stop and draw some broad distinctions between the different *styles* and *topics* of discourse. The eighteenth-century grammars and elocutionary handbooks discuss language in the context of two large categories, *prose* and *verse*. In the strictest sense, the two are defined in opposition to each other. Prose represents ordinary spoken or written language which pays no regard to meter, while verse exhibits a regularity of rhythm, accent, and metrical emphasis. As Quintilian explains, "Verse is always in some degree uniform, and flows in one strain, while the language of prose, unless it be varied, offends by monotony, and convicts itself of affectation."[8] John Walker sums up this classical concept in 1781: "The sole difference between them seems to lie in the constant, regular, and artificial arrangement of accent in the one [verse], and the unstudied, various, and even opposite arrangement in the other [prose]."[9]

The structural differences between prose and verse naturally carry many ramifications with regard to punctuation. Parkes maintains that the role of punctuation in transmitting semantic intent is far greater in verse than it is in prose. The tools of punctuation, layout, and rhyme become the primary features of a very densely packed and concise style of language. Verse calls attention to its own form in order to arouse the readers expectations which "will govern their

perception of its 'poetic' nature, stimulate close reading and cause them to ini-
tiate the special processes of interpretation required by the form."[10] The ready
perception of these poetic structures versus those of prose, the fact that they
seem to leap off the printed page, also proves to be a key element in determining
the type of subject matter and expression appropriate to this style of language.
Thus expression and structure become highly interdependent, or to put it in
rhetorical terms, the desired expression must be fitted with the appropriate language (prose or verse).[11]

Also a part of the discussion is the branding of a particular style as either masculine or feminine, according to the affective nature of the subject—serious or
more light-hearted. Walker claims that although masculine, sublime, and strong
subjects are suited to the strength and severity of prose, beautiful, didactic, and
persuasive subjects demand a smooth and elegant language. And while he
admits that all the passions may be expressed in a "poetical dress," he feels that
the benevolent ones are the most suited to verse, using such feminine adjectives
as graceful, pleasing, and amiable.[12] Quintilian weaves the nature of expression's
gestural associations into the above equation. Adding to his statement that we
must form our language to suit our delivery, he claims:

> Even the movements of the body have their rhythm; and the musical science of num-
> bers applies the percussions of measured feet no less to dancing than to tunes. Is not
> our tone of voice, and our gesture, adapted to the nature of the subjects on which we
> speak? Such adaptation, then, is by no means wonderful in the rhythm of our language,
> since it is natural that what is sublime should march majestically, that what is calm
> should advance leisurely, that what is spirited should run, and that what is tender
> should flow.[13]

But like all our efforts to prescribe and "lay down the rules" of punctuation,
we find that the attempt at strict categorization—the strong and severe, rhythmically irregular (masculine) prose on one side, and the beautiful and mild,
evenly paced (feminine) verse on the other—does not take into account the
great flexibility of language. The two contrasting styles are by no means mutually exclusive. In varying degrees and according to the subject at hand, prose
sometimes requires the smoothing, rhythmic regularity of verse, what Walker
labels "harmonious prose," and verse, the looseness and freedom available in
prose.

> [An unequal interval between accents] is so far from having a bad effect on the ear, that
> it frequently relieves it from the too great sameness to which rhyming verse is always
> liable. But if this inequality of interval is sometimes for the sake of variety necessary in
> verse, it is not to be wondered, that for a similar reason, we avoid as much as possible
> too great a regularity of interval between the accented syllables in prose. Loose and
> negligent, however, as prose may appear, it is not entirely destitute of measure: for it

may be with confidence asserted, that, wherever a style is remarkably smooth and flowing, it is owing in some measure to a regular return of accented syllables. And though
a strength and severity of style has in it something more excellent than the soft and
flowing, yet the latter holds certainly a distinguished rank in composition. The music
of language never displeases us, but when sense is sacrificed to sound; when both are
compatible, we should deprive a thought of half its beauty, not to give it all the harmony of which language is susceptible.[14]

Eighteenth- and nineteenth-century music theorists, up to their usual habits of
imitating the trends in language, also attempt to sort the expressions of music into
prose/verse categories. And like language, the boundaries of these categories are
often blurred, woven rather tightly in and among other numerous distinctions
(which are themselves not consistently drawn) together with the stylistic and
expressive, gender and gestural considerations already described. For instance, we
observed earlier that Tartini unites the instrumental style with a lively detached
expression and the vocal with a legato expression, his version of the universal alle-
gro/adagio dichotomy. Forkel, in 1788, further compares the liveliness of the
rhythmically patterned song, with its easy comprehension, to the essence of verse:
"If liveliness, particularly, is to be achieved using rhythm in music, then its musical
feet must be based on such easy and definite proportions that they can be clearly
felt without effort and trouble."[15] Georg Simon Löhlein makes a similar distinction in describing the *adagio* style: "With slow emotional melodies where many
ornaments may be used, the rhyme is not noticed as much as with joyous pieces."[16]

Mattheson, in his 1739 chapter "On the Difference between Vocal and
Instrumental Melodies," draws his parallel between verse and prose strictly along
vocal and instrumental lines, the very metrical quality of the former lending
itself most readily to the rhythmic patterns of verse:

> In poetry or prose all words have their syllabic feet, their measures also in addition to
> the rhyming and verse-composition: and these **pedes** are of the greatest strength in
> speech, as in singing and playing. Yet the meters or rhyme-schemes are not present in
> prose, i.e., the measuring of whole regular verses, lines, rhyme-terminations, etc. And
> in this vocal melody reveals another, and indeed a **thirteenth** difference from instru-
> mental melody, **because metrical music does not relate so much to the latter as with the
> former, which is very fond of verse.**[17]

As Mattheson explains, because instruments do not use words, they do not
require verse or derive emphasis according to the words. Yet his categorizations
begin to break down as he is forced to acknowledge that the meter and note
emphases of instrumental melodies are in fact derived from the very nature of
vocal melodies. Further, in place of syllabic feet and meter or rhyme schemes,
he observes that instrumental melodies, and especially dance melodies, must
adhere to their geometric progressions (i.e., regular two- and four-bar units)
even more closely than their vocal counterparts.[18]

The regular, geometric structure of dance melodies then becomes the basis by which Mattheson defines the various genera of *aria*: "Often an arietta has the same sort of repetitions as dance melodies, and is otherwise so arranged that it is easy to grasp. . . . In a word, all good concise melodies are, in a certain sense, arias or ariettas, and this last name may be attributed to every apt offspring."[19] Rousseau, in 1768, also makes the connection between aria and dance, claiming that "modern music has divers kinds of airs, each of which has reference to some sort of dance." The regularity and harmony of their proportions (their verse-like quality) is evident in their name, *air*, which Rousseau claims derives from the Roman *aera*, the "number, or the marks of the number," corresponding to the meter of the chant. "Moreover," Rousseau argues, though this word [*aera*] was originally taken only for the number or measure of the chant, in the end it was . . . used to denote the song itself."[20] Mattheson, however, finds this etymological source too far-fetched, particularly since it indicates only one "number." *Aera*, he explains, derives from *aes*, or "metal," and is therefore more likely to mean something that resounds, rather than the worth of a coin. His version of the word's origin focuses not on aria's metrical structure but on the affect of its expression: "The word aria doubtlessly derives from air, not only because all sound finds its vehicle therein; but also because a beautiful melody is to be compared with nothing more pleasant than sweet, fresh air, and is just as refreshing, if not more so."[21] Charles Masson also employs the same (essentially feminine) terminology in 1699 to describe the *Air*—"beauty," "tenderness," "gaiety," and "sweetness."[22]

The rather circuitous logic which leads Mattheson to his differentiation between the prose- and verse-like qualities of instrumental and vocal music is difficult to untangle and, as noted above, somewhat inconsistent. But a prominent part of his discussion, and also germane to the basic premise of our music/language analogy, is the notion that instrumental music very easily exceeds the natural expressions of the voice—for instance the "intemperances" one often encounters in gavottes for the piano and especially the violin. Mattheson particularly criticizes organists (with their ten fingers and two feet) who, in writing for the voice, fail to acknowledge the necessity of breathing.[23] The amateur viol player Hubert Le Blanc also focuses on the technical/mechanistic nature of music making (both vocal and instrumental) in 1740, rather disparagingly equating elaborate and physically exerting performances with the expressions of prose, and placing a high value on the physical grace with which he associates verse-like expressions. The more music imitates dances in their regularly measured phrases and natural cadences (without ricocheting bows and twisting throats), he claims, the more truly poetic it is. In his evaluation of instrumental music, Le Blanc further draws the prose/verse parallel between harmony and melody, also bringing into the dialogue the notion that everything graceful and pleasing to the eye and ear must be French. Musical poetry he calls melody (*chant*), and musical prose, harmony. Reflecting early eighteenth-century Parisian taste, he argues that the Italians try to obtain above all the one (harmony/prose), while the French sacrifice everything for the other (melody/verse).[24] Le Blanc praises the French sonatas (particularly the second and third books of Mr. Michel), "which resemble the songs of nightingales, far removed from degenerating into the vulgarity of the hissing airs by the linnet."[25] Corelli's sonatas, on the other hand, throw all but harmony by the wayside, carrying away all sense with their powerful exertions.[26] Mattheson, too, in his discussion of prose and verse, instrumental and vocal melody above, repeatedly praises the instrumental music of the French.[27] We will return shortly to this idea that French music is inherently more verse-like.

The notion that it is harmonically driven music that is capable of the greatest freedoms is also taken up by Löhlein in his 1765 essay on keyboard playing. He points out that organ fantasies (again the choice of the organ as an extreme example) are more harmonic than melodic and even freer for that reason.[28] Further, nowhere is the harmony subject to greater freedoms (or more difficult to execute) than it is in recitative, the type of composition which Löhlein feels is synonymous with the concept of musical prose. "Everyone who practices music will know what a recitative is about. It is musical prose and is like music in relationship to poetry, subjected to fewer strict rules, as in the aria or other pieces."[29]

Garcia, speaking in 1847 on the art of singing, also defines recitative according to the concept of musical prose, which "pays no regard to the number of bars or symmetry of cadences, or even to regularity of time." And like our Elocutionist Walker (who wrote in 1781), Garcia unites the strongest expressions with this style of language, and the more pleasing expressions with those of verse.

> This last type of melodic prose is wholly influenced by prosodic accents and the excitement of passion. In what may be called *melodious verse*, on the contrary, there reigns a perfect regularity—required to satisfy the rhythmical instinct. In compliance with this instinct, a complete symmetry must be established between the different parts of a melody, and they must be enclosed within certain easily perceptible limits of duration. In this way our ear may unfailingly recognize each element of a phrase, as in verse it recognizes the accents, caesura, rhyme, etc."[30]

We see the same relationship in Mattheson's illustration of how many small half members (semicolons) can be combined to present an image of despair. Mattheson explains that in arias such detailed accounts are rarely encountered since they would make for a long performance, yet these exquisite descriptions can be set well in recitative.

> Enormous is my pain; infinite are my miseries;
> The air bemoans having nurtured me;
> The world, because it supported me,
> Is worth burning simply for that;
> The stars become comets,
> To destroy this monster of nature;[31]

This relationship between the most intense expressions and the looser structures of prose, and the milder expressions with those of verse is summed up by Schulz (1774):

> No one imagines that the poet reserves only the weakest and most unimportant passages of his work for the recitative, but places the strongest outburst of passions in arias or other songs. For quite often, the opposite occurs, and of course must occur. The very lively passions, rage, despair, grief, also joy and admiration, can seldom be expressed naturally in arias when they have reached a high level. The expression of such passions will usually be uneven and discontinuous, which is utterly contrary to the flowing nature of true song.[32]

But this basic consensus (arrived at through diverse avenues and logical arguments)—that the music of prose, with its strong subjects, lacks a regularity of metrical accent and phrase structure, while the graceful and pleasing music of verse maintains a contrasting strictness—must be tempered with our understanding that as in language, the two (prose and verse) are rarely mutually exclusive. In recitative, for instance, Walker's "harmonic prose" (or prosaic verse) is very much in evidence. As the clergyman, writer, and amateur musician John Brown claims in 1789:

> The verse appropriated to recitative is of a mixed kind, consisting of the heroic line of eleven syllables, and of a line of seven syllables, with now and then a rhyme. . . . This kind of mixed verse, from the variety it affords, seems well calculated to give to the recitative as marked a resemblance to common speech as is consistent with the dignity and beauty of numbers; whilst the sparing and judicious introduction of rhyme, either to finish more highly some beautiful passage, or more strongly to point some remarkable assertion or reflection."[33]

Marpurg addresses this issue in the annotated examples of operatic recitatives which conclude his lengthy dissertation on punctuation from his *Kritische Briefe über die Tonkunst*. These include two recitatives from Hasse's opera *Ezio*, a French text from Rameau's *Zoroastre*, and, finally, a German text treated to three different possible settings for the student of recitative. The German text Marpurg feels uses far too many rhymes (a poor brand of harmonic prose), while Rameau's text (which we will discuss shortly) he mainly considers when recomposed in an "Italian guise" by various unnamed "other musicians." But Ezio's opening majestic speech in scene 2 of Act I is the most highly praised. Hasse's text (as quoted from Marpurg below) consists of lines containing eleven, seven, and also five syllables.[34] Notice especially the strategic rhymes between *torrenti* and *lamenti,* and also in the final two lines between *indistinti* and *vinti.*[35]

| | | |
|---|---|---|
| 5 | Signor, vincemmo. | (Signor, we conquered. |
| 5 | Ai gelidi Trioni | The one that mortals fear |
| 7 | il terror de mortali | is a returning fugitive |
| 7 | fuggitivo ritorna. | to freezing Trioni. |
| 5 | Il primo io sono, | I am the first one, |
| 7 | che mirasse finora | who till now could see |
| 7 | Attilla impalidir. | Attila impaled. |
| 11 | Non vide il sole piu numerosa strage | The sun has never seen such carnage |
| 11 | A tante morti era angusto il terreno. | and the anguishing earth has never seen so many deaths. |
| 5 | Il sange corse | The blood courses |
| 7 | in torbidi torrenti. | in torbid torrents. |
| 7 | Le minaccie a' lamenti | One could hear mingling |
| 5 | s'udian confuse; | the threats and laments; |
| 7 | e fra i timori, e l'ire | and the strong, the valiant, the victorious, and the vanquished |
| 7 | erravano indistinti | wander hopelessly |
| 11 | i forti, i vili, i vincitori, i vinti. | with fear and rage.) |

Mattheson, too, favors the poetic approach as "nothing penetrates the heart as much as a well-arranged rhyme scheme, especially when it is animated through an agreeable melody."

> . . . When poetic and prosaic presentations are alternately sung, the former would necessarily always please far more than the latter. The reason is that prosaic speaking always has a curious mixture of the syllabic feet and has no measured, uniform constraints by which it is easily grasped, noted and certain to the hearing. On the other hand, the ordering of the feet in poetry and the well-constituted alternation of meters, even if there were no rhyme scheme, produces something initially so certain and clear in the hearing that the mind enjoys a secret pleasure from the orderliness and accepts the performance so much the easier.[36]

Even his semicolons of despair exhibit a "sparing and judicious introduction of rhyme."

But the above examples, which are both set to music in the style of *secco recitative*, are still highly prosaic, designed to closely imitate the inflection and cadence of natural speech, albeit in a highly stylized form. Certain types of recitative take on far more of the verse-like qualities than others. For instance, as C. P. E. Bach explains, "Some recitatives, in which the bass and perhaps other instruments express a definite theme or a continuous motion which does not participate in the singer's pauses, must be performed strictly in time for the sake of good order. Others are declaimed now slowly, now rapidly according to the content, regardless of the meter, even though their notation be barred."[37] Mattheson recognizes the same need to observe a stricter meter in the case of instrumental accompaniment, but nevertheless, "such must scarcely be noticed in the singing." The style is still highly declamatory.[38]

*Arioso,* although the term is by no means applied consistently, is often used to describe these "mixed" styles.[39] And here we begin to see the difficulties in labeling the various shades of gray between that which is purely prose and that which is purely verse. *Arioso* can serve as the label for compositions which lean (in varying degrees) either on the side of one or the other. Koch (1793) places arioso in the latter category as a kind of shortened version of the aria which "must possess all the characteristics of expressive song in a very high degree."[40] Löhlein, in 1765, gives the label arioso to a *fantasia,* the product of a lesson on playing extemporaneously, but which is fundamentally dance-like, in 3/4 meter, with a few "free" elements thrown in: irregular yet even-numbered phrase lengths, expressive dissonances, interrupted passages, and short periods of imitation.[41] Mattheson uses the label *Arioso obbligato,* which, he explains, "differs from recitative and its affects only in the fact that it is to be sung according to the pulse."[42] Marpurg would have approved of this usage, stating adamantly that one ought not to use the terms "measured" and "recitative" in combination but call it something else: arioso, cantabile, or obbligato.[43] Rousseau is equally convinced that *récitatif mesuré* is a contradiction in terms:

> Every recitative, wherein we find any other measure than that of the verses, is no longer recitative. But an ordinary recitative is often changed on a sudden in music, and takes from measure and melody, . . . In the course of a recitative, a tender and plaintive reflexion takes the musical accent, and is displayed instantly by the sweetest inflexions of the music; then, being cut in the same manner by some other lively and impetuous reflexion, it is roughly interrupted to take, at a moment, the whole utterance of the words.[44]

The introduction of the verse-like qualities also has a modifying influence on the *affect* of the arioso's subjects. Mattheson explains that arioso, with its function as a narration or reflective and instructive proverb, is not as strong and stirring.[45] However, as Kirnberger explains, the arioso is still quite serious in its affect, its measured motion the most efficient of all song compositions to express a solemn feeling. The arioso is appropriate for expressing a wish, an instructive speech, or to convey a touching picture.[46] Koch uses the adjectives tender, plaintive, solemn, and eloquent.[47]

It is this "mid-style" arioso, sung according to a beat yet highly declamatory and prosodic in its accents, which is often used to describe French recitative—and not always positively. Marpurg, who built his rules of recitative from the renowned representatives of Italian opera in eighteenth-century Germany, Graun and Hasse, finds that the idiom of the melody in recitative is not much distinguished from arioso in French taste.[48] Quantz also adds (in 1752), "Their [French] recitatives sing too much and their arias too little, so that it is not always possible to divine in their operas whether a recitative or an arioso is being heard."[49] The French theorist, composer, and cellist Charles Henri de Blainville, writing in 1754, echoes this complaint: "Our recitatives sing too much, or our airs not enough."[50] Rousseau, however, defends the close relationship between recitative and air. He agrees that one must both speak and sing in opera, but the contrast should not be so great as to feel that one were say, alternating between French and German. Airs must be divided and separated by conversation but in a way that is modified by music: "'Tis by assistance of the recitative, that what is only dialogue, recital, narration in the drama, may be rendered without going out of the given language, and without displacing the eloquence of the airs."[51]

Furthermore, as we have already learned, Rousseau does not perceive French recitative as measured; the accents, emphases, and pace of the text are always the primary consideration.

> The recitative is not measured in singing. This measure, which characterizes the airs would spoil the reciting declamation; it is accent, whether grammatical or oratorical, which ought alone to direct the slowness or rapidity of the sounds; in the same manner also their elevation or lowering. The composer, in making the recitative on some determined measure, has nothing in view but to fix the correspondence of the thorough bass and music, and to denote, nearly, how the quantity of the syllables should be mark'd, cadenc'd, and the verses scann'd. The Italians never make use, for their recitative of any but the four-tim'd measure; but the French intermix their's [sic] of all sorts of measures.[52]

My purpose in embroiling myself in the difference between Italianate and French recitative is first of all to point to an issue we discussed in Part 1 regarding the extremely important national differences among punctuation practices which become more prominent the closer the music is tied to language. But secondly, the polemics (again by no means universally or consistently drawn) of a French, feminine, pleasing music of gestural ease and grace on one side, and a Germanic/Italian, masculine, and dramatic music on the other, does eventually lead us to our topic at hand—that of *interpreting rests*. Marpurg, in his criticism of French recitative, however misguided, at least gives us his version of how rests should be employed differently in a highly prosaic and a correspondingly more verse-like style of musical language.

One of Marpurg's comments about Rameau's recitative from *Zoroastre* is that "the members of the periods are nowhere distinguished from one another through small sectional pauses [*kleine Einschnittspausen*]. Everything is taken in one breath, and indeed no more syllables occur in the verse than the poet has numbered. Thus elisions appear where they should not, namely between *Abramane* and *enfin*, and between *trône* and *attend*."[53] By French standards, examples 6.4a and b illustrate typical 12-syllable alexandrine lines, the first with the *e muet* (mute e) at the end of the line on *propice*. Although not included in the syllable count, the *e muet* would, like all those in French poetry, have been customarily pronounced. The result is a feminine ending in contrast to the masculine ending of the following sentence. The medial pauses and corresponding stresses occur as expected on the sixth syllables, and the *e muets* at the end of *Abramane* and of *trône* are then naturally elided with the initial vowels of the words following them.[54]

Example 6.4. Lack of rests and sectional divisions in a recitative from Rameau's *Zoroastre*. From Marpurg, *Kritische Briefe*, vol. 2, p. 397.

However, in Marpurg's "Italianized" versions, these elisions are removed, as seen in example 6.5, and the medial pauses are indicated with *written* rests and accompanied by stronger cadential motion. This is particularly striking with the larger comma-sized point of punctuation at *trône*.

Hasse also frequently makes such departures in the scansion of his text. In example 6.6, at the end of the above-cited recitative, he makes fourteen syllables out of the last eleven-syllable line, ignoring the elisions of *i forti, i vili, i vincitori, i vinti*.[55] In doing so, he places pauses stressing "the strong, the valiant, the victorious, and the vanquished." Perhaps, as we discussed in chapter 5, we could call these commas *articuli* in the "classical" sense of the word, to be uttered like thrusts of a sword (and accompanied by the appropriate stabbing gestures). By Schulz's standards (in 1774), these lines are set very appropriately; impetuous, violent, and furious expressions require very short phrases which are more clearly separated from each other.[56]

Notice also in example 6.7, from the same recitative, the way in which Hasse calls our attention to the "remarkable assertion" created by the rhyme between *torrenti* and *lamenti*: *torrenti* is expressed with an arrival on the tonic E major, from a V[6]–I cadence (what Marpurg calls a quasi-close or *Quasischluß* and which is more or less complete). The rhyming *lamenti*, only an incomplete comma, is

Example 6.5. Marpurg's improved Italianized version of example 6.4. From Marpurg, *Kritische Briefe*, vol. 2, p. 399.

Example 6.6. The expressive effect of ignored elisions in a recitative from Hasse's *Ezio*. From Marpurg, *Kritische Briefe*, vol. 2, p. 386.

expressed as a dissonant suspended break or *schwebende Absatz*. The bass falls to $V_5^6$ of C-sharp minor with a tritone between bass and voice, and is preceded by an additional pause. Further, *minaccie* (threats), is given an emphasis with rising notes and the elision between its final syllable and the following *a'* is removed, creating two equal, four-syllable lines from the original seven. Much more is made of the sectional pauses, even where no punctuation marks occur.

Example 6.7. More on the effective use of rests from Hasse's *Ezio*. From Marpurg, *Kritische Briefe*, vol. 2, p. 386.

But do not all of these pauses, as Mattheson puts it, "mangle and constrain the melody with so many cadences"? Remember that in explaining example 4.7,

Mattheson argued that as few rests and cadences as possible should be used, every-thing expressed instead through "certain natural vocal alterations." Here we have a prime example of how important it is to understand the character of the expres-sion at hand in order to properly interpret attitudes towards the rests of musical punctuation. It is only when we recognize the very different affects portrayed through recitative and aria, that Mattheson's statement above, and his illustration in example 6.8 of the *disjunctiva* (one of three types of semicolon) begin to make sense. The semicolon in the prose-like recitative example of 6.8a requires a visible *written* rest to enhance the sense of natural speech, while the *arietta* of 6.8b (and also example 4.7) needs no such explicit indications, relying instead on the "nat-ural" vocal alterations implied by the regular rhythm and meter of their verse.[57]

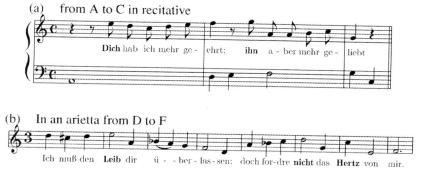

(a)  from A to C in recitative

Dich hab ich mehr ge-ehrt; ihn a-ber mehr ge-liebt

(b)  In an arietta from D to F

Ich muß den Leib dir ü - - ber-las-sen; doch for-dre nicht das Hertz von mir.

Example 6.8. Illustration of the *disjunctiva*. From Mattheson, *Der vollkommene Capellmeister*, p. 188.

The French, however, seem to be unwilling "to take on any other measure than that of verse," either through the technical display of harmonically driven instru-mental sonatas, as described by Le Blanc, or even in recitative, so that the smaller points of punctuation (written or unwritten) would receive, as Marpurg advises, a cadence or pause. French recitatives would still be highly declamatory and even pause-ridden (many rests do accompany the punctuation signs), but expressed through the very distinct rhythmic character of their language.[58] Passions are expressed in "poetical dress" by a simple noninterference with the language, enhancing neither its verse-like qualities—adjusting the meter to achieve a greater regularity of accent—nor its prose-like qualities—using disruptive pauses to empha-size emotional intensity through unevenness and discontinuity. Unfortunately, such efforts were not always understood or appreciated. Mattheson remarks that the French "proceed in their native *Recit* [*sic*] in almost all types of meter in succession, and they believe that they aid the poetic meter through such variations, which come out very unequal; thereby coming so much the closer to their natural pro-nunciation: only it seems that they err, and make such song only so much the more constrained and unintelligible, because they observe virtually no lengthening or shortening of syllables at all in their language, in an elevated style."[59] Schulz also notes that "in French recitative, all sorts of meters occur, one after the other, which is why it is very difficult to accompany, and even more difficult to grasp."[60]

The aesthetic of French recitative aside, our discussion has taught us something about the different nature and treatment of punctuation points in their respective verse-like and prose-like contexts. As we have observed, for instance in the *articuli* of example 6.6, the greater the emotional intensity, the more the flow of expression is subject to fluctuations.[61] For instance, the more serious *affect* of Haydn's Adagio from Opus 77, no. 1 (fig. 5.2) will demand a different kind of rest treatment from the more serene Mozart Piano Sonata, K.332 (ex. 5.8). Both will in turn demand a still different treatment from the eager and expectant "rests" between the two-bar units of Mozart's A-major Symphony (ex. 4.2). As we noted in our discussion of the articulative slur symbol, the specific execution associated with notational devices (including rests) will vary according to their context. For not only does prose demonstrate its difference from verse through phrases of irregular proportions, but also through a general freedom of rhythmic pacing where passionate phrases may stop and start frequently and disruptively with their anguished expressions or anxious phrases may pile in on top of each other. To quote again the words of Elocutionist Thomas Sheridan: "There is far more to observing the pauses of punctuation than their exact proportion of time; sometimes the speaker may choose to continue on in a sentence suddenly, overriding a rest, and at other times may choose to delay longer than necessary."[62]

It becomes ever more apparent that an *effective* application of musical punctuation will also be an *affective* one, with the recognition that the character of a composition's expressions must be the guiding force in determining the nature of its structural pauses. This is Forkel's general logic in 1788 and the reason for his focus on the various *affects* in defining and categorizing musical expression. In the tradition of rhetoric, musical styles are broken down into three categories: the high (church), middle (chamber), and low (theater). However, Forkel feels that "since style assumes the greatest differences from affects rather than from applications, thus must its differences naturally be seen best and most clearly through the affects."[63] He breaks down the affects into three emotional states noticeably different from each other:

1. the state of cheerfulness, of laughing, of gaiety, of a high-spirited nature.
2. the state of serious calm contentment, melancholy, or serious feelings
3. the state of intense joy, anger, despair, or of the passions.[64]

The correlation between these categories and our prose, verse, and mixed styles is immediately obvious: lively dances and simple arias and songs, the strictest verse structures, fit easily into category one; the serious, devout, and solemn chorales and ariosos belong in the second; and passionate vocal recitatives, along with similar outbursts among instrumental works and the most prose-like of sonatas, fall into the third.

As Forkel found that *affect* cuts across categories of style, so it cuts across the differentiation between prose and verse. For instance, among dances, Mattheson makes the distinction between the more intense "jubilation" of the gavotte and the "contentment and pleasantness" of the bourée.[65] He also distinguishes between different expressions in recitative, making the important connection between affect and the corresponding nature of the pauses in the case of exclamations which denote imperfect commas. A melancholy exclamation or an imperative word indicates a delay or requires reflection. However, a different kind of vocative or imperative, where there is some exclamation or command that expresses a passion or violent emotion, demands that everything be halting because of the pervading zeal.[66] For C. P. E. Bach, it is proper to broaden slightly on fermatas, cadences, and caesuras which express languidness, tenderness, or sadness.[67] Rests must also be lengthened when abrupt contrasts in character occur. According to Türk, "If a passage of gentle sensitivity follows a fiery and brisk thought, then both periods must similarly be more carefully separated than would be necessary if they were of the same character."[68]

Furthermore, not only can similar types of compositions—dances and recitatives for example—express varying affects, but an important element of the eighteenth-century musical style is the ease with which the affect of a composition can change from one moment to the next. This feature of multiple, alternating affects marks a shift from the Baroque *Affektenlehre*, where one affect was felt to govern and unify a piece. The aesthetic change was the result of new eighteenth-century philosophical and social influences on the ancient rhetorical doctrine dictating how the speaker can best move, control, and direct the emotions of the listener (in particular, the newly fashionable taste for polite conversation, which we will discuss shortly).[69] As E. W. Wolf explains, differing musical characteristics aim not merely to provide a beautiful melodic or vocal line, but more importantly to portray human emotions and passions. He adds that the emotions are apt to change frequently. Even within a single piece, some musical periods, phrases, or smaller units must be played more strongly, others more softly, according to the rise and fall of the mood. For example, sublime joy is expressed through fiery tones and strong accents, while tenderness, on the other hand, requires soft, quiet tones, delicate accents, and so on.[70] As Koch claims, this is especially true in the sonata, which can assume every character and every expression of which music is capable. Quantz also stresses: "And since in the majority of pieces one passion constantly alternates with another, the performer must know how to judge the nature of the passion that each idea contains, and constantly make his execution conform to it. Only in this manner will he do justice to the intentions of the composer, and to the ideas that he had in mind when he wrote the piece."[71] In other words, within a flowing and gentle air, one might encounter a more vehement and disruptive expression—an element of prose in the middle of verse.

Often the topics and their affects are labeled for us, even with additional visual clues towards their appropriate expression. For instance, Türk cites the first of C. P. E. Bach's Keyboard Sonatas dedicated to the King of Prussia as an example of where the expression can be heightened by *extraordinary* means (Türk's emphasis). He explains that instrumental passages marked *recitativo*, occasionally found in sonatas, concertos, and the like, "must be played more according to feeling rather than meter."[72] It is interesting to note that the two recitative passages in the second movement of Bach's Sonata, Wq 48/1, to which Türk refers, are distinguished not only by being labeled recitative, but also by the dynamic indication of *forte*. With the exception of the final two measures (also *forte*), which serve to set up the closing cadenza, the remainder of the movement is given the descriptive title and tempo indication of *Andante*, and marked *piano*. These passages exhibit the steady, moving eighth notes or "walking bass" common among contemporary definitions of the term, for instance as found in Niedt's *Musicalischer Handleitung* of 1721: "walking, orderly, evenly, neither running nor creeping, not too slowly and not too fast."[73] C. P. E. Bach's Andante is highly expressive, the opening statement (fig. 6.1), in a mournful F minor with eloquent dissonances like the diminished octave on the second eighth note of bar 2.[74] And perhaps the *piano* here is more than a dynamic, but also a character indication, serving to help reinforce the more gentle, "evenly" paced melancholy of the Andante affect and thus further enhance the dramatic contrast to the sudden textural changes and intense expressions of the highly (and explicitly) punctuated, *forte* recitatives.

Figure 6.1.  C. P. E. Bach, Keyboard Sonata in F Major Wq 48/1, 2nd movement, bars 1–11.

But even if the obviously exclamatory gestures of the violin in example 6.9 from Haydn's "Le Midi" Symphony were not part of a movement labeled Recitativo, one would easily recognize their prose-like affect.[75] How closely these gestures (the second solo violin passage in bars 11–12, marked Allegro) resemble the short interjections illustrated by Marpurg in his essay on punctuation in recitative (appendix A, §104). Haydn, like C. P. E. Bach, also supplies many clues to the nature of their expression. The solo violin's utterance, punctuated by rests, arises out of the harmony of a B$^{4}_{3}$ diminished chord, the opening leap itself emphasizing the augmented fourth interval between F♮ and B♮. Schulz, in his article "Recitativ" for Sulzer's *Allgemeine Theorie der schönen Künste*, describes such dissonances as appropriate to dark and stormy expressions.[76] The effect is enhanced by the sudden *forte* of the diminished chord and the indication of *Allegro* in the violin part. This is in stark contrast to the previous G-minor passage of very contained string arpeggiation—the second violins murmuring darkly with repeated thirty-second-note gestures—in the movement's opening tempo of Adagio, all at the dynamic of *piano* (*pianissimo* for the held tones of the two oboes).[77] Rousseau describes such an interaction between orchestra and "recitant" as the *Recitatif Obligé*, which Waring in 1779 translates as *Recitative Confin'd*—"the most touching, most ravishing, and most energetic parts of the modern measure, and which French music has not yet been able to make use of ":

RECITATIVE CONFIN'D. Is that which, being intermixt with rittornels and strokes of symphony, confines, as it were, the recitant and orchestra, one towards the other, so that they ought to be attentive in a mutual degreee . . . The actor agitated, transported with a passion which does not suffer him to go through his speech, is interrupted, breaks off, makes a stop, during which time the orchestra speaks for him; and these silences, thus filled, affect the audience infinitely more than if the actor himself spoke all that the music makes them understand.[78]

A key concept behind the notion of variable affects is that of the fantasia. We have already used the term many times to denote something in a "free" style, our fantasia-like (prose-like) sonatas. But freeness does not only denote looseness and irregularity of structure but applies to the freeness associated with invention and imagination. Fantasia is closely linked to improvisation where one is free to invent and express whatever happens to occur to one.[79] And it may just happen that one "fantasizes" in a verse-like pattern. Löhlein, as we mentioned earlier, chooses to explain the fantasia, or extemporaneous playing, within the context of the mid-style *arioso*, which maintains the structure of a dance in 3/4, with a few liberties of phrase structure. But Löhlein also describes the free, unbarred fantasia, which "observes no rules at all, in view of the meter and musical rhyme. However a certain harmonic order is nevertheless observed . . . " Löhlein adds that organ fantasies are more harmonic than melodic and even freer for that reason.[80] The free (prose-like) expressions are again correlated to that which is harmonically driven and also instrumental, sometimes pursuing, as we have

Example 6.9. Haydn, Symphony No. 7 in C Major "Le Midi," 2nd movement, bars 10–13.

already observed, such wild and strange effects that they not only take the concept of prose to an extreme, but would appear to pass beyond any analogy to language altogether. And of course, it is also the case in "imaginative" playing, that the two differing concepts of fantasia (free and strict) can be continually combined.[81]

Another term often associated with "improvisation" and "fantasia" is the fugue. The fugue represents a kind of "mixed style," sometimes written in the style of a dance, a gigue for example, yet maintaining, as Marpurg claims in his *Abhandlung von der Fuge* (1753–54), a "certain element of seriousness."[82] Mattheson feels that for this latter reason, the fugue should be written in duple meter rather than the "light skipping motion" of triple meter.[83] However, dance-like or not, the fugue, as Marpurg explains, does not exhibit the normal formal patterns of sections but is continuous from beginning to end.[84] This is due to the subject of the fugue which Mattheson defines as the chase: one voice chases the other and there is little resting or stopping until the whole chase has run its course.[85] Also, as Schulz (174) states, serious feelings require long phrases which are merged one into another.[86]

However Fux (and Mattheson also) makes the point that this relationship between voices—one part fleeing, pursued by the other—"is actually nothing but what is explained by imitation."[87] Imitation, of which Mattheson considers fugue to be the mother, is where "one voice, so to speak, converses with the other after the manner of a conversation, throws out questions, gives answers, is of a different opinion, secures approval, is in agreement, accepts opposition, etc."[88] Forkel also remarks of J. S. Bach that he "considered his parts as if they were persons who conversed together like a select company."[89] We proposed earlier in chapter 1 that eighteenth-century theorists somewhat forced the issue in applying the punctuation analogy to such strongly imitative and conversational textures as the fugue. Mattheson argues, using the example of J. S. Bach's C-major unaccompanied Violin Sonata (ex. 1.8), that such forms, since they have "little resting or stopping in them," exhibit only a disguised and minimized punctuation (a full stop functioning as a comma). Reicha, however, felt the need to adapt the evaded cadences of the fugue to conform to the more prevalent and clearly defined structures of the eighteenth century (ex. 1.9). Of course, imitative textures with long lines and disguised cadences did not entirely disappear from eighteenth-century composition. And although Mattheson's very modified punctuation analogy (Reicha's as well) may comment most on the zeal of our theorists in adapting the analogy to all of music's expressions, it nevertheless leads to another possible interpretation of the rest: that of the "restless" rest, signifying the chase, eagerness, perhaps playfulness, argument, debate, and a whole host of affects and topics that demand that the phrases be piled up, rushed together, interrupted, etc.

The reader will note that the term *conversation* has been invoked a number of times in this chapter: to describe the relationship between the piano and strings in the gavotte-like and developmental passages of Mozart's Piano Trio, by Rousseau to indicate the nature of a recitative inserted between two arias and the style of the *Recitative Confin'd*, and finally, within the context of sparring partners in a fugue.[90] Conversational attributes, as discussed in the section "Dialoguing a Melody" in chapter 3, p. 000, were applied in a variety of ways and at many levels, from very specific narratives or programs to mere marketing ploys designed to capitalize on the eighteenth-century fascination with the social activity and its influence on public and private speech, writing, and by extension, music. Thus if affect cuts across boundaries of style, so does conversation—at home in verse-like as well as prose-like structures. While conversation is typically described in terms of amiability and conviviality, representing all that is quintessentially galant (French and feminine) with its easy movement from one topic to another, nevertheless it is also capable of producing more serious affects: in the learned fugue, among the "sentiment-laden" dialogues of sonatas, trios, etc.; in the dramatic concerto (as described by Keefe and Will); and every gray area in between these expressions. As we have learned from Reicha, dialogue can be presented through regular and symmetrical, clearly defined phrases; more intensely through overlapping, elided phrases; or most dramatically in broken utterances.

We can observe a number of these imitative, conversational techniques woven into the texture of the very verse-like Minuetto from Mozart's Clarinet Quintet, K.581 (1789).[91] In example 6.10, the viola and cello present, in confident *forte* tones, a cheerful and elegant four-bar phrase. A two-bar caesura is perhaps also perceptible, although the long "expressive" slur in bar 10 does minimize the sense of a nuance between the first and second beats which would enhance the effect. This first phrase of the minuet's B section is then answered in bar 13 by the combination of viola and second violin, the first violin also emerging from its eighth-note, alternating half-step pattern to join them, even signaling or inviting their entry with the change and with a dynamic drop to *piano*. However, just before the violins are able to complete this responsive phrase (which they do on the downbeat of bar 16), the cello and viola, joined by the clarinet also on the downbeat of bar 16, interrupt them with an additional comment. This secondary thought, begun on the pickup to bar 16, is then concluded with a cadence on the dominant in bar 20, the strongest point of punctuation thus far. The result is a 3+5 organization operating within with the more regular 4+4 phrase structure of the opening *period*'s extended second half. Coinciding with the dominant cadence and "compounding" the phrase as Koch would say (or dialoguing phrases through "supposition" to use Reicha's terminology), the viola and cello take up the murmuring eighth-note pattern begun by the first violin and taken over by the clarinet. A back-and-forth dialogue ensues, each voice stepping in before the other has had time to finish. Meanwhile, the violins happily carry on with four-bar phrases, beginning a new segment with the pickup to bar 21. An assertive, *forte* restatement of the minuet's A-section *period* then occurs, beginning on the pickup to bar 25, with its easily recognizable layout of two, four-bar phrases—a clear and characteristic incise occurring between beats 2 and 3 of bar 26, and a somewhat less obvious phrase division in the corresponding bar 30 also on the downbeat of bar 16. Clear dynamic contrasts reinforce this structure. The result is that the regular rhythmical and metrical pattern of eight-, four-, and even two-bar units, which we expect of such verse-like minuets, remains essentially inviolate; the symmetrical structure is readily perceptible. But within this structure, through interruptions and suppositions of the phrases, additional dialogues among the five instrumentalists are allowed their freedom of expression and play.

Imitative textures like those we have just observed in the verse-like minuet from Mozart's Clarinet Quintet will naturally affect the nature of its punctuation in a manner very different from the "restless rests" of Mattheson's more serious fugue, which will in turn differ from the style of punctuation among conversing members of a trio in a sonata movement based on a gavotte, or yet between "recitant" and orchestra as in Haydn's "Le Midi" Symphony. The diverse contexts and frequency with which we encounter conversational attributes in eighteenth-century music gives some credence to Blainville's [27] statement in 1767 that "all melody" must be so "conversed" through full stops and commas. Such a concept of conversation (and its punctuation) is rather overwhelming. Like verbal conversation or the *Art*

Example 6.10. Mozart, Clarinet Quintet, K.581, 3rd movement, bars 9–32.

*of Communication* itself, each situation, its venue and participants, is unique and spontaneous—lively, pleasant, humorous, also dramatic, argumentative, etc. It is therefore impossible to define and pinpoint once and for all the precise style of punctuation appropriate to musical conversation. Conversational punctuation must instead be considered genre by genre, piece by piece, even moment by moment. But what we can and should comprehend from our acknowledgment of the subject's potential breadth is its fundamental influence on eighteenth-century composition—the way in which the concept of musical conversation itself embodies the important and predominant musical aesthetic of rapidly changing affects.

Let us now conclude this chapter with a stab at what I imagine Mattheson would describe as one of the "greater and more imposing instrumental pieces," in which we can expect to find an "uncommon diversity in the expression of the affects" and their "divisions." We will consider the opening sentences, seen in example 6.11, from the final movement of Beethoven's Second Symphony (1803) as arranged by Beethoven as a trio for violin, cello, and piano (1805), and which is simply labeled Allegro molto.[92] The movement begins with real fury and drama. The entire orchestra, playing in unison and at the octave, barks out crisp *forte* utterances, *punctuated* by *written* rests. The opening gesture is a half step slurred to a strong-beat quarter note followed by an eighth-note rest. (One would have to give the accent to the downbeat rather than to the beginning of the slur or else the rhythmic placement would be unclear) This is followed by an accented trill C♯ leading tone, which rather than resolving to the tonic, jumps up for the falling fifth from E to A, the gesture again concluded with a rest. The two gestures together seem to shout and exclaim, "Dominant!" While one could not really call these opening bars recitative, they nevertheless exhibit strong cadential movement, which, when combined with rests, tends to emphasize the small, irregular sectional divisions. Most certainly, the quarter-note rest must be treated within the context of a prose-like subject. After the opening exclamation, we require time to recover before we can continue, abruptly changing affect with the flowing, lively passage which follows. A uniform, fiery, and brisk tempo taken throughout would, I feel, do great injustice to these two wildly different expressions which occur in the opening six measures alone.[93]

Example 6.11. Beethoven, Symphony No. 2 in D Major, 1st movement, bars 1–12. Arranged by the composer for piano trio.

Now we must also decide whether the first eighth-note rest indicates merely the absence of a note as in example 4.2 from Mozart's Symphony K.201 (where the character was much lighter and did not contain such emphatic gestures) or if it also, in the present context of a strong affect and a prose-like topic, denotes a mark of punctuation. Perhaps the opening paired slur, with the accent on the dissonant seventh of the chord marks a kind of imperative or vocative exclamation, much as Mattheson describes. What would this sound like? The rest need not be very prominent—after all, these exclamations are only types of incomplete commas. We do not want to detract from the drama of the quarter-note rest, but we do want to convey the sense of astonishment or excitement, and indeed expectation which such a punctuation mark can convey. Perhaps simply giving equal accents to the two gestures would convey this, as I think the *sforzando* on the third beat suggests that we should. We want to avoid the sense of absolute meter here to enhance the speech-like qualities.

As we continue in a "lively" and "flowing" manner, we notice that our adjectives have suddenly swerved to the language of verse, as indeed has this passage between bars 3 and 6. We are merrily on our way in a predictable four-bar phrase (with perhaps a little two-bar inflection by the right hand of the keyboard between the third and fourth quarters of bar 4): $I^6$–$V^6$–$I$–$IV$–$I_4^6$–$V$—yet again we do not come to rest on the tonic but immediately, in *forte* tones, drop from the tonic to the dominant in a kind of half cadence. Rather than an affirmative arrival on D major, it seems to ask a question, rising a whole step in the upper voices. Perhaps the question is whether we shall ever really settle in the tonic key of D. We want to stop and ponder this question, having been abruptly taken out of the serene world of verse. The whole passage is then repeated, and then this time we can affirm D major in bar 12. Again a conversational style is implied, although with a more dramatic alteration of affect than we observed above in the Clarinet Quintet, K.581. This kind of effect of question and confirmation is discussed by Telemann [13], in his passage on punctuation in recitative. He explains that "a question raised can at the same time be an exclamation, or vice versa," and adds that "a sentence in a long speech may be repeated quite a few times, either with the original meaning or with a new or contradictory meaning." Grétry, writing in 1789, also suggests that we take advantage of such possibilities: "When one repeats a verse, it is not bad, I think, . . . to make the repose first that of the comma, and then a final repose the last time. It would be like saying with indecision, Yes, I will go see you . . ., and then more affirmatively, Yes, I will go see you."[94] So Beethoven says, "D major?" and then affirms "yes, D major," and is immediately off again.[95]

What we have achieved and learned from these few examples of Mozart, Haydn, Beethoven, Bach, and others, has been based on broad principles of the manner in which *rests* behave according to the prose-like or verse-like nature of the musical language being used. In order truly to take on our subject in all its complexity, we must fully grasp the *fantasia* (conversational) nature of musical composition and performance in the mid- to late eighteenth century, becoming immersed in the details of its numerous and changeable "topics," its various stylistic attributes—rhythmic, accentual, gestural, harmonic, melodic—and above all its governing *affects*. And although our focus is instrumental music, we must include the topics and forms of the vocal arts from which instrumental music frequently draws its materials, especially those which are the most language-specific and therefore contain the most detailed information with regard to punctuation. Our categorizations of prose, verse, and mixed styles can help, but the task is no less a daunting one, particularly when we consider the rich variety which can exist within very similar styles: *secco* recitative vs. accompanied recitative and arioso, dance for dancing vs. dance for playing or singing, and not least, those differences which are drawn along national lines.

The multiformity among compositional styles is such that no single source on musical punctuation can take into account every type of even its own subject. The pooling together of all the surviving sources cannot give us anything like a complete picture of musical punctuation practices in the eighteenth century, a broad period of time undergoing continual change. This was doubtfully ever achieved at any given point in time even in the eighteenth century. Punctuation, after all, is only one element among the continually evolving and shifting theories regarding human communication which music adopts to describe and guide its expressions. Our best effort, therefore, from which a great deal of interpretive insight can be gained, will be to explore a few of the most detailed case studies in musical punctuation in each of our broad categories, prose and verse, keeping in mind the very personal interests and biases, as well as the larger philosophical and societal influences which are so much a part of this vibrant, living, and breathing *Art of Interpreting Rests*.

*Part Three*

# Case Studies in Musical Punctuation

# Chapter Seven

# Musical Prose—F. W. Marpurg's Essay on the Punctuation of Recitative

Recitativo semplice is most natural because its bare notes are placed not only within the natural range of each voice but also notated and distributed so as to perfectly imitate natural speech such that one can distinguish each part of each period, and indicate question marks, exclamation marks and full stops. All of this is expressed through the melody, which varies concurrently with the motion and diversity of the tonalities, which in turn vary in accordance with the different meanings of the words, and according to the various sensations that the composer wants to excite in the listeners' souls.

—Pietro Lichtenthal, 1836

Music and language, as we established in chapter 6, agree on a general categorization of subject matter according to prose and verse, where in the strictest sense the one expresses strong subjects through an irregularity of rhythm, metrical accent, and phrase structure, while the other expresses milder subjects through a contrasting homogeneity. Music and language, however, inevitably disagree as to which category presents the greater challenges for the composer and performer. There is so much music in spoken verse and so much speech in musical prose, the basis for the continuing analogy between the two, that the nearer one medium approaches the other, the greater the difficulty. In verse, as Elocutionist John Walker states in 1781, it is sometimes necessary to sacrifice sense for sound in order to regularize the cadence and flow of language, to turn the more predominant structures of language (those of prose) into that which is more musical. The resulting "affinity between poetry and music," Walker claims, increases the difficulty in reading verse. Because verse requires an alteration in the inflections of prose, elegant readers of verse often verge on what is called *sing song*, and those who are less elegant produce a "whining cant."[1] Jacob Schuback, writing in 1775 on the subject of musical declamation, also comments on the very tenuous relationship between the structures of song and those of natural (prose-like) speech. A composer who has a firm grasp on the rules of declamation will find little pleasure in setting a text to the most verse-like musical expressions, the strophic songs and lieder. In fact, if in the composition something appears to work well—that is, sound and sense happen to coincide—one is better off simply crossing it out as an only greater disappointment lies in wait.[2]

Thus it is that the expressions that most closely imitate spoken language (or prose) demand the greatest departures from music's most predominant structures (those of verse). None more so than the Italian *recitativo semplice* or *secco* variety of recitative (as described above by Pietro Lichtenthal), whose "bare notes" must conform most precisely to the accents, emphases, and pauses of proper declamation. There is naturally a vast "grey" area between strict musical prose on one side and strict musical verse on the other. As we discussed in chapter 6, this includes forms like the *arioso* and the accompanied class of recitative, where the instruments express a definite theme or continuous motion which does not participate in the singer's pauses, the singing style nevertheless remaining highly declamatory. Marpurg remarks in 1762, for instance, that because the language of recitative seeks to imitate natural speech, and should not in any real sense be sung, one does not have the freedom as one does in the *arioso*, to use feminine endings instead of masculine ones, but must always treat masculine endings as masculine and feminine endings as feminine.[3] In other words, for a more verse-like expression, one does not have the *difficulty* of so exactly imitating speech. As Mattheson also explains, in 1739, "Much more art and skill would be required in composing a single **recit**, with all of its affects and caesuras [*Einschnitte*], also **NB**. in singing, than to compose and perform ten arias of the usual type."[4]

The more language-like the musical expression, the more specialized must be the knowledge of the analogous art. This is Koch's 1793 argument:

> The technical treatment of the handling of a recitative requires quite specific rules, most of which seem to be derived from the art of good declamation. It has its wholly characteristic cadence and phrase-ending formulas, which deviate completely from those typical of formal song. . . . One can thus understand the reason why I have not taken up vocal composition (in which the treatment of recitative makes up by far the lengthiest subject) in the plan of this treatise.[5]

Koch and many of his contemporaries maintain that the study of composition should begin with the shortest pieces, with the well-defined, symmetrical, and regular phrase structures belonging to the melodies of short compositions like dances, odes, and songs. According to the espoused principle of periodicity, their well-defined units of one, two, and four bars become the building blocks for increasingly larger units (ultimately movement-length forms) with the single sentence or *period* comprising the most basic, yet complete, compositional unit.

On the one hand, following Koch's sound logic, we would be well advised to begin with the verse-like examples of musical punctuation which are in fact most "musical." Yet at the same time, it has been a fundamental assumption in our analogy that language is the more accessible, familiar way to explain concepts which are otherwise difficult to express in purely musical terms. Our format thus far has been to establish the punctuation practices of language first, and then examine their musical adaptations with regard to composition and performance. Therefore, we will begin by tackling what are some of the most detailed and specific applications of musical punctuation through a study of music's most speech-like form, *secco* vocal recitative.

## The Grammatical and Rhetorical Formulas of Vocal Recitative

In our examination of musical punctuation's very fundamental application to vocal recitative, our focus will be Friedrich Wilhelm Marpurg's extensive essay from volume 2 of his *Kritische Briefe über die Tonkunst,* by far the most thorough eighteenth-century source on the subject. Marpurg's periodical, published in Berlin between 1759 and 1764, is presented in the form of letters to famous musicians, written on behalf of an imaginary society and designed to engage middle-class and amateur musicians as well as highly trained professionals.[6] Among the set of twenty letters dedicated to the subject of recitative, the final fourteen (more than two-thirds of them!) are devoted solely to a highly meticulous description of the individual punctuation signs and their various cadential and melodic formulas. These fourteen letters, dated July 31, 1762 to October 30, 1762, comprise three parts: the first concerning punctuation's grammatical and rhetorical components in language; the second and third addressing the subject of musical punctuation generally, and then specifically through its expression of the grammatical and rhetorical signs in recitative.

I have provided a translation of the second and third parts, both highly relevant for our purposes, in appendix A. They will form the basis for our discussion, enabling us not only to examine Marpurg's specific rules for the punctuation of recitative, but also to perceive how his essay is reflective of the general spirit with which the analogy was adopted. Our aim will be to apply our understanding to a "wordless" recitative by Telemann (in his E-minor Sonata for Viola da gamba and Continuo from *Essercizii musici*), which closely follows Marpurg's models and which profits from the application of his concepts. I will indicate specific passages under discussion by using Marpurg's own sectional numbering system. I do not include in my translation the analyses of complete recitatives with which Marpurg concludes his essay: two examples from Hasse's opera *Ezio,* one from Rameau's *Zoroaster,* and various anonymous settings of a German poetic text. These have been discussed in part, in chapter 4 in the context of *written* and *unwritten* rests, and again in chapter 6 in detailing different possible approaches taken in the direct musical setting of Italian, French, and German prose.

Marpurg claims that his set of rules is derived primarily from the recitatives of Graun and Hasse, both renowned composers representing Italian opera in mid-eighteenth-century Germany.[7] We must remember that although Marpurg speaks on behalf of a much revered and widely cultivated Italian musical form, his bias is still essentially German, and the attitudes he expresses are not necessarily an accurate portrayal of mid-eighteenth-century Italian (or French) attitudes on the subject. Other North German composer/theorists like Mattheson, Schulz, Türk, and Telemann also offer useful commentary which largely corroborates and augments Marpurg's ideas about the punctuation of recitatives. Unfortunately there is relatively little eighteenth-century commentary from the Italians themselves.[8] But a few of the documents that are available from composers Domenico Corri (1780–1810) and Vincenzo Manfredini (1797) and the castrati Pier Francesco Tosi (1723) and Giambattista Mancini (1774) do provide valuable information with regard to punctuation-related issues of recitative such as notation, ornamentation, and gesture.

## Written and Unwritten Conventions

In the effort to ensure the proper execution of a recitative's various commas, colons, and periods (the desire to control an all-too-fallible language), Marpurg devotes a great deal of attention to how musical punctuation should be represented visually. Punctuation is, we must always remember, essentially a visual phenomenon which becomes effective only when readers are trained to appreciate the nuances of its printed conventions. Much of Marpurg's attention is directed at the practice of employing *written* rests at points of punctuation, which, as we established in chapter 6, are generally more appropriate in depicting the declamatory and impassioned recitative-like styles than they are among the "certain natural vocal inflections" of cheerful and smoothly flowing verse-like melodies with their regular and symmetrical phrase structures. In recitatives, Marpurg explains, the members of the *periods* must be distinguished from one another through *written* rests, to depict the necessary breaths which the singer must then make.[9] Throughout the essay, Marpurg repeatedly stresses the composer's (and singer's) responsibility in this regard, particularly for the larger units of speech. For instance, in §105, where a little word like *o* is part of a vocative or imperative, as in *O wacht, und betet* (Oh watch, and pray), then it must not be separated by a small dividing rest. But when *o* or *ach* functions as a kind of exasperated sigh in itself, as in *Ach, daß ein Mensch kan unversöhnlich seyn!* (Ah, how irreconcilable man can be), then a written/sung pause is required in order to convey the full sense of the expression. Similarly, as we see in Marpurg's second example of the dash (§108), the pause as Fulvia entreats her lover, *Ma senti—* (But hear—), and then turns desperately to beseech, *—Ah! Genitor, per me favella* (—Ah! Father, speak for me), is so dramatic that it requires not one, but "twofold rests" in order "to make the singer attentive to the manner of his exe-cution if the dash alone does not do it."

The concern over notational practices and the appropriate use of rests extends also to the manner in which the declamatory voice and the accompa-nying bass correspond to their natural accents. In addition to the fact that accented syllables at the ends of phrases (according to their feminine or mas-culine nature) must fall on strong beats (§§81–83), so must the familiar V–I cadence of the bass at the end of the recitative fall with its appropriate empha-sis. As explained in §85, the bass should receive its "proper incise [*Einschnitt*]," a *written* rest under the vocal cadence. This then allows the bass's arrival on the tonic, following the vocal cadence, to occur on a strong beat. A notational style which omits this important rest, "is of no use, because the progression of the har-mony cannot be explained logically in this manner."

The manner (and visual representation) of the cadence's harmonic resolu-tion, to which Marpurg refers, is an important factor in determining the nature of the recitative's final period. In §§86 and 87, Marpurg is adamant that the antepenultimate of the cadence, a $V_2^4$ chord (the fourth of the closing note which has above it the chord of the second and the augmented fourth), must resolve to a $I^6$ chord (the chord of the sixth) before proceding to the dominant. Marpurg suggests that a place marker or *Custode* should appear over the rest with the figure 6 under it, signaling the first-inversion tonic chord which should be played not with the bass, but "with the three voices of the right hand alone." Mattheson is in agreement with Marpurg regarding the necessity of the domi-nant chord's correct resolution, but indicates (as seen in ex. 7.1) that the bass may also participate. He inserts a footnote into the 1728 edition of Johann David Heinichen's *Der Generalbass in der Komposition*, weighing in on the latter's discussion of how to treat this cadence "whose harmony seems totally to lack any appropriate resolution." Mattheson states: "Of course, the recitative cadence would always, I repeat, always have to be resolved in the following manner [ex. 7.1], as is now and then the case."[10]

Example 7.1. Harmony of the recitative cadence. From a footnote by Mattheson inserted in J. D. Heinichen's *Der Generalbass in der Komposition*, 674.

Telemann contrasts the very complete *formal cadence*, as described above by Marpurg and Mattheson, with the *cadenza trunca*, or broken-off cadence. This latter abbreviated cadence, demonstrated in example 7.2, creates a different set of effects appropriate in different dramatic contexts. As Telemann explains, in his *Singe-, Spiel- und Generalbass-Übungen* (1733), "In operas one plays the cadences immediately, as the singer pronounces the last syllables, but in cantatas, one usually plays them afterward."[11]

Example 7.2. Illustration of the *cadenza trunca*. From G. P. Telemann, *Singe-, Spiel- und Generalbass-Übungen*, No. 40, Toback.

Pier Francesco Tosi, however, warns in 1723 of a "tedious chanting that offends the ear with a thousand broken cadences in every opera, which custom has established though they are without taste or art." Yet, he adds, "to reform them all would be worse than the disease; the introducing every time of a final cadence would be wrong. But if in these two extremes a remedy were necessary, I should think that among a hundred broken cadences, ten of them, briefly terminated on points that conclude a period, would not be ill-employed."[12] Mattheson also admits (regarding ex. 7.1), "But since such boring cadences (which nevertheless constantly occur in theatrical situations) would tend to tire the listener and often seem to delay the singer unnecessarily, it may be that the opportunity has been taken to abbreviate the procedure. . . . Nevertheless, no one should be restrained from expressing a better opinion."[13] Johann Joseph Fux seems to support this looser interpretation in his *Gradus ad Parnassum* of 1725, maintaining that in recitative one should pay attention less to the harmonies than to the expression of the meaning of the words. His implication is that unresolved harmonies can be appropriate if textually driven: one is allowed to depart from the rules of harmony because "the bass does not move in a way that allows the dissonances to be resolved as usual."[14] Fux explains that in the case of the period (*punctum*) where another sentence is introduced immediately, a formal cadence is then commonly employed to mark the separation (ex. 7.3a). However, if the thought is completed, then the period should be made as in example 7.3b.[15]

Example 7.3. The cadence of the period. From Fux, *Gradus ad Parnassum*, p. 278.

The wide range of opinions (and visual representations) among eighteenth-century musicians regarding the nature of both the formal and broken-off cadence has spawned serious discussion within the field of performance practice: When and under what circumstances should either one or the other be employed? Should a composer's explicit notational practices be observed, or do implicit performance conventions override them? Dieter Gutknecht, in his extensive examination of the subject (2005), proposes that eighteenth-century cadential execution, its timing and treatment of dissonances, was far more varied than performance practices today would suggest.[16] Such evidence contributes to our understanding of the vital role played by these punctuating cadences (more than merely stock ending formulas) in conveying the meaning and import of a text. At stake is not only "correct" execution, but whether or not those cadences that require it are given their due solemnity and ceremony, while others that participate in a larger dramatic context are allowed to end more precipitately and briskly, even jarringly with unresolved dissonances, such that unfolding events may proceed more directly.

The notation of the singer's appoggiatura, which signals the final cadence, also receives its individual share of attention and scrutiny. In §84 Marpurg is most adamant that this appoggiatura should be *written*. He far prefers the feminine cadence (especially at the end of a recitative) and its characteristic falling fourth. If a masculine cadence must be used, then a stepwise appoggiatura should be employed, thereby avoiding any resemblance to the feminine cadence (and the resulting incorrect text setting).[17] It is reprehensible, Marpurg explains, that one should write in a way other than as one would sing. Further, singers lacking sufficient insight can become confused and led astray, particularly in the middle of a recitative. By this latter comment, Marpurg implies that appoggiaturas should not be inserted where the smaller points of punctuation occur. Indeed in both of his examples from Hasse's *Ezio*, appoggiaturas appear only in the context of full cadences. Telemann, however, states and indicates, through musical examples from the preface of his *Harmonischen Gottes-Dienst* (1725–26), that appoggiaturas may be inserted (even when not written) at lesser points of repose: "Singers must be careful not to sing the notes always as they are written, but now and then to make use of what is known as the accent."[18] "Now and then," in Telemann's illustrations appears to be "all the time." Yet as Frederick Neumann points out in 1982, Telemann's purpose is pedagogical and "the fact that he added appoggiaturas to all masculine and feminine cadences does not really undermine the reservation of 'occasionally.' "[19]

Our discussion brings up the larger question of the degree to which ornamentation is generally appropriate among the commas, colons and periods of recitative. Which embellishments and liberties, which a singer naturally takes to add import and meaning to his or her delivery, are suitable? Schulz is very clear on the subject: "Because recitative is not really sung, but is declaimed through musical notes, it must therefore not contain mellismatic ornamentation."[20] He admits that a feeling singer does not refrain from adding (here and there where the beauty of the affect allows) suspensions, anticipations, trills only rarely, and appoggiaturas. He adds that while these effects may appear simple enough on paper, they are nevertheless very difficult to execute and a mediocre singer will get better results simply by singing each note of each syllable as it is set. Even then the subtle nuances necessary in performance require considerable skill. Here Schulz provides an example highlighting a thread now very common in our discussion of punctuation, the inherent imprecision of notation. He presents a passage from Graun's *Tod Jesu*, in which the words *Er sinkt* (He sinks) are expressed through two tones falling on the same syllable (ex. 7.4a).[21] As Schulz explains, the rare sensitive singer sings instead the passage as shown in example 7.4b.

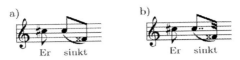

Example 7.4. Notes which should be held longer than the notation implies in a passage from Graun's *Tod Jesu*. From Sulzer, *Allgemeine Theorie der schönen Künste*, s.v. "Recitative" (Schulz), vol. 4, p. 11.

Domenico Corri, a student of Porpora in Naples from 1763 to 1767, generally condemns the notational standards that do not make explicit the necessary appoggiaturas, embellishing turns, and, as Schulz describes above, those notes which should be held longer than their notation implies:

> It is this imperfection in noting, which has hitherto rendered the execution of vocal music, particularly recitative, so difficult, that this last, (in itself, beyond a doubt, the highest species of vocal music), is almost impracticable; . . . Indeed, either an air, or recitative, sung exactly as it is commonly noted, would be a very inexpressive, nay, a very uncouth performance; for not only the respective duration of the notes is scarcely even hinted at, but one note is frequently marked instead of another, as is the case where a note is repeated, instead of that note with its proper *appoggiatura* or grace. Sometimes again, an *appoggiatura* is marked instead of a note which ought to receive, perhaps the particular emphasis of the voice, and be even longer than that which immediately follows[.][22]

Corri, as we have previously observed, takes the attitude that notation needs to be improved through the introduction of additional signs to correct its deficiencies. But, as we have also observed, such an attitude is not necessarily practical; the use of too many signs can lead to confusion rather than the intended clarity. One must instead learn to recognize the clues regarding affect and expression which govern notation's implicit conventions. Türk suggests that in keyboard music, when an idea is supposed to be executed in a "defiant" and "sharply accented" manner, then the inclusion of appoggiaturas would be inappropriate "because through them the melody would receive a certain smoothness which, in such cases, would not be desirable."[23] Similarly, Giambattista Mancini claims in 1774 that a singer, in rendering an "aria of invective" that demands "great fervor for the action," takes the meaning and emphasis completely away if he uses the appoggiatura to accompany such exclamatory words as "*Tyrant, Cruel, Implacable,* and so forth." This admonition against an overuse of the appoggiatura, however, applies only to serious song: "If he who sings in Buffo style emphasizes it, not only does he not commit an error, but he earns applause; because this same over-emphasis, which results in laughter in serious song, reaps approbation in Buffo style."[24] The Italian composer Vincenzo Manfredini, writing in 1797, feels that all ornaments other than the appoggiatura are inappropriate to *secco* recitative and allows very brief embellishments on "uninteresting or indifferent" words in the text, but never in lively or affective recitatives where the words are, for example: anxious, cruel, punishing, barbarous, treacherous, scornful, furious, pitiful, sorrowful, etc.[25] Thus the consensus is that the use of ornaments and appoggiaturas (written or unwritten), generally rare according to the declamatory nature of recitative, must correspond to the expression of the syllables and words. As these additions often occur at sectional and cadential moments, they play an important role in determining the nature of the punctuation—the sense of rest and closure which they convey, as well as the force of expression.

## So Few Signs, So Many Expressions

Marpurg concludes his lessons on the musical expression of the grammatical punctuation points in true Enlightenment spirit, with a neatly ordered and clearly laid out summary of the subject's main points (§§97–99). As Marpurg explains, the grammatical punctuation marks of language and the punctuation formulas of musical recitative can each be divided into three basic categories. Their combined musical expression can then be briefly recounted according to three basic rules. But in spite of his effort to control his subject through these succinct, clarifying lists, Marpurg presents a dizzying array of treatments for any given point of punctuation: the cadence which applies to the proper full stop can be either full (*ganz*) or elliptic (*elliptisch*); the improper full stop, which includes the colon, semicolon, and the full comma (these signs being interchangeable according to the context), receives either a regular break or a quasi-close; and the half comma receives a suspended break, which according to its strength and nature can be either consonant or dissonant, produced with either a static or altered bass, and a either a rising or falling melody. Marpurg's dilemma is a familiar one—how to define and prescribe the innumerable nuances and expressions of spoken (and sung) language, which nevertheless only a few punctuation symbols must convey.

Matcheson's list of punctuation formulas is equally complex. Like Marpurg, Mattheson ascribes two levels of cadences for the period. Both are what he calls formal (*förmlich*) closes occurring at the end of a *period*, but the full (*gäntzlich*) cadence is used only at the final conclusion. Similarly, Mattheson describes a hierarchy of cadences which can accompany the divisions within the period. Like Marpurg's full and half commas, Mattheson distinguishes between a variety of perfect (*perfectum*) and the imperfect (*imperfecte*) commas, of which the latter sometimes tolerate a very concise cadence but never a full one. The semicolon never has a full cadence, much less a complete one, but among its different manifestations, the *disjunctiva* calls for more division or separation (sometimes even real opposition) in the character of the melody than does the *relativis*, where nothing adverse or contrary should appear. The colon can be accompanied by a full close with rests, but if, for instance, a narration should follow, then the melody requires a sense of indecision.[26]

Each of Marpurg's punctuation formulas, including the rhetorical marks which we will discuss in the following section, "Elocution," can be manipulated in a great variety of ways to convey the subtle (and not so subtle) differences within the rhythms, inflection, and force of the declamation. As Marpurg explains, this can be achieved not only through the motion of the bass and the underlying harmony, but also through melodic contour and degrees of dissonance between melody and harmony. Here Marpurg strikes a nice middle ground regarding the harmony vs. melody polemic which we discussed in chapter 4. Recognizing the important interdependence between the two, he warns: "It is a mistake some musicians make that all the different parts of speech can always be distinguished **either through the motion of the bass alone or through the formulas of the melody alone**. . . . In order to give the punctuation marks their proper musical characteristics, one must pay attention to both the bass and the singing voice, and also the harmony and the melody." Marpurg demonstrates this in §95, providing examples where the melodic formulas remain the same, but different manipulations of the harmony yield either a *full cadence*, a *quasi-close*, or a *suspended break*. He then illustrates the opposite, how different degrees of repose can be achieved while the harmony remains the same, but the singing voice is manipulated through rising and falling melodies. Notice also in his examples of the regular break or the *quasi-close* (§§92–93), how he balances the two voices in order to avoid a sense of complete closure. The bass and the melodic voice of the final chord are rarely both the chord root, but if they are, the dominant is then in inversion.[27] In his examples of the *suspended breaks* (§94), which mark the smallest divisions or the half commas, he balances the degree of dissonance relative to the final harmony, the stepwise or leaping, downward or upward inflection of the melody—all of which anticipate the remainder of the thought in different ways.

The fluidity of the various punctuation formulas is also evident in Marpurg's terminology. He employs a highly descriptive (though at times rather obscure) language to describe his punctuation categories. The full cadence or *ganze Cadenz* is a very specific term used to describe the most complete punctuation formula, the fomal close discussed above which can be used occasionally within a recitative (particularly a long one), but most appropriately at its conclusion. To use the cadence elsewhere is entirely incorrect, for instance after a colon before a quotation as illustrated in §111. In such a case, the words purportedly spoken become completely disjoint when a formal cadence has already occurred before they begin. Marpurg's second category of punctuation formulas include the harmonies adapted from the full cadence, those employing inversions of and substitutions for chords in the full cadence, as well as those from the "less complete" half cadence or *halbe Cadenz* and the deceptive cadence or *unterbrochne Cadenz*. But Marpurg does not label the formulas in this category as types of *Cadenzen* but rather as *Absätze* or *Schlüße* (breaks or closes). He further "clarifies" these terms as *ordentlichen Absätze* (regular breaks) or *Quasischlüße* (quasi-closes). He employs the term *Absatz* again in his third category of punctuation formulas, the harmonically incomplete cadences which contain only simple incises or *Einschnitte* in the melody, describing them as *schwebenden Absätze* or suspended breaks. In the context of the question mark (§103), Marpurg further employs the German Latinized term for caesura (*Cäsur*) to describe the rhythmic nature of the stops which occur in the middle of a recitative. The importance of these technical nuances cannot, I think, be overestimated. The meanings of words like *Cadenz, Absatz, Schluß, Einschnitt,* and *Cäsur* (let alone their adjectival qualifiers) are, as we have already discussed, difficult to capture in modern translation and easily merge into one another: where exactly are the lines drawn between an *Einschnitt* and a *Cäsur,* an *Absatz* and a *Schluß,* and a *Cadenz?*[28] Yet at the same time, Marpurg's use of these terms and categories highlight the very supple nature of punctuation and the way the "humanly inconstant voice" of the living speaker continually refuses to be pinned down and precisely prescribed by neatly ordered lists and categories.

The elliptic cadence (*elliptische Cadenz*) is particulary interesting in regard to its categorization. Described by Marpurg as a shortened version of the full cadence, it is also a very effective device used in recitative to hold open the speech and propel it forward. After the dominant, one leaves out the tonic and instead proceeds to another key. Marpurg is adamant that these cadences have the value of full cadences and are not to be confused with the deceptive cadences of arioso style. But he admits that they can occasionally be used instead of the regular break. Most importantly, he adds, "it is easily perceived that [elliptic cadences] are nowhere to be found but in the middle of a recitative." Schulz also describes such cadences as having the value of complete but not full cadences. He emphasizes that these and similar cadences of a passionate nature are not to be used where a formal close of the period (*förmliche Schlußperiode*) is required. From the dominant, one moves not to the expected tonic, but according to the nature of the expression, to a more or less remote key. Schulz provides three examples of such expressions, shown in example 7.5: a) fierce and appropriate for intensifying feelings, b) for subsiding passions, and c) weak and sad.[29]

Example 7.5. Cadences of a passionate nature. From Sulzer, *Allgemeine Theorie der schönen Künste*, "Recitative" (Schulz), vol. 4, p. 15.

Marpurg does not explicitly indicate dynamics in his examples, but their role in the expression of such cadences is vital. As Schulz states in his twelfth rule of recitative, "the piano and forte with their shadings should be observed according to the content of the text."[30] One can easily imagine a forte dynamic accompanying the more vehement and insistent expression of the first example, with a range of softer dynamics for the subsiding expression of the second example and the abrupt, poignant shift of the third. Schulz comments that unfortunately neither the dynamics nor the changing affects are clearly marked for the singer, but it would perhaps be better if such were, since one can little depend on the singer's ability to perceive them.[31]

There are simply not enough signs to indicate all the nuances which accompany the punctuation marks of recitative. Neither would it be particularly helpful to so overcrowd the page with such detailed rhythmic, embellishing, dynamic, and affective information. Even an enumeration and categorization of all that the skilled singer must consider in order to convey these elements of musical punctuation necessarily leaves out so much vital information.

## Elocution

Ultimately what evolves from our discussion is that in order for recitative to be persuasive, it must embody all the elements of good Elocution—the proper and effective use of voice and gesture. Our sense of this comes to the fore in Marpurg's discussion of the four rhetorical punctuation marks (the question, exclamation, parenthesis and dash), and the colons before quotations. The rhetorical signs, as we mentioned earlier, employ the same basic punctuation formulas as the grammatical signs. But these extraordinary or exceptional signs, *außerordentlichen Abtheilungszeichen* as Marpurg calls them, are distinguished from the regular (*ordentlichen*) signs through the way the melody, rhythm, and harmony are manipulated to create the special emphases and heightened emotions which accompany them.

As we established in the section "Elocution and the *Honnête Homme*" in chapter 2, p. 47, gesture also bears no small role in the effective communication of the text: the elegant stance of the head and body, changes in countenance demanded by the text, and the all-important movements of the arms and hands: the commencing, terminating, suspended, and discriminating gestures within what can be called a *period of gesture*. For Giambattista Mancini, gesture is a crucial element in the execution of recitative's punctuation marks (grammatical as well as rhetorical). He devotes the entire concluding chapter of his *Practical Reflections on the Figurative Art of Singing* (1774) to the subject, entitling it "Recitative and Action." Recitatives, he claims, ought to be sung "in a natural and clear voice, which gives the just and complete strength to every word; which distinguishes the commas and the periods; in a manner which enables the listener to understand the sense of the poetry."

> But above all; even if the recitative be given with the necessary changes of voice, pauses and periods, it will always be languid and flaccid if it is not accompanied by a suitable action. This it is which gives the strength, the expression, and the vivacity to discourse. Gesture is the thing which marvelously expresses the character of that personage which one wishes to represent. The action, finally, is that which forms a true actor; hence, according to Tullius [Marcus Tullius Cicero] himself, all the greatness and beauty of the actor, consist in the action: *actio, actio, actio.*[32]

Mancini adds that one must learn to move the feet, carry the arms gracefully, and generally move the whole body with elasticity and grace—all of which is best achieved through the study of dance. Also of special importance is the countenance and the ability to change expression naturally, at precisely the right moment according to the words and music.[33] Marpurg, with his focus on the compositional rules of recitative and its proper notation, does not explicitly address the issue of gesture. But these essential counterparts to the emphases and accents of the voice are readily conceived through his very picturesque and affective descriptions of the rhetorical punctuation marks. One can easily imagine the necessary adjustments of the countenance to express sentiments he describes as "magnanimous," "assured," "joyful," "tender," or "painful." Similarly evoked are the movements of the body to accompany the momentum and contour of the melody: arms and hands raised in question or reaching out in supplication; emphatic, abrupt movements expressing vehement exclamations and exasperated sighs; the turns and asides heralded by the lowered voices in parentheses and the dissonances of dashes; and of course, the complete cessation of all movement with the final, full cadences of periods.

A key element for Marpurg in portraying the nature of a declamation is melodic inflection, the use of either rising or falling gestures in conjunction with the progression of the harmony. Marpurg first introduces the concept in the context of defining the nature of regular breaks and quasi-closes (§§92 and 94). These are the punctuation formulas through which the expression of the question and exclamation are primarily created (a complete cadence can be used in cases where the text of a recitative closes with an exclamation). However, it is in Marpurg's analysis of the recitative from Act I, scene 2, of Hasse's *Ezio* (§119, not included in the appendix A translation) that this concept is explained most clearly. Marpurg states that breaks (*Absätze*) with rising notes are to be used only where a question or exclamation or some other special emphasis occurs. This is also born out in his description of the question (§101), where he explains that it is the nature of the melody alone which distinguishes the question from the other kinds of purely grammatical divisions, "the close of which is regularly marked with **rising notes**, leaping or stepwise according to the nature of the harmony." He further warns against abusing the effect where no such question, exclamation, or special emphasis exists in the text.

The question, as Marpurg explains, can be created out of the formula of the suspended break as well as the quasi-close. But, he notes, again in the context of §119 cited above, the resulting effect can vary considerably. Rising notes accompanying suspended breaks, which serve only to hold open the melody without ending it, create a very different effect than they do when applied to the more complete periodic cadences. Among suspended breaks, the heightening or intensification of the notes is employed partly for variety and partly to give through the voice, a certain swing to the progression of the underlying harmony, or indeed often an emphasis. Marpurg observes this effect in Hasse's very appropriate setting of the sentence, *Ai gelidi Trioni il terror de mortali fuggitivo ritorna* (The one that mortals fear is a returning fugitive to freezing Trioni) (see ex. 7.6).

Example 7.6. The effect of rising notes used to accompany *suspended breaks* in a recitative from Act 1, scene 2 of Hasse'sa *Ezio*. From Marpurg, *Kritische Briefe*, p. 385.

As seen in the example, the notes rise in intensity over a second inversion dominant chord. The suspended break of the first phrase, *Ai gelidi Trioni* (to freezing Trioni), rises to a dissonant augmented fourth between melody and bass. The second phrase, *il terror de mortali* (the one feared by mortals), then rises with increasing tension from this held dissonance (a static note suspended break). The concluding phrase rises with a final emphasis on the third, accented syllable of *fugitivo* (fugitive) and then naturally subsides with *retorna* (return) and a feminine quasi-close ($V_2^4$–$I^6$). Marpurg adds that the difference between the effect of rising notes over suspended breaks vs. stronger periodic cadences can be observed even more clearly when one does away with the *written* rests (which in such cases are necessary primarily in order to guide inexperienced singers). It is always the combination of harmony and melodic contour which imparts the sense of punctuation.

In §103, Marpurg describes a similar way in which emphasis is created through rising notes. This is done in the context of the type of poetic foot used to express the question (as well as other points of punctuation) in the middle of a recitative. Most commonly, Marpurg explains, the dactylic ending is used, but an iambic caesura is also possible. Remember that classical rhetorical concepts of rhythm and clausulae played an important role for eighteenth-century musicians in determining both the nature of *commas, colons,* and *periods* and the character produced by the flow of their feet. Schulz, like Marpurg, stresses the importance of attending not just to the final syllable of a *period,* but to the key points of emphasis: "The special kinds of cadences, by which questions, fierce exclamations, and severe commanding sentences are distinguished, must be made not only out of the last syllable of the sentence, but especially out of the main word, where the sense of these figures of speech is based."[34] Marpurg implicitly defines the dactyl and iamb accentually, the former as a stressed syllable followed by two unstressed syllables, and the latter as an unstressed syllable followed by a stressed syllable. In both examples of §103, two caesuras occur, the first expressed by a suspended break, the second with a regular break or quasiclose. In all cases the melody rises with the stressed syllable. Most intersting is the manipulation of the dactyllic caesura at *lieben den* in the sentence, *Wie sollte man nicht lieben den der die Liebe selber ist?* (How can one not love he who is love personified?) Marpurg explains that this caesura is no less dactylic than the more obvious dotted-eighth–sixteenth–quarter rhythm at *selber ist.* If the note at *den* were the same as the sounding note $g^1$ of the weak second syllable of *lieben,* the rhythm would be more obvious. But a $b^1$ is taken instead of the repeated $g^1$ to give *den* [Jesus] an emphasis, and presumably a certain gestural swing to this important midpoint of the question.

Of course not all questions require a raised melody. In §102, Marpurg explains that the melody may fall where tender and painful questions occur. When many questions immediately follow one another, again the melody can fall, preferably by leap rather than stepwise. Mattheson also feels that questions can be expressed with a falling melody. He explains that many composers are rigid in the idea that questions must always be expressed with an upwardly rising voice. While it is true that a real question does raise doubt, still there are other kinds of questions which are posed in such a way that, although they ask, really express little or no doubt. For instance, the question "Can I administer medicine, if I am perishing myself?" is really making the point that no one who requires aid himself would be able to assist another. Questions can also be conveyed such that some doubt appears, and yet the voice need not ascend. As

Mattheson explains, "An imperfect consonance is most appropriate for this, when for example the question closes on a sixth, whether one would do it ascending or descending: that does not always matter, especially in recitative." However, Mattheson adds, the most typical expression of the question is when it closes on the fifth (as we find in many of Marpurg's examples).[35]

Like the question, the vocal gestures of the exclamation, and therefore the nature of its melody and harmony, are very dependent on the affect of the words uttered. As Marpurg explains in §104, joyful exclamations are generally expressed with upward leaps of a major third, a fourth, or a fifth, while sad affects tend to spring downward with a minor third, a fourth, or a fifth, or perhaps with a rising augmented fourth or a falling diminished fifth. The gestures of the violin in the recitative from Haydn's "Le Midi" Symphony (ex. 6.9) immediately come to mind: two joyful leaps of a fourth and a fifth, followed by the more lamenting fall of a diminished fifth. The simple divisions in the melody which accompany the violin's gestures, eighth- and sixteenth-note rests over a static bass, also closely resemble the way Marpurg feels short exclamatory formulas should be expressed. Longer exclamatory phrases, however, would require the harmony of a quasi-close, the melody still rising for a joyful affect and falling for a sad one. But again Marpurg adds an important caveat to his rules: alterations can always be made according to the nature of the harmony, the degree of rise or fall of the affect, and other circumstances (for instance where many exclamations follow one another and there are musical reasons to make these divisions with alternating rising and falling leaps).

Mattheson gives the exclamation (where it consists of a phrase) a threefold distinction which is made according to its affect. In the first case, the reigning passion is joy. Nothing but lively and rapid movements of sound and especially large and wide intervals are used to comprise "astonishment," "joyous acclamation," or a "rousing command." The second type includes all wishes or heartfelt yearnings; all entreaties, appeals, and laments; and also fright, dread, and terror. The latter require melodic vehemence, also best expressed through rapid or fast sounds. However yearnings, where grief is paramount, use sometimes large intervals but not common ones, and where tenderness reigns, small and extraordinary intervals must be used. The third type, which Mattheson would just as soon discard, he describes as the true scream, or pure despair. This calls for confused and unruly intervals such as major and minor thirds appearing together, etc. The frenzied tumult desired for the accompaniment of such impious, wicked screams, is well suited to the Pyrrhic meter of two short syllables.[36]

The very theatrical asides, or parentheses, where the actor/singer might literally turn to the side or raise a hand to one side of the mouth for the enclosed words, are expressed musically with a similar degree of digression. Marpurg suggests in §107 that the parenthetical melody (surrounded by rests) should be immediately lowered, returning afterwards to the interrupted progression. Mattheson feels that parentheses are really not very musical and might just as well be dispensed with in the melodic discipline. However, because they occasionally appear in arias, and more often and more fittingly in recitative, he proceeds to explain the two kinds. The first are those which digress a great deal from the text. In such a case, and very much as Marpurg describes above, the melody would have to be lowered for the digression. In other cases, however, where the interpolated text has a becoming continuity with the remainder of the presentation, or contains only short exclamations, then one does not need an unusual division of the melody and pauses and rests are not at all suitable.[37]

Even more dramatically, the dash, according to Marpurg, marks a sudden stop or ellipsis. This is created through a dissonance where the resolution is delayed or played afterwards by the bass. In the first example of §108, from the opera *Demophonte*, Marpurg offers two possible executions of the dash which follows Matusius's words *Und die einzige Hofnung—* (And the only hope—). As Marpurg explains, Matusius might pause of his own accord in order to learn the disposition of Timantes, in which case I can imagine a worried Matusius turning expectantly towards his friend. Alternatively, Timantes might interrupt Matusius's assertion. In this case, I would imagine a more abrupt pause, Matusius's emphatic gesture at *only hope* receiving additional force through Timantes' interruption of *Die, werthster Freund, besteht in der Flucht* (which worthiest friend, lies in flight). Either way, Marpurg insists, nothing but a dissonance can be used. Matusius and Timantes respectively conclude and begin on the same diminished fifth interval between voice and bass, part of a first-inversion A dominant chord, which only finally resolves to D minor with a masculine cadence on the last word and syllable, *Flucht*.

The punctuation of dialogue, as depicted above by the dash, requires great skill and attention in order to convey its natural hesitations, interruptions, sudden changes of thought, and moments of drama and tension. This is also evident in the series of rules which Marpurg gives regarding the expression of the colon before a quotation of "one's own or someone else's words." Marpurg begins, in §109, with a very straightforward case, where the quoted words begin immediately after a short *colon*. The voice rises in expectation of the quoted words, and their arrival coincides with a change of key. But he soon moves on to describe the many challenges presented by the setting of quotations: where the quoted words are contained in an arioso and must be clearly distinguished from the colon which precedes it; where a quotation and a question appear together, whereby the first merges entirely into the other; and how to avoid a number of pitfalls through different manipulations of melodic contour, the motion of the bass, degrees of dissonance, and rhetorical accent and emphasis. For instance, in the third example of §109, Marpurg notes the difficulty of setting all the "he saids" and "she saids" (or in this case the "I saids") of recounted dialogue. Marpurg explains that not only must the singer make a short stop after the *written* pause which follows the words, *sag ich*, but he must also do so at the suspended comma between the words *viel Menschen* and *sag ich*, even if no pause is evident. As we learned from Jean-François Marmontel in the section "The Art of Conversation" in chapter 2, p. 52, such usage tends "to retard the vivacity of dialogue and make the style listless where it should be more animated." Indeed as Marpurg concludes, "thus can this kind of quotation, which is not easy to compose, be expressed as well as is possible."

In the seventh example of §109, Marpurg comments on the way that the setting of No. 1 so effectively "befits the pituresque sound of the speaker's intention." The whole momentum of the melody—the downward sweep of *Großmüthig* outlining a G dominant chord, followed by a raised voice at *spricht er*, and a "natural" feminine meter for the arrival on the first inversion C-major chord—achieves this admirably. In contrast, the downwardly inflected vii°6–I masculine cadence of No. 2 better befits the words *Großmüthig spricht er* (humbly he spoke), than the original sentiment *Demüthig spricht er* (magnanimously he spoke). Similarly inappropriate is the use of a dissonance, illustrated in §110, to indicate the colon before a quotation which is then resolved at the beginning of the quoted words. While such might appear to be a clever trick (once tried by "a certain famous composer"), it nevertheless goes completely against the nature of the punctuation. As Marpurg explains, the exclamation *O! welche herrlichkeit hat der, der sprechen kann:* (Oh! What magnificence has he who can speak:) posesses a certain assurance, and should raise no doubts—doubts which certainly would be raised by the occurrence of a dissonant diminished fifth between bass and voice at the colon.

These detailed, thoughtful, and expressive descriptions of punctuation in recitative by Marpurg and others demonstrate so well the many elements which music can contribute to enhance the sentiments of language. In music, Marpurg argues, one has in fact "far more means" of distinguishing among the different parts of an expression. And although he makes this statement with particular regard to the expression of quotations in the middle of a recitative, its relevance applies not only to "these cases," but also to "all others."[38] As Elocutionist Joshua Steele also claims, the symbols of music can be used "to explain more precisely "the *melody and measure* of speech," its "*accent, emphasis, quantity, pause,* and *force.*"[39] The reciprocal nature of the punctuation analogy—the semantic qualities that language brings to music and the rhythmic, harmonic, and melodic elements that music brings to language—is perhaps most evident in this union of song and speech, music and prose.

## A Wordless Recitative by Telemann

Let us now consider how Marpurg's principles might be applied to the performance of an instrumental recitative where words, and the semantic information which they would otherwise have imparted, are absent. For our purposes, I have chosen a straightforward recitative, which closely imitates the style of its vocal counterpart—the *Recitativo* from Georg Phillip Telemann's E-minor

Sonata for Viola da gamba and Continuo, given below in example 7.7.[40] Of course we cannot claim that Marpurg's 1762 study of recitative could have in any way influenced Telemann in the composition of his sonata, already published by 1740. But it is reasonable to assume that Telemann would have applied his considerable knowledge and experience with vocal music to his instrumental compositions—experience which would have had a great deal in common with Marpurg, as well as other North German composer/theorists like Mattheson, Schulz, and Türk. Telemann, although he is known today primarily for his instrumental music, was a prolific composer of both sacred and secular vocal works and wrote at least twenty-nine operas (and perhaps as many as fifty if his own claims are to be believed).[41] Vocal music, as we discussed in Part 1, was considered in the eighteenth century to be the preeminent form of musical expression, its practices absorbed, often quite overtly as in the present Recitativo, by those of instrumental composition.[42] Further, it would have been presumed in the eighteenth century that the experienced musician would possess a certain degree of skill and knowledge regarding not just one, but both the vocal and instrumental arts. Telemann, for instance, states in his preface to the *Fortsetzung des harmonischen Gottesdienstes* of 1731–32, that he has included information in the score regarding both the vocal and thorough-bass parts, "which make the cantatas more convenient for private services and occasions where not all the instruments are available or desired, so that a single performer may play the smaller notes while singing the larger ones, or play both parts."[43]

Example 7.7. G. P. Telemann, Sonata for Viola da Gamba and Continuo in E Minor, 3rd movement.

As we now proceed with the Recitativo from Telemann's Viola da gamba Sonata, we must keep in mind all that we understand about recitative, its potential to express the most intense *affects* through rhythmic freedoms, fluctuating paces,

and frequent starts and stops—in other words, the punctuated phrases of passionate expressions. Telemann's Recitativo and Arioso pair is dramatically positioned at the center of the sonata, preceded by a lush Cantabile and spirited
Allegro and followed by a highly virtuosic Vivace, each of these movements in
the tonic key of E minor. The recitative opens with a C♯ diminished chord and
descending diminished triad, whose arrival on the third beat creates a dissonant
augmented fourth between melody and bass, immediately grabbing our attention. We sense at least a strong affect, and perhaps a rather excited or "defiant"
one. The momentum towards and through this initial masculine "cadence" on
an F♯ dominant chord is also strong. The type of division is what Marpurg would
describe as a *suspended break*, and the punctuation a kind of half comma (or even
an "unwritten" one), which I express as a comma in parentheses. Perhaps the
opening diminished chord gesture might also be perceived as an exclamation
(of Marpurg's first variety), with a dark affect indicative of the falling diminished
fifth. In either case, the degree of repose is slight and anticipatory of what is to
follow.

The two chords which make up the second phrase division consist of a B$_5^6$
dominant, the resolution of the preceding F♯ dominant, which itself resolves to
a root position E-major triad. The first chord is a dissonant one with a diminished fifth between melody and bass, but the following third beat is a consonant
one and this time signifies a *regular break* or a *quasi-close* (V$_3^6$–I). The cadence is,
as Marpurg would claim, of the stronger variety, derived from the full cadence,
where the dominant chord is in first inversion and its tonic in root position.
However, the cadence is weakened by the support in the melody voice with the
mediant G♯, which acts as a leading tone to the E-major chord which is not only
a resolution of the B dominant, but also functions as the dominant of A minor.
Thus a V–I$^6$ progression is created and another *quasi-close* on beat three of bar 3.
In fact, up to this point we have been moving forward in a series of dominant
chords—the F♯ dominant of B, which is in turn the dominant of E, which is the
dominant of A. This final moment of tension and release in the sequence
(V/V/V–V/V–V–i if one wished to express it this way) is the strongest thus far.[44]
And even though the A-minor chord is in first inversion, the final melodic note
is the tonic.

As to punctuation marks, I imagine a full comma in bar 2. The affect is still
agitated after the first half comma, but as the harmony moves from dissonance
to consonance, we are slightly calmed. It is as if we might rest, but then the
melody rises up with an added more plaintive and lingering afterthought which
closes the three-bar phrase. In bar 3, I could probably argue equal cases for a
colon or an improper full stop. The melodic line is remarkably similar to the
closing gesture of the full cadence. Here, perhaps, is an appropriate place for a
"smoothing" appoggiatura. Telemann's abrupt switch to the minor mode in bar
3 does create a special tender affect. This is first signalled by the surprising rise
from g♯ to f♮$^1$, a note of emphasis and therefore also a key to the emotional

content. The harmonic underpinning additionally contributes to the effect. The minor third relationship in the bass between the E-major chord on beat 3 of bar 2 and the A⁶-minor chord of bar 3 signifies, according to Schulz, that which is "weak" and "sad." This is one of the cadences listed among those of a "passionate nature" used where a *period* is concluded, but without a formal close (example 7.5c).

Our choice of dynamics should support these harmonic and melodic effects. Moving from the more vehement and *forte* expressions of the opening, a softer *piano* accompanies this more tender, reflective moment in a minor key. The keyboard player, according to Schulz, should supply shorter, crisp notes for the louder dynamics and then longer notes for softer, sad expressions.[45] C. P. E. Bach similarly describes the use of a slower arpeggiation of chords for recitatives of a more *affettuoso* nature and detached, resolute, unarpeggiated chords for those which are noisy and furious.[46] The poignancy of the moment in Telemann's bar 3 can be further enhanced by expressively altering the durations of the rhythms, which, as Corri and Schulz explain, is "scarcely even hinted at" in the notation. A little lingering in the melody over the f♮¹ followed by a general loss of momentum and unevenness among the repeated d¹ eighth notes helps signal the sense of subsiding passions and coming to rest as we approach this *regular break*. However the arrival point is still only a i⁶ chord and the melodic line which follows finds a quick reserve of energy, rising up joyously with the leap of a fifth to an A dominant chord and a renewed sense of purpose. The length of the pause is not as long as anticipated and I place a colon at this point.

We want also to consider the appropriate gestures of the gamba player throughout these opening measures—how the player's bow arm (à la Cambini) and position at the instrument can mimic the movements of the orator or singer. I imagine the gamba player concluding the long sequence of lively running eighth notes in the 6/8 meter of the Allegro with a final up-bow gesture on e (performed with an underhand bow grip, the equivalent of a final down-bow on the violin or cello). In the same animated and brisk character with which the entire movement was played, the arm comes to rest at the player's side to indicate a formal close. The commencing gesture in bringing the bow back to the string to begin the recitative must be made with a contrasting seriousness and determination, indicative of the opening diminished chord struck by the harpsichord and the bow strokes which will slice through the descending diminished triad. The countenance must also assume the appropriate intensity of expression. Nothing rests at the first half comma (or exclamation). The whole body is poised in a kind of silent crescendo of expectation. But then at the upbeat f♯, the countenance begins to clear and the bow begins to ease with the sense of backing off slightly from the downbeat a♮ eighth notes in bar 3 and awaiting further developments on the g♯ leading-tone comma. As a gamba player, I would want to imagine the stance of a singer first poised forward towards the audience, the arm stretched out with a sense of urgency and then shifting one's weight back away, but still held up in expectation with the new discriminatory thought. The impulse of the next gesture falls on the tender interval between f$^1$ and the repeated d$^1$ eighth notes, held through the remainder of the descent to a. The countenance assumes a concerned expression and the bow moves quickly across the instrument to reach for the upper note, and then to soothe and caress. Again I imagine the singer's stance shifting forward in a kind of sympathetic entreaty. However this suspended gesture at the colon does not last long, with a new joyous leap of a fifth from a to e$^1$ for the second half of the *period*.

In bar 4, the bass note c♮ natural becomes a c♯ and the A-minor chord becomes an A$^6_5$ dominant chord beginning a new circle of fifths pattern. The A dominant resolves to its D which is itself a V$^4_2$ of the following G chord, which is in turn a V$^6_5$ of the following C-major triad. As in bar 1, beat 3 of bar 4 displays a dissonant augmented fourth between melody and bass, another *changing note suspended break*, or in the language of punctuation, a half comma. There is also something of a questioning element to this moment. If we consider the f♯ and g sixteenth notes as simply written-out embellishments, then the "real" interval, the one between the e and the final f♯ quarter note, is a rising one. Whether or not we want to place an actual question mark here, this sense of seeking confirmation does give a certain swing and gestural propulsion to the underlying harmony. This is then contrasted by a downward slope and slight relaxation, still with an exuberant affect, into the quasi-close in bar 5, another V$^6_5$–I cadence with a mediant upper voice as in bar 2.[47] The C chord of bar 5 serves in retrospect as the subdominant of G major, followed by a V$^4_2$ dominant, which, combined with the higher tessitura of the melody, immediately propels us into the typical closing gesture of the falling fourth and the final V–I full cadence. Confident tones and gestures are appropriate throughout this second half of the *period*. The gamba player crescendos through the questioning gesture of bar 4, reaching forward to the audience, "Am I not right to be so pleased?" then shifting back and answering, "Yes, indeed I am." Then with final, perhaps exclamatory gestures, the keyboard player leads us grandly into the Arioso in G major.

Regarding this final cadence, we should also observe that it is *written* much as Marpurg prescribes. The bass dominant receives its "proper incise" (as do all of the sectional divisions) following the vocal cadence (a feminine one as the Italians favor and presented with a *written* falling fourth), and moves to the tonic on the strong beat. But does Telemann intend a formal cadence here, or is the performance convention of a broken-off cadence (associated with more theatrical, operatic styles) called for instead? If the latter and the bass cadence is allowed to occur simultaneously with the viol's cadential appoggiatura, then the suggested resolution of the D$^4_2$ dominant chord to a first-inversion G chord "in the right hand alone" cannot be made. Through this unresolved dissonance, the character of the concluding *period* would then have a more headlong, precipitate feel to it, the confident paired Arioso in G major receiving less of a separation. On the other hand, the recitative is already quite concise, consisting of only a single *period*. Therefore the potential tedium arising from a string of long, drawn-out cadences (or alternately the tedious "chanting" from so many broken cadences) is not at issue. I would be more inclined to opt for the grander, full conclusion, which Telemann describes as belonging to the cantata model, especially since the tonic arrival of the bass cadence also marks the downbeat and beginning of the Arioso. Either way, one's choice of execution must be based on the degree of repose and effect desired from the punctuation point, both the way in which it concludes the sequence of thoughts and connects to the new ideas which follow.

Thus the overall structure of Telemann's Recitativo consists of a single *period* composed of two three-bar phrases, each with a kind of 2+1 interior organization. All the points of punctuation fall on the third beats of the bars and the result is highly symmetric, but at the same time loosely formed, or what we might call *harmonic prose*. True to its nature, the recitative is full of starts and stops (two half commas, two full commas, a colon, and a period—some of these also suggestive of question and exclamation marks); varying affects (from determined and purposeful to weakened and sad, and back again with energy and assurance); the accompanying variations of rhythm, stressing now this syllable then that one; and the associated degrees of forward momentum and repose. Our attention to the rests and points of punctuation, rather than creating a number of disjunct starts and stops, has quite the opposite effect, conveying the momentum and communicative intent of the impassioned musical statement. The more familiar one becomes with vocal recitative—not only compositional studies like those of Marpurg, Mattheson and Schulz, but the actual recitatives of sacred and secular works which served as their models—the more the gestures of punctuation, which so define the genre, begin to reveal themselves.

Of course, the suggestions we have given for the performance of Telemann's recitative are only that, suggestions. There are certainly many effective means of conveying such instrumental utterances, and an infinite number of subtle and spontaneous dynamic, rhythmic, and gestural nuances with which the performer can work, and which it is simply not possible (or desirable) to indicate in the score. We have barely tapped the surface of the ways in which instrumental music borrows from this powerful and expressive language, and for an extensive, though by no means complete list of such borrowings, I refer the reader to David Charlton's 1982 article "Instrumental Recitative: A Study in Morphology and Context, 1700–1808" and Herbert Seifert's *Das Instrumentalrezitativ vom Barock bis zur Wiener Klassik* (1975). It should be kept in mind that *recitative* passages are not always specifically identified, as in the case of Telemann's Recitativo, and also C. P. E. Bach's Sonata (fig. 6.1) and Haydn's "Le Midi" Symphony (ex. 6.9). Eighteenth-century composers instead relied on a player's visual recognition of the signifying shapes and gestures. The player is also left to determine the style of recitative being borrowed—*secco* vs. the *accompanied* or *obbligato* recitative—and the necessary degree of adherence to overall meter. As the recitative begins to take on the more measured qualities of the latter style, the manner in which the text is delivered, and in consequence, how the rests of musical punctuation are treated, will naturally be affected. Or alternatively, we might say, the practices of *musical prose* will have to be adapted as they begin to assume properties belonging to those of *musical verse*—the "opposite" fundamental application of musical punctuation, and also our subject for the next chapter.

# Chapter Eight

# *Musical Verse—Johann Mattheson's "Curious Specimen" of a Punctuated Minuet*

In this chapter we begin to know and to practice the connection of melodic sections with regard to their rhythm and punctuation. To attain this objective the shortest compositions common in music are chosen first, because the different possible ways of connecting their few melodic sections can be most easily perceived and imitated. These short compositions are:

1. the current dance melodies
2. the melodies to odes and songs, and
3. all short pieces arbitrarily arranged with respect to the meter, the rhythm, the length, the punctuation, and the tempo.

—*Heinrich Christoph Koch, 1793*

In the previous chapter, on recitative, we discussed the way in which musical punctuation seeks to express the most predominant structures of language, those of prose. In this chapter, we now turn the tables to view musical punctuation, still as it seeks to imitate language, but from the perspective of music's most predominant structures. The general consensus among eighteenth-century music theorists, as expressed above by Koch, is that the basics of musical punctuation are to be derived from the most recognizable and distinctly defined forms of the day, what we are describing as the verse-like structures of music. These verse forms come in both vocal and instrumental varieties, but it is the latter which best depict the pleasing regularity of meter, accent, and cadence. True, the melodies to songs and odes (the chorale and figured melodies) make good punctuation models: John Gunn [45] adapts forty favorite Scotch airs for the violoncello (or the violin or German flute) in 1793 as familiar models for the study of proper phrasing; and Türk recommends in 1789 "short songs set for the clavichord by good composers."[1] But the character of these melodies still depends on the contents of the poetry, and their overall form on the structure of the strophes. These compositions, according to Koch, presuppose a certain knowledge of vocal music and the rules of language, a two-sided and therefore more difficult branch of composition.[2] And as we understand from Schuback, even for those who have acquired the necessary knowledge of declamation, the manipulation of poetry to the rhythm and meter of melody is a matter of constant compromise and little pleasure.[3] And Mattheson's writes that instrumental melodies, and especially dance melodies, must adhere to their "geometric progressions" even more closely than their vocal counterparts.[4] Therefore, the best place to begin our study of punctuation in music's verse-like subjects is with the simple, flowing melodies of small, instrumental dance pieces. The representation of language at its "most musical" is in fact a kind of instrumental, nonverbal form.

Eighteenth-century theorists also maintained that an understanding of phrase structure among the various dance melodies would ultimately lead the way towards an understanding of music's larger compositions with their multiform interior organizations. As Schulz explains in 1774:

> If beginners were diligent in familiarizing themselves with the execution of the different dances, which are so easy to feel and so manifold, indeed which have all manner of phrase divisions, they would soon observe how the accents and divisions [*Einschnitte*] must be marked in order to make both perceptible; they would then also, as often occurs in sonatas and solos, more easily learn to recognize the connecting melodies among phrases of two, three, or more measures.[5]

Echoing Schulz, Türk also recommends the diligent practice of various dance compositions "as an aid to learn how to feel phrase divisions."[6] Kirnberger, too, advises: "Every beginner who wants to become well grounded in composition is advised to become familiar with the disposition of all types of ballets, because all types of characters and rhythm occur and can be observed most accurately in them."[7]

The best dances with which to "learn how to feel phrase divisions" tend to have two basic attributes: first, they have pleasing characters appropriate to simple textures and regular, clearly delineated phrases; and second, they have retained in their day a continuing popularity as social and theatrical dances. Koch's list of the "current dance melodies"—the *gavotte, bourrée, polonaise, anglaise* or *contredanse, march*, and *minuet*—all fit the bill, described using terms like gay, pleasant, lively, sprightly, brisk, simple, pretty, etc. Koch gives the *polonaise* the fairly strong affect of "solemn gravity," but still this does not mar the regularity of its "rhythmical sections of an even number of measures."[8] The march too, although it is sometimes "sublime and splendid," has the aim of "facilitating a complete equality of steps."[9] Not on Koch's list, however, is a dance like the *allemande* which qualifies on neither of the above accounts—both serious in character, and having early on developed an independent instrumental form functioning as a kind of extension to the *prelude* of the Baroque suite. Johann Gottfried Walther, for instance, compares the allemande in 1732 to a rhetorical proposition out of which flows the remaining parts of the suite—the courante, sarabande, and gigue.[10] Similarly

Marpurg describes the allemande in 1762 in terms of complex harmonic development and thickly interwoven, imitative textures:

> The main object of an Allemande is a well-worked series of different kinds of alternating harmonies, the melody of no voice particularly projecting above the others. The different voices should work against each other with a similar strength, although primarily through the upper and middle voices; it is not only through the melody that one observes the allemande.[11]

Marpurg adds that the melody of the allemande does maintain a regular metrical orientation, characterized by a "short-note upbeat" to the bar, but one is also likely to encounter clauses or phrases containing odd numbers of measures, for example seven or nine.

The graceful minuet of French origin, on the other hand, remained one of the most popular social dances of aristocratic Europe throughout the eighteenth century.[12] By mid-century it was the only important Baroque dance surviving as a popular form and, not coincidentally, it continued in its purely instrumental guise to exhibit every espoused value of the typical classical style with its clearly delineated harmonic movement and phrases of even and symmetrical numbers.[13] The melodic and harmonic patterns of the eight-bar minuet became so standardized and predictable that compositional games were made of them. Kirnberger notably, in *Der allezeit fertige Polonoisen- und Menuettencomponist* of 1757, created tables of individual minuet measures, assembled in such a way that eight throws of the dice would yield an eight-bar phrase cadencing on the dominant, and another eight throws a concluding return to the tonic.[14] The minuet became, in one sense, the epitome of what was considered "good taste" among eighteenth-century polite society—representing all that is physically graceful and charming, and providing great pleasure and agreeable entertainment.

Throughout the eighteenth century, minuets were incorporated into countless classical chamber works and symphonies, and in the hands of eminent composers became highly sophisticated compositions (e.g., the minuets of ex. 4.10 from Beethoven's First Symphony and ex. 6.10 from Mozart's Clarinet Quintet). Christopher Hogwood describes a number of clever techniques incorporated into the very adaptable and attractive form: the mixing of high and low styles—aristocratic fanfares and dotted rhythms juxtaposed with Hungarian music, Turkish elements, or quotations from familiar and local German melodies; contrapuntal ingenuity involving canons and cryptic devices like mirror constructions; as well as the introduction of uneven phrase units, fermatas, and pedal-point harmonies which test the movement's danceability.[15] Yet at the same time, the minuet's essentially "galant" attributes made the compositions exceedingly suitable for the "fair sex," a designation which, for some eighteenth-century critics, severely diminished the form's aesthetic value. Johann Adam Hiller, writing in 1766, denounces the French, feminizing nature of minuets, likening their inclusion in symphonies to "beauty spots" (a French cultural emblem) on the face of a man: "They give the music a foppish appearance, and weaken the manly impression made by the uninterrupted sequence of three well-matched, serious movements, wherein lies one of the greatest beauties of execution."[16]

But the fact remains that however deprecated or marginalized, the minuet was nevertheless a primary ingredient in the development of what we have come to call the "classical style," its influence felt particularly through its role as a didactic paradigm for the composition of instrumental music. The appeal of the minuet was twofold—at once so supremely simple that it could be reduced to a dice game, yet this same simplicity and regularity making it the perfect teaching medium for the ways in which individual phrases could be combined, varied, and manipulated into complex, symphony-length movements. More often than any of "the current dance melodies," it was the minuet, embodying the fundamental principles of periodicity (small phrases linked to form increasingly larger ones), that was employed as an initial exercise in the art of musical punctuation. Mattheson set the standard in 1737 with his "little minuet," replete with punctuation marks, poetic feet, numerical proportions, and rhetorical emphases, "so that everyone may see what such a little thing consists of, when it is not a monster, and so that one would learn to make a sound judgment in moving from trifling matters to the more important."[17] Riepel, in 1752, sets his student the task of composing a simple minuet in order to "begin with the small and insignificant, so that we will soon achieve something greater and more praiseworthy."[18] Thirteen years later, in 1765, Löhlein punctuates and analyzes a minuet which both reminds us of Mattheson's and incorporates much of Riepel's terminology. And at the end of the century, the minuet is again being put through its paces by Koch in 1793; he makes the minuet his initial focus in the second chapter of volume 3 of his *Versuch einer Anleitung zur Composition*: "The Connection of Melodic Sections into Periods of Short Length, or the Arrangement of Short Compositions." He discusses in detail, with numerous musical examples, the ways in which the four melodic sections and cadential formulas of the minuet's two *periods* can be combined and manipulated.[19]

These minuets, "trifling" and "insignificant" as their critics and proponents purport them to be, nonetheless raise a number of important issues and present some critical questions for the modern performer and interpreter.[20] Mattheson's minuet in particular has received repeated attention, yielding a number of puzzled (and puzzling) responses—including Mathis Lussy's 1873 description of the example as "a curious specimen of musical punctuation" and a "strange analysis, remarkable for the time in which it was made," as well as Ernst Apfel's 1976 discussion of the "internal metrical (rhythmical) problem" of the minuet.[21] As it is the earliest, most detailed, and most cited example of its kind, one could hardly write a book on the subject of musical punctuation without including a discussion of what has come to be known as Mattheson's minuet. And as we begin to delve into its details and the history of its reception and interpretation, we uncover what I can only describe as "a surprisingly complex and lively picture of pointing theory." We will therefore make the case of Mattheson's minuet the focus of our study, enlisting the help of Löhlein, who also provides detailed information with regard to punctuation, together with what we can glean from Koch and Riepel. The interpretive efforts of others, like Lussy's and Apfel's cited above, will also be of great service as we focus our discussion on some of the important matters relative to the subject of musical punctuation: classical rhetorical concepts of rhythm and meter; punctuation's various grammatical and rhetorical elements; gesture (particularly as it relates to dance); written and unwritten rests; articulation; and governing all of these elements, *affect*.[22] As in our discussion of recitative, we will take into consideration both the limits of our study (a book could be written on minuets alone) and the biases of our sources.[23]

## The Minuet as a Compositional Model

We will begin by presenting the four minuets put forth as compositional models by Mattheson, Riepel, Löhlein, and Koch.[24] As we have already stated, our main focus will be that of Mattheson's "strange analysis" (reproduced for the reader in both modern notation [ex. 8.1] and facsimile [figs. 8.1 and 8.2]). This "little" minuet is so fully packed with the visual aids of punctuation that it is necessary to break down our discussion into three categories or tiers of analysis. First we will look at the basic structure of the dance form, commenting on the larger points of punctuation—its *periods, colons,* and *semicolons*—according to general cadential and melodic motion. Second, we will examine the smaller phrase units of the *comma,* looking more closely at the gestural nature of the two-bar dance step and the implications for the instrumental performer. And third, we will magnify our lens one more level to look within these smallest units of punctuation to analyze the "sound feet" from which they are constructed—the metrical placement of short and long syllables—and related information regarding accent and emphasis, which will take us even deeper into the history of the dance and the earliest known minuet step patterns.

### A. *Mattheson*—Kern melodischer Wißenschafft *(1737),* Der vollkommene Capellmeister *(1739)*

I. Le Menuet, *la Minuetta,* be it made in particular for playing/singing/dancing, has no other affect than **moderate cheerfulness** [*mässige Lustigkeit*]. If the melody of a minuet is only sixteen measures long (for it cannot be shorter), then it will have at least some commas, a semicolon, a few colons, and a few periods in its make-up. Many a person would scarcely think that; yet it is true. At some places, if the melody is of the proper type, one can even clearly perceive the **emphasis**, not to mention the accents, question marks, etc. The numerus sectionalis or geometric relationship, and the rhythmus, or arithmetic relationship are both indispensable for all kinds of dances, and gives them the proper measure and form. In the minuet here we want to show such an example, which can serve as a model for analysis of all the others.

Example 8.1. Johann Mattheson's punctuated minuet.

Here now is a complete melodic paragraph or **combined sentence** of 16 measures, which become 48. It consists of two periods or **sentences**, which (like the following caesuras [*Einschnitte*]), are increased through repetition by a third of the whole, and are marked with three points (∴) under their final notes. In this paragraph there is not only a **colon**, or member [*Glied*]; but also a **semicolon**, or half member [*halbes Glied*], which one recognizes by their usual signs (:) (;). One also encounters three **commas**, which become nine, and which are indicated with the familiar little comma stroke (,).[25] The threefold emphasis however, we have indicated with so many asterisks (*). The sectional number or **geometric proportion** is 4 here, as with all good dance melodies, and there are four crosses (†) as indicators. The **rhythms** [*Rhythmi*] or sound feet [*Klang-Füsse*] of the first and second measures are used again in the fifth and sixth, $\smile — | — \smile — |$. Those stated later in the ninth and tenth measures are heard again immediately in the eleventh and twelfth, from which arithmetic uniformity arises. And that is the entire analysis in eight parts.

Figure 8.1. Facsimile of example 8.1 from *Kern melodischer Wissenschafft*, pp. 109–10.

Figure 8.2. Facsimile of example 8.1 from *Der vollkommene Capellmeister*, p. 224.

## B. *Riepel*—Anfangsgründe zur musicalischen Setzkunst *(1752)*

The following is a summary of the principles laid out by the teacher for his pupil in the course of a lesson on minuet composition, including one of the student's final and more successful efforts:

1. Even numbers of measures are pleasing to the ear in all compositions and are especially required in a minuet.
2. Each part should consist of no more than eight measures.
3. The beginning and theme must be clearly separated into recognizable two- and four-measure [*Zweyern oder Vierern*] segments.
4. Perfectly moving or imperfectly moving notes [*vollkommen oder unvollkommen erhebende Noten*] are required until the cadence. Two imperfect measures should not follow in succession, nor should a stationary measure [*unbeweglich Note*] be used anywhere in the minuet except at the end of both parts.
5. The measures in the second part must bear a similarity to those of the first part. Complete coherence is required of a minuet just as much as in a concerto, an aria, symphony, etc.
6. A minuet should ascend in the first part and fall back in the second.
7. The most expert composers of minuets make a clear distinction between the fourth and fifth measures. If the fourth measure consists of perfectly moving notes, then the fifth should contain imperfectly moving notes, or the reverse.

Example 8.2. Riepel's minuet.

*Pupil:* May I now claim that I know how to write an orderly minuet?

*Teacher:* You must never boast. The rules alone don't make the difference. For if another wrote a minuet whose organization was not as clear, but whose melody was livelier, then perhaps such a minuet would be far more popular among the amateurs than one of yours that obeys the rules and has the correct proportions.

## C. *Löhlein*—Clavier-Schule (*1765*)

At (*) there is a musical **comma**, or **caesura** [*Einschnitt*]. At (*a*) is more the sense of a **full stop**, or a shorter musical **period**, than a **phrase section** [*Absatz*], yet one could take it for a **colon**. At (*b*) the first **period** ends, and the musical thought is concluded through a cadence in the relative major in the nature of a full stop. Now the second part of a new period begins. At (**) is a caesura, which the progression, as two short clauses, requires. At (*c*) is a phrase section (**colon**), which combined with the previous caesura[26] makes a four bar phrase [*Vierer*]. Finally the complete sentence or the second period is ended through a cadence (full stop) on the tonic [d].

Example 8.3. Löhlein's minuet.

## D. *Koch*—Versuch einer Anleitung zur Composition (*1793*)

The *minuet*, which, above all other dance melodies, is taken up most often in our modern compositions, moves (1) in a brisk 3/4 meter, which can begin not only on the upbeat, but also with the downbeat. If it is arranged for dancing, then (2) its melodic sections [*melodischen Theile*] must have a rhythmical relation of an even number of measures; and (3) it must consist of two sections or reprises each containing no more than eight measures.

. . . This short composition [by Haydn] has the most perfect unity.[27] It consists of four melodic sections and contains only a single main idea, which, however, is modified

Example 8.4. Koch's example of a minuet.

in various ways. This is the first four-measure phrase [*Vierer*], which initially appears as a I-phrase [*Grundabsatz*], but immediately afterward has been repeated and changed into a closing phrase [*Schlußsatz*]. In the second section, the phrase which is a V-phrase [*Quintabsatz*] and with its repetition is the closing phrase is essentially the very same phrase; it has merely been given a different turn. The phrase has been played in contrary motion and through a passing modulation has been given more variety. From this it is apparent that a single phrase can indeed be sufficient for such a short composition if the composer knows how to give it a different direction and connection so that the whole, despite its unity, obtains nevertheless the necessary variety.[28]

## *1. Four- and Eight-Bar Structure: Period, Colon, and Semicolon*

As basic compositional models these minuets all observe the standard, defining characteristics of the dance form. And as one would expect of such verse-like subjects, their punctuation leaps off the printed page. Immediately obvious in all of the minuets is the sixteen-bar form divided into two eight-bar *periods*, which are in turn divided into four-bar groups.[29] Mattheson calls this four-bar structure, which one expects of good dances, the geometric proportion or the ratio of how many times an antecedent value contains or is contained by a consequent value (e.g., 16 bars containing 4 bars 4 times).[30] Koch agrees with Mattheson that sixteen bars is the ideal length for such compositions, adding that the four, four-bar phrases are not only the most common and useful, but also the most pleasing to one's sensibilities.[31]

Koch distinguishes among the four sections according to whether or not they cadence.[32] The two sections that contain cadences are the second and fourth (those ending in bars 8 and 16), dividing the whole into two small *periods* or sections. Koch's example of Haydn's minuet demonstrates the scenario where both of these cadences occur in the main key. Riepel's and Löhlein's, however, correspond to another example Koch gives where the first cadence, usually at the end of the second phrase again, closes in a subsidiary key. In the major mode, this secondary key is the major key of the fifth (the dominant) as in Riepel's minuet, and in minor it is either the minor key of the fifth or, as in Löhlein's example, the major key of the third.[33] The sense of closure created within the two-*period* form is therefore greater for the second *period*, cadencing as it does in the home key. Mattheson's minuet, however, functions slightly differently. It operates as a consolidated minuet/trio model with a *da capo* back to the first *period*. The first *period* appears much like the others, with a tonic cadence in bar 8, but the second *period* cadences on the relative major.

Koch further details the sections that do not end with cadences but merely with phrase endings, the phrases that conclude in bars 4 and 12. Four punctuation formulas are possible for these interior divisions, where either the subsequent cadences (as we discussed above) occur both in the main key, or where one is in a secondary key: (I,V), (I,I), (V,I), and (V,V). Haydn's, Riepel's, and Löhlein's all correspond to the first case, where the first melodic section closes with a phrase-ending on the triad of the main key (a I-phrase), and the third section with a phrase-ending on the triad of the fifth, (a V-phrase). Mattheson's is also perhaps closest to the I,V model, the first phrase closing on the tonic key, and the third phrase closing on the dominant of the second *period*'s key.

Thus the intermediary phrases of our minuet models are all quite similar and we shall look to Löhlein and Mattheson to describe the nature of their punctuation points. In both cases the first phrase of the first *period*, which closes on a tonic, receives a larger point of punctuation than the first phrase of the second *period*, which closes with a half cadence. If we were discussing two sentences of text, we might say that logically, the two, four-bar phrases of the second *period* are more connected than the two, four-bar phrases of the first *period*. Löhlein toys with the idea of placing a kind of imperfect, shorter period in the latter case, but since there are many possibilities in such situations (as we encountered in our discussion of recitative), he admits that it could also be considered as a colon. Mattheson scales down the relationship and gives bar 4 a colon, and the lesser close of the half cadence in bar 12 a semicolon.[34]

The colon, according to Mattheson, is used to present a cause, effect, narration, example, conclusion, and other similar effects. With the exception of the present case, Mattheson provides no musical examples of the colon (a separate chapter would be required in order to do so). But he does offer a few descriptions from which we can glean something of the content as it is portrayed through the melody.[35] If a *narration* is to follow, the melody should be indecisive. In the case of a *quotation* or otherwise thoughtful saying, then not only must the melody be interrupted, but the key must also be altered. In all of these cases, one can have a fairly clear sense of what is to follow, but cadences must be avoided before the narration or quotation is brought forward; in other words, the colon indicates an expectant pause. However, in the case of *conclusions* or *similes*, an expectant pause is not necessary; one can in fact have an anticipatory cadence, as we find in both Mattheson's and Löhlein's minuets.[36] Löhlein's cadence, for which he has given us both the melody and the bass, is quite strong—what Marpurg describes in his *Principes du clavecin* (1756) as a perfect cadence where the bass moves from the dominant to the tonic and the treble from the second or seventh degree to the tonic.[37] The cadence, however, is a feminine one, moving from a "good" strong beat to a "bad" weak beat. Mattheson's cadence is probably also a perfect one and even a masculine one, reaching the tonic harmony on the downbeat. The sense of complete closure is undermined by the movement of the treble from the third degree to the tonic on a weak beat. The pause should convey a true conclusion of thought, but with the sense that the speaker has more to say. I think the time should be taken from the third quarter note of the bar, perhaps as much as an eighth note, but always with care so as not to disrupt the overall verse-like structure of the dance. The second four bars should then also begin quite strongly, to emphasize the beginning of the new phrase and the introduction of additional information.

Unlike the colon, the semicolon (which divides Mattheson's second period) can occur before the grammatical sequence of words is completed, thus achieving a lesser degree of repose. The second period begins in the relative D major, after a cadence on the tonic B minor at the conclusion of the first period. The melody rises up in a stepwise pattern, descends and briefly rests on the dominant A in bar 12, and then begins a descending, leaping pattern for a full cadence in D major. Mattheson describes three types of semicolon (with musical examples): the *disjunctivis*, the *oppositis*, and the *relativis*. The *relativis* requires a similarity of sounds and intervals, which, while not adverse or contrary, still manage to retain their diversity and variation to some extent. The *oppositis*, on the other hand, demands contrasting sounds: pitches which reverse their course, and intervals which run against one another through abrupt alterations of the key, pulse, etc. The *disjunctivis* indicates a separation of ideas, but without real contrast or opposition. Koch's very similar phrases would have to fall in the category of the *relativis*, but perhaps Mattheson's semicolon is the *disjunctivis*, where ideas are differentiated from one another, but there is no opposition in them. In Mattheson's minuet paragraph then, we have an idea that is stated, and then concluded or similized, followed by two contrasting yet not oppositional aspects of the same or similar idea. In all of the minuets, we observe this same general structural form (though not necessarily the same interior content), a form that presents a very standardized minuet "layout" for these *colons, semicolons,* and *periods*, where at no point is the overall perception and clarity of the structure's symmetry disrupted.

## 2. *The Comma and the Two-Bar Dance Step*

We now come to the level of punctuation mark, the comma, which reflects the important basic unit of the minuet dance step—four small steps requiring six quarter-note beats to execute, the equivalent of two bars in 3/4 time, often notated as 6/4 in dance tutors. A great variety of minuet step-units evolved over time, particularly among the more elaborate dances choreographed for the theater, but among the ballroom dances, a few notable step patterns emerge. Two of the most popular patterns are provided in figure 8.3: the *pas de menuet à deux mouvements*, the steps falling on beats 1, 3, 4, and 5 of the two-bar unit, and the more difficult *pas de menuet à trois mouvements*, the steps falling on beats 1, 3, 4, and 6.[38]

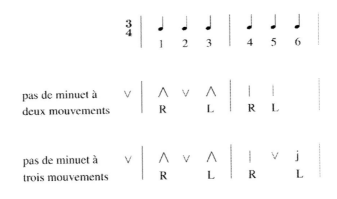

Figure 8.3. Two common minuet step patterns; table 1 in the article "Minuet" in *Grove Music Online*, edited by L. Macy (2005). Used by permission of Oxford University Press, Inc.

The sense of repose that the harmony creates to accommodate this two-bar level of the dance unit need not be very strong. For instance, in bar 2 of

Löhlein's minuet, we have a quick half cadence on the third beat, and in Mattheson's minuet, a simple progression in the opening two bars from tonic to subdominant. The sense of these "cadences" is reminiscent of Marpurg's suspended caesura in recitative which he used to designate a half comma. But unlike recitative, the caesuras of verse-like subjects, even important points like the semicolons, colons and periods described above, serve primarily to delineate the regularity and symmetry of the form. They need not be emphasized by so many rests and cadences, but only, as Mattheson states, through "certain natural vocal alterations." The French violin teacher and dancing master Pierre Dupont, in his *Principes de violon* of 1718 (2nd ed. 1740), provides a valuable example of how the gesture of this two-bar step pattern and rhetorical unit of a comma might be achieved. In the minuet example of figure 8.4, he directs the violinist with *ts*, indicating the French term *tirer* (to pull) and the equivalent of the down-bow, and *ps* for the term *pousser* (to push) and the equivalent of the up-bow, in order that these respectively heavy and light gestures should correspond to the strong and weak beats within the phrases.[39] Note the extra down-bow at the beginning of bar three (and by correlation in bars 6, 11, and 15) supporting the two-bar division within the four-bar phrase unit.

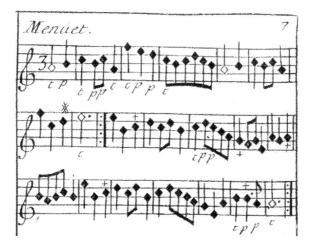

Figure 8.4. Bowing a minuet. From Pierre Dupont, *Principes de violon par demandes et par réponce*, 7.

These gestures of the violin bow, like a conductor's baton, beautifully depict the phrase structure of the minuet, mirroring the grace of the dance itself. One can perhaps imagine Dupont himself, with his dancing master's fiddle, easily marking out the two-bar units as he guides his students through the min-uet's paces. We want, therefore, to take a closer look at the subtleties of this string-playing mechanism—particularly as it reflects the French, and more specifically the Lullian style of playing.[40] The influence of French opera was strong in the prosperous, culturally rich, and cosmopolitan city of Hamburg, where Mattheson resided his entire life. Mattheson was enthralled by the glamor and magnificence of the Hamburg Opera, the most important opera center in Northern Europe in the early eighteenth century—its elaborate pro-ductions said to rival those of Paris itself. Here Mattheson would have encoun-tered the French-influenced works of Johann Georg Conradi and Johann Sigismund Kusser (who had studied under Lully in Paris), and very probably would have heard Lully's *Acis et Galetée* when it was performed in Hamburg in 1689.[41] In addition, the ballet masters employed by the Hamburg Opera in the late seventeenth and early eighteenth centuries were almost exclusively French.[42]

Georg Muffat, the German organist and composer who sought to introduce the French style of playing to Germany, gives us a sense of what was so distinc-tive about the performance of ballets in the French-Lullian manner. Muffat describes two primary characteristics: "It focuses on what is most pleasing to the ear, and it indicates the meter of the dance so exactly that one can immediately recognize the type of piece, and can feel the impulse to dance in one's heart and feet at the same time."[43] Part of the effect created by the French ensemble was the result of the rather rigidly prescribed set of bowing rules, a uniformity in practice not yet known, according to Muffat, in either Germany or Italy. In his *Florilegium secundum* (1698), Muffat provides an example (ex. 8.5) of a minuet in which he juxtaposes the more random German and Italian bowing practices with those of the Lullian style.

Those who indiscriminately play the first note of a measure up-bow are in direct con-flict with this way of playing. This often happens among the Germans and Italians in triple time, especially if the first note is shorter than those following. This opposite view and this transgression of the most important Lullian rule results in a great difference in the sound, both in the first notes and in those which follow.[44]

Example 8.5. The German/Italian versus Lullian Style of Bowing.

This "most important Lullian rule," or what has come to be called "the rule of the down-bow" for every first strong beat of the bar, can feel rather clumsy and cumbersome—especially on a modern violin with metal or metal-wound strings and a comparatively heavy Tourte bow (although with practice, it is definitely possible and can be highly effective). But with the lighter mechanism of a gut-strung violin and short dance bow, weighted primarily where it is held by the hand towards the frog, this gesture can be quite easy and natural, even subtle. As Muffat explains, "The greatest skill of the Lullists lies in the fact that even with so many repeated down-bows, nothing unpleasant is heard, but rather that the length of the lines is wonderfully bound up with a marvelous liveliness, an astonishing uniformity of beat with the variety of movements, and a sensitive beauty with lively playing."[45]

I can imagine, for instance, how the Minuet I from J. S. Bach's Suite in G Major for Unaccompanied Cello might benefit from such an observance through the bow of the two-bar gesture and its important strong and weak beats. Whether, in the eight-bar *period* of example 8.6, one should choose to use the upper Lullian-styled set of bowings or the lower more "indiscriminate" set, a small nuance or lifting of the bow between bars 2 and 3 and again between bars 6 and 7 would enable the punctuation to "leap off the printed page."[46] I believe the listener would then be able to hear the entire period structure together with its "sensitive beauty" and "liveliness" much more easily than he or she would through a performance that aims at "length of line" by means of legato eighths directed solely towards their cadential goal. Surely, too, there would be a strong visual component, as well as auditory, to a consistent correlation of strong beats with inherently strong gestures—which would be even more impressive when executed by a full string ensemble (like Lully's band) in an orchestral minuet. It is important to remember that instrumental musicians often played on stage, costumed and incorporated into the theatrical performance.[47]

As our excursion into violin bowing reveals, the rhythmic nature of the melody is a key component of the two-bar phrase segment. We will be looking more closely

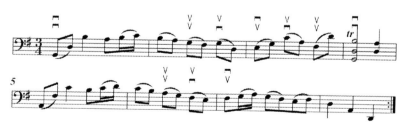

Example 8.6. J. S. Bach, Suite for Unaccompanied Violoncello in G Major, BWV1007, Minuet I, bars 1–8.

at the nature of musical *meter*, the placement of the feet, their short and long syllables, on either strong or weak beats within the two-bar dance unit. But for now, we want to consider how the feet are combined in the production (or absence) of comma-sized units. Riepel explains that the rhythmic grouping of the feet into two-bar units can be achieved either by their contrast to the bars that follow them, or by a contrasting relationship within the pairs themselves, always maintaining, of course, a natural progression from one to another. It is through an effort to explain this concept that Riepel introduces the three categories of a measure's rhythmic motion, which we discussed in chapter 4: it moves either perfectly (i.e., ♩ ♩♩♩ or ♩ ♫♫) or imperfectly (i.e., ♩ ♩ ♩. or ♩ ♩ ♪), or is dead (i.e., ♩ ♩). His criticism of his student's initial attempt at a minuet (rule no. 4) is that he has "not clearly enough separated the beginning, or the theme, into recognizable two- or four-measure segments," using "sometimes stationary measures, sometimes too many measures of stepwise running notes, where on the contrary, perfectly or imperfectly moving notes are required in a minuet until the cadence."[48] However, if we examine the final effort of Riepel's student, we observe that generally the two- and four-bar phrases exhibit a nice combination of imperfectly and perfectly moving measures.

But most minuets do not conform to these compositional rules, and the "rhythm" of their measures is not a reliable means of determining whether phrases divide into four-bar and, more particularly, the smaller two-bar groups. Riepel himself admits that "rules alone do not make the difference," in whether or not a minuet is composed effectively. For instance, the only measures in Bach's minuet (ex. 8.6) that are not perfectly moving, are bars 4 and conceivably bar 8, which I imagine to be a cadential, stationary one—the cello voice, conveying both harmony and melody, can create here the illusion of a "dead" dotted half note d at the same time that the bass outlines the typical descending fifth and octave. Mattheson draws our attention to what he calls the "arithmetic uniformity" of his sound feet. The first two feet, which are a combination of imperfectly and perfectly moving measures and are followed by a comma, are repeated again after the colon. However the feet that repeat in bars 9 and 10 and then in 11 and 12, also separated by a comma, are all perfectly moving (although not rhythmically uniform).[49]

Regarding the existence of two-bar units in the Haydn minuet example given by Koch, we refer to his own assertion that, "in the examples concerning these punctuation forms, the melodic sections were for the most part formed so that there were no perceptible incises. If, however, melodic sections which contain incises are occasionally used, they are either complete or incomplete incises." Koch adds that in the present case, we really deal only with complete incises of two measures, which stand in a punctuation relationship only with that segment immediately following and which makes the phrase complete.[50] The question is, do we perceive any of these two-bar incises in Haydn's minuet? Haydn uses perfectly moving measures of uniform and steady quarter notes. Riepel would no doubt consider this minuet to be one of the very effective livelier varieties whose melodic organization is nevertheless not as clear. And I think we can assume an overall brisker tempo for this minuet than for the others in the group, which would tend to lessen the effect of two-bar units.[51] Note also that the final four bars of Mattheson's second *period*, which are not divided by a comma, exhibit a similar uniform and perfectly moving rhythm. But at the same time, it is possible that the effect of Haydn's two-note slurs, which appear in the first two bars of each four-bar unit, serve to create something of the same lilting effect as would imperfectly moving measures of half notes and quarter notes. In the second *period*, the bass moves in just this way. One can perhaps insist on two-bar phrases, but this must be done in varying degrees according to the sense of the harmonic and melodic rhythms and contours. The minuet's lively character and the overall unity of the melodic material, which Koch himself describes, will also tend to temper the effect of the two-bar nuance within the four-bar phrase.

This last comment, that one could somehow *insist* on the two-bar punctuation unit, raises some important questions for the instrumental performer. For instance, in example 8.6, from Bach's First Cello Suite, are we insisting too much to claim two-bar incises within its lively and perfectly moving four-bar phrases? Or for that matter in the Menuetto (marked Allegro molto e vivace) from Beethoven's First Symphony (ex. 4.10)? Further, does such an insistence impose a kind of rigidity (however elegant and graceful) onto a composition which our composer/theorists would themselves describe as more "praiseworthy" than their "little" and "insignificant" compositional models? Naturally, the answers to these questions are not straightforward, for neither is freedom and complexity in phrase structure limited to minuets in the larger "for playing" category, nor are the more strictly composed minuets "for dancing" lacking in sophisticated, expressive details.

The minuet models presented by theorists tend to maintain, as we have remarked in the examples of Mattheson, Riepel, Löhlein, and Koch, a rigidity of even-numbered phrasing, and more particularly four- and eight-bar phrases. Mattheson firmly places his standard, sixteen-bar punctuated minuet in the "for dancing" category. Koch, too, is very clear that only in minuets not designed for a dance can the reprises be of arbitrary length (longer than eight measures) and the melodic sections of an uneven number of measures.[52] A similar phenomenon is observed among dance manuals: Daube, in his *Anleitung zur Erfindung der Melodie und ihrer Fortsetzung* (1797–98), insists that it is ignorance of the regular 2+2 and 4+4 phrasing that has produced so many undanceable minuets with irregular phrasing, such as those in symphonies; and Johann Georg Albrechtsberger quotes Riepel in declaring in 1790 that symmetrical phrasing must be adhered to only in dancing but is not appropriate in longer pieces such as arias, symphonies, trios, and quartets.[53] As Rebecca Harris-Warrick states in 2000, "*All* of the surviving minuet choreographies are set to music that not only has an even number of measures, but that usually has four-bar phrase lengths."[54]

However, outside the compositional models, there is much practical evidence to the contrary, among minuets for dancing as well as for playing. Harris-Warrick observes that the minuets of Lully, and indeed those by many composers of the seventeenth century, do not adhere to four- and eight-bar phrasing as the norm for dance music.[55] Tilden A. Russell, in his 1999 comparison between minuets danced at balls versus those learned in lessons—a repertoire found in almost 100 *recueils* of dance tunes published throughout the eighteenth century, observes that merely one collection in four contains only minuets in which the number of measures is divisible by four.[56] And Riepel (through the voice of his student describing dances in a beer hall) notes that while two, four-bar phrases will produce a cheerful, yet somewhat serious response from dancers, two three-bar phrases will cause everyone "to jump around as if they were crazy." More generally Riepel adds (this time in the voice the teacher) that the use of uneven phrases (not only three- and five-bar phrases, but also those of seven and nine) "procures a little trip into an uncharted land of musical delights, which would otherwise be impossible and must eternally banish one to a state of misery."[57]

The discrepancy between theory and practice may in part be explained by a certain degree of flexibility and fluidity in the relationship between the physical dance and the music. While minuets tend to consist of eight- and sixteen-bar phrases, the typical Z floor pattern, normally consisting of six minuet step-units, generally requires twelve bars of music to execute. This suggests, according to Meredith Little, "that a frequent lack of coincidence between music and dance was enjoyed." Although presumably (but not necessarily always) this "pleasant tension" would be resolved at the end of the 100 to 200 bars usually required for the minuet performance.[58] Also, a large part of the minuet's popularity and longevity as a social dance lies in its ability to absorb a great variety of steps into the basic six-beat pattern, and at the same time to adapt the same steps to a great variety of different airs. Giovanni-Andrea Gallini, director of dance at the Theatre Royal in the Haymarket and collaborator with Haydn in London, wrote in 1762: "If one tune does not please the performer, he may call for another; the minuet still remaining unalterable."[59] Harris-Warrick maintains that even among amateur dancers, the appearance of irregular phrase structures would not have been perceived as problematic. And certainly, in the case of minuets composed for the theater, the choreography would not have been restricted to the typical step variations performed at ballroom dances, but would have easily incorporated one-step units in order to adjust to phrases of odd numbers.[60]

We want, as Harris-Warrick advises us, to dispel the myth that dance steps force composers into a "metrical straitjacket," and also to note that irregularity in phrasing is only one of the many possible expressive devices of dance music—including harmony, melody, rhythm, meter, tempo, and key—just to name a few. Harris-Warrick argues that seventeenth-century dance music tends to have a much freer approach to phrase structure than the dance music of the eighteenth century, which having so clearly defined a metrical template, perceives any deviation from the underlying dance pattern as a deliberate distortion.[61] But it is not necessary to conclude from this that those minuets that do conform to the principles espoused by eighteenth-century theorists, function as "straitjackets" for their performers. We should also heed Hogwood's caution not to undervalue minuets that adhere to the more formal, standard constructions of the dance, in particular Haydn's early efforts at symphonic minuets.[62] I hope to convince the reader, as we look now more closely at the interior rhythms and metrical nature of Mattheson's minuet, that an observance of the two-bar dance unit—the little extra down-bows and "certain natural vocal alterations," so fundamental to the construction of the dance, ultimately expands rather than confines one's expressive range. Within what Hogwood terms this "nuance of pronunciation," we can begin to grasp the immense appeal and popularity of the very engaging, flexible, and attractive minuet form.

## 3. Meter: Good Beats and Bad Beats, Accent and Emphasis

We will begin our close look at the relationship between meter, punctuation, and the two-bar minuet dance unit by briefly revisiting the "problem" of the tie (or the hemiola formed by the tie) between bars 6 and 7 of Mattheson's minuet. As we suggested in chapter 5 (ex. 5.21, p. 146), the fact that the tie crosses the division of the comma does not in and of itself eliminate the point of punctuation. The *expression* of the notes has changed, that is, the downbeat of the melody may not receive its customary degree of stress in all parts, but this need not sound so very different from, for example, the eighth-note rests in bars 3 and 13 of Löhlein's minuet (ex. 8.3, p. 210). Furthermore, the bass can provide (in varying degrees according to the nature of the harmony) the necessary accent at the beginning of the phrase segment, thereby diminishing (again in varying degrees) the sense of a cross-rhythm or hemiola.

Others, however, have offered different interpretations. Lussy, writing in 1873, chooses simply to omit the tie, rewriting the first beat of bar 7 as an eighth note $b^1$ followed by an eighth note $c\sharp^2$.[63] Ernst Apfel, on the other hand, gives the tie his full consideration, perceiving it as an intrinsic part of the composition's "internal metrical problems." Apfel feels that the resulting hemiola isolates the final measure and working backwards, proposes the measure grouping shown in figure 8.5. Part of Apfel's analysis is based on the manner in which he interprets the strong and weak beats of Mattheson's poetic feet. Apfel feels that because the downbeat quarter note in Mattheson's minuet is weak, labeled ⌣, and the downbeat of bar 2 is strong, labeled —, then the rhythm of the entire minuet is based on a progression of weak bars followed by strong bars. He also notes that the rising emphasis of the melody, the leap up to the f♯$^1$ leading to the g$^1$ of bar 2, supports this relationship. Thus the closing measures of both *periods* and both the *colon* and *semicolon* are strong, and the beginning measures are weak (see fig. 8.6). Apfel admits that this interpretation is somewhat questionable, but nevertheless feels that it explains away most of the problems, comparing the task of musical metrics to the "squaring of a circle."[64]

$$\|: 1 + (3 \times 2) + 1 :\|(:) \ 1 + (3 \times 2) + 1 \ (:)\|d.c.$$

Figure 8.5. Measure grouping of Mattheson's minuet according to Ernst Apfel in "Ein Meneutt bei Johann Mattheson," p. 299.

$$\|: \smile — \smile — \smile — \smile — :\|(:) \ \smile — \smile — \smile — \smile — (:)\|d.c.$$

Figure 8.6. Weak/strong orientation of Mattheson's minuet according to Ernst Apfel in "Ein Meneutt bei Johann Mattheson," p. 299.

One can certainly hear Mattheson's minuet with this tendency. In fact it has all the hallmarks of modern phrasing practice, where figurations have the sense of leading forward from one point of stress to the next in an upbeat formation. One could also imagine a similar rendition of the minuet from Bach's First Cello Suite (ex. 8.6), the opening eighths acting as pickups to the b's of beat 2 and bar 2. But at the same time, such an interpretation, where the first measures function as upbeats to the stronger second measures, suggests a complete controversion of the minuet's rhythm—a phrasing that overrides all of Mattheson's punctuation marks and contradicts everything we have come to understand about the nature of the dance and its two-bar unit. As represented in the chart of dance steps (fig. 8.3), the dancer makes a plié on the upbeat, rising to a straightened position on the ball of the foot with the arrival of the downbeat. In addition, remember that the dancers were thinking in measures twice as long as those in the music—6/4 rather than 3/4. Dancing masters would even beat the time of the minuet in two large beats: a downward motion of the arm for the first "good" measure, and an upward one for the following "bad" or "false" measure. As the French musician and theorist Loulié explains in 1696, the reason for using 6/4 instead of two bars of 3/4 "is because in 3/4 the good beat is not distinguished from the false beat; and it is for this reason that dancers beat the Minuet in 6/4 although it is notated in 3/4."[65] The Lullian bowing described earlier also supports this sense of a strong opening downbeat. Muffat complains specifically about the use of up-bows in cases where the "first note is shorter than those following," illustrating in example 8.5 the same quarter-note–half-note rhythmic configuration under discussion. Certainly a skilled player (on either Baroque or modern equipment) could disguise the "weak" effect of beginning with an up-bow, but then we lose that sense of gestural playing which, as Muffat claims, seems to "indicate the meter of the dance so exactly."

Although no commentary contemporary to Mattheson's minuet seems to suggest an interpretation of the opening measure as "weak," still there is considerable evidence even in the eighteenth century for a need to justify such a metrical placement of short and long notes on respectively strong and weak beats. What is fascinating here is not the rather ordinary rhythmic pattern and its placement, but the evident need on the part of eighteenth-century musicians to explain, prescribe, and regulate every expressive element within their domain. The result is the adaptation of complex classical concepts of rhythm and meter, and particularly the much-debated accentual and/or quantitative nature of poetic feet. As we discussed in the section "Rhythm and Meter" in chapter 3, p. 75, Mattheson cleverly sidesteps the problematic issue by invoking both qualities in his discussion of "sound feet" at different times and for different purposes. Thus by referring only to the quantitative quality of an *iamb*, consisting of "one short and one long sound," he can in the case of dance composition, justify its setting contrary to the eighteenth-century accentual rules of meter, with the short syllable on the strong downbeat and the long syllable on the weak second and third beats. And there can be no doubt that Mattheson considers the opening foot of his minuet to be an iamb. He states, and illustrates explicitly in example 8.7, that the iamb, its character "moderately gay, not hasty or running," and also "quite tender with a noble simplicity," belongs to "true minuets and their composition, as has been done sensibly by Lully."[66]

Menuet

Example 8.7. Use of the iamb in minuets. From Mattheson, *Der vollkommene Capellmeister*, p. 165.

Riepel, on the other hand, presents a very different explanation of how a short syllable followed by a long syllable can be so metrically placed on a strong downbeat. Furthermore, as becomes apparent in the following lesson on prosody (presented within the context of recitative), this type of pattern can never be considered an iamb, but instead a kind of varied trochee: a long short pattern, or a half note followed by a quarter note.[67] The teacher begins with example 8.8, where the first syllables of *Lebe* and *alle* are both long and therefore placed in an accented position.

Example 8.8

He then demonstrates to his student in example 8.9 how the short second syllables of the above *trochees* can be lengthened, a freedom permitted in all good
compositions.

Example 8.9

The student remarks that it may be very well for a composer to knowingly take
such liberties, but wouldn't the listener then perceive the new rhythm as an
iamb? But the teacher is quick to correct this misconception. An iamb could
never be set in this way, with the accented syllable in an unaccented position. An
iamb must be set as in example 8.10.

Example 8.10

The teacher adds that an iambic setting does not suit the text of example 8.10.
An iambic setting requires an iambic text, where the second syllable receives the
stress, as in example 8.11.

Example 8.11

Such a setting is so clearly correct, the teacher continues, that iambs set otherwise in song, as in the following example 8.12, where the stressed syllable is
placed within the measure, really "gets one's hackles up."

Example 8.12

The student is in full agreement (and note the abundant use of
punctuation with which his zeal is expressed). "How abominable! — Even

though the long notes occur on long syllables, etc. Oh miracle of harmonious nature! — — Thesis and Arsis have their effect, each for itself! — And how — — — —"

Koch would, I imagine, offer a different explanation to either proposed by Mattheson or Riepel when the melody is in this way varied or decorated, or "as the meter in music possesses something exclusively its own—something not known in poetry" (see p. 24). In a case like this, the accompanying voices would then take over the role of preserving the sense of metrical stress. We have already observed how this rule can affect the treatment of Mattheson's tie (or the effect of a hemiola) in bars 6 and 7. But also in the case of his supposedly "displaced" iamb, the motion of the bass can serve to reinforce the sense of a strong opening down beat. Ernst Wilhelm Wolf addresses the issue in 1785 by making a distinction between the appearance of a note versus its actual role, also noting (as Riepel's student does in ex. 8.9) the difficulty in identifying these accents for noncomposers:

A strong note can sometimes be very short without losing its strong accent. Likewise, a weak note can be longer and still receive a weak accent. In such cases we say that the strong notes are internally long [*innerlich lang*] and externally short [*ausserlich kurz*], and that the weak notes are internally short and externally long. (In vocal composition much depends upon this distinction, and therefore many people who are not themselves composers can easily misjudge the degree of accent.)[68]

Another aspect of our discussion, particular to Mattheson's minuet, is the traditional use of the short-long iambic rhythm in the earliest forms of the French dance. This is particularly in combination with, as Mattheson states (and demonstrates in ex. 8.7), the contrasting trochee—the latter frequently following the former. Mattheson adds that the trochee is often varied, and I think this is essentially what we have here in the second measure of his punctuated minuet.[69] As depicted in example 8.13, the iamb/trochee (¾ ♪♩ | ♩♪) is in fact the rhythm of the earliest known minuet step, the music (for oboe band) and choreography surviving from the comic *mascarade, Le mariage de la grosse Cathos* (1688) by André Philidor *l'aîné*.[70] The step pattern of this minuet, preserved in a system of notation invented by Jean Favier, is completely different, in both execution and timing, from all versions of the step-unit preserved in the more common Feuillet notation of the eighteenth century. The step-unit, which would have been used exclusively for the first 24 bars of the minuet (performed with the form of AABBAABB), does bear a superficial resemblance to Feuillet's *minuet step of three movements*. It consists of the standard two-bar unit, the music in 3/4 and the dance in 6/4, and contains four changes of weight with three bends and rises (see fig. 8.3). However, as described by Harriss-Warrick and Marsh, "the timing of Favier's *pas de menuet*—its quick first and last *demi-coupés* contrasting with the deliberate

Example 8.13. André Philidor *l'aîné, Le mariage de la grosse Cathos*, Act 5, Menuet.

quality of the central *mouvement*—lends a completely different character to the step-unit."[71]

Rhythm and gesture play such an important role in the punctuation of dances that it is worth considering the frequency of use for this late seventeenth-century minuet step of Favier's. Its basic rhythmic pattern appeared frequently among the minuets of Lully's (Mattheson's stated authority on minuets) *tragédies en musique*—for instance, at the end of the fourth act in *Belleraphon*, the Troupe d'Astrée dansante from *Phaéton*, and in the flute duet at the end of act 4 in *Atys*. The pattern was also adopted by Keiser, Kusser's successor at the Hamburg Opera, whom Mattheson praised as "the greatest opera composer in the world."[72] Note how, in example 8.14, from the minuet at the end of the second act in Keiser's *La forza della virtù* (first performed in 1700), the long-short syllables of the trochee are often varied.[73] The text that accompanies the first appearance of the minuet tune, supports the idea of a strong opening downbeat in spite of the iambic rhythm in the music: *Meine Krönung zu beehren.*

**Menuet**

Example 8.14. Reinhard Keiser, Minuet from *La forza della virtù*, end of Act 2, bars 1–8.

The pattern appeared not only in the works described above, but also in other minuets by Philidor, Lalande, Campra, Jean-Philippe Rameau, Jean-François Dandrieu, Gaspard Le Roux, Henry Purcell (in the chorus of "Fear no danger" from *Dido and Aeneas*), J. S. Bach, and of course, Mattheson—just to name a few.[74] Did Mattheson see this minuet step danced, or perhaps even dance it himself? We know that Mattheson's parents, hoping their son would one day achieve a position among Hamburg society (as an aspiring *honnête homme*), made the fashionable accomplishment of dancing a part of his formal education.[75] And given Mattheson's own statement regarding the importance of knowing every step, turn, and leap of the feet in dance, it is very possible that he imagined the Favier step incorporated into his own punctuated minuet. Or perhaps the earlier Favier minuet steps were completely supplanted by those preserved in eighteenth-century Feuillet notation—the characteristic short-long-long-short rhythm continuing to be used while the step which accompanied it had ceased to be performed.[76] Either way, eighteenth-century composers of minuets inherited the earlier French rhythmic pattern, which had then somehow to conform to important contemporary German theories (adapted from ancient Greek and Latin principles) regarding prosody and the metrical placement of poetic feet. The result is the foregoing rather cumbersome and intricate explanations of theorists like Mattheson, Riepel, and Koch. But in addition to revealing the rigor with which these eighteenth-century theorists pursued their linguistic analogies, we are also left with a very vivid sense, founded in the movements of dance, of the important two-bar minuet phrase unit. More particularly, we understand the very distinctive gestural impulse lent by the dance's historically charactaristic iamb/trochee rhythm with its associated quick first and last demi-coupés.

Another key feature of Mattheson's minuet and the iamb/trochee rhythmic pattern involves the punctuation-related issue of rhetorical accent and emphasis. As we explained earlier, grammatical accents are those which mark the "good" beats and "bad" beats of the bar. The expressive, rhetorical accents, on the other hand, are what Mattheson refers to as *emphases*. Emphases can occur on any note and correspond to places of dissonance or rhythmic syncopation—especially raised notes though also sometimes lowered notes; they are generally not subjected to any kind of regularity, taking possession of a single note or several consecutive notes, long notes or short notes, and occurring on both accented and unaccented beats.[77] Now perhaps it is because Mattheson is careless and unclear in the number of repeats he requires in his minuet, and appears to indicate only two asterisks in the version of the minuet in *Der Vollkommene Capellmeister* (fig. 8.2). Or perhaps it is because these two asterisks appear on the bar lines while the third asterisk (which resembles more of a small, smudged dot as it appears in the version in *Kern melodischer Wissenschafft*—see fig. 8.1) seems to fall on the third beat of bar 11. But interpretations of the "threefold emphasis indicated by so many asterisks" vary considerably.

Some theorists choose to avoid the issue entirely: Unger, writing in 1969, omits all symbols relating to both poetic feet and the "threefold emphasis," and Carl Dalhaus, in his article "Melodie" in the second edition of *Die Musik in Geschichte und Gegenwart*, presents only the first *period* of the minuet, also leaving out both asterisks. Lussy, however, claims that the asterisks in the first and fifth measure, which he places directly under the two f♯$^2$s, indicate the triple emphasis. And he makes a special point at the end of his discussion of the minuet to call our attention to Mattheson's use of the term *emphasis* (*accent pathétique*), describing it as "an accented note foreign to the time and rhythm," and occurring at the syncopated f♯$^2$ of the first bar, at the adjacent high notes g$^2$–f♯$^2$–g$^2$ in bar 2, and again at the adjacent diminished seventh interval in bar 6 between g$^2$ and a♯$^1$. He makes no mention of the e$^2$ in bar 11. In 1917 Wiehmayer seems to have taken his cue from Mattheson's statement that "as the principal rule, such emphasis would almost always require a raising, and in fact a perceptible though not large raising . . . for often a semitone can accomplish it best."[78] Wiehmayer places the asterisks on the dotted quarter note g$^2$s of bars 2 and 6, half steps away from the preceding f♯$^2$.[79] The emphasis in bar 11 is then comfortably expressive of the same general concept. Apfel also suggests that this might be the proper interpretation.

　　Both of these latter interpretations are consistent with Mattheson's definition of emphasis as described above. Indeed, in many of the minuets that employ the iamb/trochee rhythmic pattern, one encounters small accentual turns and trills on either one or the other of these half notes (as we see in Mattheson's quantitative illustration of the iamb in example 3.5). We might also bring in the terminology of *agogic* accents here, coined by Riemann in 1884 and used to describe emphases created through duration rather than dynamics or metrical position. The concept of agogic accentuation and accent is also closely linked to that of *tempo rubato*, the deliberate lengthening of certain notes (for example the e$^2$ in bar 11) for expressive reasons, but without disrupting the overall sense of the meter.[80]

　　Part of the confusion over where to place the points of emphasis is similar to the difficulty encountered with Koch's use of his "distinctive signs" (△ and □) which we discussed in chapter 4. Sometimes the symbols of punctuation are placed on the main beat of the caesura gesture, sometimes on the final note, and sometimes unclearly straddling a number of notes. For this reason, I have also included facsimile copies of Mattheson's minuet in figures 8.1 and 8.2. As the minuet appears in *Kern melodischer Wissenschafft*, we see that not only the third asterisk falls on the third beat, but also the semicolon in bar 12, which in *Der vollkommene Capellmeister* falls on the bar line.[81] Perhaps it is simply a question of typesetting and both of these symbols should in fact fall on the bar line (as I have illustrated them in ex. 8.1).[82] And in a way, a placement of the symbols on the third beats is not so very different from a placement on the bar line; the appearance of Löhlein's internal punctuation marks on third beats has not been problematic. We have decided that in expressing punctuation signs in a verse-like minuet, the time should be taken from the concluding notes of the bar, without disrupting the overall meter, and marking the beginning of the next phrase with an accent appropriate to its place within the larger period structure (according to Türk's concept of metrical hierarchy). A point of emphasis also occurring at the conclusion of the bar (whether it is placed under the final beat or the bar line) might be interpreted similarly. In a sense this allows us to subscribe to both of the above theories of emphasis concerning the $f\sharp^2$ and $g^2$. Both the concluding note of the first bar and the way in which the following bar is begun would be affected. In this way the asterisk points to the very special rhythmic and gestural relationship between the contrasting iamb and trochee, and also to the point of expectation after the $e^2$ in bar 11 before the descending, concluding phrase of bars 13–16. Little and Jenne also note the potentially expressive relationship between the poetic feet and the two-bar dance unit: "There are many possibilities of the way in which the four steps are timed with the six beats producing numerous counter rhythms between dance and music, a relationship from which the dance derives enormous strength."[83] Mattheson concurs, explaining that emphasis "points toward the emotion and illuminates the sense or meaning of the performance."[84]

Where then does this discussion of the relationship between poetic feet and meter, and grammatical and rhetorical accent and emphasis bring us? On the grammatical level there can be no doubt that we have a strong opening bar with a strong downbeat, followed by a weaker bar with a weaker down beat. However, overlaying this, the rhetorical emphasis of the syncopated and contrasting rhythms, together with their heightened pitch, leads us forward, in intensity of expression and also probably in increasing dynamics, towards the second bar. However, after the comma in bar 2, the grammatical accents reassert themselves, with the beginning tone $c\sharp^2$ receiving a slightly lesser accent than its counterpart in the first bar, and the downbeat of bar 4 receiving an even lesser one. The expressive intensity is relaxed, and in "moderate cheerfulness" we cadence at the colon. The phrase is then repeated with a slight variation through the introduction of the $a\sharp^1$ and a stronger close at the first full stop. Similarly bar 9 initially asserts its proper, dancing grammatical accents, but above this, through its rising line, maintains a sense of forward momentum with the $e^2$ in bar 11 as the greatest point of anticipation. Bar 12 then expresses the customary downward inflexion of the semicolon, after which the regular grammatical accents resurface for the remaining, lively phrase of four *vollkommen*, perfectly moving bars. As Koch states, the expressive accents, the emphases, are more prominent than the grammatical, which are generally part of the background, and thus we have our multitiered analysis.[85]

The result is not as rigid as either a strict strong/weak or weak/strong orientation and allows us to perceive the many layers of grammatical and rhetorical punctuation, as I think Mattheson intends we should. The expressive emphases do not override the underlying regularity of the periodic structure, and neither do their metrical accents prevent seemingly contrasting rhythmic and melodic tendencies from occurring. These principles apply not only to academic, compositional models, but also to well-known, highly crafted minuets of the standard literature—like the minuets and trios of examples 4.10, 5.16, 5.22, 6.10, and 8.6 by Beethoven, Bach, and Mozart. The many rhythmical and metrical elements are all allowed to operate at their own level. The four- and especially two-bar nuances of the basic minuet punctuation form become the backdrop by which we can appreciate not only the deviations from the standard format, but also the dance's fundamental expressive potential and the immense appeal it held for both composers and performers in the eighteenth century. As we learned from Parkes, the role of punctuation in transmitting semantic intent is far greater for the verse-like forms than those of prose. The tools of punctuation, layout, and rhyme become the primary features of a very densely packed and concise style of language. It becomes the performer's responsibility to aurally and visually call attention to the poetic form of the dance, thereby arousing the listener's expectations and bringing to their attention the expressive details within.

# Afterword

I find, in the end, that I come to the same general conclusion that eighteenth-century composers, theorists, and performers did themselves: except for didactic purposes, it is not, after all, desirable to insert directly into musical notation the punctuation marks of language; these are, in effect, already implicit in the notation. The more specificity and detail we demand from our notation, the less helpful it becomes, rigidly prescribing that which is animate and spontaneous, and sometimes so subtle and intangible that any attempt at written expression renders it essentially ineffectual. Ironically, it is our arrival at such a seemingly negative conclusion regarding the usefulness of our analogy, which is the great lesson that the concept of musical punctuation has been able to teach us.

The concept of musical punctuation, like punctuation itself, is inextricably bound up with the history of the written process. The great pains we have taken to learn to read our musical notation—to rediscover its implicit conventions—has enabled us to identify the many rhythmic, metric, accentual, affective, melodic, and harmonic clues of musical punctuation. These indicators, in combination with a composition's expressive dynamic and articulative information, give us real insight (if not the precise semantic content) into where the pauses of punctuation occur, the nature of the material they divide, and where they fall on the scale from scarcely perceptible to highly conspicuous. We have observed that very often long musical lines are achieved not by maintaining a continuously sustained sound, always leading forward over bar lines toward the resolution of dissonant harmonies, but instead by creating a sense of prolonged expectation through the skillful manipulation and punctuation of multiple short phrases, which frequently stop on the dominant and leading-tone structures (in essence, the way eighteenth-century sentences are themselves constructed).

The conventions of eighteenth-century notation teach us not only about the kind of *voice* we should use in executing the pauses of musical punctuation, but also their accompanying *gestures*: the elegant stance of the head and body and becoming attitude at one's instrument; the changes in countenance demanded by frequent shifts in *affect*, so characteristic among eighteenth-century compositions; and the all-important movements of the arms and hands (the sweep of the violinist's bow, the pianist's arm poised to strike the keys). Thus the important physical mechanics of sound production and the acquisition of technical facility in singing and playing must also be carefully integrated, even choreographed, according to a composition's expressive content and structure: minuets must dance in two-bar step-units, laments must droop and weep, impassioned speech must be accompanied by emphatic and theatrical gestures, etc.

However, our own efforts to rediscover the punctuation points embedded in eighteenth-century musical notation merely reflect the even greater struggle faced by eighteenth-century musicians (and their linguistic counterparts) with the recognition of punctuation's crucial role in controlling what had come to be regarded as an all-too-human and fallible language. Eighteenth-century musicians felt an overwhelming need to understand fully the diverse stylistic, logical, grammatical, and rhetorical components of musical punctuation, upon which (according to the various philosophical, scientific, political, and social values of Enlightenment thought) correct and persuasive discourse depended. The need to prescribe systematically the usage of each and every comma, colon, and period, while maintaining all the while an enormous respect for the living language—as it is conversed and communicated among members of an ensemble and an assembled audience. This, I believe, is the most important aspect of the present study for the reader to retain: an understanding of the close, intimate relationship between speaker and text, performer and score, that eighteenth-century musicians sought to achieve. Their very detailed analyses of musical punctuation (often carried out at the level of one- and two-bar phrase units, individual rhythmic gestures, and points of emphasis) are always conceived with an expressive communicative intent. Performance, far from being divorced from the analytic process, is in fact its driving force. "We must," in the words of Elocutionist Thomas Sheridan, "make the living language, as it ought to be, our first object of attention; and consider the written one, as it should be, only in a secondary light."

The best performances of eighteenth-century music, to my mind, are achieved by instrumentalists (and singers) who are able to convey both a deep recognition and an understanding of the punctuation-related structures and patterns imbedded in musical notation, but who are also continually engaged with the analytic and interpretive process. They strive moment by moment, gesture by gesture, always according to the context of the performance, to bring the musical language alive with its *resting points of the spirit* —to persuade, to excite, to soothe, to touch—in short, to move the minds, appetites, and wills of women and men.

# Appendix A

# *Translation of Marpurg's Lessons on Musical Punctuation, from His* Kritische Briefe über die Tonkunst, *vol. 2*

**Letter CIX**
**Twelfth Installment of the Lessons on Recitative.**
Berlin, September 4, 1762.

**Part Two.**
**On Musical Punctuation in General.**[1]

### §. 78.

Before we take up the musical expression of the various grammatical and rhetorical punctuation marks, and give to each part of speech its appropriate formula of division, we want first, to become generally acquainted with punctuation marks in music.

### §. 79.

In **the arioso style** one encounters 1) full cadences; 2) half cadences; 3) rhythmic; and 4) suspended breaks [*schwebende Absätze*]. Just as full cadences are more perfect than the half: so also are those rhythmic breaks, which are derived from the full cadence, more complete than those which originate from the half; further, among suspended breaks, those which involve consonant intervals are more complete than those which involve dissonant intervals.

### §. 80.

In **the recitative style** one encounters 1) full cadences; 2) elliptical or shortened full cadences; 3) regular breaks [*ordentliche Absätze*],[2] and 4) suspended breaks [*schwebende Absätze*].[3] The mechanical nature of these formulas of division will be shown presently.

§. 81.

Provisionally it is to be noted that, since expression imitates natural speech in recitative and is not actually to be sung, one does not then have the same freedom in this style, as in arioso, to conclude a word with a feminine ending in a masculine manner; rather, one must treat masculine endings as masculine and feminine endings as feminine. The following examples err in this regard:

§. 82.

One observes in the second example how the vocal part ends with the same closing formula as the bass. This was formerly very fashionable in bass recitatives, and still currently appears in French recitative. But since Italian recitative requires one manner of singing, whether for treble, alto, tenor, or bass, it does not at all tolerate this and similar kinds of bass formulas.

## First.
## On Full Cadences in Recitative.

§. 83.

The bass in the full cadence, generally prepared by the fourth or the sixth of the closing tone [tonic], progresses from the dominant to the closing tone.[4] While in proper song feminine cadences are allowed only in certain cases: in recitative they are given preference over the masculine, especially at the end of the recitative. It would do well that our poets always end their recitatives with a feminine rhyme as the Italians do. Otherwise a composer can not use feminine cadences.

### (a) Example of feminine cadences.

Among these cadences are those with a falling fourth, as in the four first numbers, [which are] more customary at the end of recitatives in the secular style than those with a repeated note, as in the fifth number.

### (b) Example of masculine cadences.

The best of these masculine cadences is that of the first number.

§. 84.

Regarding the **manner of notating** the feminine cadence with its falling fourth, it is to be noted that the last two notes are written by certain composers differently than they are sung, for example,

This notational style is without doubt reprehensible, because one should write in a natural way and for no other purpose than as one sings; and because many singers, lacking sufficient insight, can become confused and led astray, especially in the middle of a recitative.

§. 85.

Further some are accustomed to anticipate the next to last bass note of the cadence, namely the dominant, without the insertion of a pause, as in the following manner:

Hence, this notational style is of no use, because the progression of the harmony cannot be explained logically in this manner, as will become evident in the following §; and in addition to these faults, are yet two others in the second number, namely **first**, that the bass does not receive its proper incise [*Einschnitt*];[5] (for the final note c must fall not on a bad, but on a good beat;) and **second**, that a longer note is tied to a smaller note. This kind of tie belongs only between a half and a whole note, but not between a quarter and a half note. I know that many great composers have themselves made this mistake. But mistakes remain mistakes, wherever they are found. In general, this mistake can be put down to carelessness, because one always saves the recitative, as a supposed trifle, to the last when arias, choruses, etc., and everything else are already finished. Then all becomes a rush, and the recitative is just hurriedly scrawled without the slightest consideration. Yet experience teaches us that very many composers set quite pretty choruses and arias, etc., but cannot set a single recitative correctly in all its parts: the recitative is therefore not such a trifle that it can be written half asleep—. As in No. 2 with the incise of the bass, mistakes occur in the following example in the upper and lower voices:

### §. 86.

I come now to the **harmony** of full cadences. What I have to mention in this regard concerns the **antepenultimate of the cadence,** or the note which pre-cedes the dominant, especially where the fourth of the closing note has above it not the perfect triad but the chord of the second [*Secundenaccord*] with the aug-mented fourth, for example.[6]

Everybody knows that after the harmony of the augmented fourth, the bass must descend. Since the bass rises here, so the question arises as to how such a liberty can be explained. To progress from the chord of the second to the chord of the domi-nant, which can be the perfect triad as well as the seventh chord, is not only wrong, but in certain positions of the right hand can lead to the error of fifths and octaves, if the perfect triad precedes the chord of the second over the same bass note.

### §. 87.

A few composers solve the problem by using the six-four chord instead of the chord of the second over the note of the fourth in question; at the rest play the seventh and fifth of this chord and proceed afterward as:

**Singstimme.**

**Generalbaß.**

I wish to make no objection against this procedure in the case where the six-four chord applies. But what if this is not possible and the chord of the second must be used? There is no other solution than to employ the ellipsis where the pause in the bass occurs, and to strike without the bass the chord of the sixth [*Sextenaccord*] at the closing tones of the vocal part, as in No. (a).[7] One can recognize that this explanation is not incorrect, because some conscientious composers even show the chord of the sixth together with the bass properly on paper, as one sees in No. (b). This manner of notation in the second number, even though it is regular, appears nevertheless to me not exemplary, because it causes the inexperienced thorough-bass player to strike the bass note of the chord of the sixth, in this case e, which should not in fact be struck. But in order nevertheless to show the chord of the sixth, which should be made **with the three voices in the right hand alone**, I consider there to be no better method, than to mark the chosen bass note with a place marker [*Custode*] and to set the figure 6 under the pause, as in No. (c).

**Singstimme.** (a)      (b)      (c)

**Generalbaß.**

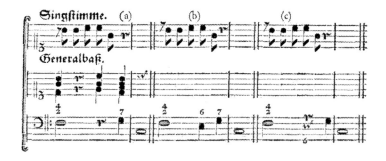

§. 88.

Generally speaking, the **use** of full cadences occurs both in the course of and at the end of a recitative. However, they should not be used in the middle of a recitative, particularly a short one, without good cause, as has occurred in the past.

## Second.
## On Elliptical Cadences in Recitative.

### §. 89.

The **elliptical cadence** is a shortened full cadence, in which one leaves out the closing tone and proceeds immediately after the dominant to another key, for example.

### §. 90.

In these elliptical cadences, the dominant often becomes confused with the fourth of the key, as:

and so on.

### §. 91.

The elliptical cadences in recitative are not at all to be confused with the interrupted cadences of the arioso style, for they have the value of complete cadences even though they can occasionally be used instead of the regular break. Moreover it is easily perceived that they are nowhere to be found but in the middle of a recitative.

## Letter CX
## Thirteenth Installment of the Lessons on Recitative.
### Berlin, September 11, 1762.

## Third.
## On Regular Breaks or Quasi-closes in Recitative.[8]

§. 92.

The **regular breaks** or **quasi-closes** of recitative are both masculine and feminine. They consist of a succession of two harmonies, of which the first can be
either dissonant or consonant. The last however, with whose entry the quasi-
close is made, must be consonant. Here are a few formulas which must be considered above all in terms of the progression of the bass and the underlying
harmony, since the singing voice can be formed in many ways according to the
nature of the declamation, the number of the words, and other circumstances.
**Yet the close must always occur with falling notes**, except in certain cases which
will be explained below that require the opposite, namely **rising notes**. Finally,
all formulas occur in both major and minor modes, **except those which are for
minor modes alone**, but to save space they will appear here in only a single
mode. These formulas originate only in the **following four ways:**

1) **concerning the last two chords belonging to the full cadence;** namely the
   dominant chord, which can be both the perfect triad as well as the seventh
   chord, and the chord on the final note, for example in C major g b d f and
   c e g; and in A minor from e g♯ b d and a c e. The **last note** of a quasi-close
   of this type is always the final tone or the mediant in both the bass and the
   melody, as illustrated in the following example.

and so on.

All these formulas work equally well for both minor as well as major keys. If one wishes a masculine cadence, the last melody note is left out.

2) **concerning the diminished seventh chord on the leading tone in the minor key, and the triad of the final tone.** The last note again is always a final or a mediant, as:

These formulas occur only in minor modes.

3) **concerning the two chords, which in other musical styles form half cadences.** Here the last bass note is either a dominant, as in the first four numbers; or a mediant, as in the fifth number.

Just as the first four formulas find their proper arrangement in major modes, so the last one does in minor.

4) **concerning both chords, which in the arioso style form an interrupted cadence from the dominant to the sixth**, as:

§. 93.

Among these **four kinds** of quasi-closes, **the first two**, namely the one which is derived from the full cadence, and next, the one where the penultimate chord is a diminished seventh, are the **most complete**. The last two are **less complete**. Moreover, all formulas which do not agree with one or another of these four types in terms of the progression and nature of the harmony, cannot be quasi-closes.

**Fourth.**
**On Suspended Breaks.**

§. 94.

**Suspended breaks,** which can be either masculine or feminine, consist only in a simple incise in the melody either over a static bass; or it changes together with the bass. We have therefore **two kinds** of suspended breaks.

**1) Example of the first kind.**

and so on.

One observes in the preceding examples, α) that in terms of the underlying harmony, the suspended breaks of this kind can be **consonant** and **dissonant**; β) that they can both occur with only one note or a repeated note, as well as with a leap of a third, fourth, or fifth; η) that these leaps can be **falling** as well as **rising**. The difference between rising and falling, and consonant and dissonant breaks will be explained in course.

## 2) Example of the second kind.

and on and on.

One will gather from the preceding examples, which are possible in different styles, 1) that these suspended breaks with two-fold harmonies can be both **consonant** and **dissonant** relative to the final chord and 2) that they can be made with both a **rising** and a **falling** melody.

## Part Three.
## On the Expression of the Grammatical and Rhetorical
## Punctuation Marks in Recitative.

### §. 95.

It is a mistake some musicians make that all the different parts of speech can always be distinguished either **through the motion of the bass alone** or **through the formulas of the melody alone.** As long as our music is conceived harmonically, this will be impossible. As evidence I will provide only a pair of examples.

Here the melodic formulas are all the same. However the first example contains a full cadence, the second a quasi-close, and the third only a suspended break.

The progression and harmony of the bass is the same in both numbers. But anyone who notes that the melody falls in the fourth number and instead rises in the fifth, will easily perceive that just as both tone formulas cannot express the same thing, neither can the rise and fall of the voice in natural speech be used towards the same end.

§. 96.

What follows from all this? This, that in order to give the punctuation marks their proper musical characteristics, one must pay attention to both the bass and the singing voice, as well as to the harmony and the melody.

§. 97.

If one examines the inner value of grammatical punctuation marks, one finds they can be sorted into the three following,

1) into the proper full stop;[9]
2) into the improper full stop. The colon belongs here, together with the semicolon, and in certain cases the full comma; and
3) into the half comma.

§. 98.

Similarly we employ no more than three punctuation formulas in musical recitative. In fact there are basically no more than three such formulas, namely

1) the **cadence**, though its species is either **full** or **elliptic**;
2) the **quasi-close**, whose strength is either **more** or **less** complete; and
3) the **suspended break**, whose strength and type is either **consonant** or **dissonant**, and is produced with either a **static** or **altered** bass, likewise either **rising** or **falling**.

**Letter CXI**
**Fourteenth Installment of the Lessons on Recitative.**
Berlin, September 18, 1762.

§. 99.

In consequence of the preceding explanations, the lessons on grammatical punctuation and their musical expression can be briefly recounted in the following manner:

1) Where there is a complete thought or period, there belongs a **full stop**.
2) But the speech is either continued from the same matter or not.
   α) In the latter case, where a **full stop** is **proper** or **complete**, the **cadence** is used in the composition of recitative.
   β) In the first case where the **full stop** is **improper** or **half**, a **quasi-close** or **consonant incise** is used in music; the former if the presentation is long; the latter if it contains only a few words, or just a single word.
3) Within a period, a thought hangs more or less together.
   α) In the latter case, where either a **colon, semicolon** or **full comma** occurs, as these signs can be properly interchanged according to the context, the **quasi-close** is used in composition.

β) In the first case, where nothing but a written or unwritten **half comma** occurs, a **suspended break** is used in composition.

### §. 100.

Before I clarify the matter with general examples, and make a few specific remarks here and there, we wish to become familiar with the **four rhetorical punctuation marks,** and the **colons before quotations.**

### First.
### On the Question Mark.

### §. 101.

The expression of the **question** in the recitative style is borrowed from the harmony of the quasi-close and also often from the suspended break. Nothing but the nature of the melody distinguishes the question from the other kinds of purely grammatical divisions, the close of which is regularly marked with **rising notes**, leaping or stepwise according to the nature of the underlying harmony. One sees the following formulas.

### 1) Borrowed from quasi-closes.

and on and on.

The most complete formulas, with which one can close a recitative if the text demands it, are the **first two** numbers for the **minor**; the **third** and **fourth** for the **major**, and the **fifth and sixth** for **both modes**. The formulas in numbers 7, 8, and 9, where the bass is always a mediant rather than a dominant or final note as in the preceding numbers, have formerly been remarkably abused in both modes; not when a **question** or **exclamation** or some special emphasis is evident in the final word, where there would be no objection to its use, but when not the slightest trace of a question or emphasis, etc. exists in the text.

### 2) Borrowed from suspended breaks.

and so on.

The place for an expression of this kind is in the middle of a recitative, 1) If the question contains only a few words or even just a single one; and 2) if many questions follow one another where the latter borrows its treatment from the regular break.

### §. 102.

When an exception to the rule is noted to occur, 1) for tender and painful questions, and 2) when many questions immediately follow one another, it is permissible now and then to allow the melody to fall; preferably by leap rather than stepwise, as for example.

§. 103.

The **dactylic endings** in music are permitted for the question as for any of the other stops in the middle of a recitative, for example

The most common closing dactyl is seen at **selber ist**. However the kind of caesura [*Cäsur*] at **lieben den** is no less dactylic, which one understands especially if one replaces the note b at **den** with the repeated g of the preceding note. Here the note b was taken in order to emphasize the word **den**. The example could be written with iambic caesuras as follows:

### Second.
### On the Exclamation Point.

§. 104.

The **exclamation point** consists of either only a short exclamatory formula, which can be a vocative or an imperative, as well as an interjection; or it consists of a phrase. **In the first case** it is expressed through a simple incise in the melody, namely either by a leap or by repeating a note. If the affect is joyful, it regularly leaps upward with a major third, a fourth, or a fifth. If the affect is sad, it regularly leaps downward with a minor third, fourth, or fifth; similarly often with a rising augmented fourth or a falling false [diminished] fifth. **In the second case**, the harmony of a quasi-close accompanies the melody, which regularly ends rising for a joyful affect and falling for a sad one. I say **regularly**, because an alteration can be made according to the nature of the harmony, the degree of rise or fall of the affect and other circumstances. One observes the following example.

If one, as at the end of the second number, omits the exclamation point in writing: it is nevertheless appropriate in composition to end the phrase, which the exclamation has brought about, with a rising melody and thereby draw attention to its meaning. In the third number, the exclamation formula falls, yet the vocative ends by rising. In the fourth number, the opposite happens, whereby the exclamation formula rises, and the vocative descends.

In an example, such as number six, where so many exclamations follow one another, and where an incise must be made at each word, there are musical reasons to make these incises with alternating rising and falling leaps, even if the same affect is present for all.

§. 105.

Where the text of a recitative closes with an exclamation, one can, according to the nature of the circumstances, end the music with a partial close or a complete cadence, for example.

**With a cadence.**

**With a quasi-close.**

When the little word **o** is connected with a vocative or imperative: it must not be separated through a small dividing rest before its main word. The case is different with the word **ach**; or when the little word **o** is used instead of **ach**, as could happen, for example, in number twelve.

§. 106.

When an exclamation and a question follow one another, one must not forget to mark the question, for example.

## Letter CXII
### Fifteenth Installment of the Lessons on Recitative.
Berlin, September 25, 1762.

### Third.
### On the Parenthesis.

§. 107.

Among the different possible styles, it is generally most correct, and for recitative most suitable, to express an **inserted sentence** musically by setting it with a somewhat lowered melody, returning afterward to the interrupted progression, for example

### Fourth.
### On the Dash.

§. 108.

The **dash**, which marks an ellipsis or an aposiopesis,[10] can without doubt be eas-ily expressed in no other way than by a dissonance, whose resolution is either delayed or given over to the thorough bass. Or if it is in a recitative dialogue, it can be left to the other conferring person. In the arioso style, pauses are similarly ben-eficial to employ. One sees this in the following example from the recitative style.

### First example.

As **Matusius** and **Timantes** in the opera **Demophontes**, which both Graun and Hasse have set, confer over the danger with which the king's anger threatens them: thus speaks the worried Matusius about their safety:

| | |
|---|---|
| **Und die enzige Hofnung** | **And the only hope—** |

and Timantes answers:

| | |
|---|---|
| **Die, werthster Freund, besteht** | **Which, worthiest friend,** |
| **in der Flucht.** | **lies in flight.** |

Matusius might pause of his own accord in order to learn the disposition of Timantes; or Timantes might interrupt him: either way, Matusius can not do other than end with a dissonance. Timantes, however, must resolve the dissonance, and complete that which is missing in the speech of Matusius; and in the process finish the rhetorical figure and at the same time satisfy the music.

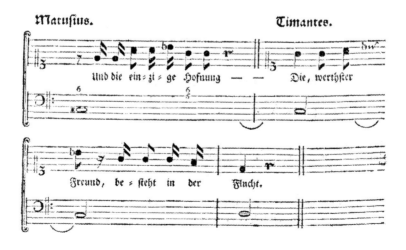

### Second example.

**Aerius**, in the opera of this name, after his victorious arrival from the Catalonian field, reproaches his bespoken bride, **Fulvia**, that she treats him with too much deference, and as a result he has decided that she is no longer the one for him. She returns his reproach with the words,

| | |
|---|---|
| **Oh Dio! Son quella.** | **Oh, Heaven! I am still the same.** |
| **Ma senti—.** | **But hear—.** |

Here she breaks off and requests her father, Maximus, to speak in her place.

| | |
|---|---|
| **—Ah! Genitor, per me favella.** | **—Ah! father, speak for me.** |

This was set by Graun in the following way.

Here not only is the ellipsis beautifully expressed, but at the same time a very successful change is made in the key at *ma*. The twofold rests after *senti* can serve to make the singer attentive to the manner of his execution if the dash alone does not do it.

### Letter CXIII
### Sixteenth Installment of the Lessons on Recitative.
Berlin, October 2, 1762.

### Fifth.
### Of the Colon before a Quotation.

§. 109.

The **grammatical colon before a Quotation of one's own or someone else's words** can sometimes be expressed through a simple incise in the melody over a suspended bass; and sometimes through the formula of a quasi-close, and in fact better with a rising rather than a falling melody. For one does not naturally allow the voice to sink at a quotation, but on the contrary, raises it. Besides, if there are no other circumstances to the contrary, it is good, as soon as the foreign words etc. begin, to change the key [modulate].

## First example.

Although the incise with the formula of the descending fifth in the second number has very frequently been used before quotations, the rising fifth in the first number is nevertheless better for the reason just cited.

## Second example.

If the harmony has already changed at the pause after the colon, and the **Arioso** then follows, the quoted passage is undoubtedly very clearly distinguished from that which precedes it.

**Third example.**

Here between the words **viel Menschen** and **sag ich** is a suspended comma, which the singer must mark with a short stop, even if no pause is indicated; and after **sag ich**, a similarly appropriate stop is indicated through a pause: thus this kind of quotation, which is not easy to compose, can be expressed as well as is possible.

**Fourth example.**

Here a quotation and question appear together, whereby the first merges entirely into the other.

**Fifth example.**

Here, the formula of the quotation is added to the proper rhetorical accent at **nicht**, which every raised melody already requires.

**Sixth example.**

The quotation effectively occurs already at **und spricht**, which is why at **Angesicht**, as is common, the falling quasi-close is used.

**Seventh example.**

Of the two numbers, the first is so much more expressive, because the words **spricht er** are expressed not only with the voice raised, and with a feminine meter as is natural in speech, but also because the whole momentum of the melody befits the picturesque sound of the speaker's intention; just as would be the case with the second number if one set the words **demüthig spricht er** [humbly he spoke] under it.

§. 110.

A certain famous composer once tried to indicate the colon before a quotation by a dissonance, which resolves at the beginning of the quoted words, as:

As astute and well conceived as this trick appears to be: yet in the first place, it goes against the nature of punctuation, in that the clarity suffers by it. If one considers afterward, that the exclamation: **O! welche herrlichkeit hat der, der sprechen kann** [Oh! what magnificence has he who can speak] possesses a certain assurance, and should raise no doubts: so one observes that the expression with the dissonance is not what it should be. The following simple expression, which is likewise set in the key of D minor, appears to me more adapted to the sense of the text, and also to be more genuine; namely:

§. 111.

It is a mistake to express the colon before a quotation with a complete cadence, for example.

## Appendix B

# Chronological Chart of Punctuation References

## Sources

1. Quintilian, *Education of an Orator*; trans. John Selby Watson, 2:239–40 [9.4.122–125].
2. Gioseffo Zarlino, *Le istitutioni harmoniche*, Part 3, 211–12; trans. Marco and Palisca, 124–25.
3. Thomas Morley, *A Plaine and Easie Introduction to Practicall Musicke*, 178.
4. Charles Butler, *The Principles of Musik in Singing and Setting*, 97.
5. Christopher Simpson, *A Compendium of Practical Musick*, 141.
6. Thomas Mace, *Musick's Monument*, 109–10, 130.
7. Anonymous, *A Treatise of Stops, Points, or Pauses*, 3–5.
8. Friedrich Erhardt Niedt, *Musicalischer Handleitung*, Part 3, 51; trans. adapted from Poulin and Taylor, 266–67.
9. Johann Beer, *Musikalische Diskourse*, 142–43.
10. François Couperin, Preface to *Pièces de clavecin: Troisième livre*.
11. Johann Leonhard Frisch, *Bödikers Grund-Sätze*; in Stefan Höchli, *Zur Geschichte der Interpunktion im Deutschen*, 172–73.
12. Johann Joseph Fux, *Gradus ad parnassum*, 277–78; trans. from Lester, *Between Modes and Keys*, 206–9.
13. Georg Philipp Telemann, Preface to *Fortsetzung des Harmonischen Gottesdienstes*; trans. adapted from Swack, vi–vii.
14. Michel Blavet, Preface to *Sonate*, Op. 2, no. 2, *"La Vibray" pour flûte traversière et basse continue.*
15. Claude Buffier, *A French Grammar on a New Plan*, 149–50.
16. Girolamo Gigli, *Regole per la Toscana Favella*, 219; trans. provided by Alessandra Campana.
17. Johann Mattheson, *Der vollkommene Capellmeister*, 182–91; trans. adapted from Harriss, 383–90.

18. Lorenz Mizler, *Neu eröffnete musikalische Bibliothek*, 2:246–47; Meinrad Spiess, *Tractatus musicus compositorio-practicus*, 131–32. Mizler quotes and summarizes Mattheson extensively. Spiess quotes Mizler almost verbatim, excluding the quote included under the comma column.

19. John Mason, *An Essay on Elocution, or, Pronunciation*, 21–23.

20. Johann Joachim Quantz, *Versuch einer Anweisung die Flöte traversiere zu spielen*, 74, 104–5; trans. adapted from Reilly, 88, 122.

21. Johann Christoph Gottsched, *Kern der Deutschen Sprachkunst aus der ausfürlichen Sprachkunst*, 34–37.

22. Leopold Mozart, *Versuch einer gründlichen Violinschule*, 33, 107–8; trans. adapted from Knocker, 36, 101.

23. Robert Lowth, *A Short Introduction to English Grammar*, 158.

24. Friedrich Wilhelm Marpurg, *Kritische Briefe über die Tonkunst*, 2:309.

25. Georg Simon Löhlein, *Clavier-Schule*, 178; trans. adapted from Wilson, 7.

26. Denis Diderot and Jean le Rond d'Alembert, *Encyclopédie, ou Dictionnaire raisonné*, s.v. "Ponctuation," 13:15–16.

27. Chares Henri Blainville, *Histoire générale, critique et philologique de la musique*, 157.

28. Jean-Jacques Rousseau, *Dictionnaire de musique*, s.v. "Ponctuer." The entry to *punctuate* does not appear in the 1779 English translation by Waring.

29. Johann Philipp Kirnberger, *Die Kunst des reinen Satzes in der Musik* 1:96–98; trans. Beach and Thym, 114–16.

30. Johann Georg Sulzer, *Allgemeine Theorie der schönen Künste*, s.v. "Vortrag" (by J. A. P. Schulz).

31. Jacob Schuback, *Von der musicalischen Declamation*, 13–15.

32. Michael Johann Friedrich Wiedeburg, *Der sich selbst informirende Clavierspieler* 3:252.

33. Johann Adam Hiller, *Anweisung zum musikalisch-ziertlichen Gesange*, 26.

34. John Walker, *Elements of Elocution*, 1:7–8.

35. Domenico Corri, *A Select Collection of the Most Admired Songs, Duetts, &c.*, 1:2–3.

36. Johann Christoph Adlung, *Umständliches Lehrgebäude*; from Höchli, *Zur Geschichte der Interpunction im Deutschen*, 239–42.

37. William Jones, *A Treatise on the Art of Music*, 46–47.

38. Christian Friderich Daniel Schubart, *Ideen zu einer Ästhetik der Tonkunst*, 358.

39. Anton Bemetzrieder, *Introduction to General Instructions on Music*, vi–vii.

40. Joseph Robertson, *An Essay on Punctuation*, 18, 77, 84, 90.

41. Heinrich Christoph Koch, *Versuch einer Anleitung zur Composition* 2:342–45; trans. adapted from Baker, 1–2.

42. André Grétry, *Mémoires, ou Essais sur la musique* 1:240–41.

43. Daniel Gottlob Türk (1789), *Klavierschule*, 343–44; trans. adapted from Haggh, 332–33.

44. Georg Friedrich Wolf, *Kurzgefasstes musikalisches Lexicon*, 57, 156.

45. John Gunn, *The Theory and Practice of Fingering the Violoncello*, 68; from Graves, 372.
46. John Wall Callcott, *A Musical Grammar*, 274–99.
47. Antoine Reicha, *Traité de mélodie*, 10, 11, 23.
48. Nicolas Étienne Framery, *Encyclopédie méthodique: Musique*, s.v. "Ponctuation" (by Momigny), 2:279.
49. William M. D. Kitchiner, *Observations on Vocal Music*, 72–73.
50. Pierre Baillot, *L'art du violon*, 163; trans. adapted from Goldberg, 289.
51. Alexandre Choron and J. Adrien Lafage, *Nouveau manual complet de musique vocale et instrumentale, ou, Encyclopédie musicale*, Part 2, vol. 1, 51.

52. François Antoine Habeneck, *Méthode théorique et pratique de violon*, 107.
53. Manuel Garcia, *École de Garcia*, 17–18; trans. Paschke, 48.
54. Ch. P. Girault-Duvivier, *Grammaire des grammaires*, 339–45.
55. Simon Sechter, *Die Grundsätze der musikalischen Komposition* 1:54–55; trans. adapted from Chenevert, 153–55.
56. Mathis Lussy, *Traité de l'expression musicale*, 13, 26; trans. adapted from Glehn, 44, 64–65.
57. Rudolph Westphal, *Allgemeine Theorie der musicalischen Rhythmik seit J. S. Bach*, 107.
58. Hugo Riemann, *Musik-Lexicon*, 1st ed., s.v. "Phrasierung."
59. Josef Hofmann, *Piano Questions Answered*, 98–99.
60. Diran Alexanian, *Traité théorique et pratique du violoncelle*, 33; trans. Fairbanks.
61. Jacob Fischer, *Erläuterungen zur Interpunktions-Ausgabe*, 3, 17.

## Notes

The [L] after an author's name refers to the references in the chart which use vocabulary from language sources—dictionaries, encyclopedias, grammers, and rhetorical treatises—rather than musical sources. Footnotes in the original sources are indicated by an asterisk * in the chart.

Chronological Chart of Punctuation References

| Treatise | Comma | Semicolon | Colon | Period |
|---|---|---|---|---|
| **1**<br>**Quintilian**<br>**[L]**<br>**ca. AD**<br>**92–95** | A *comma* according to my notion, is a certain portion of thought put into words, but not completely expressed; by most writers it is called a part of a *member*. The following examples of it Cicero affords us: "Was a house wanting to you? But you had one. Was money superabundant with you? But you were in want." | | A *member* is a portion of thought completely expressed, but detached from the body of the sentence, and establishing nothing by itself. Thus, "O crafty men!" is a complete member, but, abstracted from the rest of the period, has no force, any more than the hand or foot, separated from the human body. | There are two kinds of it; one simple, when a single thought is expressed in a rather full compass of words; the other consisting of members and commas, which may contain several thoughts … It ought fairly to terminate the sense; it should be clear, that it may be easily understood; and it should be of moderate length that it may be readily retained in the memory. |
| **2**<br>**G. Zarlino**<br>**1558** | Church musicians write rests in their chants not for ornament but out of need, because it is impossible to sing their chants straight through without resting. So they devised signs to place at points where the performers were to breathe.… It must be remembered, as many of the ancients observed, that this kind of pause must not be placed except at the ends of grammatical phrases (*clausule*) or periods (*punti*) of the text to which the music is set. Composers must observe this rule in order that the parts of the text will be distinguishable, and the sentences heard as intended. | | | |
| **3**<br>**T. Morley**<br>**1597** | … but to shewe you in a worde the use of the rests in the dittie, you may set a crotchet or minime rest above the coma or colon, but a longer rest than that of a minime you may not make till the sentence bee perfect, and then at a full point you may set what number of rests you will. Also when you would expresse sighes, you may use the crotchet or minime rest at the most, but a longer than a minime rest you may not use, because it will rather seeme a breth taking than a sigh.… Lastlie you must not make a close (especiallie a full close) till the full sence of the words bee perfect.… | | | |
| **4**<br>**C. Butler**<br>**1636** | Minim- and Crotchet-rests answer to Semicolons, Commas, Breathings and Sighs.<br>Improper and Imperfect Cadences answer to Points of Impefect sens, [Commas, and Semicolons.] | | Semibrief-rests one or more answer to a Period, or to a Colon: which also is of Perfect sens.<br>So like with, Primari Cadences Perfect, which close the Harmoni, answer firstly to Periods ending the Ditti; or form principal part of it: and Secundari, to Colons or Interrogations. | |

Chronological Chart of Punctuation References

| Treatise | Comma | Semicolon | Colon | Period |
|---|---|---|---|---|
| **5**<br>**C. Simpson**<br>**1667** | You must also have respect to the Points of your Ditty; not using any remarkable *Pause* or *Rest*, untill the words come to a full point or period. Neither may any *Rest*, how short soever, be interposed in the middle of a word; But a sigh or sobb is properly intimated by a *Crochet* or *Quaver Rest*. | | | |
| **6**<br>**T. Mace**<br>**1676** | The last of All, is the *Pause*; which although it be not a *Grace*, of any performance, not likewise *Numbered* amongst the *Graces*, by others, yet the performance of It, (in proper Places) adds much *Grace*: And the thing to be done, is but only to make a kind of *Cessation, or standing still*, sometimes *Longer*, and sometimes *Shorter*, according to the *Nature*, or *Requiring* of the *Humour* of the *Musick*....<br><br>And forget not especially, in such *Humours*, to make your *Pauses, at Proper Places*, (which are commonly at the *End* of such *Sentences*, where there is a *Long Note*), as easily you will know how to do, if you give your mind to regard *such Things*, which give the *Greatest Lustre in Play*, as I have already told you. | | | |
| **7**<br>**Anonymous**<br>**[L]**<br>**1680** | It is a Note of imperfect Sens, and by it a Sentence is divided into several parts:  At each of which parts, where the comma is placed, the voice must be stayed a littl, but the Tenour of it is still to be kept up.<br><br>A Comma is a Breathing Stop: No more, Stop at it while you may tell one. Therefore, | It is a Note of an imperfect distinction in the middl of the member of a Sentence, as it were between the parts of a composed Speech, and Notes a longer Stop than a Comma.<br><br>Where Semi-Colon placed is; There you, May pleas to make a Stop, while you tell Two. | It is a Note of perfect Sens, but not of a perfect Sentence, and that becaus, either the part preceding, without the following; or the following, without the preceding, cannot be well understood.<br><br>A Colon is a longer Stop; Therefore, Stop at each Colon, while you may tell Four. | It is a Note of perfect-Sens, and of a perfect Sentence, is always to be placed after it, and is a longer Stop than a Colon.... And sound the Word next before the Period a littl longer than the rest, with a Cadency; or letting fall of your voice a littl.<br><br>To Stop, while you tell Sir, do not forget, where you do see a Period to be set. |
| **8**<br>**F. E. Niedt**<br>**1717** | Similarly, the verses or commas must not be split or mangled, as happened in the preceding example: where in, "and should the jealousy etc.," the composer separated "and should" with a short rest, which is incorrect, in that no comma belongs here and the sense only becomes torn and spoilt by it. The composer must carefully observe where one speech ends and another begins, which is indicated by a *Colon* (:), *Semicolon* (;). *Punctum* (.), and the like. He must also observe the question mark and other signs as well as the commas, and must plan well ahead that the notes fit properly with the text, and his sentences arranged so that he will not pass for, or be considered as either a musical pedant or madman [Pedanten oder Phantasten]. | | | |

Chronological Chart of Punctuation References

| Treatise | Comma | Semicolon | Colon | Period |
|---|---|---|---|---|
| **9**<br>**J. Beer**<br>**1719** | Concerning a Peculiar Musical Comma [Von einem absonderlich *commate musico*]. This is more easily understood through the example of the Delphine Oracle's well-known answer to the soldier's question: Whether he will remain in the war, or come out with his life. To him it is answered thus: "Ibis redibis non morieris in bello." Now because of the lack of commas, two different interpretations can be made from this sentence … when one places the comma after "redibis," it has the sense, "you will come back, and not die in the war," but if one places the comma after "non," it denotes the contrary…. | | | |
| **10**<br>**F. Couperin**<br>**1722** | One finds a new sign in the figure (,); it is for marking the end of melodies or harmonic phrases, and to make clear that it is necessary before going on at the end of a melody, to put a little separation between it and that which follows. This separation is in general nearly imperceptible, but if one does not observe this little silence, persons of taste will notice that something in the execution is missing. In a word, it is the difference between those who read without pause, and those who stop at periods and commas. These silences should be felt without altering the bar. | | | |
| **11**<br>**J. L. Frisch**<br>**[L]**<br>**1723** | The comma is a stroke, which separates every circumstance, even if it is indicated in only a word, from the others. In speaking, one remains somewhat quiet, or leaves off a little for the sake of clarity. It is the most necessary sectional division. | The semicolon, or comma with a point over it (;) is a sign, which the simple-minded are happily able to leave out, and place a comma or a colon in its stead. But then even the learned themselves do not really know where it should be used. | One places the colon or double point (:) where a part of the sense of the words ends, but yet more follows. In such cases, it would become monotonous if one were to keep reading, and would [likewise] sound bad if one were to anticipate the final tone and alter the voice. | The full stop is the easiest sign (.). One uses it, where a sense of either part of the speech, or the whole speech concludes. One holds it the longest, and gives the final words a falling tone. |
| **12**<br>**J. J. Fux**<br>**1725** | Concerning Recitative Style. … In addition, the following punctuations of rhetoric should be observed too: the comma, colon, semicolon, period, question mark, exclamation point, and parentheses: for everything should be in one of these divisions. … Knowing how to use all these punctuations is learned more by use and by observing the works of good composers than by rules. | | | |

Chronological Chart of Punctuation References

| Treatise | Comma | Semicolon | Colon | Period |
|---|---|---|---|---|
| **13** **G. P. Telemann** **1731** | The commas, colons, semicolons, and full stops etc., are of no little importance: their thoughtless confusion can lead to an ambiguous [or] even a distorted meaning; especially if the poet employs a laconic (choppy) style, using many points, so that the composer himself must take up smaller phrase divisions. Many figures of speech are of no less concern to composers than to poets: A question raised can at the same time be an exclamation, or vice versa; questions may be doubtful, affirmative, [or] negative; should they all be expressed in the same way, regardless?... Speech is interrupted by pain or joy, rage or shyness, etc. A sentence in a long speech may be repeated quite a few times, either with the original meaning or with a new or contradictory meaning. Just as a speaker alters the quality of his voice according to the subject, the composer should do the same. | | | |
| **14** **M. Blavet** **1732** | I have always observed, among students, a difficulty in suitably recovering the breath: so that most often, they confound one phrase with another, or they interrupt a melody which should be played all in one breath. To avoid such confusion, I thought to place the letter h in the places where one should breath, especially in the types of melody like the Rondeaux or other small character pieces, where all the grace depends on the arrangement of the phrases and in their cleanness and precision, which one cannot achieve without breathing easily and in the correct resting places. | | | |
| **15** **C. Buffier** **[L]** **1734** | The comma serves to distinguish Nouns, Verbs, Adverbs, and the parts of a Period, not necessarily connected together. | The semicolon shews the sense less perfect than the colon, and more so than the comma. | The colon is frequently used in the middle of a Period, or to signify that the sense is not so complete as the point would express. | The full point signifies that the Period is complete, and the sense entirely finished. |
| | Pointing is the manner of employing several characters, to distinguish the different parts of a discourse.... This practice, which these latter ages have introduced, is of exceeding great benefit to Grammar, by preventing several ambiguities arising from the relation of words to one period rather than to another. By an omission of pointing, invincible difficulties have arisen in the holy scripture, in the exposition of the principles of religion, in the publication of laws, and contracts of the utmost importance to society. | | | |
| **16** **G. Gigli** **[L]** **1734** | Full Stops and Commas indicate that suspension which we must make when speaking in order to denote an interruption or some sense of completion in our reasoning. | | | |
| | The Comma signifies a sort of interruption, and a short pause in the speech. | The Semicolon signifies an interruption which still has qualities of conclusion. | The Colon is used when the period can stand by itself but something is missing. | The Full Stop marks the full conclusion of the idea or proposition. |

Chronological Chart of Punctuation References

| Treatise | Comma | Semicolon | Colon | Period |
|---|---|---|---|---|
| **17**<br>**Johann Mattheson**<br>**1739** | Now since a Comma in speech represents that which in the human body is the Articulus or the joint; thus by comparison the *Colon* indicates a membrum and **whole member**, as the Greek name implies; but the semicolon (:) indicates only **half** of one. | | | |
| | In short, the *Comma* is a little part of the sentence through which the discourse obtains a small division [Einschnitt]: although there is not a rhetorical but only a grammatical and imperfect meaning: for very often a single word requires its own comma. | The semicolon has yet its own characteristic, namely this, that it often occurs even before the grammatical sequence of words is completed; which however does not occur with the Colon, since that actually requires a formal grammatical sense. Nonetheless, the complete meaning of the whole rhetorical presentation or structure is yet to come. | The *Colon* indicates more than the preceding divisions [Einschnitte] since it **includes a larger part of speech, and contains one complete grammatical idea**; although everyone observes that still more is to follow for the completion of the rhetorical presentation. And, just for the last reason given, the *Colon* can in fact not be subject to a complete final cadence in melody, but indeed a pause, an expectant one. | The concept of a period obliges me not to make a **formal** close in the melody before the sentence is finished. But the concept of a paragraph prohibits me from using a **full** cadence anywhere except at the end ... With various periods (the very last excepted) I can also interrupt and pause **formally** ... For one uses not only periods, though mostly these; but also occasionally the question and exclamation marks, which, as the period, can unexpectedly close a sentence, indeed frequently an entire compound sentence. |
| **18**<br>**L. Mizler 1742**<br>**&**<br>**M. Spiess 1745** | One can express it with one or two eighth-rests or with a quarter-rest, or also according to the nature of the meter, with a half-note rest. Yet it is not always necessary to represent commas through rests, in that they can also appear through certain natural falls of the voice. | The semicolon represents the middle point between a comma and a colon, including such expressions as a separation, an object, or something which relates to something else. At a semicolon, one must make a larger division [Einschnitt] in the melody than at a comma. | A colon, which comprehends a larger part of speech, and a complete grammatical thought, permits a longer delay, and even though no complete closing cadence occurs, still there is an expectant rest (clausulum desideratam). | The full stop is indicated through a formal cadence, and the final one at the end through the full close in the tonic key. |
| **19**<br>**J. Mason**<br>**[L]**<br>**1748** | You are not to fetch your Breath (if it can be avoided) till you come to the Period or Full Stop; but a discernible Pause is to be made at every one, according to its proper Quantity or Duration. A Comma stops the Voice while we may privately tell *one*; a Simi-colon *two*; a Colon *three*; and a Period *four*. Where the Periods are very long, you may take Breath at a Colon or Simi-colon; and sometimes at a Comma, but never where there is no Stop at all. | | | |

Chronological Chart of Punctuation References

| Treatise | Comma | Semicolon | Colon | Period |
|---|---|---|---|---|
| **20** **J. J. Quantz** **1752** | If a piece begins with a note on an upbeat; which beginning note may only be the last note of the bar or may occur after a preceding rest; or if there is a cadence and a new idea begins, breath must be taken before the repetition of the principal subject or the beginning of the new idea, so that the end of the preceding idea and the beginning of the one that follows are separated from one another.... Musical ideas that belong together must not be separated; on the other hand, you must separate those ideas in which one musical thought ends and a new idea begins, even if there is no rest or caesura [Einschnitt]. This is especially true when the final note of the preceding phrase and opening note of the following one are on the same pitch. | | | |
| **21** **J. C. Gottsched** **[L]** **1754** | **The smallest separation of certain words, which do not belong together, one observes through a comma [Beistrich].** But one must take care, to use neither too many, nor too few, but to hold the middle road. Too many commas halt the reading too much; but too few, make a script not clear enough: since one does not always remember where one should insert a small pause. | **One sets a semicolon [Strich-punct] where either a new re-mark on the same matter, or the same remark on another matter is made.** | **If in one period, two sepa-rate remarks occur, then one sets a colon [Doppelpunct] between them....** Since they belong somewhat together, one separates them only through a colon; but not through a full stop. | **After a short sentence, where the sense is complete and can be understood on its own, one makes a full stop [Schlußpunct].** This also con-tributes much in reading to-wards the proper time to stop, and pause some: in order that it can be the better under-stood. Namely where no full stop stands; one must then read on, and has no time to fetch a breath. But at a full stop. one can pause and take in a new breath. |
| **22** **L. Mozart** **1756** | There are three reasons why the rest was discovered to be a necessity in music. **Firstly, for the convenience** of singers and wind players, in order to give them a little respite during which to take breath. **Secondly, from necessity,** because the words in songs require punctuation and because in many compositions one or other of the parts often has to remain silent if the melody is not to be spoilt and made unintelligible. **Thirdly, for the sake of elegance.** The human voice glides quite easily from one note to another; and a sensible singer will never make a break unless some special kind of expression [Ausdrückung], or the **phrase divisions [Abschnitte]** and caesurae [Einschnitte] demand one. *The phrase divisions and caesurae are the *Incisiones, Distinctiones, Inerpunctiones,* and so on. But what sort of animals these are must be known to great grammarians, or better still, rhetoricians or poets. But here we see also that a good violinist must have this knowledge. For a sound composer this is indispensable, for otherwise he is the fifth wheel on the wagon: for the diastolica (from Διαστολή) is one of the most necessary things in melodic composition. | | | |

Chronological Chart of Punctuation References

| Treatise | Comma | Semicolon | Colon | Period |
|---|---|---|---|---|
| **23**<br>**R. Lowth**<br>**[L]**<br>**1762** | | The Semicolon is double of the Comma. | The Colon is double of the Semicolon. | The Period is a pause in quantity or duration double of the Colon. |
| **24**<br>**F. W. Marpurg**<br>**1762** | Quaver | Crotchet | Minim | Semibrief |

One admits in all languages, 1) that the punctuation marks [Unterscheidungszeichen] are created in order to divide the boundaries of sense in a speech; 2) that, the greater the connection of sense, the smaller the punctuation sign must be; and the reverse, that, the lesser the connection of sense, the greater the punctuation sign must be; and 3) that of the punctuation signs, the **full stop** is the greatest, and the **comma** is the smallest; that the **colon** comes next after the full stop, and that the **semicolon** amounts to only half as much as the colon.

| Treatise | Comma | Semicolon | Colon | Period |
|---|---|---|---|---|
| **25**<br>**G. S. Löhlein**<br>**1765** | | | | |

It has been stated that, to the orator and poet as well as to the musician, a correct relationship between period and rhyme is essential. But what is a **Period** in music? It is precisely that which it is in poetry: **a number of rhythms [Anzahl von Rhytmen]** containing a certain thought, comprised by means of a musical **period [Punctum]** or cadence [Schlußfall]. The **rhythm** (numerus sectionalis, or section), [Einschnitt] is a part of the numero or section [Absatze], which is the same as the caesura in poetry.

| Treatise | Comma | Semicolon | Colon | Period |
|---|---|---|---|---|
| **26**<br>**D. Diderot**<br>**[L]**<br>**1765** | The usual characters of *punctuation* are the comma [virgule], which marks the least of all the pauses, an almost imperceptible pause;<br><br>The art of *punctuating* boils down to a firm understanding of the principles of this proportion. | the semicolon [point & une virgule], which designates a slightly larger pause; | the colon [deux points], which announces a rest again a little more considerable; | and the period [le point], which marks the greatest of all the pauses.... |

*Punctuation* is the art of indicating in writing, through the accepted signs, the proportion of the pauses that one should make in speaking.

| Treatise | Comma | Semicolon | Colon | Period |
|---|---|---|---|---|
| **27**<br>**C. H. Blainville**<br>**1767** | | | | |

Indeed, all melody in music must be reasoned, conversed [dialogué] so to speak, phrased, rounded: that which follows must relate to that which preceded it; it must have full stops, commas, that is to say the sense of completion and repose, or a suspension like the hemistich in verse; lastly it must be a discourse, or rather a picture whose harmony and melody are the colors, which together refine the movements, the characters of the passions, or the different phenomena of nature. In a word these diverse cadences and vehicles are rests for light that create play and movement, to make things turn, as one says of figures in a painting.

## Chronological Chart of Punctuation References

| Treatise | Comma | Semicolon | Colon | Period |
|---|---|---|---|---|
| **28**<br>**J. J. Rousseau**<br>**1768** | Ponctuer. It is, as a term of composition, to mark the more or less perfect rests, and to divide the phrases accordingly as one feels them through the modulation, and through the beginnings, the endings, and the greater or lesser connections of the cadences, as one feels all these things in discourse, through the aid of punctuation. | | | |
| **29**<br>**J. P. Kirnberger**<br>**1771** | Just as a paragraph in speech consists of segments [Einschnitten], phrases [Abschnitten], and sentences [Perioden] that are marked by various punctuation symbols such as the *comma* (,), *semicolon* (;), *colon* (:), and *full stop* (.); the harmonic paragraph can also consist of several segments, phrases, and periods. In a long section [Abschnitt] the chord progression can be divided into individual periods and smaller resting points, where the ear is not completely satisfied and permanently put to rest yet is allowed to rest momentarily.... There are three main types of cadences [perfect cadence, half cadence, interrupted cadence], the first of which produces complete repose and thus can be used to conclude main sections of a composition. The other two types do not produce complete repose, yet can also be used to conclude main sections; they are also suitable for dividing such sections into periods. Each of these three main types can be varied or modified in many ways, whereby the feeling of rest which they provide is more or less weakened. The result is a great variety of smaller resting points that are achieved only by the harmonic progression. | | | |
| **30**<br>**J. A. P. Schulz**<br>**1774** | The phrase divisions [Einschnitten] must be clearly and correctly marked. The phrase divisions are the commas of the melody, which in speech must be made perceptible by a small resting point. This happens, if one either leaves off a little on the last note of a phrase, and again firmly places the first note of the following phrase; or when one lets the tone sink a little [at the end of the phrase], and again raises it with the beginning of the new phrase. *The word **phrase** will be taken here in its broadest meaning, encompassing both the Einschnitte, and the Abschnitte and Perioden of song. | | | |
| **31**<br>**J. Schuback**<br>**1775** | Musical **punctuation** [musicalische **Interpunction**] concerns the duration of the pauses, or so to speak musically, the rests, which a composer makes, and the method by which he observes whether a full stop, colon, comma, exclamation point, or question mark occurs.... If in a part [Absatze] of a rhetorical declamation. the listener anticipates that more should follow, or if the sense is already satisfactorily expressed, or if the complete conclusion of the passage is still to be reached, this is made apparent through the voice in the last word, and afterwards through a momentary silence, according to the circumstances. It is the same with song. But the composer effects this sense by means of the harmonies or the bass line, which either leaves the ear in uncertainty, or calms it down, in order to express whether the end of a paragraph is already reached or something further is expected. | | | |
| **32**<br>**M. J. F. Wiedeburg**<br>**1775** | On the cadence. In song a cadence is made almost at the end of each sentence, even when the words of the song do not have periods at the end of each sentence. But really a formal cadence should not be made in the melody, unless a period occurs in the hymnbook, since a cadence ends a musical speech as does the full stop at a period. But because the meaning of each sentence does come to a pause and thereby similarly causes a full stop or pause in the singing, so the cadence (or a musical colon or caesura [Einschnitt]) is quite fitting. In playing preludes or Fantasias the cadence is often not necessary, and instead should be applied only rarely, yes should even be avoided in a skillful manner, as we will see forthwith. | | | |

Chronological Chart of Punctuation References

| Treatise | Comma | Semicolon | Colon | Period |
|---|---|---|---|---|
| **33** **J. A. Hiller** **1780** | | | | The easiest rule [of good performance, with regard to text and music] is probably that of **punctuation**, without which an oration can not even have its proper sense and understanding, let alone its strength and emphasis. One easily feels that after a comma or semicolon, the proposition of a speech is not brought to an end, but something must follow in order to bring it to the point which one calls a period and is most often marked with a full stop. The voice of the orator is accustomed to sink at the approach of a full stop, and in music, it is generally indicated by the presence of a full cadence. The question mark raises the voice of the orator, as it does the voice of the singer in music. The exclamation mark similarly indicates a raised voice, and at the same time, a strengthened tone, for both the orator and singer. |
| **34** **J. Walker** **[L]** **1781** | | | | The period is supposed to be a pause double the time of the colon; the colon, double the semicolon; and the semicolon, double that of the comma, or smallest pause; the interrogation and exclamation points are said to be indefinite as to their quantity of time, and to mark an elevation of voice; and the parenthesis, to mark a moderate depression of the voice, with a pause greater than a comma. |
| **35** **D. Corri** **ca. 1782** | | | Thus for example, one of the most important articles in the execution of music (vocal music in particular) is the proper division of the PERIODS; as is evident from hearing good singers often break in upon the sense and the melody, for want of knowing how to take breath in the proper places. To assist the performer in this particular, two signs are introduced; one ✱ to enable him to distinguish at sight the musical periods where a pause is always necessary; and another ✱ to direct him in taking breath where the period is too long, or when a particular exertion of the voice is required. | |
| **36** **J. C. Adlung** **[L]** **1782** | | The semicolon partially separates several members [Glieder] of a sentence, if they are of some length, such that the comma alone cannot provide enough clarity; ... | It is used only in cases where the sentences are of considerable length.... If they are short, a simple comma is adequate. | The full stop separates complete sentences and periods and stands in a speech where one takes a fresh breath. |
| **37** **W. Jones** **1784** | In common Time, it is very usual to make a stop, equivalent to a Comma, after three fourths of the first Bar; another stop, equivalent to a Colon or Semicolon, after three fourths of the second Bar: the first clause containing the first or principal subject, the next a second or subordinate Subject. Sometimes the first comma is found at three fourths of the second Bar: and another stop at the correspondent part of the fourth Bar; or, in pieces which allow a latitude, the Composer omits the second stop, and continues the air at his pleasure, to avoid formality; ... | | | |
| **38** **Schubart** **1784–85** | *Recitativ.* Musical declamation or speech.... One must completely internalize rhythm [Rhythmus], and understand precisely the prosody of language; in order to observe keenly the highs, the lows, the rise and fall of speech. [One must] observe with the strictest conscientiousness each comma, colon, period, question mark, each exclamation, each thought and sign of expectation, in a word, each distinctive sign [Unterscheidungszeichen] of speech. | | | |

Chronological Chart of Punctuation References

| Treatise | Comma | Semicolon | Colon | Period |
|---|---|---|---|---|
| **39** **Bemetz-rieder** **1785** | In major the consonances of the sixth the fourth the third and the second, and in minor the consonances of the sixth the fourth the fifth without alterations and even of the tonick, form at times very slight separative rests, if introduced by harmonics at the distance of a fourth whether above or below: this rest may be compared to that of a comma in discourse. <br><br> … represented by crotchets or fourths of a note, and those of the dissonant and soliciting harmonies by crotchets or fourths of a note. | The third pause of the scale (that of the semicolon) is much varied; it is in music the suspensive, interrogative, exclamative, and admirative rest. The harmonics of the sixth and of the fourth are suspensive rests, … the dissonances of the fifth and of the second are interrogative rests, … the dissonance of the fourth in the minor mood with alteration of the fourth and the sixth is exclamative and admirative, … <br><br> … represented by minims with a dot | The consonance of the fifth is the second pause of the scale, it is a separative rest, which answers to the idea of the colon; in both moods it is solicited or called for by the consonances of fourth, sixth and octave; and by the dissonances of second, fourth and sixth; in major the consonance of the second solicits also the pause of the fifth. <br><br> … represented by minims or half notes | The consonance of the tonick is the first and principal pause in the scale, the initial and final rest, which expresses in music a full stop or period: in major and minor it is solicited prepared or called for by the consonances of fourth and fifth, and by the dissonances of second fifth and *sensible* seventh; besides which it may in major be solicited by the consonance of the second. <br><br> … represented by semibreves or whole notes |
| **40** **J.** **Robertson** **[L]** **1785** | A Comma is a Greek word, which properly means a segment, or a part *cut off* a complete sentence. But in its more usual acceptation, it signifies the POINT, by which a period is subdivided into its least constructive parts. In reading, it requires a small rest, or a short pause. | A Semicolon signifies *half a member*. The point, which bears its appellation, is used for dividing a compounded sentence into two or more parts, not so closely connected, as those, which are separated by a comma; nor yet so independent on each other, as those, which are distinguished by a colon. In reading, a semicolon requires a longer pause than a comma. | This word in Greek signifies a *member*, or a large division of a period. It is used when the preceding part of the sentence is complete in its construction; but is followed by some additional remark or illustration, naturally arising from the foregoing member, and immediately depending on it in sense, though not in syntax. | A period properly signifies a *circuit*, or a sentence, in which the meaning is suspended, till the whole is finished…. In reading, a period requires a full stop, that is, a complete pause, or a perfect interval of silence. |

Chronological Chart of Punctuation References

| Treatise | Comma | Semicolon | Colon | Period |
|---|---|---|---|---|
| **41** **H. C. Koch** **1787** | Certain more or less noticeable resting points of the spirit [Ruhepuncte des Geistes] are generally necessary in speech and thus also in the products of those fine arts which attain their goal through speech, namely poetry and rhetoric, if the subject that they present is to be comprehensible. Such resting points are just as necessary in melody if it is to affect our feelings. ... For lack of a completely suitable term and on account of its similarity to the labeling of the larger and smaller resting points in speech, we shall call this **melodic punctuation** [melodische Interpunction]. * ... for example, the full stop ends the periods of speech in the same way as the cadence closes the periods of melody; the phrase [Absatz] and incise [Einschnitt] differentiate the melodic sections of the period just as do the semicolon and comma the smaller parts of the periods in speech. | | | |
| **42** **A. E. M. Grétry** **1789** | Above all, it is necessary to attend to the musical punctuation [ponctuation musicale], from which will result the verity of declamation. The mathematical relationships which exist between the tones, are as they are in nature, like the physical proportions of the human form: but it is the attitude, the expression, the passion, which animates a statue; in the same way declamation animates the tones. What a vast arena for the musician! I have said that music is a discourse: it has then, like verse and prose, the pauses and inflections of the comma, the colon, the exclamation point, the question mark and the full stop. The musician who misses them, either doesn't hear his music, or doesn't understand the words. | | | |
| **43** **D. G. Türk** **1789** | The **Phrase Member** [**Einschnitt**], as the smallest member, is like that which would be separated by a comma (,). If it is especially wished to include the Caesura with these, then one would have to compare it with the Caesura of verse. | A musical **Phrase** [**Rhythmus**] can be compared with the smaller parts of speech which are indicated by a Colon (:) or a Semicolon (;). | | A musical **Period** (or **Section** [**Abschnitt**]), of which there can be several in a main section, would be like that which is called a **Period** in speech, and which is separated from that which follows by a full stop (.). |
| **44** **G. F. Wolf** **1792** | Einschnitt. There is not yet complete agreement regarding the explanation of these and several expressions of the kind; that is why what one calls the Einschnitt, another gives the name Caesura. It is best, if one understands by the Einschnitt the smallest members [Glieder], which in speech are separated by a comma; several of which represent a Period, and each of which is by and large called a Rhythmus. — One has newly begun to indicate the Einschnitt through the following symbol, as ": which for the unpracticed is a good method of recognizing them and establishing their execution, for instance in Türk's easy sonatas.  Rhythmus. — One also understands by the **Rhythmus**, the Einschnitt. Thus a Rhythmus of two or three measures is the same as an Einschnitt of two or three measures. A Rhythmus can be compared with the smaller parts of a discourse which one indicates by a colon or a semicolon. | | | |

Note: In the row for D. G. Türk 1789, a spanning introductory text reads: "I have often said that a complete composition could be suitably compared to a speech, for as the latter itself may be divided into smaller and larger parts or members, so is this also true of music."

Chronological Chart of Punctuation References

| Treatise | Comma | Semicolon | Colon | Period |
|---|---|---|---|---|
| **45**<br>**J. Gunn**<br>**1793** | There are certain general principles which take place both in the structure and performance of proper air or melody. ... One remarkable quality it possesses, in common with speech, is that of rhythm, or the subdivision of an air into phrases, less or more conclusive, corresponding to sentences, and their component smaller members in discourse; ... With a view, therefore, to a more methodical study of air, ... I have, in a supplementary work, selected almost the whole of the original Scotch airs, ... The several subdivisions, or phrases, are marked with an asterisk on the concluding note of the phrase, which is to be separated from the following by a short rest like those used in the separation of the different sentences, and their parts, in common discourse; Indeed it will be even proper to pursue the analogy with language still further, in the method of studying these airs, namely, to learn one phrase, in its proper time and expression, before proceeding to the next, in the same manner that sentences in a language are analyzed and construed. | | | |
| **46**<br>**J. W.**<br>**Callcott**<br>**1810** | A phrase (*Einschnitt*) is a short melody, which contains no perfect nor satisfactory musical idea.... In musical punctuation, this sign seems analogous to that of the comma (,) in language. | A section (*Absatz*) is a portion of melody formed by two regular phrases, the last of which is terminated by a cadence. This sign seems analogous to that of the semicolon (;) in language. In the Arioso or Legato style of music, it is usual to find sections which are not subdivided into phrases. | | The period consists of one or more sections, occasionally interspersed with independent feet, phrases or codettas. The period always ends with a radical cadence, like the section, and answers to a full stop (.) in language. |
| **47**<br>**A. Reicha**<br>**1814** | What distinguishes and separates one idea from another, are the points of repose; ... The melody has different means of indicating these reposes; 1) by a note which is longer than the preceding one; 2) by a rest; 3) by the beat of the measure on which the cadence is made; 4) by certain notes of the scale which nature demands.... In general, there is a strong analogy between the cadences in music and grammatical punctuation. | | | |
| | One can call the quarter cadence a comma and designate it with the sign (,). | One can designate the half cadence with the sign (;) or (:). | | One can designate the perfect cadence with a full stop (.). |
| **48**<br>**Framery**<br>**1818** | TO PUNCTUATE. In execution, it is to attack the first note of each unit of sense which needs to be separated from that which precedes it; it is to reinforce the shape of the phrase by giving emphasis to the tones which require it, and make clear which note terminates the sense, not only by the silence which follows, but again by the proper inflection, and a different attack.<br><br>*To punctuate* in composition, is to cadence the musical discourse and directly phrase it; it is to place the fundamental note in the bass every time that the upbeat [levé] or the downbeat [frappé] of the cadence requires it, according to the conclusion of a reprise or a part. | | | |

## Chronological Chart of Punctuation References

| Treatise | Comma | Semicolon | Colon | Period |
|---|---|---|---|---|
| **49** W. Kitchiner 1821 | | | | There are certain Musical phrases, and subdivisions of Notes—which, like words, require punctuation to make them immediately and distinctly intelligible. The principal care of those who compose Music to Words, ought to be, that their Notes justly express the meaning and spirit of them— "The sound should be an echo to the Sense." If Composers would first attend to the accurate punctuation of the Words,—and then, over the several *Stops*—introduce *Rests* of defined value,—equivalent to the Stops;—it would in a great degree prevent that playing at cross-purposes which now so often occurs, to the great perplexity of both the Singer and the Accompanist—and is inevitable, from the musical technicals.—*ad libita*—marks for pauses, &c. being so indefinite that no two persons estimate them exactly alike. |
| **50** P. Baillot 1835 | | MUSICAL PUNCTUATION. Notes are used in music as words are used in speech; they serve to construct a phrase or form an idea. Consequently, we must use full stops and commas in music just as we do in written language, to distinguish periods and members and render it easier to understand. [*One remarks that the silences expressed in music by the quarter, eighth or sixteenth rests, are the equivalent of the full stops and commas used in discourse.] But the slight separations, the very short silences, are not always indicated by the composer; it is therefore necessary for the performer to introduce them, when he sees that they are needed, by letting the final note of a phrase member, or of the entire period, die away. In certain cases, he can even cut off the full value of these notes. | | |
| **51** A. Choron & J. Lafage 1838 | | | In the examination of phrases or melodic periods, two principle objects first grab our attention: These are 1) their endings or their points of repose which distinguish the various parts; 2) the length of these same parts and the connection between them, which we discover principally by the number, or the quantity of measures which they contain. The first constitute that which we call musical *punctuation*; the others, that which in a sense restricts, we properly designate the rhythm. The portions of the melody, determined by the points of repose, are of two kinds, according to those which form a complete or incomplete sense: in the first case they can remain alone, and form a phrase of greater or lesser length: in the second, they must join one or more other portions in order to form a phrase or period, they take the name then of members, that is to say, phrase members. | |
| **52** F. A. Habeneck 1840 | | | In melody as in discourse, there are periods, phrases, and members or figures [dessins]. A period can contain many phrases. A phrase can contain many figures. In order to phrase well, it is necessary to divide the figures, phrases, and periods in such a manner that they can be easily understood by the listeners; and to do this, it is necessary to distinguish clearly the beginning and end of each figure, phrase, and period. We call this *musical punctuation*. If all melodies were conveniently divided [by rests], the art of phrasing would not be difficult. But there are many where one does not find a rest at the end of a period and where, nevertheless, the figures should be separated, the one from the other, by a certain abandoning of the sound. | |
| **53** M. Garcia 1847 | Good melodies, like speeches, are divided by pauses, which are regulated, as we have explained earlier, by the distribution and length of the several ideas composing such melodies. Nevertheless, under certain circumstances, the melodic period is displayed without any pause whatever, and without interruption in the uniform movement of its notes. Our ears, however, will easily recognize the points at which pauses should be introduced. | | | |

Chronological Chart of Punctuation References

Punctuation is the art of distinguishing, by certain recognized signs, the phrases among them, the incomplete meanings which constitute these phrases, and the different degrees of subordination suitable for each. A good punctuation, says Rollin, provides discourse with clarity, grace, and harmony; it relieves the eyes and spirit of the speakers and the hearers, by making them aware of the order, coherence, and the connection and distinction of the parts; by giving them natural pronunciation, and by dictating to them, as the sense demands, proper boundaries and different kinds of repose.

| Treatise | Comma | Semicolon | Colon | Period |
|---|---|---|---|---|
| **54** <br> **Ch. P. Girault-Duvivier** <br> **[L]** <br> **1851** | A *comma* indicates the least of all the pauses, a pause nearly imperceptible. | A *semicolon* indicates a stronger pause than the comma. | The *colon* expresses a repose again more extensive than the semicolon. | One distinguishes three kinds of *points*: the *full stop*, the *question mark*, and the *point of wonder* or the *exclamation point*. |
| **55** <br> **S. Sechter** <br> **1853** | Just as the comma is the least noticeable resting point in speech, so also are such points in music. Even a leap in the fundamental bass from the 4th to the 7th scale degree, or from the 7th to the 3rd, is sufficient to indicate such a resting point, as also is a leap from the 6th to the 3rd. All of the fundamental bass progressions which were given with regard to the semicolon can also hold for the comma; the fundamental bass will either be entirely concealed, or made less decisive through the upper voice. | As the semicolon is neither so restful as the period nor so expectant as the colon, so also are the resting points in music which can take their place. In this case the fundamental bass moves either from the 1st to the 4th scale degree, from the 4th to the 1st, 6th to the 2nd, or 3rd to the 6th. Of course, the fundamental bass can likewise proceed as in the complete and half cadence; but it is either concealed or it is made less decisive by the progression of the upper voice. | Just as the colon excites attention, so also does the half cadence. The lower voice, if it is itself the fundamental bass, leaps from the 1st or 2nd scale degree to the 5th; or, if it is not the fundamental bass, moves up from the 4th scale degree to the 5th when it is the third, or from the 6th scale degree to the 5th when it is the fifth of the fundamental bass. | Just as the full stop is calming, so also is the perfect cadence or full cadence, where the lower voice, now the fundamental bass, descends from the 5th scale degree to the 1st and the upper voice, which after the lower voice is most prominent, moves from the 9th or 7th scale degree to the 8th. |

Chronological Chart of Punctuation References

| Treatise | Comma | Semicolon | Colon | Period |
|---|---|---|---|---|
| **56** **M. Lussy** **1873** | Bad phrasing [rhythmer] is like bad punctuation and bad accentuation in reading; ... Just as the punctuation of a grammatical phrase demands short or long pauses according to the sense of the words or groups of words which it has to separate, so all cadences require rests or pauses of a corresponding length to suit the musical sense or the group of sounds to which they form the close. The different *cadences*, which are comparable to the ends of phrases, phrase members, hemistiches, and the incises of an air, present all the elements of a musical phraseology, and are termed: the *perfect cadence*, the *imperfect cadence*, the *interrupted cadence*, the *half cadence*, the *quarter cadence*, &c., corresponding to the full stop, semicolon, colon, question mark, exclamation mark, suspension, and comma. | | | |
| **57** **R. West-phal** **1880** | It is from vocal music that the observance of the caesuras at the ends of colons [units of several metrical feet belonging to the same rhythmic unit and held together by one main accent] came to be regarded as indispensable in instrumental music as well. Certainly it is not always the composer who marks these caesuras; the performer himself must discover their places and convey them precisely to the listener. The latter is achieved through the appropriate nuances for each colon, a legato delivery if no rests occur within the colon, and the first lifting of the legato with the caesura. This basic condition for a clear and tasteful execution, which is unfortunately increasingly neglected, cannot be recommended too strongly. | | | |
| **58** **H. Riemann** **1882** | By **phrasing**, one describes the marking off of a single element of a melody through musical performance [Vortrag]. Phrasing is not difficult when the composer has indicated through the use of the legato curve [Legatobogen] how far a phrase extends within the larger whole; but unfortunately such cases occur only too seldom, and even our best masters have, especially in the piano movement, only very poorly hinted at the phrasing. The idea of introducing a new sign to facilitate the delimitation of phrases (colons), perhaps that of the comma which is customarily used as a sign for breathing in singing exercises (suggested by R. Westphal in his *Rhythmik* [1880] but already in use beforehand by Lebert and Stark in their Klavierschule), is worth heeding. In any case, it is little advisable to use the legato curve, because it has on occasion become confused with the tie (slur), a symbol which has also become known to include in its meaning notes which should be performed staccato. Frankly brackets ⌐——— would greatly distort the musical notation, while little hooks ' would be scarcely noticeable. — In an additional sense, one also understands by phrasing, the more refined nuances of performance, the diverse accents (see Accent), crescendo and diminuendo, stringendo and ritardando, extensions of individual notes in order to achieve greater expression, etc. See Expression [Ausdruck]. | | | |
| **59** **J. Hofmann** **1909** | Can you give an amateur a concise definition of phrasing and a few helpful suggestions as to clear phrasing? Phrasing is a rational division and subdivision of musical sentences, and serves to make them intelligible. It corresponds closely with punctuation in literature and its recitation. Find out the start, the end, and the culminating point of your phrase. The last-named is usually to be found upon the highest note of the phrase, while the former are usually indicated by phrasing slurs.... The regular way to conclude a phrase, or observe a pause, as you say, is to lift the arm from the keyboard and keep the wrist perfectly limp, so that the arm carries the loosely hanging hand upward. | | | |

Chronological Chart of Punctuation References

| Treatise | Comma | Semicolon | Colon | Period |
|---|---|---|---|---|
| **60** **D.** **Alexanian** **1922** | The "Legato." So far, the exercises have required the use of all the bow. We will now occupy ourselves with the fragmentary use of the latter. I cannot omit a few general remarks on this subject, although I know that their full purport will not be realized until after the study of intensities [dynamic oppositions or fluctuations]. In violoncello-playing nothing (unless it be the fingering) is so personal as the choice of bowing. And yet it is only after having formed a well balanced bow-technique that it will be possible to think of regulating, one's self, the "articulations" (or divisions of the strokes of the bow) after one's own conceptions of musical punctuation, and also according to the prominence that one wishes, from personal taste, to give rather to this note than to that one. | | | |
| **61** **J. Fischer** **1926** | Explanation of Signs. The punctuation marks of grammar (, ; : ? !) I use faithfully as the signs for the members of musical sentences. For the period, I use this form ⊙. & is that which in writing is the customary sign for and. Standing *between* two time units (notes or pauses), it denotes the *close fitting, close separating* bond between both adjacent sentence parts. & and ⊃⊂, standing *below* a note or pause, are the signs for *sentence interconnection* (accumulation or intertwining); it indicates that the relevant current value belongs to both the preceding and the following part of the sentence. ∩ and ⊃ are signs for *sentence emphasis*. ∩ indicates the heavy, ⊃ the light accent (ictus). The ictus should be portrayed with the same delicacy as the metrical accent; an intentional, reasoned stress beyond a rhythmical, truly musical delivery. | | | |

# Notes

## Introduction

*Epigraph.* South Bay Toastmasters, "Invocation and the Pledge of Allegiance," http://www.southbaytoastmasters.org/handbook/invocation.htm (accessed November 15, 2004; site now discontinued).

1. Robert Pinsky, interview by Scott Simon, *Weekend Edition-Saturday*, National Public Radio, February 28, 1998.

2. Restore Our Pledge of Allegiance, "Pledge History," http://www.restorethepledge.com/history.html.

3. Ken Lynn, "The Origin and Meaning of the Pledge of Allegiance," *Freethought Today*, May, 1999, http://www.ffrf.org/fttoday/1999/May99/lynn.html.

4. "Lawmakers Blast Pledge Ruling," *CNN.com*, June 27, 2002, http://archives.cnn.com/2002/LAW/06/26/plege.allegiance.

5. "Senators Call Pledge Decision 'Stupid,'" *CNN.com*, June 27, 2002, http://archives.cnn.com/2002/ALLPOLITICS/06/26/senate.resolution.pledge/index.html.

6. "Pledge History," http://www.restorethepledge.com/history.html.

7. M. B. Parkes begins his history of punctuation by stating, "PUNCTUATION is a phenomenon of written language, and its history is bound up with that of the written medium" (*Pause and Effect: An Introduction to the History of Punctuation in the West* [Berkeley: University of California Press, 1993], 1). John Lennard also claims that "punctuation is a feature only of written language, and could not begin to develop until writing was fully established" (*But I Digress: The Exploitation of Parentheses in English Printed Verse* [Oxford: Clarendon, 1991], 2).

8. Paul Henry Saenger, *Space between Words: The Origins of Silent Reading* (Stanford, CA: Stanford University Press, 1997), 11.

9. Parkes, *Pause and Effect*, 69. Roy Harris is particularly critical of Parkes's historical simplification in this matter. As a linguist he wants to know more about how writing came to be regarded as an autonomous mode of visual communication. However he does not disagree with the basic course of events, and for our purposes, Parkes's summary will suffice. Roy Harris, review of *Pause and Effect*, *Language Sciences* 16 (1994): 333.

10. Parkes, *Pause and Effect*, 88.

11. Ibid., 5–6.

12. There is some controversy as to who actually wrote the Pledge of Allegiance. Both Francis Bellamy (1855–1931) and James B. Upham (1845–1905) worked for

*The Youth's Companion*, but credit is generally given to Bellamy. "Pledge History," http://www.restorethepledge.com/history.html.

13. "National School Celebration of Columbus Day," *The Youth's Companion*, September 8, 1892, 446.

14. Dr. John W. Baer, "The Pledge of Allegiance: A Short History," 1992, http://history. vineyard.net/pledge.htm.

15. "National School Celebration of Columbus Day," *The Youth's Companion*, 446.

16. The Encyclopedia Britannica uses the following form: "I pledge allegiance to my Flag and the Republic for which it stands; one Nation indivisible, with Liberty and Justice for all," *Encyclopedia Britannica Online*, s.v. "Pledge of Allegiance to the Flag of the United States of America," http://search.eb.com/eb/article? tocld=9060389.

17. For information regarding early uses of the semicolon, see Parkes, *Pause and Effect*, 86.

18. *Encyclopedia Britannica Online*, s.v. "Pledge of Allegiance to the Flag of the United States of America."

19. There is of course still some gesture associated with the pledge. As we begin we stand, placing our right hands over our hearts. Then when the recitation has been completed, we drop our hands and return to our seats.

20. *Funk and Wagnalls Standard Dictionary* (New York: Harper and Row, 1983), s.v. "Basic Style Manual" (by Alice Ottun), 991.

21. Paul A. Robinson, *Opera, Sex, and Other Vital Matters* (Chicago: University of Chicago Press, 2002) 305–6.

22. Lynne Truss, *Eats, Shoots and Leaves: The Zero Tolerance Approach to Punctuation* (London: Profile Books, 2003), 95–96.

23. Joseph Robertson, preface to *An Essay on Punctuation* (London, 1785).

24. Claude Buffier, *A French Grammar on a New Plan, Translated into English* (London, 1734). The 1734 English translation is clearly based not on Buffier's original *Grammaire françoise sur un plan nouveau, pour en rendre les principes plus clairs & la pratique plus aisée* (Paris: Chez N. Le Clerc, 1709), but on the enlarged and revised version, *Grammaire françoise sur un plan nouveau, avec un traité de la prononciation des e, & un abrégé des régles de la poésie françoise* (published in Paris in 1723, and again in 1729 and 1732). 149. See also appendix B, entry 15.

25. Trevor Butterworth, "Two countries Separated by a Semicolon," *Financial Times Weekend Edition*, September 17/18, 2005.

26. David Crystal, *Language and the Internet* (Cambridge: Cambridge University Press, 2001), 164; Nicholson Baker, "The History of Punctuation," in *The Size of Thoughts* (New York: Random House, 1996), 73.

27. Sarah Lyall, "Punctuation an Unlikely Subject for Bestseller," *New York Times*, January 5, 2004, http://www.nytimes.com/2004/01/05/books/05GRAM.html.

28. See appendix B, entry 50, and also entry 30.

29. See pp. 110–12.

30. James Webster, "The Triumph of Variability: Haydn's Articulation Markings in the Autograph of Sonata No. 49 in E flat," in *Haydn, Mozart, and Beethoven: Studies in the Music of the Classical Period*, ed. Sieghard Brandenburg (Oxford: Clarendon, 1998), 34.

31. Jacob Schuback, *Von der musicalischen Declamation* (Göttingen: Vandenhoecks Wittwe, 1775), 28.

32. See appendix B, entry 42.

33. Mary Sue Morrow, *German Music Criticism in the Late Eighteenth Century* (Cambridge: Cambridge University Press, 1997), 4–18; Alan Kors, ed., *Encyclopedia of the Enlightenment*, 4 vols. (Oxford and New York: Oxford University Press, 2002), s.v. "Music" (by Thomas Christensen).

# Chapter One

*Epigraph.* Thomas Mace, preface to *Musick's Monument* (London, 1676; facsimile ed. in 2 vols., Paris: Éditions du centre national de la recherche scientifique, 1958–66), pref., 118.

1. Mark Evan Bonds, *Wordless Rhetoric: Musical Forms and the Metaphor of Oration* (Cambridge, MA: Harvard University Press, 1991), 68. See also Brian Vickers, *In Defense of Rhetoric* (Oxford: Clarendon, 1988), 361; Wilibald Gurlitt, "Musik und Rhetorik: Hinweise auf ihre geschichtliche Grundlagenheit," in *Musikgeschichte und Gegenwart*, ed. Hans Heinrich Eggebrecht, 2 vols. (Wiesbaden: Franz Steiner, 1966), 1:65.

2. Leopold Mozart, *Versuch einer gründlichen Violinschule* (Augsburg, 1756; facsimile ed., Frankfurt am Main: H. L. Grahl, 1956) 108ff; trans. Editha Knocker as *A Treatise on the Fundamental Principles of Violin Playing* (London: Oxford University Press, 1985) 102ff. See also Mozart [22], appendix B.

3. See George Barth, *The Pianist as Orator: Beethoven and the Transformation of Keyboard Style* (Ithaca, NY: Cornell University Press, 1992), 24.

4. According to Bonds, this is one of the most significant developments in musical thought over the course of the eighteenth century (*Wordless Rhetoric*, 68).

5. Jean-Jacques Rousseau, *Écrits sur la musique* (Paris: Chez Lefèvre, 1859), 229.

6. Kofi Agawu, *Playing with Signs: A Semiotic Inerpretation of Classic Music* (Princeton, NJ: Princeton University Press, 1991), 7.

7. Tom Beghin poses this in explanation of why eighteenth-century or earlier music theorists resorted to rhetorical terminology ("Forkel and Haydn" [DMA thesis, Cornell University, 1996], 19).

8. Hermann Keller, *Phrasierung und Artikulation: ein Beitrag zu einer Sprachlehre der Musik* (Kassel: Bärenreiter, 1955) 18–19; trans. Leigh Gerdine as *Phrasing and Articulation: A Contribution to a Rhetoric of Music* (London: Barrie and Rockliff, 1966) 14.

9. Truss, *Eats, Shoots and Leaves*, 70.

10. Joshua Steele, preface to *Prosodia rationalis, or An Essay towards Establishing the Melody and Measure of Speech, to be Expressed and Perpetuated by Peculiar Symbols* (London, 1775), viii.

11. Giusepe Maria Cambini, *Nouvelle méthode théorique et pratique pour le violon, divisée en 3 parties* (Paris, ca. 1795; facsimile ed., Geneva: Minkoff, 1972), 19–22; trans. Elisabeth Le Guin; see http://epub.library.ucla.edu/leguin/boccherini/contents.htm.

12. Johann Mattheson, *Der vollkommene Capellmeister* (Hamburg: Herold, 1739; facsimile ed., Kassel, Bärenreiter, 1954), 160–70; trans. Ernest C. Harriss as *Johann Mattheson's "Der vollkommene Capellmeister": A Revised Translation with Critical Commentary* (Ann Arbor, MI: UMI Reasearch Press, 1981), 344–63. See also Heinrich Christoph Koch, *Versuch einer Anleitung zur Composition*, vols. 2–3 (1787–93; facsimile ed., Hildesheim: Georg Olms, 1969), 3:13–18; trans. Nancy Kovaleff Baker as

*Introductory Essay on Composition: The Mechanical Rules of Melody, Sections 3 and 4* (New Haven, CT: Yale University Press, 1983), 66–69.

13. Brian Vickers, "Figures of Rhetoric/Figures of Music?" *Rhetorica* 2 (1984): 2.

14. This in spite of the fact that Walker would later write *Melody of Speaking Delineated* (1787). John Walker, preface to *Elements of Elocution*, 2 vols. (London, 1781), 1:xii. Walker's acknowledgment of the importance in using musical concepts to describe speech very likely came from Quintilian: "Aristoxenus the musician divides all that belongs to the voice into 'rhythm,' and 'melody in measure'; of which the one consists in *modulation*, the other in *singing* and tunes. Are not all these qualifications then, necessary to the orator, the one of which relates to gesture, the second to the collocation of words, and the third to the inflexions of the voice, which in speaking are extremely numerous?" (*Education of an Orator*, trans. John Selby Watson [London: Haddon, Brothers, and Co., 1856] 1:82 [1.10.22–23]).

15. Steele, *An Essay towards Establishing the Melody and Measure of Speech*, 24–26.

16. Koch, *Versuch einer Anleitung* 2:356; trans. Baker, 6.

17. Vickers, "Fugues of Rhetoric/Figures of Music?" 17–18; Hans-Heinrich Unger, *Die Beziehungen zwischen Music und Rhetorik im 16.–18. Jahrhundert* (Hildesheim: Georg Olms, 1969), 56.

18. J. S. Bach, *Sechs Brandenburgische Konzerte*, ed. Heinrich Besseler, *Neue Ausgabe sämtlicher Werke*, Series VII, 2 (Kassel: Bärenreiter, 1956).

19. In Unger's example, the paired slurs over the sixteenth notes on beats one and two are absent, which may have affected his placement of the comma.

20. Vickers, in his review of Barth's *The Pianist as Orator*, also finds that the fault lies not in Barth's scholarly knowledge but in the flimsy foundations of the tradition itself (review of *The Pianist as Orator: Beethoven and the Transformation of Keyboard Style*, by George Barth," *Rhetorica* 13 (1995): 98–101.

21. Vickers, *In Defense of Rhetoric*, 364.

22. Mozart, *Quartette mit einem Blasinstrument*, ed. Jaroslav Pohanka, *Neue Ausgabe sämtlicher Werke*, Series VIII, 20 (Kassel: Bärenreiter, 1962).

23. G. F. Händel, *Elf Sonaten für Flöte und Basso continuo*, ed. Hans-Peter Schmitz with a new edition by Terence Best, *Hallische Händel-Ausgabe*, Series 4, Group 3 (Kassel: Bärenreiter, 1995). Mary Oleskiewicz suggests that since the term, *flauto*, which generally meant recorder, was also used in Dresden to indicate transverse flute, this work could have also been intended for the latter instrument. See Mary Oleskiewicz, "Quantz and the Flute at Dresden: His Instruments, His Repertory, and Their Significance for the *Versuch* and the Bach Circle" (PhD diss., Duke University, 1998), 56–59, 213.

24. Charles Burney, *A General History of Music, from the Earliest Ages to the Present Period*, 4 vols. (London, 1776–89), 4:643. See Barth, *The Pianist as Orator*, 31; and Bonds, *Wordless Rhetoric*, 62–66.

25. Koch, *Versuch einer Anleitung* 2:350; trans. adapted from Baker, 4n.

26. Mattheson, *Der vollkommene Capellmeister*, 170; trans. Harriss, 363.

27. Koch, *Versuch einer Anleitung* 3:19; trans. Baker, 69.

28. J. S. Bach, *Präludien, Toccaten, Fantasien und Fugen II*, ed. Dietrich Kilian, *Neue Ausgabe sämtlicher Werke*, Series IV, 6 (Kassel: Bärenreiter, 1964).

29. Marpurg's weekly periodical *Kritische Briefe über die Tonkunst* consists of 128 letters dated from June 23, 1759 to January 15, 1763. His extensive essay on the subject of punctuation (first in language and then in music) is covered in letters 104 to 117 (July 31, 1762–October 30, 1762). The facsimile edition published by Georg

Olms in 1974 presents, in two volumes, a reprint of the original three-volume periodical as it was published in Berlin by Friedrich Wilhelm Birnstiel, 1760–64.

30. Johann Mattheson, *Der vollkommene Capellmeister*, 145; trans. adapted from Harriss, 317–18.

31. For further discussion of extramusical associations and eighteenth-century instrumental practice, see James Webster, *Haydn's "Farewell" Symphony and the Idea of Classical Style: Through-Composition and Cyclic Integration in His Instrumental Music* (Cambridge and New York: Cambridge University Press, 1991), 225–49.

32. Bonds, *Wordless Rhetoric*, 173.

33. Morrow, *German Music Criticism*, 4–18; Simon P. Keefe, "Koch's Commentary on the Late Eighteenth-Century Concerto: Dialogue, Drama and Solo/Orchestra Relations," *Music and Letters* 79 (1998): 371.

34. *Grove Music Online*, s.v. "Absolute Music" (by Roger Scruton), http://www.grovemusic.com.

35. *The New Princeton Encyclopedia of Poetry and Poetics*, s.v. "Semiotics, poetic" (by Peter Steiner), http://lion.chadwyck.com/lion_ref_ref/search. See also Patricia Bizzell and Bruce Herzberg, *The Rhetorical Tradition: Readings from Classical Times to the Present*, 2nd ed. (Boston: Bedford/St. Martin's, 2001) 1189–90.

36. Agawu, *Playing with Signs*, 5.

37. *The Oxford Companion to English Literature*, 5th ed., s.v. "Chomsky, Noam."

38. Leonard Bernstein, *The Unanswered Question: Six Talks at Harvard* (Cambridge, MA: Harvard University Press, 1976).

39. Joel Lester, in his thorough history of eighteenth-century compositional theory, explains that Koch's analogies between music and language at first appear to put him in the same category as Mattheson and others who borrowed many concepts from rhetoric. But where Mattheson's application of rhetorical terms often failed to illuminate the musical structure on its own terms, Koch's emphasis was always on the music (*Compositional Theory in the Eighteenth Century* [Cambridge, MA: Harvard University Press, 1992] 286).

40. Park Honan, "Eighteenth and Nineteenth Century English Punctuation Theory," *English Studies* 41 (1960): 102.

41. Bonds explains that the overwhelming references to musical punctuation are largely due "to important changes in musical style that are characterized by units of increasingly smaller size and slower harmonic rhythm: short, more or less symmetrical phrases replace the long, spun-out melodies of earlier generations (*Wordless Rhetoric*, 74); See also Ratner, "Eighteenth-Century Theories of Musical Period Structure," *Musical Quarterly* 42 (1956): 439.

42. Johann Philipp Kirnberger, *Die Kunst des reinen Satzes in der Musik*, 2 vols. (Berlin and Königsberg, 1776–79; facsimile ed., Hildesheim: Georg Olms, 1968), 1:100–101; trans. of 1st ed. by David Beach and Jurgen Thym as *The Art of Strict Musical Composition* (New Haven, CT: Yale University Press, 1982), 118. The first edition of vol. 1 from Kirnberger's *Die Kunst des reinen Satzes in der Musik* was published in Berlin, by Christian Friedrich Voss in 1771. According to David Beach, although the Olms reprint claims to be a photocopy of the Berlin and Königsberg edition of 1776–79, it could not be since the first volume was not printed during that time. The reprint is therefore probably a copy of either the 1771 first edition or the 1774 reprint. (Introduction to *The Art of Strict Musical Composition*, xviii).

43. Gregory Butler, "Fugue and Rhetoric," *Journal of Music Theory* 21, no. 2 (1977): 49–50.

44. Mattheson, *Der vollkommene Capellmeister*, 244, 368; trans. Harriss, 484, 695.

45. Mattheson, *Kern melodischer Wißenschafft* (Hamburg, 1737; facsimile ed., Hildesheim: Georg Olms, 1976), 146. The asterisk is omitted in the version of this example included in *Der vollkommene Capellmeister*, 368.

46. Antoine Reicha, *Traité de haute composition musicale*, 2 vols. (Paris: Zetter & Cie., 1824–25), 2:222.

47. Leonard Ratner, *Classic Music: Expression, Form, and Style* (New York: Schirmer, 1980), 271f.

48. Reicha, *Traité de haute composition musicale* 2:224–25.

49. Cambini, *Nouvelle méthode pour le violon*, 23.

# Chapter Two

1. Honan, "English Punctuation Theory," 92.

2. Jane Donawerth finds this definition of rhetoric to be more inclusive, particularly of rhetorics by women which tend not to treat either argument or persuasion (preface to *Rhetorical Theory by Women before 1900: An Anthology* [Lanham, MD: Rowman & Littlefield, 2002], xv). Bizzell and Herzberg state that because rhetoric is a complex discipline with a long history, it is less helpful to try to define it once and for all than to look at how it was defined at various points along the way, and how these definitions have shaped our understanding of rhetoric today (*The Rhetorical Tradition*, 1).

3. *Encyclopedia of the Enlightenment*, s.v. "Rhetoric" (by Thomas M. Conley); Bizzell and Herzberg, *The Rhetorical Tradition*, 792–94.

4. See Bizzell and Herzberg, *The Rhetorical Tradition*, 805, 862.

5. See Thomas M. Conley, *Rhetoric in the European Tradition*, (Chicago: University of Chicago Press, 1990) 202–6.

6. Quintilian, *De institutione oratoria*; trans. with notes by John Selby Watson as *Institutes of Oratory, or Education of an Orator*, 2 vols. (London: H. G. Bohm, 1855–56).

7. See Conley, *Rhetoric in the European Tradition*, 38. Brian Vickers states that "it was, after all, Quintilian who had first linked the two arts, urging the orator to learn from musicians flexibility in voice-inflexion, and above all 'the variation of arrangement and sound to suit the demands of the case.' Both arts, Quintilian stated, know how to adapt form to feeling, find the appropriate expression for emotions" (*In Defense of Rhetoric*, 372). See also Ursula Kirkendale, "The Source for Bach's *Musical Offering*: The *Institutio oratoria* of Quintilian," *Journal of the American Musicological Society* 33 (1980): 88–141.

8. Quintilian, *Institutes of Oratory* 1:147 [1.2.38], 2:391–92 [2.12.1]. Watson's nineteenth-century translation of Quintilian's work is highly regarded and widely accepted as providing the closest flavor to the original Latin. See Bizzell and Herzberg, *The Rhetorical Tradition*, 363.

9. It is argued that the concept of the good speaker as a good man is already familiar from Plato, Isocrates and Cicero, though perhaps none go into quite as much detail as Quintilian regarding his complete education from birth to retirement. See Bizzell and Herzberg, *The Rhetorical Tradition* 360; and also Conley's discussion of Isocrates (*Rhetoric in the European Tradition*, 17–20).

10. Bizzell and Herzberg, *The Rhetorical Tradition*, 3.

11. Quintilian, *Education of an Orator* 2:352–53 [11.3.35–39]; Parkes, *Pause and Effect*, 66.

12. Quintilian, *Education of an Orator* 2:344–45 [11.3.165–66].

13. Ibid. 2:360 [11.3.108–11].

14. Ibid. 2:371 [11.3.65–66 ]. Quintilian states: "As to the hands, without the aid of which all delivery would be deficient and weak, it can scarcely be told of what a variety of motions they are susceptible, since they almost equal in expression the powers of language itself; for other parts of the body assist the speaker, but these, I may almost say, speak themselves" (2:364 [11.3.85]). See also Robert Toft, "Action and Singing in Late 18th- and Early 19th-Century England," *Performance Practice Review* 9, no. 2 (1996): 151.

15. Quintilian, *Education of an Orator* 2:239–40 [9.4.122–25].

16. Saenger, *Space between Words*, 11.

17. "There is little evidence that before the sixth century, guides to *phrasing* (punctuation) originated with the author" (Parkes, *Pause and Effect*, 9–11).

18. Saenger, *Space between Words*, 11.

19. Parkes, *Pause and Effect*, 9–10. See also Nicholson Baker, *The Size of Thoughts: Essays and other Lumber* (New York: Random House, 1996) 75.

20. Saenger, *Space between Words*, 72. Word separation is believed to have developed in Ireland in the late seventh century (see Lennard, *But I Digress*, 2).

21. Parkes, *Pause and Effect*, 4.

22. Ibid., 4, 66.

23. Quintilian, *Education of an Orator* 1:97–99 [2.2.4–12].

24. I must confess to having told this rather simplistic story of a vying gramatical and rhetorical punctuation in an earlier form of the present manuscript. See Stephanie Vial, "Take Pause: Musical Punctuation in the Eighteenth Century" (DMA hhesis, Cornell University, 2000).

25. David Cram, "Seventeenth-Century Punctuation Theory: Butler's Philosophical Analysis and Wilkins' Philosophical Critique," *Folia Linguistica Historica* 8 (1989): 310–11. For Cram, a more consistent, optimal use of punctuation is achieved in the eighteenth century, following a period of great fluctuation in practice in the seventeenth century. Park Honan tells the same story but where it is the eighteenth century which witnesses a great diversity in practice and the nineteenth century that achieves a better balance in usage ("English Punctuation Theory").

26. Parkes, *Pause and Effect*, 90–92.

27. Quintilian, *Education of an Orator* 2:221–23 [9.4.44–51].

28. Ibid. 2:227 [9.4.66–70]. See also Parkes, *Pause and Effect*, 66.

29. Quintilian, *Education of an Orator* 2:239–40 [9.4.121–31]. This kind of rhythm will become important in our distinction between prose and verse in chapter 6.

30. Parkes, *Pause and Effect*, 87.

31. Truss, *Eats, Shoots and Leaves*, 178–79.

32. From R. J. Scholes and B. J. Willis's 1990 study, "Prosodic and Syntactic Functions of Punctuation: A Contribution to the Study of Orality and Literacy." Saenger, *Space between Words*, 52.

33. Conley, *Rhetoric in the European Tradition*, 111–20.

34. Parkes, *Pause and Effect*, 81.

35. Ibid., 70, 81, 86–88.

36. James Murphy claims that it is clear from the outset that Ramus considered Aristotle and his followers, Cicero and Quintilian as a related group. Carole

Newlands and James J. Murphy, introduction to Petrus Ramus, *Arguments in Rhetoric against Quintilian* (Dekalb: Northern Illinois University Press, 1986) 7-9.

37. Bizzell and Herzberg, *The Rhetorical Tradition*, 679.

38. Ramus, *Arguments in Rhetoric against Quintilian*, 150.

39. Ibid., 154.

40. Parkes, *Pause and Effect*, 88-89.

41. Conley, *Rhetoric and the European Tradition*, 143-44.

42. "Rhetoric from late 1600s on, whether secular or sacred, was deeply discredited by the assumptions that rhetoric is no more than tropes and figures and, even if there were more to it, is unworthy of serious study" (Bizzell and Herzberg, *The Rhetorical Tradition*, 577).

43. Francis Bacon, *The Tvvoo Bookes of Francis Bacon: Of the Proficience and Aduancement of Learning, diuine and humane*. (London: Henrie Tomes, 1605), 17, http://wwwlib.umi.com/eebo/image/611/.

44. Conley, *Rhetoric in the European Tradition*, 154.

45. Bizzell and Herzberg, *The Rhetorical Tradition*, 796; Conley, *Rhetoric in the European Tradition*, 168.

46. Conley, *Rhetoric in the European Tradition*, 199-200.

47. Bizzell and Herzberg, *The Rhetorical Tradition*, 791.

48. Bacon, *The Tvvoo Bookes of Francis Bacon*, 17-18; Conley, *Rhetoric in the European Tradition*, 167-68.

49. Bizzell and Herzberg, *The Rhetorical Tradition*, 795.

50. Ibid., 794; Conley, *Rhetoric in the European Tradition*, 170.

51. Conley, *Rhetoric in the European Tradition*, 170.

52. Ibid., 165.

53. Bizzell and Herzberg, *The Rhetorical Tradition*, 794.

54. Parkes, *Pause and Effect*, 89.

55. Ibid., 89-90.

56. Thomas Sprat, *The History of the Royal-Society of London for the Improving of Natural Knowledge* (London: J. Martyn and J. Allestry, 1667); see Parkes, *Pause and Effect*, 90.

57. Bizzell and Herzberg, *The Rhetorical Tradition*, 794-95.

58. Conley, *Rhetoric in the European Tradition*, 174; Bernard Lamy, *The Art of Speaking: Written in French by Messieurs du Port Royal; In Pursuance of a Former Treatise, Entitled, The Art of Thinking. Rendered in English* (London, W. Taylor and H. Clements, 1708), 55.

59. John Constable, *Reflections upon the Accuracy of Style* (London: Henry Lintot, 1731), 6.

60. Bizzell and Herzberg, *The Rhetorical Tradition*, 798-99; Conley, *Rhetoric in the European Tradition*, 191-92.

61. Bizzell and Herzberg, *The Rhetorical Tradition*, 799.

62. Parkes, *Pause and Effect*, 90-91.

63. Conley, *Rhetoric in the European Tradition*, 203-5; Bizzell and Herzberg, *The Rhetorical Tradition*, 791-92.

64. Conley, *Rhetoric in the European Tradition*, 201-3. Charles Rollin, *The Method of Teaching and Studying the Belles Lettres, or an Introduction to Languages, Poetry, Rhetoric, History, Moral Philosophy, Physicks, &c., Translated from the French, In Four Volumes* (London: A. Bettesworth and C. Hitch, 1734), 1:10-11.

65. Rollin, *The Method of Teaching and Studying the Belles Lettres* 1:63.

66. Conley emphasizes the French cultural dominance of the eighteenth century with regard to fashion, letters, education and political ideas. Rollin's *Traité* and other

French works circulated all over Europe, yet no English or German rhetorics were translated into French during the same period (*Rhetoric in the European Tradition*, 203–5).

67. Among the rhetorics discussed thus far, very little attention has been paid to this fifth and final stage known as *pronunciation*. Wilbur Howell sees the eighteenth-century focus on oral delivery as in part explained by reaction to Ramist influence; *Pronuntiatio*, which "classically" received less attention than *invention, disposition*, and *style* was the only part of rhetoric which was neither attacked by Ramus nor revised during the seventeenth century. Howell proposes that the basic justification of the Elocutionists could have been that the previous immunity of *pronuntiatio* to attack entitled it to be regarded as having a continuing validity; see Wilbur Samuel Howell, *Eighteenth-Century British Logic and Rhetoric* (Princeton, NJ: Princeton University Press, 1971), 153.

68. Bizzell and Herzberg, *The Rhetorical Tradition*, 802; Conley, *Rhetoric in the European Tradition*, 215–16.

69. Hugh Blair, *Lectures on Rhetoric and Belles Lettres, in Three Volumes* (Dublin, 1783), 1:161.

70. Thomas Sheridan, *A Course of Lectures on Elocution: Together with Two Dissertations on Language; and Some Other Tracts Relative to Those Subjects* (London, 1762), 79–80.

71. Denis Diderot and Jean le Rond d'Alembert, *Encyclopédie, ou Dictionnaire raisonné des sciences, des arts et des métiers, par une société de gens de lettres*, 17 vols (Paris, 1751–65), s.v. "Ponctuation," 13:16.

72. Rollin, *The Method of Teaching and Studying the Belles Lettres* 4:391–92.

73. Sheridan, *A Course of Lectures on Elocution*, 80.

74. Blair, *Lectures on Rhetoric*, 429.

75. Parkes, *Pause and Effect*, 92.

76. Lennard, *But I Digress*, 86–87.

77. Sheridan, *A Course of Lectures on Elocution*, 75–76.

78. John Walker, *A Rhetorical Grammar, or Course of Lessons in Elocution* (London, 1785) 30. See also Robert Toft, "The Expressive Pause," *Performance Practice Review* 7 (1994): 204.

79. Michel Le Faucher, *The Art of Speaking in Publick, or An Essay on the Action of an Orator; as to his Pronunciation and Gesture*, 2nd ed. (London, 1727), 170.

80. Lennard, *But I Digress*, 83.

81. Gilbert Austin, *Chironomia, or A Treatise on Rhetorical Delivery: Comprehending Many Precepts, both Ancient and Modern, for the Proper Regulation of the Voice, the Countenance, and Gesture* (London, 1806), 135. The degree of theatricality in gesture was a subject of much discussion. Fénelon argues in 1685 that the orator's action, in both public and private speech, should appear natural and suited to the subject matter (*Dialogues on Eloquence*, trans. Wilbur Samuel Howell [Princeton, NJ: Princeton University Press, 1951], 100). John Walker, while he believes that plain speaking should be the model rather than acting, one should not then run to the contrary extreme and condemn everything that is vehement and forcible (preface to *The Academic Speaker, or A Selection of Parliamentary Debates, Orations, Odes, Scenes, and Speeches, from the Best Writers* [Dublin, 1796], vii–viii). Thomas Sheridan prefers the conversational approach to public speaking, but his fellow Irishman, Austin, believes that pantomime should be the basis for all gesture; see Bizzell and Herzberg, *Rhetorical Tradition*, 889. See also Toft, "Action and Singing in Late 18th- and Early 19th-Century England," 148.

82. Austin, *Chironomia*, 433.

83. Gilbert Austin is one of the few to provide a detailed, effective notation system to be placed above the words in the text, as well as copious pictures. Many Elocutionists express the difficulty of notating gesture. For instance, John Walker complains of the difficulty in describing actions by words and hopes that the pictures he provides will help facilitate the reader's conception. Although they may not answer all needs, they are better than no attempt at all (preface to *The Academic Speaker*, ii). Thomas Sheridan bemoans the fact that no general, practical rules on gesture can be laid down with any efficiency. This is because in the present day there are no common standards or models for imitation. The best one can hope to do is to speak from the heart and thereby convey one's sincerity (*Lectures on Elocution*, 119–21). As Dene Barnett explains, the most concrete details of the eighteenth-century art of gesture are to be culled from among the writings of actors, singers, directors, teachers, and dramaturges (Dene Barnett, with Jeanette Massy-Westropp, *The Art of Gesture: The Practices and Principles of 18th Century Acting* [Heidelberg: Carl Winter Universitätsverlag, 1987], 7).

84. Walker, preface to *The Academic Speaker*, iii.

85. Charles Batteux, *A Course of the Belles Lettres, or The Principles of Literature.*, trans. Mr. Miller (London, 1761; orig. publ. Paris, 1753), 4:203. See also Barnett, *The Art of Gesture*, 321.

86. Austin, *Chironomia*, 394.

87. Walker, preface to *The Academic Speaker*, v.

88. Toft, "Action and Singing," 156.

89. Austin, *Chironomia*, 435; Barnett, *The Art of Gesture*, 358.

90. From Johann Gottfried Pfannenberg, *Über die rednerische Action mit erläuternden Beispielen; verzüglich für studierende Jünglinge* (Leipzig, 1796); trans. in Barnett, *The Art of Gesture*, 360.

91. Toft, *Action and Singing*, 156–57.

92. Quintilian, *Education of an Orator* 2:370 [11.3].

93. Austin, *Chironomia*, 379–80.

94. From Karl August Böttiger, *Entwickelung des Ifflandischen Spiels in vierzehn Darstellungen auf dem weimarischen Hoftheater im Aprillmonath 1796* (Leipzig, 1796); trans. in Barnett, *The Art of Gesture*, 80.

95. Barnett, *The Art of Gesture*, 275.

96. Austin, *Chironomia*, 52.

97. Conley, *Rhetoric in the European Tradition*, 224; Bizzell and Herzberg, *The Rhetorical Tradition*, 802.

98. Glenn J. Broadhead, "A Bibliography of the Rhetoric of Conversation in England, 1660–1800," *Rhetoric Society Quarterly* 10 (1980): 43.

99. Kevin L. Cope, preface to *Compendious Conversations: The Method of Dialogue in the Early Enlightenment*, ed. Kevin L. Cope (Frankfurt am Main and New York: P. Lang, 1992), xii.

100. Peter Burke, *The Art of Conversation* (Ithaca, NY: Cornell University Press, 1993), 114.

101. Henry Fielding, "An Essay on Conversation," in *Miscellanies, In Three Volumes* (London, 1743) 1:99–100, 96–97.

102. Sheridan, *A Course of Lectures on Elocution*, 186.

103. The textbook, designed for home schooling, was written with her father: Maria Edgeworth and Richard Lovell Edgeworth, *Practical Education*, 2 vols. (London: J. Johnson, 1798), 2:408–9.

104. Adolf Freiherr von Knigge, *Practical Philosophy of Social Life, or The Art of Conversing with Men, in Two Volumes* (London, 1794).

105. Jennifer Georgia, "The Joys of Social Intercourse: Men, Women, and Conversation in the Eighteenth Century," in *Compendious Conversations*, ed. Kevin L. Cope, 249. Burke also describes the influence of printed conversation on actual speech, for instance treatises on subject presented in dialogue form as models for readers (*The Art of Conversation*, 118–20).

106. This is quoted by Mallet and Marmontel from the author of a preface to M. de Fénelon's *Dialogues* on eloquence; trans. in *The Encyclopedia of Diderot and d'Alembert: A Collaborative Translation Project*, s.v. "Dialogue," http://name.umdl. umich.edu/ did2222.0000.362/. Hugh Blair claims that "among the Ancients, Plato is eminent for the beauty of his dialogues" (*Lectures on Rhetoric* 3:83). See also Burke, *The Art of Conversation*, 96.

107. Constable, preface to *Reflections upon the Accuracy of Style*, iii–iv.

108. Blair, *Lectures on Rhetoric and Belle Lettres* 3:82.

109. Parkes, *Pause and Effect*, 92–93.

110. Eighteenth-century experimentation with how to indicate dialogue in theatrical works is also evident. Jean Varloot focuses particularly on Diderot's *Dorval et moi*, describing the various uses of italics, parentheses, *guillements*, and *points de suspension*, as well as the numerous verbal directions written in the margins regarding gesture and punctuation ("Diderot du dialogue à la dramaturgie: L'invention de la ponctuation au XVIIIe siècle," *Langue française* 45 (1980): 41–49.

111. From "Direct," in Diderot and d'Alembert, *Encyclopédie*. See Vivienne Mylne, "The Punctuation of Dialogue in Eighteenth-Century French and English Fiction," *Library: A Quarterly Journal of Bibliography* 1 (1979): 50.

112. Mylne, "The Punctuation of Dialogue," 45.

113. Mylne refers in particular to Samuel Richardson's multipurpose use of the dash to indicate changes of speaker, moments of drama and tension, and the characterization of conversation among foolish and pretentious people (Ibid., 60–61). Parkes also notes the influence of Richardson (master printer as well as novelist) on the practice of later authors with regard to the em-rule or dash, and a series of points (*Pause and Effect*, 93).

114. See Jennifer Georgia's discussion of *Evelina* in "The Joys of Social Intercourse," 253–55.

115. Fanny Burney, *Evelina, or The History of a Young Lady's Entrance into the World*, 3rd ed., 3 vols. (London: T. Lowndes, 1779) 2:25–26.

116. Mylne notes that the device of putting each response on a new line seems not to have been completely accepted by most printers until the nineteenth century in both England and France ("The Punctuation of Dialogue," 61).

117. Translation from *De l'Allemagne* taken from Madame the Baroness de Staël-Holstein, *Germany*, ed. O. W. Wight (Boston and New York: Houghton, Miflin and Co., 1859), 78, http://www.hti.umich.edu.

118. Diderot and d'Alembert, *Encyclopédie*, s.v. "Dialogue," 4:936; trans. in *The Encyclopedia of Diderot and d'Alembert*, s.v. "Dialogue."

119. For a discussion of the difference between English and French conversational styles, see Burke, *The Art of Conversation*, 111–12.

120. De Staël, *Germany*, 91. According to Morellet, the bad habit of interrupting is a particular French shortcoming; see Barbara R. Hanning, "Conversation and Musical Style in the Late Eighteenth-Century Parisian Salon," *Eighteenth-Century Studies* 22 (1989): 515–16.

121. De Staël, *Germany*, 92. It should be noted that the concept of the sublime, mentioned here by de Staël, plays an important role among eighteenth-century aesthetics. The first-century treatise *On the Sublime*, believed to have been written by Cassius Longinus, had become very well known and influential, particularly after its 1674 translation by the French literary critic, Nicolas Boileau. De Staël uses the term in the sense that anything "sublime" was perceived to have a very powerful emotional impact on its audience—the antithesis of that which is "vulgar." For some of the standard texts on the subject, see Cassius Longinus, *On the Sublime*, trans. T. S. Dorsch (London: Penguin, 1965); Nicolas Boileau-Despréaux, "Preface to His Translation of Longinus on the Sublime," in *Selected Criticism*, trans. Ernest Dilworth (Indianapolis: Bobbs-Merill, 1965), 43–52; Edmund Burke, *A Philosophical Enquiry into the Sublime and Beautiful* (London: Penguin, 1998), 101–27; Immanuel Kant, *The Critique of Judgment*, trans. Werner Pluhar (Indianapolis: Hackett, 1987); Frances Ferguson, *Solitude and the Sublime: Romanticism and the Aesthetics of Individuation* (New York: Routledge, 1992); Timothy Gould, "Intensity and Its Audiences: Toward a Feminist Perspective on the Kantian Sublime," in *Feminism and Tradition in Aesthetics*, ed. Peggy Zeglin Brand and Carolyn Korsmeyer, 66–87 (University Park: Penn State University Press, 1995); Jean-Francois Lyotard, *Lessons on the Analytic of the Sublime (Kant's Critique of Judgement, sections 23–29)*, trans. Elizabeth Rottenberg (Stanford, CA: Stanford University Press, 1994); Kirk Pillow, *Sublime Understanding: Aesthetic Reflection in Kant and Hegel* (Cambridge, MA: MIT Press, 2000); Eva Schaper, "Taste, Sublimity, and Genius: The Aesthetics of Nature and Art," in *The Cambridge Companion to Kant*, ed. Paul Guyer, 367–93 (Cambridge, New York, and Melbourne: Cambridge University Press, 1992); and Bizzell and Herzberg, *The Rhetorical Tradition*, 344–45.

122. Burke, *The Art of Conversation*, 112–13.

123. Jane Donawerth, preface to *Rhetorical Theory by Women*, xv–xvi.

124. Hannah More, *Essays on Various Subjects, Principally Designed for Young Ladies* (London, 1777), 57.

125. Walter Ong, *Orality and Literacy: The Technologizing of the Word* (London: Methuen, 1982) 111–12. Judith Mattson Bean, "Conversation as Rhetoric in Margaret Fuller's *Woman in the Nineteenth Century*," in *In Her Own Voice: Nineteenth-Century American Women Essayists*, ed. Sherry Lee Linkon (New York and London: Garland, 1997), 27. Katherine Ann Jensen, *Writing Love: Letters, Women, and the Novel in France, 1605–1776* (Carbondale: Southern Illinois University Press, 1995).

126. Bean, "Conversation as Rhetoric," 29–31. For more information concerning feminine styles of discourse, see Jennifer Coates, *Women, Men and Language: A Sociolinguistic Account of Sex Differences in Language* (New York: Longman, 1986); Erica Harth, *Cartesian Women: Versions and Subversions of Rational Discourse in the Old Regime* (Ithaca, NY: Cornell University Press, 1992).

127. Olwen H. Hufton, *The Prospect Before Her: A History of Women in Western Europe* (New York: Alfred Knopf, Distributed by Random House, 1996), 433–34. Burke states that the golden age of the salon was the seventeenth century and particularly in Paris (*The Art of Conversation*, 115). For more information on salons in England, Germany and Italy, and the Netherlands, see *The Encyclopedia of the Enlightenment*, s.v. "Salons."

128. Hufton, *The Prospect Before Her*, 434; Burke, *The Art of Conversation*, 116.

129. *Encyclopedia of the Enlightenment*, s.v. "Salon: France" (by Rosena Davison).

130. Dena Goodman, "Seriousness of Purpose: Salonnières, Philosophes, and the Shaping of the Eighteenth-Century Salon," *Proceedings of the Annual Meeting of the Western Society for French History* 15 (1988): 111.

131. Burke, *The Art of Conversation*, 116.

132. See Hufton, *The Prospect Before Her*, 438; and Goodman, "Seriousness of Purpose," 111–13.

133. David Hume, *Essays, Moral and Political*, 2 vols. (Edinburgh: A. Kincaid, 1742), 2:5–6.

134. Knigge, *The Art of Conversing with Men* 2:245.

135. Georgia, "The Joys of Social Intercourse," 255.

136. Robert Lowth, *A Short Introduction to English Grammar* (London, 1762), 154–55.

137. Ibid., 166–67. See also Parkes, *Pause and Effect*, 92.

138. Bizzell and Herzberg, *The Rhetorical Tradition*, 792, 802.

139. Lennard, *But I Digress*, 84.

140. Parkes, *Pause and Effect*, 92.

141. Honan, "English Punctuation Theory," 93.

142. Honan explains that David Steel, in his *Elements of Punctuation* of 1786, represents the closest the eighteenth century comes to demanding a purely syntactically based punctuation: "Grammar, which ought to be the basis of punctuation, has seldom been considered as adequate to the purpose: too much accommodation to the reader, and too little attention to grammatical construction have usually been the sources whence the doctrine of points has been deduced" ("English Punctuation Theory," 97). Parkes adds that we must interpret the remarks of such authors with caution; writers like Steel are reacting against prevailing uses rather than reflecting them (*Pause and Effect*, 4).

143. Noah Webster, *A Philosophical and Practical Grammar of the English Language* (New Haven, CT: Oliver Steele, 1807), 218.

144. Claude Buffier, *A French Grammar*, 149–50.

145. Trevor Butterworth, "Two Countries Separated by a Semicolon," *The Financial Times Weekend Edition*, September 17, 2005. See also the Introduction, p. 5, regarding American attitudes towards the semicolon.

146. Truss, *Eats, Shoots & Leaves*, 128.

147. Nicolson Baker, "The History of Punctuation," 82.

148. Crystal, *The Language of the Internet*, 37.

149. Parkes, *Pause and Effect*, 87.

150. Honan, "English Punctuation Theory," 102.

## Chapter Three

1. Koch, *Versuch einer Anleitung* 2:342; trans. adapted from Baker, 1 (my emphasis).

2. Christoph Wolff explains that Johann Christoph Gottsched preferred to use the term *Geist* for genius rather than the un-German *Genie* ("Defining Genius: Early Reflections of J. S. Bach's Self-Image," *Proceedings of the American Philosophical Society* 145, no. 4 [2001]: 475). According to Rob van Gerwen, Kant's use of *Geist* in describing art is as "the animating factor," the lively expression of the mental life of the artist (genius) ("On Exlemplary Art as the Symbol of Morality: Making Sense of Kant's Ideal of Beauty," in *Kant und die Berliner Aufklärung: Akten des IX Kant Kongresses*, 5 vols., [Berlin and New York: Walter de Gruyter, 2001], 3:557–59).

3. Claude Palisca describes Koch's very vivid use of the term, *Ruhepunkte des Geistes*, as awakening "the image of a breathing organism" (preface to *Introductory Essay on Composition of Heinrich Christoph Koch*, trans. Nancy Kovaleff Baker).

4. *Encyclopedia of the Enlightenment*, s.v "Music" (by Thomas Christensen).

5. Mattheson, *Der vollkommene Capellmeister*, 141–42, 148; trans. Harriss, 311–12, 324.

6. Daniel Gottlob Türk, *Klavierschule* (1789; facsimile ed., Kassel and New York: Bärenreiter, 1962), 340; trans. adapted from Raymond Haggh, *School of Clavier Playing by Daniel Gottlob Türk* (Lincoln: University of Nebraska Press, 1982), 329.

7. Friedrich Wilhelm Marpurg, *Kritische Briefe über die Tonkunst*, 3 vols. (Berlin: W. F. Birnstiel, 1759–64), 2:327–39; facsimile ed., 2 vols. (Hildesheim: Georg Olms, 1974).

8. Mattheson, *Der vollkommene Capellmeister*, 180–95; trans. Harriss, 386–98.

9. Schuback, *Von der musicalischen Declamation*, 4.

10. Johann Nikolaus Forkel discusses the new interest in his own chapter, "Delivery, or Declamation of Compositions": "We now posses some very valuable treatises concerning this part of musical rhetoric. Some examples are **Sulzer's** *Allgemeine Theorie* under the article, "Vortrag," **C. Ph. Em. Bach's** *Versuch über die wahre Art das Clavier zu Spielen*, **Quantz's** *Anweisung zur Flöte*, and **Tosi's** *Anleitung zur Singkunst* translated by **Agricola**, etc." (introduction to *Allgemeine Geschichte der Musik*, vol. 1 (Leipzig, 1788; facsimile ed., Graz: Akademische Druck- u. Verlagsanstalt, 1967), 59; trans. Doris Powers as "Johann Nikolaus Forkel's Philosophy of Music in the Einleitung to Volume One of His *Allgemeine Geschichte der Musik* (1788): A Translation and Commentary with a Glossary of Eighteenth-Century Terms" (PhD diss., University of North Carolina, 1995), 140.

11. Ursula Rempel describes a "teach-yourself-at-home craze" from 1770 to 1820. The "hits" of famous performers and composers were arranged for amateurs, and method books were published which implied that amateurs could become as skilled and famous as the author. Ursula Rempel, "Women and Music: Ornament of the Profession?" in *French Women and the Age of Enlightenment*, ed. Samia L. Spencer (Bloomington: Indiana University Press, 1984), 177.

12. François Couperin, preface to *Troisième livre de piéces de clavecin* (Paris, 1722; facsimile ed., Courlay: Éditions J. M. Fuzeau, 1988).

13. François Couperin, "Vingt-Quatriéme Ordre: Les jeunes seigneurs," *Quatriéme livre de pièces de clavecin* (Paris, 1730; facsimile ed., New York: Broude Bros., 1973), 36–37.

14. See Jane Clark's discussion of the way Couperin's character piece reflects Dufresnay's 1721 description of *Les petits-maîtres*: "The *petit maître* [fop] makes a point of appearing more disorganized than in fact he is . . . talks a lot and scarcely ever thinks . . . expects fortune to run after him . . . the speech of the *petit maître* is high and low, a mixture of the trivial and the sublime, of politeness and coarseness" ("Les Folies françoises," *Early Music* 8 [1980]: 167).

15. Türk, *Klavierschule*, 344; trans. adapted from Haggh, 333.

16. Ibid., 344–45; the example is from p. 345. J. A. P. Schulz makes a similar claim in his article on musical "Vortrag," first published in 1774 for Sulzer's *Allgemeine Theorie der schönen Künste*: "There is no difficulty when a phrase ends with a rest; the point of division [Einschnitt] marks itself. But when a phrase does not end with a rest, the point of division is more difficult to discover and more skill is required to mark it correctly" (in Johann Georg Sulzer, *Allgemeine Theorie der schönen*

*Künste*, 2nd ed., 4 vols. [Leipzig, 1792; facsimile ed., 5 vols., Hildesheim: Georg Olms, 1967–70], s.v. "Vortrag," 4:703).

17. Richard Maunder notes that it is very difficult to date precisely the four volumes that comprise Domenico Corri's *A Select Collection of the Most Admired Songs, Duetts, etc.* Based on the first performance dates of some of the songs in the collection, he argues that it is very unlikely that volume 1 was published before 1782 or even 1783 (Introduction to vol. 1 of Domenico Corri's *Treatises on Singing: A Four Volume Anthology* (New York: Garland, 1993), vii–viii.

18. Domenico Corri, *A Select Collection of the Most Admired Songs, Duetts, etc.*, vol. 4. *Domenico Corri's Treatises on Singing* 3:36.

19. Koch, *Versuch einer Anleitung* 2:349–50; trans. Baker, 3–4.

20. Mattheson, *Der vollkommene Capellmeister*, 38; trans. Harriss, 139.

21. Ibid., 37; 137.

22. Christian Friedrich Daniel Schubart, *Ideen zu einer Ästhetik der Tonkunst*, ed. Ludwig Schubart (Vienna: J. V. Degen, 1806), 350. Schubart, an accomplished organist and composer, was also prone to dissolute and outspoken behavior which frequently landed him in trouble with his authorities: at the University, in the Church, and among the nobility. He was imprisoned for ten years, from 1777 to 1787, for apparently insulting the mistress of Duke Carl Eugen of Württemberg. Several of Schubart's most important works date from this period of imprisonment, including his *Ideen zu einer Ästhetik der Tonkunst* (*Grove Music Online*, s.v. "Schubart, Christian Friedrich Daniel" [by David Ossenkop]).

23. Ingrid Brainard, "The Speaking Body: Gaspero Angiolini's *Rhétorique muette* and the *Ballet d'action* in the Eighteenth Century," in *Critica musica: Essays in Honor of Paul Brainard*, ed. (Amsterdam: Gordon and Breach, 1999), 19.

24. Giambattista Mancini, *Pensieri e riflessioni pratiche sopra il canto figurato* (Vienna: Nella stamparia di Ghelen, 1774), 164–65; the editions of 1774 and 1777 compared, translated, and edited by Edward V. Foreman as *Practical Reflections on Figured Singing by Giambattista Mancini* (Minneapolis: Pro Musica Press, 1996), 59.

25. Mattheson, *Der vollkommene Capellmeister*, 37; trans. Harriss, 137.

26. Charles Burney, *A General History of Music, from the Earliest Ages to the Present Period: To Which Is Prefixed, A Dissertation on the Music of the Ancients*, 4 vols. (London, 1776–89), 4:208, http://galenet.galegroup.com/servlet/ECCO.

27. Mancini, *Pensieri e riflessioni pratiche*, 161; trans. Foreman, 58.

28. Mattheson, *Der vollkommene Capellmeister*, 35–36; trans. Harriss, 134–35. These passages are also quoted by C. P. E. Bach in *Versuch über die wahre Art, das Clavier zu spielen* (Berlin: 1753 and 1762; facsimile ed., Leipzig: Breitkopf & Härtel, 1957), 122–23; trans. William J. Mitchell as *Essay on the True Art of Playing Keyboard Instruments* (New York: Norton, 1949), 152.

29. Robert Toft, *Heart to Heart: Expressive Singing in England, 1780–1830* (Oxford: Oxford University Press, 2000), 150. Thomas Bolton, *A Treatise on Singing, Containing Anatomical Observations by John Hunter on the Management and Delivery of the Voice, Second Edition* (London, 1812), 14–15. Special thanks to Robert Toft for helping me to locate Bolton's treatise.

30. C. P. E. Bach, *Versuch über die wahre Art*, 122–23; trans. Mitchell, 152.

31. Pierre Marie François de Sales Baillot, *L'art du violon: Nouvelle méthode* (Paris: Dépôt central de la musique, 1835), 267; trans. Louise Goldberg as *The Art of the Violin* (Evanston, IL: Northwestern University Press, 1991), 463.

32. Cambini, *Nouvelle méthode pour le violon*, 20; trans. adapted from Elisabeth Le Guin, http://epub.library.ucla.edu/leguin/boccherini/contents.htm.

33. Ibid.; trans. adapted from Elisabeth Le Guin, http://epub.library.ucla.edu/leguin/boccherini/contents.htm. According to a manuscript copy of the Op. 2, no.1 String Quartet (Lucca, Istituto Musicale Boccherini, D.I.33), in which the expressive markings are possibly in Boccherini's own hand, the movement is titled *Allegro comodo*, and marked *piano*. In light of these indications, Cambini's interpretation seems perhaps even more outlandish. See also Elisabeth Le Guin's discussion of Cambini's elaborate, but very appropriate response to this passage (according to contemporary expectations) in *Boccherini's Body: An Essay in Carnal Musicology* (Berkeley and Los Angeles: University of California Press, 2006), 86–88. From the incipit provided by Yves Gérard (of the first two bars only), there are no slurs connecting the quarter notes in bar 1. In bar 2 a slur occurs over the first beat, with two slurs dividing the four sixteenth-notes on the fourth beat; see Yves Gérard, *Thematic, Bibliographical, and Critical Catalogue of the Works of Luigi Boccherini*, comp. Yves Gérard under the auspices of Germaine de Rothschild; trans. Andreas Mayor (London and New York: Oxford University Press, 1969), 173.

34. Türk, *Klavierschule*, 366–67; trans. Haggh, 355–56, 519.

35. C. P. E. Bach, *Versuch über die wahre Art*, 123; trans. Mitchell, 152. Mitchell appends a footnote from Marpurg's *Der Critischer Musicus an der Spree*, Sept. 9, 1749, which expresses a similar view: "I know a great composer [C. P. E. Bach? ] on whose face one can see depicted everything that his music expresses as he plays it at the keyboard."

36. Leopold Mozart, *Violinschule*, 53; trans. Knocker, 54–57. Türk and Mattheson also explain that the listener does not want to perceive the difficulties experienced by the performer. Türk, *Klavierschule*, 366; trans. Haggh, 355; Mattheson, *Der vollkommene Capellmeister*, 36; trans. Harriss, 135.

37. Pierre Baillot, *Methode de violoncelle et de basse d'accompangement*, ed. Baillot, Levasseur, Catel, et Baudiot (Paris: Magasin de musique du Conservatoire Royal, 1804), 9. The method is a collaboration by a number of instructors from the newly established Conservatoire in Paris; trans. Elisabeth Le Guin in "'One Says That One Weeps, but One Does Not Weep': *Sensible*, Grotesque, and Mechanical Embodiments in Boccherini's Chamber Music," *Journal of the American Musicological Society* 55 (2002): 247.

38. Mattheson, *Der vollkommene Capellmeister*, 36; trans. Harriss, 135–36.

39. Ursula Rempel, "Women and Music," 174. See also *Grove Music Online*, s.v. "Women in Music, II:3, 1500–1800" (by Judith Tick); Matthew Head, "If the Pretty Little Hand Won't Stretch: Music for the Fair Sex in Eighteenth-Century Germany," *Journal of the American Musicological Society* 52 (1999): 208.

40. Le Guin, "Boccherini's Chamber Music," 245 (my emphasis).

41. Bonds also calls attention to the fact that eighteenth-century theorists felt that far more had been said on the grammar of music than on its rhetoric (*Wordless Rhetoric*, 68–71).

42. Rousseau, *Dictionary of Music*, s.v. "Phrase."

43. Mattheson states that he thinks much more highly of Quintilian's, Isidor's, and Putean's precepts than those of Demosthenes and Cicero because the former are known to be excellent musical thinkers, writers, and orators. This favoritism is largely based on the desirable brevity of their periods (*Der vollkommene Capellmeister*, 9; trans. Harriss, 58).

44. Ibid., 187; trans. adapted from Harriss, 390. *Colo* is the spelling used by both Mattheson and Harriss.

45. In a similar vein, in 1717 Niedt [8] separates "the question mark and other signs" from the colon, semicolon, and full stop.

46. Marpurg, *Kritische Briefe*, 309–10.

47. Heinrich Christoph Koch, *Musikalisches Lexikon* (Frankfurt, 1802; facsimile ed., Hildesheim: Georg Olms, 1964), s.v. "Accent." See also Sandra Rosenblum, *Performance Practices in Classic Piano Music: Their Principles and Applications* (Bloomington: Indiana University Press, 1988), 92.

48. Johann Adam Hiller, *Anweisung zum musikalisch-zierlichen Gesange, mit hinlänglichen Exempeln erläutert* (Leipzig, 1780; facsimile ed., Leipzig: Peters, 1976), 28.

49. Rousseau, *Dictionary of Music*, s.v. "AC."

50. Forkel, *Allgemeine Geschichte der Musik*, 21; trans. adapted from Powers, 77.

51. Ibid., 39; 106–7.

52. Bonds, *Wordless Rhetoric*, 72.

53. James Hepokoski and Warren Darcy explain how the small event of a "medial caesura" (a point of punctuation) in sonata form expositions can become key to understanding the larger structure ("The Medial Caesura and Its Role in the Eighteenth-Century Sonata Exposition," *Music Theory Spectrum* 19, no. 2 [1997]: 115–54). Karol Berger states in his discussion of the form of Chopin's Ballade, Op. 23, "I consider first the 'punctuation form,' the way the work is articulated into a hierarchy of parts by means of stronger and weaker cadences" ("The Form of Chopin's Ballade, Op. 23," *19th-Century Music* 20 [1996]: 47); Elaine Sisman also incorporates Koch's (and Riepel's) models of how "small units of structure—phrases—underlie dances, arias, and symphony and concerto movements" in her analysis of the second movement of Haydn's Symphony No. 14 ("Small and Expanded Forms: Koch's Model and Haydn's Music," *Musical Quarterly* 68 [1982]: 444). See also Wolfgang Budday, *Grundlagen musikalischer Formen der Wiener Klassik* (Kassel: Bärenreiter, 1983); Hermann Forschner, *Instrumentalmusik Joseph Haydns aus der Sicht Heinrich Christoph Kochs* (Munich: Emil Katzbichler, 1984).

54. Bonds, *Wordless Rhetoric*, 71–72.

55. Koch, *Versuch einer Anleitung* 3:13; trans. Baker, 66.

56. Ibid. 3:5–6; 64.

57. Ibid. 3:13; 66.

58. The word *rhythmus* has a variety of usages. For instance both Turk [43] and G. F. Wolf [44] use the term to designate the part of speech which is indicated by a colon or semicolon. But as explained in the article "Rhythmus" in Sulzer's *Allgemeine Theorie*, the term is founded on the notion of "the order of tone and movement." See Haggh, *School of Clavier Playing by Türk*, 512. Koch uses the term to describe "the length of melodic sections, and the proportion or relationship which they have amongst themselves with regard to the number of measures" (*Versuch einer Anleitung* 2:346; trans. Baker, 2).

59. Mattheson, *Der vollkommene Capellmeister*, 160; trans. Harriss, 344.

60. Ibid., 196; 405.

61. Ibid., 198; 409.

62. Steele, *An Essay towards Establishing the Melody and Measure of Speech*, 214–15.

63. Rousseau, *Dictionary of Music*, s.v. "Metric."

64. Forkel, *Allgemeine Geschichte der Musik*, 27; trans. Powers, 86–87.

65. In his chapter on Renaissance Humanism, Thomas Conley points out that the Greek tradition never displaced the Latin, but was grafted onto the key conceptions of Cicero and Quintilian (*Rhetoric in the European Tradition*, 117–19).

66. Steele, preface to *An Essay towards Establishing the Melody and Measure of Speech*, viii.

67. Ibid., 194.

68. Ibid., 2–3.

69. Ibid., 64.

70. Lord James Burnet Monboddo, *Of the Origin and Progress of Language*, vol. 2 (Edinburgh, 1774), 275.

71. John Foster, *An Essay on the Different Nature of Accent and Quantity, with Their Use in the Pronunciation of the English, Latin, and Greek Languages; Containing an Account of the Ancient Tones, and a Defence of the Present System of Greek Accentual Marks, against the Objections of Isaac Vossius, Henninius, Sarpedonius, Dr. G. and Others* (Eton, 1762), 276. Concerning whether ancient Greek verse was purely quantitative, and Latin accentual, or somewhere in between for both of them, W. S. Allen doubts that there is such a thing as an unequivocally stressless rhythm. Further, there is no need for such a distinction in order to account for the nature of Greek or Latin prosody. See W. S. Allen, "On Quantity and Quantitative Verse," in *In Honour of Daniel Jones: Papers Contributed on the Occasion of the Eightieth Birthday*, ed. David Ambercrombie, 3–15 (London: Longmans, 1964).

72. Forkel, *Allgemeine Geschichte der Musik*, 10, 27–28; trans. Powers, 61, 88–89.

73. Mattheson, *Der vollkommene Capellmeister*, 160; trans. Harriss, 344. Mattheson mistakenly credits Gerhard Johann Vossius, Isaac's even more renowned father, as the author of *De viribus rythmi, et cantu poëmatum*. However Mattheson did draw on the *Latina grammatica* by Gerhard Johann for his classification. See Hans Nehrling, "Die antiken Versfüße, ihre Problematic und Überliefung bei Johann Mattheson," in *Musik als Text: Bericht über den Internationalen Kongress der Gesellschaft für Musikforschung, Freiburg im Breisgau, 1993*, ed. Hermann Danuser and Tobias Plebuch, 2 vols., 2:34–37 (Kassel: Bärenreiter, 1998).

74. Rousseau, *Dictionary of Music*, s.v. "Rhyme."

75. See *Grove Music Online*, s.v. "Versification"; and *The New Harvard Dictionary of Music*, 1986 ed., s.v. "Prosody."

76. Antoine Reicha, *Traité de mélodie, abstraction faite de ses rapports avec l'harmonie: suivi d'un supplément sur l'art d'accompagner la mélodie par l'harmonie, lorsque la première doit être prédominante: Le tout appuyé sur les meilleurs modèles mélodiques*, 2 vols. (Paris, 1814), 1:89; trans. by Peter M. Landey as *Treatise on Melody* (Hillsdale, NY: Pendragon Press, 2000), 88. See Hanning, "Conversation and Music in the Salon," 522; and also Simon Keefe's chapter "Antoine Reicha's *Dialogue*," in which he describes Reicha's intensely systematic consideration of melody and dialogue as a theoretical landmark (*Mozart's Piano Concertos: Dramatic Dialogue in the Age of Enlightenment* [Woodbridge, UK, and Rochester, NY: Boydell Press, 2001]).

77. Reicha, *Traité de mélodie* 1:89–92; trans. Landey, 89–90.

78. The influential Viennese music theorist and prolific composer Simon Sechter, like Reciha, also describes very specific ways in which phrases, members, and periods can be distributed among two voices, "since one voice can break off at different points, while the other immediately picks up the thread." In his first example of how one imitates conversation in music, he allows the second voice to interrupt the first after only one measure. Sechter admits that this really doesn't belong in serious

compositions and rewrites the passage for one voice. He continues: "It is best if the first voice continues on uninterrupted for the first four measures of the passage until the colon, and the other voice renders the last four measures up to the period in the same manner. Thus one voice is given the antecedent phrase, the other the consequent phrase." He adds that the voices could also proceed by two measure groups; see Sechter, *Grundsätze der musikalischen Komposition*, 3 vols. (Leipzig: Breitkopf und Härtel, 1853–54), 1:84–85; trans. James Chenevert as "Simon Sechter's *The Principles of Musical Composition*: A Translation of and Commentary on Selected Chapters" (PhD diss., University of Wisconsin, Madison, 1989), 192–93.

Diderot also gives "dialogue" a specific musical definition: "Dialogue, *as a term in Music*, is a composition of at least two voices or two instruments that answer each other, and which often merge together as a duo. Most of the scenes in operas are in this sense *dialogues*. However, in Music this word applies more specifically to the organ. On this instrument the organist plays *dialogues* by the interplay of different responses or on different keyboards" (Diderot and d'Alembert, *Encyclopédie*, s.v. "Dialogue," 4:937: trans. adapted from *The Encyclopedia of Diderot and d'Alembert*, s.v. "Dialogue").

79. Mattheson, *Der vollkommene Capellmeister*, 292; trans. Harriss, 397.

80. Marpurg, *Kritische Briefe* 2:333.

81. See appendix A, §§108–11.

82. Koch, *Versuch einer Anleitung* 3:332; trans. Baker, 209. Communing with oneself can also be described as a kind of dialogue. Henry Fielding divides conversation into three sorts in 1743: "Men are said to Converse with God, with themselves, and with one another." Henry Fielding, *Miscellanies*, 97.

83. Koch, *Versuch einer Anleitung* 3:315; trans. Baker, 202–3. See also Keefe, "Koch's Commentary on the Late Eighteenth-Century Concerto," 372.

84. Sulzer, *Allgemeine Theorie der schönen Künste*, s.v. "Sonate," 4:425. Sulzer had little or no musical training and so relied on Kirnberger for help in writing the musical articles. According to Schulz, Kirnberger wrote the music articles from A to I. Schulz under Kirnberger's supervision wrote the articles from K to R, but he wrote the articles from S to Z by himself. See Lester, *Compositional Theory in the Eighteenth Century*, 240. See also *Grove Music Online*, s.v. "Sulzer, Johann Georg" (by Howard Serwer).

Sulzer's work was reprinted and expanded several times, first in 1786, the additions consisting primarily of extensive bibliographies appended to the articles, and again in 1792 with additional bibliographic information. See *Æsthetics and the Art of Musical Composition in the German Enlightenment: Select Writings of Johann Georg Sulzer and Heinrich Christoph Koch*, ed. Nancy Kovaleff Baker and Thomas Christensen (Cambridge and New York: Cambridge University Press, 1995), 15–16. Since the articles remain largely unchanged from their original 1771–74 publication, we will place them chronologically in our discussion of the treatises on musical punctuation according to the earlier date. However, volume and page numbers in the notes and bibliography will refer the reader to the more widely available 1792 edition, available in facsimile by Georg Olms Verlag (Hildesheim, 1967).

85. Schubart, *Ideen zu einer Ästhetik der Tonkunst*, 360. Compositions like C. P. E. Bach's light-hearted, playful, and technically undemanding character pieces for solo keyboard (1754–57) might also be included in the list. Ingeborg Allihn and Darrell M. Berg observe the relationship between these miniatures and the gestures of the elite Berlin friendship circle, devoted to the Enlightenment ideals of intellectual and social exchange; see Allihn, "Die Pièces Caractèristiques des C. P. E. Bach: Ein Modell für die Gesprächskultur in der zweiten Hälfte des 18. Jahrhunderts," in *Carl*

*Philipp Emanuel Bach: Musik für Europa*, ed. Hans Günter Ottenberg, 94–107 (Frankfurt: Die Konzerthalle, 1998); and Berg, "C. P. E. Bach's Character Pieces and His Friendship Circle," in *C. P. E. Bach Studies*, ed. Stephen L. Clark, 1–32 (Oxford: Oxford University Press, 1988).

86. Baillot, *L'art du violon*, 268; trans. Goldberg, 479. Rousseau claims that there can not really be such a thing as a true quartet, since it is possible to hear only two melody voices at one time. However, Momigny disagrees with Rousseau, arguing that in a conversation, at any given point, there must be a principle voice or actor on whom one's attention is focused. See Hanning, "Conversation and Music in the Salon," 523.

87. Johann Wolfgang von Goethe, *Briefwechsel zwischen Goethe und Zelter in den Jahren 1799 bis 1832* (Leipzig: P. Reclam, 1902), 193–94.

88. Hanning, "Conversation and Music in the Salon," 525.

89. De Staël, *Germany*, 77.

90. Hanning, "Conversation and Music of the Salon," 519.

91. Koch, *Versuch einer Anleitung* 3:333; trans. Baker, 209; Keefe, *Mozart's Piano Concertos*, 16.

92. Morrow, *German Music Criticism*, 12.

93. Ibid., 10.

94. Burney, *A General History of Music* 4:643. See also Richard Will's discussion of C. P. E. Bach's trio in "When God Met the Sinner, and Other Dramatic Confrontations in Eighteenth-Century Instrumental Music," *Music and Letters* 78 (1997): 182.

95. The term concerto probably originates from the Latin *concertare*, meaning both "to contend, dispute, debate," and also "to work together with someone." Both definitions of the term have been applied throughout the form's development; see *Grove Music Online*, s.v. "Concerto" (by Arthur Hutchings). For a discussion of the use of the word *concertant* in defining a general dialogue style, see Hanning, "Conversation and Music in the Salon," 520.

96. Mattheson, *Der vollkommene Capellmeister*, 234; trans. Harriss, 467.

97. Friedrich Erhard Niedt, *Musikalische Handleitung*, Part II, 2nd ed. (Hamburg, 1721; facsimile ed., Buren, Netherlands: Frits Knuf, 1976), 109; trans. Pamela L. Poulin and Irmgard C. Taylor; introduction and explanatory notes by Pamela L. Poulin, *The Musical Guide: Parts I (1700/10), 2 (1721), and 3 (1717)* (Oxford: Clarendon Press; New York: Oxford University Press, 1989), 149.

98. Koch, *Versuch einer Anleitung* 3:333–37; trans. Baker, 209–11.

99. Sulzer, *Allgemeine Theorie der schönen Künst*, s.v. "Trio," 4:599. In his article on the sonata, Schulz particularly refers to *Sanguineus und Melancholicus* as a truly passionate conversation in tones.

100. Keefe, *Mozart's Piano Concertos*, 326. See also his discussion of both cooperative as well as competitive aspects in late eighteenth-century concepts of dramatic dialogue and concerto dialogue (48–50).

101. Will, "When God Meets the Sinner ," 184–85.

102. William Jones, *A Treatise on the Art of Music, in Which the Elements of Harmony and Air Are Practically Considered* (Colchester: W. Keymer, 1784) 49–50.

103. Luigi Boccherini, *Six String Quartets, opus 32 (Gérard 201–206)*, ed. Mark W. Knoll, 2 vols. (Ann Arbor, MI: Steglein Publishing, 2003).

104. This is part of Mattheson's list of thirty-three rules concerning the four characteristics of melody discussed on pp. 61–62.

105. Mattheson, *Der vollkommene Capellmeister*, 140; trans. Harriss, 311. Matthew Head claims that Mattheson furnishes a close to comprehensive list of what constituted "easiness" in music for women ("Music for the Fair Sex," 214).

106. Johann Joachim Quantz, *Versuch einer Anweisung die Flöte traversiere zu spielen* (Berlin: J. F. Voss, 102–3; trans. Edward Reilly as *On Playing the Flute* (New York: Schirmer, 1985), 120–21.

107. *Grove Music Online*, s.v. "Women in Music" (by Judith Tick).

108. Edgeworth, *Practical Education*, 521–22.

109. Carl Philipp Emanuel Bach to Johann Nikolaus Forkel, 20 September, 1775, in *Carl Philipp Emanuel Bach Briefe und Dokumente: Kritische Gesamtausgabe*, ed. Dr. Ernst Suchalla, 2 vols. (Göttingen: Vandenhoeck & Ruprecht, 1994), 1:516. Along the same lines as the accompanied sonata which stood either on its own, or with supporting parts, the North German keyboard concerto of the 1770s also adopted flexible scoring. Small chamber accompaniments of perhaps two violins and a cello would be written into the keyboard part, allowing the soloist either to play along in the tutti sections, or be his or her own accompaniment without an ensemble (Head, "Music for the Fair Sex," 231).

110. Head, "Music for the Fair Sex," 214–16.

111. Morrow, *German Music Criticism*, 25, 27, and 43.

112. Head, "Music for the Fair Sex," 227–34.

113. Haydn to the publisher Artaria, Vienna, 25 February, 1780, in *Joseph Haydn Gesammelte Briefe und Aufzeichnungen*, from the collection of H. C. Robbins Landon, ed. Dénes Bartha (Kassel: Bärenreiter, 1965) 90. See also Daniel M. Raessler's discussion of English women pianists who exceeded the boundaries of "polite accomplishment" ("London's Dancing Dogs, or, the Other Pianoforte School," *Early Keyboard Journal* 13 [1995]: 81–105).

114. Marcia J. Citron, *Gender and the Musical Canon* (Cambridge and New York: Cambridge University Press, 1993), 106.

115. Ibid.

116. Steele, preface to *An Essay towards Establishing the Melody and Measure of Speech*, xvi–xvii.

117. As mentioned in the Introduction, the signal that I am referring to a specific quote in the chart will be indicated by a number in brackets following the citation of the author. For example Marpurg [24] is a reference to entry no. 24 of the chart.

118. Hugo Riemann, *Vademecum der Phrasierung* (Leipzig: Max Hesse, 1900), 6.

119. Parkes, *Pause and Effect*, 4.

120. Toft, "The Expressive Pause," 205–6.

121. J. J. O. de Meude-Monpas copies Rousseau's *ponctuer* entry in his own *Dictionnaire de musique* (1787), adding the prefatory sentence, "It is the synonym of to phrase" *C'est le synonime de phraser* (*Dictionnaire de Musique* [Paris: Knapen, 1787; facsimile ed., New York: AMS, 1978], s.v. "Ponctuer," 152–53).

122. Mattheson, *Der vollkommene Capellmeister*, 180–81; trans. Harriss, 380.

123. Koch, *Versuch einer Anleitung* 2:245, 3:3–6; trans. Baker, 2, 63–64.

124. Wolfgang Amadeus Mozart to Leopold Mozart, Kaysersheim, 18 December 1778, in *Briefe und Aufzeichnungen, Gesamtausgabe*, 7 vols. (Kassel: Bärenreiter, 1962–75) 2:523; Emily Anderson quite reasonably translates *punckirt* as *phrased*, but given the familiarity of such terminology in the eighteenth century, I think *punctuated* is more apt; see *The Letters of Mozart and His Family*, ed. Emily Anderson, 2nd ed.,

2 vols. (London: Macmillan; New York: St. Martin's, 1966), 642. I thank Neal Zaslaw for bringing this to my attention.

125. Riemann, *Vademecum der Phrasierung*, 1–7.

126. Mathis Lussy, *Traité de l'expression musicale: Accents, nuances et mouvements dans la musique vocale et instrumentale* (Paris: Heugel, 1874) 26–27; trans. of 4th ed. (1882) by M. E. von Glehn as *Musical Expression, Accents, Nuances, and Tempo, in Vocal and Instrumental Music* (London: Novello, 1884), 64–65.

127. Webster, *Haydn's "Farewell" Symphony and the Idea of Classical Style*, 33.

128. Bonds, *Wordless Rhetoric*, 74.

129. Morrow, *German Music Criticism*, 145–46.

130. A critic of Parkes's *Pause and Effect*, Roy Harris, complains that he offers a paucity of information about the development of different punctuation conventions in writing different European languages. Roy Harris, review of *Pause and Effect* (*Language Sciences* 16 [1994]: 334).

131. Hugo Riemann, *Musik-Lexikon*, 3rd ed. (Leipzig: M. Hesse, 1887), s.v. "Phrasierung." Riemann expanded his explanation of the term "Phrasierung" (phrasing) after the first publication of the *Musik-Lexikon* in 1882 (see appendix B, entry 58). In the third edition five years later, the term "Phrasierungsbezeichnung" (phrasing sign) is also included, and introduces a number of new signs through which the structural sense of musical thoughts can be indicated. The seventh edition of the *Musik-Lexikon* (Leipzig: M. Hesse, 1909) further includes the entry "Interpunktion, musikalische, s. Phrasierung" (Musical punctuation, see phrasing).

132. See pp. 115 and 135.

## Chapter Four

*Epigraph.* Anonymous, *A Treatise of Stops, Points, or Pauses* (London, 1680; facsimile ed., Menston, UK: Scolar Press, 1968), 6.

1. The concept that we read essentially the same musical notation today with an entirely different set of conventions than did our eighteenth- and nineteenth-century predecessors, and that in order to appreciate and understand fully the expressive nature of compositions by composers like Haydn, Mozart, Beethoven, and Schubert, we must uncover these lost conventions, was the foundation of my introduction to performance practice as a graduate student at Cornell University. I highly recommend pianist Malcolm Bilson's recently released DVD entitled *Knowing the Score* (Ithaca, NY: Cornell University Press, 2005) in which he examines this issue, demonstrating his ideas (accumulated over decades of experience from his extensive concertizing and teaching) about the differences between articulation, tempo, and pedaling on an eighteenth-century Viennese piano and a modern Steinway.

2. Koch, *Versuch einer Anleitung* 2:361–62; trans. Baker, 8–9. One will also notice that in the second example of each group, Koch does not always reproduce exactly the same music. However these variations (the absent eighth-note pickup to bar 3 of figure 4.1d or bar 2 in figure 4.1f) do not affect the concept of the implied rest.

3. Joseph Riepel, *Anfangsgründe zur musicalischen Setzkunst: Nicht zwar nach alt-mathematischer Einbildungs-Art der Zirkel-Harmonisten, sondern durchgehends mit sichtbaren Exempeln abgefasset*, 5 vols. (Regensburg: E. F. Baders, 1752–86), 1:147–237; reprint

in vol. 1 of *Sämtliche Schriften zur Musiktheorie*, 2 vols., 1:147–237 (Vienna: Böhlau, 1996) (references refer to Böhlau edition).

4. Nancy Baker admits that her placement of Koch's punctuation symbols is perhaps the most serious editing she did in translating his *Introductory Essay on Composition*. She felt that Koch's indications were not consistent, placed sometimes at the caesura note, sometimes at the last note of the section, or straddling two notes, neither of which seem to be appropriate (preface to *Introductory Essay on Composition*, xxiv). I think Baker has basically understood the sense of the issue and I generally concur with her version of Koch's examples, which place the symbol consistently under the final note of each phrase segment.

5. Koch, *Versuch einer Anleitung* 2:352–53; trans. Baker, 4 (the brackets are mine).

6. Ibid. 2:353–54; 5. For convenience sake, we will from here on (as Baker does) dispense with the terminology "resting point of the spirit" and use simply "resting point" in its place.

7. Ibid. 2:360; 8.

8. See also Habeneck [52] (1840), Garcia [53] (1847), and Westphal [57] (1880).

9. Robert Donington, *The Interpretation of Early Music* (New York: St. Martin's Press, 1974), 470.

10. C. P. E. Bach, *Versuch über die wahre Art*, 129, 254; trans. Mitchell, 160, 375.

11. Keller, *Phrasierung und Artikulation*, 18–19; trans. Gerdine, 14.

12. Keller explains that Fischer's 1926 "punctuated edition" of classical works remains only an experiment (ibid., 19; 15). See Jacob Fischer, *Erläuterungen zur Interpunktions-Ausgabe* (Berlin-Lichterfelde: Schlesingerische Buch- & Musikhandlung, 1926), 3. Donington also states that "very little attempt is made to suggest phrasing in notation" (*The Interpretation of Early Music*, 470).

13. Nicolas Étienne Framery, *Encyclopédie méthodique: Musique*, 2 vols. (Paris: chez Panckoucke, 1791–1818), s.v. "Ponctuation" (by Momigny), 2:275–76.

14. Koch, *Versuch einer Anleitung* 2:345; trans. Baker, 2.

15. Steele, *An Essay towards Establishing the Melody and Measure of Speech*.

16. Riemann describes Koch's efforts differently, claiming Koch to be a great advocate for the improvement of notation. See chapter 3, p. 92.

17. Mozart, *Sinfonien*, edited by Hermann Beck, in *Neue Ausgabe sämtlicher Werke*, Series IV, 5 (Kassel: Bärenreiter, 1957). I thank John Hsu for bringing this very appropriate example to my attention.

18. Hugo Riemann, *Musik-Lexikon*, 4th ed. (Berlin: Max Hesse, 1894), s.v. "Phraseierung," 814.

19. Türk, *Klavierschule*, 340–41; trans. Haggh, 330.

20. Ibid., 346; 334–35.

21. In Sulzer, *Allgemeine Theorie der schönen Künste*, s.v. "Vortrag," 4:703.

22. *Grove Music Online*, s.v. "Versification (Italian)" (by Tim Carter).

23. Marpurg, *Kritische Briefe* 2:391.

24. Ibid.

25. In Sulzer, *Allgemeine Theorie der schönen Künste*, s.v. "Recitativ," 4:9.

26. Heinrich Schütz, forward to the *Görlitz Tablature Book*, in *Neue Ausgabe sämticher Werke*, vol. 40 (Kassel: Bärenreiter, 1988), xix.

27. Keller, *Phrasierung und Artikulation*, 20; trans. Gerdine, 16–17.

28. Mattheson, *Der vollkommene Capellmeister*, 185; trans. Harriss, 386.

29. Ibid. Fux also claims that very often the comma is continued without a break, such as when the meaning of the text demands such continuity (Johann Joseph Fux,

*Gradus ad Parnassum* [Vienna, 1725]; facsimile ed., New York: Broude, 1966); trans. Joel Lester in *Between Modes and Keys* (New York: Pendragon, 1989), 207.

30. Mattheson, *Der vollkommene Capellmeister*, 185–86; trans. Harriss, 387.

31. Jean-Philippe Rameau, *Traité de l'harmonie reduite à ses principes naturels* (1722), trans. with an introduction and notes by Philip Gossett (New York: Dover, 1971), book II, chap. 19.

32. Joel Lester proposes that after the middle of the eighteenth century, all music theorists used at least some portions of Rameauian harmonic theory, which nevertheless did not prevent them from discussing in a meaningful way many of the linear (melodic) aspects of the music of their time. He adds that the harmony/melody dichotomy, which some twentieth-century scholars impose, is mostly irrelevant to eighteenth-century music (*Compositional Theory in the Eighteenth Century*, 124, 190–91). For further discussion of the melody vs. harmony issue, see Nancy Baker, preface to *Koch's Introductory Essay*, xv–xviii; Nola Reed Knouse, "Joseph Riepel and the Emerging Theory of Form in the Eighteenth Century," *Current Musicology* 41 (1986): 47–50.

33. Kirnberger, *Die Kunst des reinen Satzes in der Musik* 1:98; trans. Beach and Thym, 116.

34. In Sulzer, *Allgemeine Theorie der schönen Künste*, s.v. "Vortrag," 4:703.

35. Mathis Lussy, *Traité de l'expression musicale*, 44–45; trans. adapted from Glehn, 92.

36. Joseph Riepel, *Anfangsgründe zur musicalischen Setzkunst* 1:25–26; trans. Knouse in "Joseph Riepel and the Emerging Theory of Form," 52.

37. Beethoven, Symphony No. 1, in *Werke*, ed. Beethoven-Archiv, Bonn under the direction of Joseph Schmidt-Görg, Series I, 1 (Munich: G. Henle, 1961).

38. In this context, *Pf* refers to *poco forte* or somewhat loudly, a dynamic degree less than *forte*. See Haggh, *School of Clavier Playing by Daniel Gottlob Türk*, 505n.

39. Türk, *Klavierschule*, 335–36; trans. Haggh, 325. See also Kirnberger, *Die Kunst des reinen Satzes* 2:115, 124; trans. Beach and Thym, 383, 392.

40. E. W. Wolf, "Vorbericht als eine Anleitung zum guten Vortrag beim Clavierspielen," preface to *Eine Sonatine, Vier affectvolle Sonaten und ein dreyzehnmal variirtes Thema* (Leipzig: Breitkopf, 1785), iii; Christopher Hogwood, "A Supplement to C. P. E. Bach's *Versuch*: E. W. Wolf's *Anleitung* of 1785," in *C. P. E. Bach Studies*, ed. Stephen L. Clark (Oxford: Clarendon Press; New York: Oxford University Press, 1988), 139.

41. In Sulzer, *Allgemeine Theorie der schönen Künste*, s.v. "Vortrag," 4:705. Türk (see chap. 5, p. 132) and Beer [9] offer different sentences for much the same purpose.

42. Türk, *Klavierschule*, 346; trans. Haggh, 335.

43. This is Kirnberger's explanation of good beats and bad beats in quadruple meter (*Die Kunst des reinen Satzes in der Musik* 2:124; trans. Beach and Thym, 392).

44. Türk, *Klavierschule*, 337; trans. Haggh, 326.

45. Koch, *Versuch einer Anleitung* 2:373; trans. Baker, 14.

46. The notion that measures or groups of measures can be organized analagously to the way beats are organized into measures is often referred to as "hypermeter," a term first used in this way by Edward Cone in 1968 (*Musical Form and Musical Performance* [New York: Norton, 1968]). See also William Nathan Rothstein, *Phrase Rhythm in Tonal Music* (New York: Schirmer Books; London: Collier Macmillan Publishers, 1989); Joel Lester, *The Rhythms of Tonal Music* (Carbondale: Southern Illinois University Press, 1986).

47. Türk, *Klavierschule*, 336; trans. Haggh, 326.

48. Bonds and Ratner seem to misunderstand the grammar of Koch's subject and predicate in ex. 4.1. They include the e² quarter note as part of the subject, although according to *the melodic rule*, it belongs to the predicate (Ratner, *Classic Music*, 441; Bonds, *Wordless Rhetoric*, 76).

49. For further reference to *the melodic rule*, see Michel de Saint-Lambert, *Les principes du clavecin* (Paris, 1702; facsimile ed., Geneva: Minkoff, 1974), 26–27; Quantz, *Versuch einer Anweisung die Flöte traversiere zu spielen*, 295–300; Kirnberger, *Die Kunst des reinen Satzes* 2:125; Koch, *Versuch einer Anleitung* 2:368–71; Simon Sechter, *Grundsätze der musikalischen Komposition*, 64; Lussy, *Traité de l'expression musicale*, 44.

50. Türk, *Klavierschule*, 346–47; trans. Haggh, 335 (my emphasis).

51. In Sulzer, *Allgemeine Theorie der schönen Künste*, s.v. "Vortrag," 4:705. In his musical examples of the "external accents" which begin new phrases or segments (*Ab- oder Einschnitte*), E. W. Wolf also indicates cases where the beginnings of phrases occur in different parts of the measure. Wolf, *Anleitung zum guten Vortrag*, IV; trans. Hogwood, "E. W. Wolf's Anleitung," 139.

52. In Sulzer, *Allgemeine Theorie der schönen Künste*, s.v. "Vortrag," 4:704.

53. Türk, *Klavierschule*, 342–46; trans. Haggh, 331–35. See also Sulzer, *Allgemeine Theorie der schönen Künste*, s.v. "Vortrag," 4:704; and G. F. Wolf [44] (1792).

54. Riepel, *Anfangsgründe zur musicalischen Setzkunst* 1:147.

55. Koch, *Versuch einer Anleitung* 2:363; trans. Baker, 9.

56. Facsimile of symbols ©1993 from Vol. 1 of *Domenico Corri's Treatises on Singing*.

57. See chapter 5, p. 135.

58. Reproduced by arrangement with Broude Brothers Limited.

59. Leo Treitler, "The Beginnings of Music-Writing in the West: Historical and Semiotic Aspects," *Language and Communication* 9 (1989): 202–3.

60. Keller, *Phrasierung und Artikulation*, 20; trans. Gerdine, 16. Emilio de' Cavalieri's (1600) uses a different symbol for what he calls the *incoronata*, •S•: "This sign indicates the incoronata, which is to serve for taking breath and to give time for making some gestures." These breath marks in the music correspond to each point of punctuation in the text: colon, comma, and period, and a few others besides. Emilio de' Cavalieri, *Rappresentatione di Anima, et di Corpo* (Rome, 1600; facsimile repr. Farnborough, UK: Gregg, 1967). See also Donington, *The Interpretation of Early Music*, 471.

61. Parkes, *Pause and Effect*, 307. According to Keller, Beethoven used this same double stroke once in his posthumously published Piano Trio in E-flat Major in order to emphasize an especially declamatory section (*Phrasierung und Artikulation*, 81; trans. Gerdine, 104).

62. Hugo Riemann and Carl Fuchs, *A Practical Guide to the Art of Phrasing* (New York: G. Schirmer, 1890), 10.

63. Ibid., 10–13.

64. Riemann, *Vademecum der Phrasierung*, 6–7.

65. See, for instance, Wiehmayer's editions of the following works, all of which are given the title of "Neue instruktive Ausgabe": Johann Sebastian Bach, *Das wohltemperierte Clavier* (Magdeburg, Germany: Heinrichshofen's Verlag, 1915); Johann Sebastian Bach, *Französische Suiten* (Magdeburg: Heinrichshofen's Verlag, 1910); Ludwig van Beethoven, *Sonaten* (Magdeburg: Heinrichshofen's Verlag, 1911); Franz Schubert, *Impromptus und Moments musicaux,*: op. 90, op. 94, op. 142 (Magdeburg: Heinrichshofen's Verlag, 1913). See also Keller, *Phrasierung und Artikulation*, 24; trans. Gerdine, 21.

66. I think one can observe particularly in Fischer's [61] (1926) punctuation efforts, the tendency towards micromanagement, applying far too many symbols at far too detailed a level without real respect for the performance process.

67. Marpurg, *Kritische Briefe* 2:310.

68. Toft, "The Expressive Pause in England," 208–9. Donington also adds: "A sense of phrasing is so intimate and incommunicable a part of interpretative musicianship that very little attempt is made to suggest it in notation" (*The Interpretation of Early Music*, 470).

69. Cambini, *Nouvelle méthode pour le violon*, 19. Translation adapted from Elisabeth Le Guin, http://epub.library.ucla.edu/leguin/boccherini/contents.htm.

70. Keller, *Phrasierung und Artikulation*, 11; trans. Gerdine, 4.

71. Riemann and Fuchs, *A Practical Guide to the Art of Phrasing*, vii–viii.

72. Manuel Garcia, *École de Garcia: Traité complet de l'art du chant* (Paris: Author, 1847; facsimile ed., Geneva: Minkoff, 1985), 20; 1847 and 1872 eds. collated and translated by Donald V. Paschke as *A Complete Treatise on the Art of Singing*, 2 vols. (New York: Da Capo, 1972), 1:49.

73. See the discussion of this passage in Toft, "The Expressive Pause in England," 211.

74. Corri, preface to *A Select Collection of the Most Admired Songs, Duetts, &c.* 1:1–2.

75. Rousseau's *Dissertation on Modern Music* gained little attention and was a significant personal cost for him to get published. However, Rousseau's system was eventually adopted in the nineteenth century by the Galin-Paris-Chevé school and then spread throughout Europe and to Japan, China, and other parts of Asia, where a version of it is still being used today. See John T. Scott, introduction to *Essay on the Origin of Languages and Writings Related to Music*, in vol. 7 of *The Collected Writings of Rousseau* (Hanover, NH: University Press of New England, 1998), xvi; also available online at http://www.netlibrary.com.

76. Rousseau, *Writings Related to Music*, trans. John T. Scott, 33–34.

77. Baillot, *L'art du violon*, 156–57; trans. Goldberg, 278.

78. Parkes, *Pause and Effect*, 114.

## Chapter Five

*Epigraph.* Keller, *Phrasierung und Artikulation*, 11; trans. Gerdine, 4.

1. *The New Harvard Dictionary of Music*, 1986 ed., s.v. "Articulation."

2. Rosenblum, *Performance Practices in Classic Piano Music*, 144.

3. Donington divides punctuation into two subcategories, *Articulation* and *Phrasing* (*The Interpretation of Early Music*, 470–81).

4. Ratner, *Classic Music*, 190–96.

5. Robin Stowell, *Violin Technique and Performance Practice in the Late Eighteenth and Early Nineteenth Centuries* (Cambridge: Cambridge University Press, 1985), 283.

6. Keller complains of the rarity in finding a musician to whom the difference between phrasing and articulation has become entirely clear (*Phrasierung und Artikulation*, 12; trans. Gerdine, 4.)

7. Charles Dickens, *Our Mutual Friend* (New York: The New American Library of World Literature, 1964), 103.

8. The use of articulation with regard to language and speech seems to have been an early and natural application, existing side by side with its anatomical usage. As a

verb form, the past participle, *articulated*, was the first to be used. *The Oxford English Dictionary*, 1989 ed., s.v. "Articulate-Articulus."

9. In another quote (see p. 106), Mattheson also uses the word *Gelencke* to refer to the points of punctuation, literally calling them *joints*, or as Harriss translates them, *articulations*.

10. J. J. O. de Meude Monpas, *Dictionnaire de Musique*, s.v. "Articulation."

11. Vickers also quotes Peacham's 1593 description of *articulus* as a figure "very convenient to expresse any vehement affections: in peaceable and quiet causes it may be compared to a semi-breefe in Musicke, but in causes of perturbation and haste it may be likened to thicke and violent strokes in fight, or to a thick and thundring peale of ordinance." These analogies, Vickers explains, "update Quintilian's metaphor of sword-fighting" (*In Defense of Rhetoric*, 313, 326).

12. Giovanni Antonio Piani, *Sonate a violino solo* (Paris, 1712; facsimile ed., Madison, WI: A-R Editions, 1975), 2.

13. The notion of a specific "articulated" bow stroke appears in a number of French string treatises, particularly in those for the violin. L'Abbé le fils explains that the "articulated bow stroke" (*Le coup-d'Archet Articulé*)—many thirty-second notes with dots under a slur—should be played with a very free wrist and each of the notes should be articulated with a perfect evenness (*Principes du violon* [Paris, 1761; facsimile ed., Paris, Centre de documentation universitaire et S. E. D. E. S., 1961], 54). Jacob-Joseph-Balthasar Martinn distinguishes between the *martelé*, which should be articulated with firmness and vivacity at the tip of the bow, and the *staccato* (depicted like Piani under a slur), which form in succession articulated or detached notes executed with one stroke of the bow. In his discussion of the *détaché*, no mention of *articulation* is made (*Méthode élémentaire pour le violon* (Paris: Frey, ca. 1810), 92–93. See also David Boyden, *The History of Violin Playing from Its Origins to 1761* (Oxford: Clarendon, 1990), 414; and Donington, *The Interpretation of Early Music*, 474.

14. J. J. C. de Mondonville, *Les sons harmoniques* (Paris, 1738; facsimile ed., Paris: UCP, 1979), 3. Can we make a case (based on the nature of the rhetorical figure *articulus*) for the former (dots) requiring a more violent stroke than the latter (strokes)? Boyden also feels that there is a distinction between the *detaché* and *articulation* (*The History of Violin Playing*, 414). Robert Riggs, however, makes the point that while there are several eighteenth-century treatises which do differentiate between the performance of staccato dots and strokes, the majority of treatises, and perhaps the most influential and relevant ones, do not employ a dual system. Riggs, "Mozart's Notation of Staccato Articulation: A New Appraisal," *Journal of Musicology* 15 (1997): 233.

15. Baillot, *L'art du violon*, 100–110; trans. Goldberg, 171–91. Baillot also introduces *articuler* to describe two means of expression achieved by the left hand. "Let the fingers fall from high enough above the string that they have some force and much suppleness, and in such a way that they move as evenly as possible." Another means of expression is the "light articulation of soft notes" (*Articuler . . . dans les sens doux*). "The violinist can make a barely audible, light sound of the fingers hitting the string while he produces *flautando* sounds" (152; 269, 270).

16. This usage dates back in French sources to the thirteenth century (*Trésor de la Langue française*, 1974 ed., s.v. "Articuler").

17. Jacques Hotteterre, *Principes de la flûte traversiere* (Paris, 1720; facsimile ed., Geneva: Minkoff, 1973), 21.

18. Meude-Monpas, *Dictionnaire de Musique*, s.v. "Articulation."

19. We have mentioned that *Articulation* does appear in Meude-Monpas's 1787 French dictionary. While much of Meude-Monpas's material is copied directly from Rousseau's *Dictionnaire*, this entry is not, a fact perhaps explained by Meude-Monpas's additional focus on *Poètes lyriques, les Versificateurs, les compositeurs, Acteurs, Exécutants, etc.* Probably one of the first such entries in a truly musical dictionary appears in an 1864 American dictionary: "This word [Articulation] is one of the most important in the musician's vocabulary. It refers equally to vocal and instrumental performance; to words and to notes; and includes that distinctness and accuracy of expression which gives every syllable and sound with truth and perspicuity, and forms the very foundation of pathos and grace" (John Moore, *Complete Encyclopædia of Music* [Boston: J. P. Jewett, 1854], s.v. "Articulation").

20. It must be admitted that German usage of the term *Artikulation* is rare in general. For instance, the word does not appear in any form in Grimm's *Deutsches Wortebuch* published in Leipzig in 1854. Goethe (1749–1832) uses the word only three times and solely in connection with the human body and skeleton (*Goethes Werke*, CD-ROM [Cambridge, England: Chadwyck-Healey, 1995], s.v. "Artikulation").

21. Quantz, *Versuch einer Anweisung die Flöte traversiere zu spielen*, 61.

22. Quantz, *On Playing the Flute*, trans. Reilly, 71.

23. Quantz, *Essai d'une méthode pour apprendre à jouer de la flûte traversière* (Berlin: Chrétien Frédéric Voss, 1752; facsimile ed., Paris: Aug. Zurfluh, 1975), 62.

24. Baroque flutist and Quantz authority Mary Oleskiewicz was of great service in interpreting this word "Aussprache" or "aussprechen." It is her opinion that the use of aussprechen in chap. VI, sec. III, para. 1 should be translated "pronounce," as the equivalent French passage reads *prononcer*. She feels that in this passage and the one above, both of which concern the tonguing and use of syllables, "articulation" in the modern sense of the word does not enter into it.

25. Keller, *Phrasierung und Artikulation*, 12; trans. Gerdine, 4 (my emphasis).

26. In 1957, just as a new edition of Tartini's *Traité des agréments de la musique* was being prepared by Erwin R. Jacobi, a manuscript written and signed by Giovanni Francesco Nicolai, one of Tartini's distinguished pupils, was discovered in Venice by the scholar Pierluigi Petrobelli. Nicolai's manuscript was found to contain not only all the material from the 1771 French edition (until now the sole surviving source for the treatise), but also entirely new chapters and sections by Tartini, including the chapter "Rules for Bowing" under discussion (*Traité des agréments de la musique*, ed. Erwin R. Jacobi [Celle: H. Moeck, 1961], 46, 55, Supplement p. 2). Special thanks to Giuseppe Gerbino for translating this passage from Nicolai's manuscript.

27. See Rosenblum, *Performance Practices in Classic Piano Music*, 144. See also discussion of the vocal/instrumental dichotomy on p. 24.

28. The theoretical possibility that it was Tartini who copied from Leopold Mozart's violin tutor can be disregarded. See Pierluigi Petrobelli, "The School of Tartini in Germany and Its Influence," *Analecta musicologica Int.* 5 (1968): 1–17; Jacobi, preface to Tartini, *Traité des agréments de la musique*, 46.

29. See Bernard Harrison, *Haydn's Keyboard Music; Studies in Performance Practice* (Oxford: Clarendon, 1997) 36–40; Rosenblum, *Performance Practices in Classic Piano Music*, 144–51.

30. Türk, *Klavierschule*, 356; trans. Haggh, 345.

31. C. P. E. Bach, *Versuch über die wahre Art*, 127; trans. Mitchell, 157.

32. Türk, *Klavierschule*, 356; trans. Haggh, 345.

33. The distinction was perhaps not as clear as it might have been in the eighteenth century. Francesco Geminiani confusingly uses the word *staccato* and its symbol (a stroke over the note) to describe both how one shortens the last note of a phrase and in the general expression of a series of short notes appropriate to a piece of a lively character (*The Art of Playing on the Violin* [1751; facsimile ed., London: Oxford University Press, 1951]).

34. Mozart, Piano Trio in C Major, K.548, ed. Wolfgang Plath and Wolfgang Rehm, in *Kammermusik, Neue Ausgabe sämtlicher Werke*, Series VIII, 22/2 (Kassel: Bärenreiter, 1986).

35. Türk, *Klavierschule*, 359; trans. Haggh, 347–48. See also Rosenblum, *Performance Practices in Classic Piano Music*, 150.

36. Koch, *Versuch einer Anleitung* 2:364–65; trans. Baker, 10.

37. Lussy, *Traité de l'expression musicale*, 45. I have not translated the French word *incise*, since we have already become familiar with it through Nancy K. Baker's use of the term to translate Koch's *Einschnitt*, the German equivalent of the comma, which she claims he uses both for the point of division, the incision, and for the section preceding it (*Introductory Essay*, 2n). Glehn has translated Lussy's term as *section* (Glehn, *Musical Expression*, 70).

38. Lussy, *Traité de l'expression musicale*, 31; trans. Glehn, 70.

39. Note that the two-bar slurs beginning in bars 7 and 11 are Lussy's adaptations and do not appear in Mozart's own version as seen in ex. 5.8.

40. Lussy, *Traité de l'expression musicale*, 32–33; trans. Glehn, 72.

41. Ibid., 31; 71.

42. E. W. Wolf, "Anleitung zum guten Vortrag," viii; trans. Hogwood, 148.

43. See Stowell, *Violin Technique and Performance Practice*, 29–30.

44. Mozart, *Violinschule*, 135; trans. Knocker, 123–24. Mozart describes the execution of two-note slurs in a similar manner at the beginning of the same chapter. For a summary of eighteenth-century concepts of the short slur, see Rosenblum, *Performance Practices in Classic Piano Music*, 158–63.

45. E. W. Wolf, "Anleitung zum guten Vortrag," viii; trans. Hogwood, 149.

46. Koch, *Versuch einer Anleitung* 2:364; trans. Baker, 10.

47. Mozart, Piano Sonata in F Major, K.332, ed. Wolfgang Plath and Wolfgang Rehm, in *Klaviermusik, Neue Ausgabe sämtlicher Werke*, Series IX, 25/2 (Kassel: Bärenreiter, 1986).

48. Koch, *Versuch einer Anleitung* 2:411–12, 453; trans. Baker, 34, 55.

49. Türk, *Klavierschule*, 340; trans. adapted from Haggh, 329.

50. Ibid., 340–41; 329–30.

51. Harrison, *Haydn's Keyboard Music*, 39–40.

52. Türk, *Klavierschule*, 340; trans. Haggh, 506.

53. Ibid., 355; 344.

54. Rosenblum, *Performance Practices in Classic Piano Music*, 174.

55. Joseph Joachim to Johannes Brahms, 20 May, 1879, in *Johannes Brahms im Briefwechsel mit Joseph Joachim*, ed. Andreas Moser, 2 vols. (Tutzing: Hans Schneider, 1974), 2:164.

56. Brahms writes "bei uns es viel zu kehren" which probably best translates as, "in our house, there is much to sweep." Here Brahms is also referring to Joachim's earlier discussion of the different methods of notating the *staccato* and *portato* for the violin player. Brahms to Joachim, 30 May, 1879, in *Briefwechsel* 2:168.

57. Joachim to Brahms, 20 May, 1879, in *Briefwechsel* 2:164.

58. See also Mattheson, *Der vollkommene Capellmeister*, 184; trans. Harriss, 384; Simpson [5]; Niedt [8]; Quantz [20]; Mozart [22]; and Hiller [33].

59. Türk, *Klavierschule*, 355; trans. Harriss, 344.

60. François Antoine Habeneck, *Méthode théorique et pratique de violon* (Paris: Canaux, 1840), facsimile ed. in *Violon: Les grandes méthodes romantiques de violon*, vol. 4, ed. Ncolas Fromageot (Courlay: Éditions J. M. Fuzeau, 2001), 115. Antoine Reicha gives a clear definition of what is meant by a figure or *dessin*: "Accordingly, a melodic segment is nothing but a small idea, which must have a pause (which in music is called a cadence) which distinguishes it from the following idea. Such a segment, or melodic idea, we will call a *dessin*." Reicha, *Traité de mélodie* 1:10; trans. Landry, 14.

61. Joseph Hofmann, *Piano Playing with Piano Questions Answered: A Little Book of Direct Answers to Two Hundred and Fifty Questions Asked by Piano Students* (New York: Doubleday, Page & Co., 1909), 98–99 (my emphasis).

62. Riemann and Fuchs, *A Practical Guide to the Art of Phrasing*, 10. In the third edition of his *Musik-Lexikon* (1887), Riemann explains that, unfortunately, the term "phrasing" is often used in the sense of articulation, and that this has been the cause of much misunderstanding (s.v. Phrasierung).

63. Schenker refers the reader to C. P. E. Bach's description of the basic eighteenth-century slur execution, and explains: "The masters know only one type of slur, the legato slur; it indicates that a series of notes are bound together" (Heinrich Schenker, "Abolish the Phrasing Slur," *The Masterwork in Music, Vol. 1 (1925)*, trans. William Drabkin [Cambridge: Cambridge University Press, 1994], 21–22).

64. Joseph Haydn *Zwei Streichquartette, op. 77, 1779*, with remarks by László Somfai (autograph facsimile ed., Budapest: Editio Musica, 1980), 2b (reference refers to original manuscript).

65. Somfai subscribes to this interpretation explaining that, "in his last period Haydn noticeably strives to suggest 'phrasing,' in the nineteenth century sense of the word, here and there at important points, going beyond the elementary bowing instructions (legato slurs, staccatos) which can essentially be called only 'articulation.' . . . This more developed 'phrasing,' in comparison with the traditional 'articulation,' is principally seen in the contrast between bars 3 and 7: in bar 3, the long bow above the staccato strokes does not indicate some sort of portamento (unlike the true staccatos of bar 7) but points to a performance in a long line including staccato and legato over one and a half bars, as opposed to the marcato-style performance of bar 7 which is broken up chord by chord" (remarks to Haydn, *Zwei Streichquartette, op. 77, 1779*, 79–80 [reference refers to facsimile edition]).

66. James Webster makes the point in his article on Haydn's articulation practices, that the importance of articulation in analysis is diminished if it is perceived as supplemental or merely providing clarification (to the performer) of the real substance of music (Webster, "The Triumph of Variability," 62–63).

67. Somfai, in Haydn, *Zwei Streichquartette, op. 77, 1779*, 88.

68. Webster, "The Triumph of Variability," 36–37.

69. Haydn, *Streichquartette "Opus 76," "Opus 77" und "Opus 103,"* ed. Horst Walter, in *Werke*, ed. Joseph Haydn-Institut, Köln, under the direction of George Feder, Series XII, 6 (Munich: G. Henle, 2003).

70. Also known as *Gran Partita*, as it was later called. Wind Serenade in B♭, K.361, in *Neue Ausgabe sämtlicher Werke*, ed. Daniel N. Leeson and Neal Zaslaw, Series VII, 17/2 (1979); see Mozart, *Grande quintetto pour le piano forte, hautbois, violon, viola et violoncelle*, arranged by C. F. G. Schwencke (Hamburg: Jean Auguste Böhm, 18–).

71. While pre-Tourte bows lend themselves easily to lively, detached expressions, they are also capable of producing very sustained sounds with smooth connections between up-bows and down-bows.

72. Joseph Haydn, *30 berühmte Quartette für 2 Violinen, Viola und Violoncello*, ed. Andreas Moser and Hugo Dechert (Frankfurt: C. F. Peters, 1918).

73. Joseph Haydn, *30 Celebrated Quartets for Two Violins, Viola and Cello*, ed. Reinhold Jockisch (New York: International Music Company, 1972).

74. This passage presents some difficulties to the cellist. One would want to arrive (with the other string players) on a down-bow in bar 4, but then one needs to find a way to sneak in an up-bow before bar 5, which also needs to begin with a down-bow. Probably the International Edition's suggestion to place the two eighth notes on the up-bow is a good one. The trick is to do this without creating the sense of a new gesture, but to draw the new bow as part of the impulse and sound created by the B♭ dotted half note.

75. According to James Webster, the label of "Imperial" given to Symphony no. 53 is neither relevant to contemporary programmatic associations nor Haydn's own expressive compositional content (*Haydn's "Farewell" Symphony*, 238).

76. Symphony no. 53 was one of the most frequently arranged of Haydn's symphonies; see Wheelock, *Haydn's Ingenious Gesting with Art: Contexts of Musical Wit and Humor* (New York: Schirmer Books, 1992), 225, 38n. See also Wheelock's discussion of the symphony's circulation in London, particularly the Andante movement as it was arranged for voice and piano and set to a number of different texts ("Marriage à la Mode: Haydn's Instrumental Works 'Englished' for Voice and Piano," *Journal of Musicology* 8 (1990): 362).

77. Cambini, *Nouvelle méthode pour le violon*, 21–22. This reference applies to all quotes from Cambini in the ensuing discussion. Le Guin provides a complete translation alongside the original French for Cambini's analysis of this phrase by Haydn. See http://epub.library.ucla.edu/leguin/boccherini/contents.htm.

78. The expressive indications which Cambini adds to both this example from Haydn and fig. 3.3 from Boccherini are clearly intended for instructive purposes only. A brief examination of his own string writing (from his quartets and concertos) reveals a much more standardized notational practice—far fewer dynamic and bowing indications, and no fingering suggestions that I could find.

79. Haydn, *Sinfonien um 1777–1799*, ed. Sephen C. Fisher and Sonja Gerlach, in *Werke*, Series I, 9 (Munich: G. Henle, 2002).

80. Türk, *Klavierschule*, 357; trans. Haggh, 346.

81. Willner describes three distinct types of hemiola: cadential hemiolas, which do not affect the metrical structure; expansion hemiolas, which allow two bars to occupy the span of one; and contraction hemiolas, which let two bars occupy the span of three. In a follow-up article, he also identifies the frequently occurring overlapping hemiola—two successive two-bar hemiolas that overlap because they are collapsed onto three bars; Channan Willner, "The Two-Length Bar Revisited: Händel and the Hemiola," *Göttinger Händel-Beiträge* 4 (1991): 208–31; and idem, "More on Handel and the Hemiola: Overlapping Hemiolas," *Music Theory Online* 2, no. 3 (March,

1996). This latter article sparked a debate between Willner and David Schulenberg regarding the listener's (or analyst's) ability to perceive such complex hemiola structures. See David Schulenberg, "Commentary on Channan Willner, 'More on Handel and the Hemiola,'" *Music Theory Online* 2, no. 5 (July 1996); and Channan Willner, "Handel, the Sarabande, and Levels of Genre: A Reply to David Schulenberg," *Music Theory Online* 2, no. 7 (Nov., 1996); http://www.societymusictheory.org/.

82. Meredith Little and Natalie Jenne, *Dance and the Music of J. S. Bach* (Bloomington: Indiana University Press, 1991), 75.

83. Tilden A. Russell, "Minuet Form and Phraseology in *Recueils* and Manuscript Tunebooks," *Journal of Musicology* 17 (1999): 406–7.

84. Patricia M. Ranum, "L'hémiole chantée: Quelques réflexions sur les 'réflexions' de Herbert Schneider," *Revue de musicologie* 79 (1993): 229. Herbert Schneider claims in his article that hemiolas were not reserved for cadences but could occur even at the beginning of a dance or chorus and were a recurring feature of the formal structure. The quote from Ranum, above, is her particular response to Schneider's claim that the reason discussion of the hemiola is so absent from the historical treatises is that the device was of such common usage that one had no need to speak of it (Schneider, "Structures métriques du menuet au XVIIe siècle," *Revue de Musicologie* 78 [1992]: 27–65).

85. Ranum, "L'hémiole chantée," abstract.

86. Koch, *Versuch einer Anleitung* 3:22; trans. adapted from Baker, 72.

87. Mozart, *Violinschule*, 44; trans. Knocker, 46. For further discussion of whether or not the second note of a tie should be restruck, see Paul Badura-Skoda, "A Tie is a Tie is a Tie: Reflections on Beethoven's Pairs of Tied Notes," *Early Music* 16, no. 1 (1988): 84–88.

88. Quantz, *Versuch einer Anweisung*, 253; trans. adapted from Reilly, 277.

89. For additional examples of "hemiola bars" from Mattheson, see the minuets from suites 5, 11, and 12 of his *Pieces de clavecin* (1714), and the minuet from Sonata VI for violino or Traverso solo and continuo from *Die brauchbare Virtuoso* (1720).

90. See also the discussion of Ernst Apfel's analysis of Mattheson's minuet, p. 221.

91. Beethoven, *Klaviersonate II*, edited by Hans Schmidt, in *Werke*, edited by Beethoven-Archiv, Bonn, under the direction of Joseph Schmidt-Görg, Series VII, 3 (Munich: G. Henle, 1961).

## Chapter Six

*Epigraph.* Mattheson, *Der vollkommene Capellmeister*, 208; trans. adapted from Harriss, 426.

1. Parkes adds that this might explain why principles advocated in the discussions of punctuation sometimes appear not to correspond with practice (*Pause and Effect*, 4–5).

2. From *Peri Epideiktikon*, which contains two treatises ascribed to Menander, ca. AD late third or early fourth century. Vickers borrows the coinage "taxonomania" from D. Shackleton Bailey (1986) (*In Defense of Rhetoric*, 60–61).

3. Ratner, *Classic Music*, 9–30.

4. Mozart, *Kammermusik*, ed. Wolfgang Plath and Wolfgang Rehm, in *Neue Ausgabe sämtlicher Werke*, Series VIII, 22/2. This description of a gavotte is taken from

Koch's chapter explaining "the connection of melodic sections with regard to their rhythm and punctuation" (*Versuch einer Anleitung* 3:17, 40–43; trans. Baker, 67, 78–80).

5. Koch refers to "the sonata, with its varieties, the duet, trio, and quartet" (ibid. 3:315; 202).

6. Mattheson, *Der vollkommene Capellmeister*, 225; trans., Harriss, 453–54.

7. Ratner, *Classic Music*, 233.

8. Quintilian, *Education of an Orator* 2:225 [9.4.60].

9. Walker, *Elements of Elocution* 1:148.

10. Parkes, *Pause and Effect*, 114.

11. Vickers, *In Defense of Rhetoric*, 80. Kofi Agawu also links the definition of musical topics with the concept of expression. He draws the conclusion that since everything in a composition is assumed to be at least potentially expressive, than any division between structure and expression is at best fragile (*Playing with Signs*, 30).

12. Walker, *Elements of Elocution* 1:177.

13. Quintilian, *Education of an Orator* 2:243 [9.4.138–39].

14. Walker, *Elements of Elocution* 1:142–45.

15. Forkel, *Allgemeine Geschichte der Musik*, 26–27; trans. Powers, 86–27.

16. Georg Simon Löhlein, *Clavier-Schule* (Leipzig, 1765), 187; trans. Dora Jean Wilson as "Georg Simon Löhlein's *Klavierschule*" (PhD diss., University of Southern California, 1979), 395.

17. Mattheson, *Der vollkommene Capellmeister*, 209; trans. Harriss, 427.

18. Ibid., 209; 427–28.

19. Mattheson, *Der vollkommene Capellmeister*, 212; trans. Harriss, 433.

20. Rousseau, *Dictionary of Music*, s.v. "Air."

21. Mattheson, *Der vollkommene Capellmeister*, 212; trans. Harriss, 432. According to the *Oxford English Dictionary*, *aera* is a late Latin term meaning "a number expressed in figures," with an early etymology as the plural of *aes*, or brass (money) (*Oxford English Dictionary* online, s.v. aera, http://dictionary.oed.com/).

22. Charles Masson, *Nouveau traité des règles pour la composition de la musique* (Paris, 1699; facsimile ed., New York: Da Capo, 1967), 27.

23. Mattheson adds that some wind instruments also require special breath control. A trumpeter, for instance, should be given short, somewhat interrupted melodies, whereas an oboe and bassoon can handle longer ones (*Der vollkommene Capellmeister*, 206; trans. Harriss, 422).

24. Hubert Le Blanc, *Defense de la basse de viole contre les entreprises du violon et les prétensions du violoncelle* (Amsterdam: Pierre Mortier, 1740; facsimile ed., Geneva: Minkoff, 1975), 9–10.

25. Little is known about Mr. Michel, who was a violinist of some fame and believed to be either Italian or born in Italy. His eight books of violin sonatas in the French style are contemporaneous with the sonatas of Jean-Baptiste Senaillé (1687–1730) (F.-J. Fétis, "Michel," in *Biographie universelle des musiciens et bibliographie générale de la musique*, 2nd ed. (Paris: Firmin-Didot, 1860–65).

26. Le Blanc, *Defense de la basse de viole*, 15.

27. Mattheson, *Der vollkommene Capellmeister*, 206, 210; Harriss, 422, 428.

28. Löhlein, *Clavier-Schule*, 187; trans. Wilson, 395.

29. Ibid., 100; 343. Fux also states, in 1725, "Recitative style is nothing other than speech expressed by means of music, or, in other words, oratorical speech" (*Gradus ad Parnassum*, 274; trans. in Lester, *Between Modes and Keys*, 204).

30. Garcia, *École de Garcia*, 15; trans. adapted from Paschke, 47. Choron and Lafage begin their 1838 chapter on phrases ("Des Phrases") with the statement that one can compose in both prose and verse. They go on to explain that *recitative* moves without measure, while *air* maintains constant and uniform punctuation formulas placed at equal distances, and especially in opening phrases (Alexandre Choron and Adrien Lafage, *Nouveau manual complet de musique vocale et instrumentale*, 6 vols. in 11 [Paris: Roret, 1836–39], part 2, vol. 3, 133–34).

31. (Unsäglich ist mein Schmerz; unzehlbar meine Plagen; / Die Lufft beseuffzt, daß sie mich hat genehrt; / Die Welt, dieweil sie mich getragen, / Ist bloß darum Verbrennens werth; / Die Sterne werden zu Cometen, / Mich Scheusal der Natur zu tödten;); Mattheson, *Der vollkommene Capellmeister*, 189–90; trans. Harriss, 393–94.

32. Sulzer, *Allgemeine Theorie der schönen Künste*, s.v. "Recitativ," 4:6. Koch quotes the same passage (*Versuch einer Anleitung* 3:236–37; trans. Baker, 167).

33. John Brown, *Letters upon the Poetry and Music of the Italian Opera; Addressed to a Friend* (Edinburgh: Bell and Bradfute, 1789) 7–9.

34. Herbert Seifert sees this same eleven- and seven-syllable pattern in the Piano Sonata, Op. 1, no. 2 by G. Rutini (1748) ("Das Instrumentalrezitativ vom Barock bis zur Wiener Klassik," in *De Ratione in Musica: Festschrift Erich Schenk*, ed. Theophil Antonicek, Rudolf Flotzinger, and Othmar Wessely [Kassel: Bärenreiter, 1975], 114). See also David Charlton, "Instrumental Recitative: A Study in Morphology and Context, 1700–1808," in *Comparative Criticism: A Yearbook*, ed. E. S. Schafer (London: Cambridge University Press, 1982), 151.

35. Special thanks to Giuseppe Gerbino, who patiently explained Italian versification and these verses to me.

36. Mattheson, *Der vollkommene Capellmeister*, 196; trans. adapted from Harriss, 405–6.

37. C. P. E. Bach, *Versuch über die wahre Art*, 314; trans. Mitchell, 421.

38. Mattheson, *Der vollkommene Capellmeister*, 213; trans. Harriss, 435. Vincenzo Manfredini also explains that accompanied recitatives require the actor to execute his part strictly in tempo (*Regole armoniche: O sieno precetti ragionati per apprender la musica* [Venezia: Presso Adolfo Cesare, 1797] 70). Türk argues that passages marked *recitativo* in instrumental compositions "would have a poor effect if they were played strictly according to the specified values of the notes." But the "quickening and hesitating" he advocates to approximate the way an orator would declaim the words should only be used when one is playing alone or with a very attentive accompanist (*Klavierschule*, 371; trans. Haggh, 360).

39. *Grove Music Online*, s.v. "Arioso."

40. Koch, *Versuch einer Anleitung* 3:237–38; trans. Baker, 168.

41. Löhlein, *Clavier-Schule*, 177–78. trans. Wilson, 385–97.

42. Mattheson, *Der vollkommene Capellmeister*, 212; trans. Harriss, 433.

43. Marpurg, *Kritische Briefe* 2:255.

44. Rousseau, *Dictionary of Music*, s.v. "Recitative Measur'd." This issue of whether recitative can adhere to a strict tempo is taken up in discussions by modern scholars on instrumental recitative. David Charlton, for example, explains that in discussing instrumental recitative, one need not limit oneself to the freedom from strict tempo ("Instrumental Recitative," 151).

45. Mattheson, *Der vollkommene Capellmeister*, 212; trans. Harriss, 432–33.

46. Sulzer, *Allgemeine Theorie der schönen Künste*, s.v. "Arioso," 1:214.

47. Koch, *Versuch einer Anleitung*, 3:237; trans. Baker, 168.

48. Marpurg, *Kritische Briefe* 2:398.

49. Quantz, *Versuch einer Anweisung*, 316; trans. Reilly, 329.

50. Charles Henri de Blainville, *L'esprit de l'art musical* (Geneva, 1754; facsimile ed., Geneva: Minkoff, 1974), 52.

51. Rousseau, *Dictionary of Music*, s.v. "Recitative."

52. Ibid. See also Lois Rosow, "French Baroque Recitative as an Expression of Tragic Declamation," *Early Music* 11 (1983): 472.

53. Marpurg, *Kritische Briefe*, 398. According to Joel Lester, although Marpurg considered himself Rameau's publicist in Germany, he seemed to be unfamiliar with much of Rameau's writings (*Compositional Theory in the Eighteenth Century*, 150).

54. *Grove Music Online*, s.v. "Versification" (by Graham Sadler).

55. "In practice, elisions and diphthongs can be handled with some flexibility by the poet, and also by the composer, as required." *Grove Music Online*, s.v. "Versification" (by Tim Carter).

56. Sulzer, *Allgemeine Theorie der schönen Künste*, s.v. "Melodie," 3:378. See also Ratner, "Eighteenth-Century Theories of Musical Period Structure," 440.

57. Also, in expressing his semicolons of despair, each unit (*comma* and *semicolon*) is delineated by visible rests (Mattheson, *Der vollkommene Capellmeister*, 190–91; trans. Harriss, 391–95).

58. "Since the sixteenth century, spoken French has developed a rhythmic character distinct from that of any European language. On the one hand it makes only slight difference between long and short syllables; on the other, it has largely eliminated word-stress in favor of group-stress: a word will normally be accented only if it is the last of a group" (*Grove Music Online*, s.v. "Versification" [by Graham Sadler]).

59. Mattheson, *Der vollkommene Capellmeister*, 213–14; trans. Harriss, 435.

60. Sulzer, *Allgemeine Theorie der schönen Künste*, s.v. "Recitativ," 4:8.

61. As Sandra Rosenblum also explains, in 1988, "Rests are more at home in lines of sharply etched motivic groups and unusually expressive passages, or in music of declamatory recitative-like or arioso styles, than they are in smoothly flowing melodies and serene environments" (*Performance Practices in Classic Piano Music*, 368).

62. Sheridan, *A Course of Lectures on Elocution*, 75–76.

63. Forkel, *Allgemeine Geschichte der Musik*, 44; trans. Powers, 114. See also Vickers, *In Defense of Rhetoric*, 80.

64. Forkel, *Allgemeine Geschichte der Musik*, 44; trans. Powers, 115.

65. Mattheson, *Der vollkommene Capellmeister*, 225–26; trans. Harriss, 453–54. Mattheson is somewhat unique in his depiction of the gavotte affect's intensity. Most others considered the affect to be one of moderate gaiety, avoiding any extremes of emotional expression; see, for example, *Grove Music Online*, s.v. "Gavotte" (by Meredith Ellis Little).

66. Mattheson, *Der vollkommene Capellmeister*, 186–87; trans. Harriss, 388–89.

67. C. P. E. Bach, *Versuch über die wahre Art*, 129; trans. Mitchell, 161. The paragraph that contains the above statement appears only in the 1787 edition of C. P. E. Bach's *Versuch*.

68. Türk, *Klavierschule*, 342; trans. adapted from Haggh, 331.

69. *Grove Music Online*, s.vv. "Affects, theory of the," and "Rhetoric and Music," (by George Buelow). Claude Palisca attributes the new eighteenth-century conception of emotions as fleeting, constantly shifting, and conflicting reactions of the mind and body to internal, external, and imaginary stimuli as the result of the work by psychologists David Hume and David Hartley (*Grove Music Online*, s.v. "Baroque"); See also Rosenblum, *Performance Practices of Classic Piano Music*, 10.

70. E. W. Wolf, "Anleitung zum guten Vortrag," iii; trans. Hogwood, 138.

71. Quantz, *Versuch einer Anweisung*, 107; trans. Reilly, 125.

72. Türk, *Klavierschule*, 370–71; trans. Harriss, 359–60.

73. Niedt, *Musicalischer Handleitung*, Part II, 109; trans. Poulin and Taylor, 148. This is Mattheson's corrected definition for the revised second edition. Niedt originally (1706) defined the term as "very slow" (*gantz langsam*). For further discussion of the term, see *Grove Music Online*, s.v. "Andante" (by David Fallows).

74. Carl Philipp Emanuel Bach, *Sei Sonate per cembalo: che all' Augusta Maestà di Federico II, Ré di Prussia D.D.D.* (Nuremberg, 1742; facsimile ed., New York: Performers' Facsimiles, 1986). Thanks to David Schulenberg for useful discussion concerning this sonata.

75. Haydn, *Sinfonie*, ed. Jürgen Braun and Sonja Gerlach, in *Joseph Haydn Werke*, Series I, 3 (Munich: Henle, 1990; my condensing of score).

76. Sulzer, *Allgemeine Theorie der schönen Künste*, s.v. "Recitativ," 4:9, 18.

77. A number of narratives have been applied to this movement and its paired Adagio in G major (a double concerto for violin and cello with accompanying concertante flutes). James Webster ponders whether we might consider the latter as a pastoral (signified by the prominent flute writing) and the recitative, by way of contrast, as representative of Hades, thus telling a story first of confrontation with death and then salvation. I agree with Webster that more is at stake here than H. C. Robbins Landon's concept of the Recitativo as an operatic parody or David Charlton's suggestion of a domestic quarrel depicted in the spirit of comic irony. The exclamatory gestures above, and the truly anguished sighs and gestures of the movement's concluding solo violin passages, suggest to me a genuine effort to borrow the language of recitative to depict music's most intense and passionate expressions; see Webster, *Haydn's "Farewell" Symphony*, 240–41.

78. Rousseau, *Dictionary of Music*, s.v. "Recitative Confin'd."

79. Gregory Butler discusses the link between the term "fantasia," as a short imagined contrapuntal texture, and stage four, *memoria*, of the rhetorical process ("The Fantasia as Musical Image," *Musical Quarterly* 60 [1974]: 602).

80. Löhlein, *Clavier-Schule*, 187; trans. adapted from Wilson, 395.

81. Ratner, *Classic Music*, 308–14.

82. See Alfred Mann, *The Study of Fugue* (New York: Dover, 1987), 154.

83. Mattheson refers to the importance of meter in determining *affect* (*Der vollkommene Capellmeister*, 387–88; trans. Harriss, 727). Kirnberger also stresses the important role meter plays in a melody's ability to express various emotions and sentiments, indicating as Mattheson does that 3/4 demands a light execution. See his fourth chapter, on tempo, meter and rhythm, in *Die Kunst des reinen Satzes* 2:105–53; trans. Beach and Thym, 375–417. Türk devotes a large part of his chapter "Concerning the Expression of the Prevailing Character" to the prominent role meter plays in determining whether a heavy or light execution is demanded (*Klavierschule*, 360–65; trans. Haggh, 349–53).

84. Mann, *The Study of Fugue*, 56.

85. Mattheson, *Der vollkommene Capellmeister*, 368; trans. Harriss, 695–96. Fux makes the same analogy in 1725: "Fugue takes its name from the words *fugere* and *fugare*—to flee and to pursue—a derivation confirmed by a number of eminent authors" (see Mann, *The Study of Fugue*, 80).

86. Sulzer, *Allgemeine Theorie der schönen Künste*, s.v. "Recitativ," 4:378.

87. Mann, *The Study of Fugue*, 80, 154.

88. Mattheson, *Der vollkommene Capellmeister*, 331; trans. from Gregory Butler "Fugue and Rhetoric," *Journal of Music Theory* 21, vol. 2 (1977): 64.

89. The fugue is described in sources throughout the eighteenth century as a conversation, argument, debate, diatribe, or battle among various voices. *The New Harvard Dictionary of Music*, 1986 ed., s.v. "Fugue" (by Ernest D. May).

90. See also Simon Keefe's discussion of the role of dialogue in the fugue. Keefe, *Mozart's Piano Concertos*, 28–30, 51–52.

91. Mozart, *Quintet mit Bläsern*, ed. Ernst Fritz Schmid, in *Neue Ausgabe sämtlicher Werke*, Series VIII, 19/2 (Kassel: Bärenreiter, 1958).

92. Beethoven, Symphony No. 2, ed. Bathia Churgin, in *Werke*, edited by the Beethoven-Archiv, Bonn under the direction of Joseph Schmidt-Görg, Series I, 1 (Munich: G. Henle, 1961).

93. In early thesis meetings with my committee as a student at Cornell University, Malcolm Bilson brought up the opening of this second symphony, explaining that he always wants the *rest* after the opening two measures to be lengthened before the following dance-like passage begins. He suggested that my topic would be worth pursuing if I could come up with good reasons why one should wait at this point. I hope that I have in fact accomplished this, and as always, I appreciate his ability to suggest what prove to be some of the most interesting and illuminating musical passages to work with.

94. André Grétry, *Mémoires, ou Essais sur la musique*, 3 vols.(Paris, 1789, 1797), 1:313. (The 1797 edition is a reprint of the first edition, 1789, with two additional volumes.)

95. It is not shown in ex. 6.11, but here is a truly compounded phrase, where the end of one segment coincides with the beginning of another (bar 12).

## Chapter Seven

*Epigraph.* Pietro Lichtenthal, "Recitativo," *Dizionario e bibliografia della Musica*, vol. 2 (Milan: A, Fontana, 1836; repr., Bologna: Forni, 1970). Thanks to Emanuele Senici for the above translation, and to Gary Moulsdale for bringing the passage to my attention.

1. Walker, *Elements of Elocution* 1:173–80.

2. Schuback, *Von der musicalischen Declamation*, 31–32.

3. See appendix A, §81.

4. Mattheson, Preface to *Der vollkommene Capellmeister*, 23; trans. Harris, 59. Niedt also explains that recitative is "by the by, a difficult style until one becomes accustomed to setting it properly in accordance with natural speech" (*Musicalischer Handleitung*, Part III, 2nd ed. (Hamburg, 1717; facsimile ed., Buren, Netherlands: Frits Knuf, 1976), 48; trans. Poulin and Taylor, 264–65).

5. Koch, *Versuch einer Anleitung zur Composition* 3:239–40; trans. Baker, 168–69.

6. This is done in a similar spirit to the fictitious cast of characters created and described by Addison and Steele for the London *Spectator* as a means of forming and raising the standard of public opinion in manners, morals, art, and literature. Like the *Critische Musicus an der Spree* (1749–50) and the *Historish-kritische Beiträge zur Aufnahme der Musik* (1754–62), the *Kritische Briefe* was edited and written primarily by Marpurg, himself. In addition to the extensive series of articles or "letters" on recitative, the *Kritische Briefe* contains book and music reviews, translations of foreign

works, articles on theory and aesthetics (including his arguments with Kirnberger about the fugue and with Georg Andreas Sorge regarding the value of Rameau's theories), as well as fifty-nine short compositions by contemporary musicians; see Lester, *Compositional Theory in the Eighteenth Century*, 233–34; and *Grove Music Online*, s.v. "Marpurg, Friedrich Wilhelm" (by Howard Serwer).

7. This Marpurg states in the very first of his letters on recitative (*Kritische Briefe* 2:253).

8. Frederick Neumann notes the lack of eighteenth-century Italian documents on eighteenth-century recitative ("The Appoggiatura in Mozart's Recitative," *Journal of the American Musicological Society* 35 [1982]: 122.

9. Marpurg, *Kritische Briefe* 2:398 (§129).

10. Johann David Heinichen, *Der Generalbass in der Komposition* (Dresden, 1728; facsimile ed., Hildesheim: Georg Olms Verlag, 1969), 674. See Dieter Gutknecht, "Performance Practice of Recitative Secco in the First Half of the Eighteenth Century," *Early Music* 33 (2005): 474.

11. Telemann, "No. 40, Toback," in *Singe-, Spiel- und Generalbass-Übungen* (1733; facsimile ed., Leipzig: Zentralantiquariat der DDR, 1983).

12. Pier Francesco Tosi, *Observations on the Florid Song*, trans. Mr. Galliard and ed. with additional notes by Michael Pilkington (orig. in Italian, 1723; London: Stainer and Bell, 1987), 32.

13. See Heinichen, *Der Generalbass in der Komposition*, 674. Gutknecht adds that Heinichen also considered the use of the correct harmonic resolution in the progression of the final cadence inappropriate, as it would tend to slow down or interrupt the momentum of the dramatic action. ("Performance Practice of Recitative Secco," 475).

14. Fux, *Gradus ad Parnassum*, 276; trans. in Lester, *Between Modes and Keys*, 205–6.

15. Ibid., 207–8. Fux also explains that the period can be made in the same way as the colon if the sentence and the thought are finished but the speech continues with the same subject. Ibid., 278; trans. in Lester, 207–8.

16. Gutknecht, "Performance Practice of Recitative Secco," 473–94. For further discussion of the eighteenth-century recitative cadence, see Winton Dean, "The Performance of Recitative in Late Baroque Opera," *Music and Letters* 58 (1977): 389–402; and Sven Hansell, "The Cadence in 18th-Century Recitative," *Musical Quarterly* 54 (1968): 228–48.

17. Schulz expresses the same opinion, but more strongly. One should not write masculine cadences as in no. 2 of Marpurg's examples of masculine cadences, because "when the grace note is observed in performance, it becomes effectively feminine." Although Schulz admits that even Graun himself has a few times been known to make such errors (Sulzer, *Allgemeine Theorie der schönen Künste*, s.v. "Recitativ," 4:15).

18. Georg Philipp Telemann, *Harmonischer Gottes-Dienst*, vol. 1 (1725; facsimile ed. presented by Susi Möhlmeier and Frédérique Thouvenot, Courlay: Éditions J. M. Fuzeau, 2002), 5.

19. Neumann, "The Appoggiatura in Mozart's Recitative," 118.

20. Sulzer, *Allgemeine Theorie der schönen Künste*, s.v. "Recitativ," 4:8.

21. Ibid. 4:11.

22. Corri, *A Select Collection of the Most Admired Songs* 1:2.

23. Türk, *Klavierschule*, 205–6n; trans. Haggh, 197–98, 467.

24. Mancini, *Pensieri, e riflessioni* practiche, 97–98; trans. Foreman, 36. See also Neumann, "The Appoggiatura in Mozart's Recitative," 122.

25. Manfredini, *Regole armoniche*, 71. See also Neumann, "The Appoggiatura in Mozart's Recitative," 123.

26. Mattheson, *Der vollkommene Capellmeister*, 186–89; trans. Harriss, 388–93. Fux, as we have already observed, details more than one manner of treating the *period*: applying the same formula as the *colon* if the sentence and thought are finished but the speech continues with the same subject, and more conclusive terminations if the thoughts require greater separation. His *colons* exhibit the equivalent of a *quasi-close*, both examples showing a tonic close in the melody, and his *commas* and *semicolons* use both the static note and changing note variety of the *suspended break* (*Gradus ad Parnassum*, 277–78; trans. in Lester, 207–8.)

27. Joel Lester argues that it is Marpurg's ability to separate theory from practice which, as in this case, enables him to appreciate both sides of an issue: Mattheson's that harmony always arises from melody, since in order for harmony to be present there must be at least two melodies, one higher and one lower; and Rameau's that no simple melody can be conceived that does not first have its basis in harmony. According to Lester, such flexibility is what explains the great popularity and influence of Marpurg's practical works (*Compositional Theory in the Eighteenth Century*, 234–35).

28. For a detailed discussion of German usage, see Raymond Haggh, *School of Clavier Playing by Daniel Gottlob Türk*, 504–12.

29. Sulzer, *Allgemeine Theorie der schönen Künste*, s.v. "Recitativ," 4:15.

30. Ibid., 9.

31. Ibid., 18.

32. Mancini also offers his opinion regarding the degree of theatricality deemed appropriate to gesture. He notes that it has been the considered opinion of the "professors" that the chamber recitative is rendered differently from that of the theater and again differently from that of the parlor or church. Although for his part he cannot see that there is any reason why this should be the case (*Pensieri, e riflessioni*, 169–70; trans. Foreman, 61).

33. Ibid., 171–72, trans. Foreman, 62.

34. Sulzer, *Allgemeine Theorie der schönen Künste*, s.v. "Recitativ," 4:9.

35. Mattheson, *Der vollkommene Capellmeister*, 193; trans. Harriss, 399. Schulz also describes this setting where the voice is the fifth instead of the third of the bass. Sulzer, *Allgemeine Theorie der schönen Künste*, s.v. "Recitativ," 4:16.

36. Mattheson, *Der vollkommene Capellmeister*, 193–94; trans. Harriss, 399–401.

37. Ibid., 194–95; trans. Harriss, 401–3. Koch describes a similar concept of parenthesis in the context of purely instrumental music, where incidental melodic sections are interpolated within a larger melodic section. The length of the interpolated material is proportional to the length of the melodic segment or phrase into which it is inserted, serving to enhance the sentiments being expressed. Koch, *Versuch einer Anleitung* 3:228–29; trans. Baker, 160–61.

38. Marpurg, *Kritische Briefe* 2:333.

39. Steele, preface to *Prosodia rationalis*, viii.

40. Georg Philipp Telemann, *Essercizii musici, overo, Dodeci soli et dodeci trii à diversi stromenti* (Hamburg: Presso dell'Autore, 1739–40; facsimile ed., New York: Performers' Facsimiles, 1996).

41. Brian Stewart states that Telemann was the most important composer of German-language opera in the first half of the eighteenth century (*Grove Music Online*, s.v. "Telemann, Georg Philipp" (by Brian Stewart).

42. David Charlton comments on the high incidence of "wordless recitatives" which occur in scores of the highest quality and have been written by Europe's finest composers. He notes that what is remarkable is the very exactitude of the imitation taking place, in spite of the absence of concrete words ("Instrumental Recitative," 150).

43. Georg Philipp Telemann, preface to *Fortsetzung des harmonischen Gottesdienstes*, [Hamburg, 1731–32], ed. and trans. Jeanne Swack (Albany, CA: PRB Productions, 1996), v. Swack explains that the second collection of cantatas in the *Fortsetzung des harmonischen Gottesdienstes* differs from its predecessor, the *Harmonischer Gottes-Dienst* of 1725–26 in three important ways: its scoring requires two obbligato instruments rather than one; the structure of the cantatas is standardized to a pair of arias framing a single recitative (the cantatas in the *Harmonischer Gottes-Dienst* sometimes begin with a recitative); and the cantatas were probably not composed from the start as solo cantatas, but may have been arranged from fully scored cantatas (x).

44. Edward O. D. Downes describes such *ad infinitum* dominant progressions as very common to the eighteenth-century style of *secco* recitative and very well suited to representing the tension and relaxation of speech ("*Secco* Recitative in Early Classical Opera Seria [1720–80]," *Journal of the American Musicological Society* 14 [1961]: 59).

45. Schulz adds that in the keyboard part, *forte* is often indicated by quarter notes and quarter-note pauses, and for *piano*, when the affect becomes soft or sad, longer notes appear with tenuto written over them (Sulzer, *Allgemeine Theorie der schönen Künste*, s.v. "Recitativ," 4:18).

46. C. P. E. Bach, *Versuch über die wahre Art*, 270; trans. Mitchell, 422.

47. David Charlton divides the vocal shapes of recitative into two groups: questioning ones based on the dominant chord and confirmatory ones based on the tonic chord ("Instrumental Recitative," 151–52).

# Chapter Eight

*Epigraph.* Koch, *Versuch einer Anleitung zur Composition* 3:39–40; trans. Baker, 78.

1. Türk, *Klavierschule*, 347; trans. Haggh, 336.

2. Koch, *Versuch einer Anleitung zur Composition* 3:50–51; trans. Baker, 83.

3. Schuback, *Von der musicalischen Declamation*, 31–32.

4. Mattheson, *Der vollkommene Capellmeister*, 209; trans. Harriss, 427.

5. Sulzer, *Allgemeine Theorie der schönen Künste*, s.v. "Vortrag," 1:706.

6. Türk also refers students to Schulz' article on *Vortrag* for more instruction concerning musical punctuation (*Klavierschule*, 347; trans. Haggh, 336).

7. Kirnberger, *Die Kunst des reinen Satzes*, 202; trans. Beach and Thym, 216.

8. Stephen Downes explains that it was in the late eighteenth century, amidst a politically unstable Poland, that the *polonaise* began to assume a heightened emotional quality, eventually becoming a keyboard work for the salon rather than court dancing. *Grove Music Online*, s.v. "Polonaise" (by Steven Downes).

9. Koch, *Versuch einer Anleitung* 3:39–51; trans. Baker, 78–83.

10. Johann Gottfried Walther, *Musicalisches Lexicon* (Leipzig: W. Deer, 1732), s.v. "Allemande."

11. Friedrich Wilhelm Marpurg, *Clavierstücke mit einem practischen Unterricht für Anfänger und Geübter* (Berlin: Haude und Spener, 1762–63), 21–22; see also *Grove Music Online*, s.v. "Allemande" (by Meredith Ellis Little and Suzanne G. Cusick).

12. The origin of the minuet is unknown but records indicate that it was danced in the court of Louis XIV by the 1660s. *Grove Music Online*, s.v. "Minuet" (by Meredith Ellis Little).

13. Ibid. Meredith Little intimates that the many applications of the minuet form (in symphonies and chamber works) never lost their association with the actual practice of dance accompaniment.

14. Johann Philipp Kirnberger, *Der allezeit fertige Polonoisen und Menuettencomponist* (Berlin: G. L. Winter, 1757). See also Christopher Hogwood, "In Defense of the Minuet and Trio," *Early Music* 30 (2002): 239–40; Stephen A. Hedges, "Dice Music in the Eighteenth Century," *Music and Letters* 59 (1978): 181.

15. Hogwood, "In Defence of the Minuet and Trio," 241–43. For more discussion of inventive techniques applied to the minuet, with particular reference to Haydn, see Gretchen Wheelock's chapter "Humorous Manners and the 'Really New Minuet'" in her, *Haydn's Ingenious Jesting with Art*, 55–89.

16. Quoted in Matthew Head, "Like Beauty Spots on the Face of a Man: Gender in Eighteenth-Century North-German Discourse on Genre," *Journal of Musicology*, 13 (1995): 144. Christopher Hogwood also provides a number of similar criticisms leveled at the minuet and its inclusion in both symphonies and chamber works in general ("In Defense of the Minuet and Trio," 237).

17. Mattheson, *Kern melodischer Wißenschafft*, 109; *Der vollkommene Capellmeister*, 224; trans. Harriss, 451.

18. Riepel, *Anfangsgründe zur musicalishen Setzkunst* 1:21; trans. in Knouse, "Joseph Riepel and the Emerging Theory of Form," 51. See also Sisman, "Small and Expanded Forms," 448.

19. Koch, *Versuch einer Anleitung* 3:17–80; trans. Baker, 78–95.

20. Mark Evan Bonds comments that "even though Mattheson, Riepel, and Koch all emphasize the use of small-scale dance forms (especially the minuet) in teaching composition, all three ultimately deprecate the aesthetic value of such forms" (*Wordless Rhetoric*, 50).

21. Mathis Lussy, *Traité de l'expression*, 26–27; trans. von Glehn, 64–65. Ernst Apfel, "Ein Menuett bei Johann Mattheson," *Die Musikforschung* 3 (1976): 296.

22. In addition to the interpretations of Mattheson's minuet by Lussy and Apfel, we will also be referring to the following discussions: *Die Musik in Geschichte und Gegenwart*, 2nd ed. (Kassel; New York: Bärenreiter; Stuttgart: Metzler, 1994–), s.v. Meliodie, section C, Melodielehre (by Carl Dahlhaus); Unger, *Die Beziehungen zwischen Musik und Rhetorik*, 56; and Theodor Wiehmayer, *Musikalische Rhythmik und Metrik* (Magdeburg: Heinrichsofen, 1917), 28–29.

23. In our chapter on recitative, we discussed the German adaptation of an Italian musical form. In this chapter we now work with the German adaptation of a primarily French form.

24. The citations for the minuet compositional models of exx. 8.1–8.4, which we will be referring to repeatedly in this section, are as follows: Mattheson, *Kern melodischer Wißenschafft*, 109–10; idem, *Der vollkommene Capellmeister*, 224–25; trans. adapted from Harriss, 451–53; Riepel, *Anfangsgründe zur musicalischen Setzkunst*, 21–29; trans. adapted from Knouse, "Joseph Riepel and the Emerging Theory of Form," 51–54;

Löhlein, *Clavier-Schule*, 178–81; trans. adapted from Wilson, 380–83; and Koch, *Versuch einer Anleitung* 3:47, 58–60; trans. Baker, 79, 85–87.

25. Here Mattheson is inconsistent. The only way to end up with 48 measures is to repeat both sentences, the first one being then heard four times (AABBAA). But the only way to have nine commas is to play the second sentence only once, and the first sentence still four times (AABAA).

26. Here Löhlein refers to the place marked (***). The use of a different number of asterisks at each caesura carries no information with regard to their respective weights, but is simply like marking them a, b, and c.

27. This minuet is the third movement of a divertimento for two violins, flute, oboe, violoncello, and bass in G Major, H:2/1, composed before 1766.

28. Koch adds that often, in minuets, truly different melodic sections are connected.

29. There is a type of minuet composed of three-bar phrases, often designated *menuet de Poitou*. However many other pieces labeled as such use four-bar or varied constructions. Many, including Mattheson in his *Das neu-eröffnete Orchestre* (1713), claim that the minuet grew out of the *branle* from the French province of Poitou, but there remain a number of questions surrounding this hypothesis and the origin of the minuet is still unknown; see Rebecca Harris-Warrick, "The Phrase Structure of Lully's Dance Music," in *Lully Studies*, ed. John Hajdu Heyer (Cambridge: Cambridge University Press, 2000), 34.

30. This definition of the geometric proportion comes from Alexander Malcolm, *A Treatise of Musick, Speculative, Practical, and Historical* (1721; facsimile ed., New York: Da Capo, 1970), 98–100. See also John Mason, *An Essay on the Power of Numbers* (London, 1749; Facsimile ed., Menton, UK: Scolar Press, 1967), 28, in which he quotes Malcolm.

31. Koch, *Versuch einer Anleitung* 3:53; trans. Baker, 84.

32. Koch, like Marpurg in his essay on the punctuation of recitative, reserves the term, cadence, for only the largest points of division. See the section "So Few Signs, So Many Expressions" in chapter 7.

33. Koch, *Versuch einer Anleitung* 3:57–103; trans. Baker, 85–105.

34. Lussy and Wiehmayer represent the colon in bar 4 in Mattheson's minuet as a semicolon in spite of the fact that the text (which they both quote verbatim) indicates that in the minuet, "not only is there a colon, but also a semicolon." The same error is reiterated by Dalhaus in his *MGG* article and then by Apfel. This may stem from the fact that the first colon in *Kern Melodischer Wißenschafft* (see fig. 8.1) is somewhat smudged and looks like a semicolon. Lussy also places a colon rather than a full stop at the end of the second period.

35. Mattheson's discussions of semicolons and colons all occur within the context of texted music, many of them in terms of recitative. However we assume that the general principles apply here.

36. Mattheson, *Der vollkommene Capellmeister*, 191–92; trans. Harriss, 396–97.

37. Marpurg's chapter on cadences appears only in the French version of *Anleitung zum Clavierspielen* (Friedrich Wilhelm Marpurg, *Principes du clavecin* (Berlin: Haude et Spener, 1756), 45–46; trans. in Elizabeth Loretta Hays, *F. W. Marpurg's Anleitung zum Clavierspielen (Berlin, 1755) and Principes du clavecin (Berlin, 1756): Translation and Commentary* [PhD diss., Stanford University, 1977], chap. VIIIa, 2–6).

38. Both of these steps are described in Pierre Rameau's *Le maître à danser* (1725). See also Little and Jenne, *Dance and the Music of J. S. Bach*, 64–65.

39. Pierre Bonaventure Dupont, *Principes de violon par demandes et par réponce*, 2nd ed. (Paris: Boivin, 1740), 7.

40. *Grove Music Online*, s.v. "Dupont, Pierre" (by Neal Zaslaw).

41. Beekman C. Cannon, *Johann Mattheson: Spectator in Music* (New Haven, CT: Yale University Press, 1947), 23–26. See also *Grove Music Online*, s.v. "Mattheson, Johann" (by George J. Buelow).

42. Dorothea Schröder, "Das Ballett an der Hamburger Gänsemarket-Oper, 1678–1749," in *Tanz und Musik im ausgehenden 17. und im 18. Jahrhundert* (Michaelstein/Blankenburg: Institut für Aufführungspraxis, 1993), 28.

43. Georg Muffat, *Florilegium secundum: Für Streichinstrumen, in Partitur mit unterlegtem Clavierauszug*, ed. Heinrich Rietsch, in *Denkmäler der Tonkunst in Österreich* 4 (Vienna: Artaria, 1894–1895), 44; trans. in David K. Wilson, *Georg Muffat on Performance Practice* (Bloomington: Indiana University Press, 2001), 104.

44. Ibid., 46, 53; trans. adapted from Wilson, 40.

45. Ibid., 47; trans. adapted from Wilson, 41.

46. Ex. 8.6 is my interpretation of Anna Magdelena's manuscript copy. See Johann Sebastian Bach, *Sechs Suite für Violoncello Solo*, in *Neue Ausgabe sämtlicher Werke: Faksimile-Beiband zum kritischen Bericht*, Series VI, 2 (Kassel: Bärenreiter, 1991).

47. Rebecca Harris-Warrick and Carol G. Marsh, *Musical Theatre at the Court of Louis XIV: "Le mariage de la grosse Cathos"* (Cambridge: Cambridge University Press, 1994), 8.

48. Riepel, *Anfangsgründe zur musicalischen Setzkunst* 1:22; trans. Knouse, 51–52.

49. It is not obvious that Mattheson's application of the concept of arithmetic uniformity conforms to the classical mathematical use of the term, which is based, as Alexander Malcolm (1721) explains, on the number of units by which an antecedent value exceeds or comes short of a consequent value. The repeating feet in Mattheson's minuet do not follow as regular an arithmetic pattern as does, for instance, the sequence 4, 8, 12, 16, 20, 24, 28, etc, where the difference between each number is four (*A Treatise of Musick*, 98–100).

50. Koch, *Versuch einer Anleitung* 3:72–73; trans. Baker, 90–91.

51. For discussion of minuet tempo indications, see Rebecca Harris-Warrick, "The Tempo of French Baroque Dances: Evidence from 18th-Century Metronome Devices," *Society of Dance History Scholars* 5 (1982): 14–23; Klaus Miehling, "Die Tempi von Gavotte und Menuett im ausgehenden 17. und im 18. Jahrhundert," in *Tanz und Musik im ausgehenden 17. und im 18. Jahrhundert* (Michaelstein/Blankenburg: Institut für Aufführungspraxis, 1993), 28; idem, "Das Tempo bei Mozart," in *Mozart-Jahrbuch* (Salzburg: Internationalen Mozart-Kongreß, 1991), 625–32; Frederick Neumann, "How Fast Should Classical Minuets Be Played," *Historical Performance* 4, no. 1 (1991): 3–13.

52. Koch, *Versuch einer Anleitung* 3:48; trans. Baker, 79.

53. Judith L. Schwartz and Christena L. Schlundt, *French Court Dance and Dance Music: A Guide to Primary Source Writings, 1643–1789* (Stuyvesant, NY: Pendragon Press, 1987), 87–88, 123.

54. Harris-Warrick, "Lully's Dance Music," 39; note her emphasis on the word *all*.

55. Ibid., 55.

56. Russell, "Minuet Form and Phraseology," 399. I think Russell somewhat overstates his case. Most of the examples he details in his article do observe at least an even number of measures and some of his claims to odd-numbered phrasing and phrase asymmetry are based on what I believe are misinterpretations of hemiolas and

notational devices which appear to isolate individual measures, but which in fact do not. See in particular his examples 8 and 11, pp. 407 and 410.

57. Riepel, *Anfangsgründe zur musicalischen Setzkunst*, 30, 38. See Russell, "Minuet Form and Phraseology," 401; and Hogwood, "In Defense of the Minuet and Trio," 243.

58. The repeats of the 8+8 pattern are not long enough for a complete minuet performance and would have to be combined with at least one other bipartite piece (Little and Jenne, *Dance and the Music of J. S. Bach*, 65; see also Little's article "Minuet" in *Grove Music Online*.

59. Giovanni-Andrea Gallini, *A Treatise on the Art of Dancing* (London, 1762), 176. See Russell, "Minuet Form and Phraseology," 386; and Hogwood, "In Defence of the Minuet and Trio," 247.

60. Harris-Warrick, "Lully's Dance Music," 40-43.

61. Ibid., 55-56.

62. Hogwood, "In Defense of the Minuet and Trio," 240-43.

63. See above, note 21 in this chapter.

64. Apfel, "Ein Menuett bei Johann Mattheson," 299.

65. Little and Jenne, *Dance and the Music of J. S. Bach*, 68.

66. Mattheson, *Der vollkommene Capellmeister*, 165; trans. Harriss, 352.

67. Riepel, *Harmonisches Sylbenmaß* (Regensburg: E. F. Baders, 1752-86; facsimile ed. Vienna, Böhlau Verlag, 1996), 2:7-8.

68. E. W. Wolf, "Anleitung zum guten Vortrag," iv; trans. Hogwood, 139-40. Türk uses the same terminology. See Türk, *Klavierschule*, 92; trans. Haggh, 91.

69. Mattheson, *Der vollkommene Capellmeister*, 165-66; trans. Harriss, 352-53. The trochee, according to Mattheson, is best suited to peasant dances or lullabies and cradle songs, as it possesses something satiric yet rather innocent—nothing of the serious nor mordant. Mattheson also illustrates the dotted quarter-eighth-quarter rhythmic pattern as a variant of the *dactyl*. But this very common foot, suited to both serious and light-hearted melodies, still gives a similar metrical effect, even if not an actual *trochee*. ibid., 165-66; 354-55.

70. Harris-Warrick and Marsh, *Musical Theatre at the Court of Louis XIV*, 53-54, 144-48.

71. Ibid., 111.

72. Cannon, *Johann Mattheson*, 25.

73. Reinhard Keiser, *La forza della virtù* (facsimile ed., New York: Garland, 1986).

74. Ibid., 80; Little and Jenne, *Dance and the Music of J. S. Bach*, 70.

75. Cannon, *Johann Mattheson*, 19.

76. Harris-Warrick and Marsh, although not proposing that Favier's minuet step timings should replace those of Feuillet notation, do suggest that the steps would be applied appropriately in minuets by Lully or other composers whose tunes share Favier's step rhythm (*Musical Theatre at the court of Louis XIV*, 116).

77. Mattheson, *Der vollkommene Capellmeister*, 174-80; trans. Harriss, 369-79.

78. Ibid., 175; trans. Harriss, 370. See also note 22 in this chapter.

79. Wiehmayer, *Musikalische Rhythmik und Metrik*, 28-29.

80. Hugo Riemann, *Musikalische Dynamik und Agogik: Lehrbuch der musikalischen Phrasierung* (Hamburg, 1884). Late nineteenth-century writers like Lussy and Riemann recognized the agogic accent as a key element of expression within the context of the metrical phrase unit; see *Grove Music Online*, s.vv. "Agogic" and "Accentuation," (both by Matthias Thiemel).

81. Apfel proposes that the semicolon could be placed after the first quarter b¹ of bar 13, or less probably the second quarter b¹ of bar 12. (*Ein Minuett bei Johann Mattheson*, 297).

82. The most recent edition of Mattheson's *Der vollkommene Capellmeister* places the semicolon on the bar line, but leaves the third asterisk on beat three of bar 11 as in *Kern Melodischer Wissenschafft* (Johann Mattheson, *Der vollkommene Capellmeister*, ed. Friederike Ramm [Kassel, Basel, London, New York, and Prague: Bärenreiter, 1999], 333).

83. Little and Jenne, *Dance and the Music of J. S. Bach*, 64–65.

84. Mattheson, *Der vollkommene Capellmeister*, 175; trans. Harriss, 370.

85. Koch, *Musikalisches Lexikon*, s.v. "Accent," 51–52; See also Rosenblum, *Performance Practices inlassic Piano Music*, 92.

# Appendix A

1. I have chosen to translate the term Marpurg uses here, *Unterscheidungszeichen* (the signs which differentiate one part from another), as "punctuation." This is both for greater ease and for the reason that Marpurg seems to equate the two. He begins letter CIV (July 31, 1762) with the heading, *Von der grammatischen und rhetorischen Interpunction, oder von den Unterscheidungszeichen einer Rede* (*Kritische Briefe* 2:309).

2. I translate *ordentich* as "regular" since Marpurg seems to use the term in the sense of what regularly or normally (according to the rules) happens. For instance, in §104, he writes that for joyful exclamations, the melody normally (*ordentliche Weise*) leaps upward, but when the affect is sad, it normally (*ordentliche Weise*) leaps downward. And as we observed on p. 190, Marpurg contrasts the more typical or regular (*ordentlich*) grammatical punctuation marks from the exceptional or extraordinary (*außerordentlich*) rhetorical punctuation marks.

3. This category of punctuation formulas is rather obscure. As Marpurg defines it in the context of recitative, it consists of the most incomplete harmonic progressions. But it is difficult to know exactly what is being suspended or left out. Perhaps Marpurg is referring to the suspension of sense at these points, which requires the remainder of the musical *period* in order to become complete. In a letter to me (September 2007), David Beach, acknowledging Marpurg as a great thinker, described his particualar use of the term *schwebenden Absätze* as "downright fuzzy."

4. Marpurg uses the term *Schlußton* (literally "closing tone") instead of the more specific tonic or *Tonika*.

5. I translate *Einschnitt* here as incise, in part for lack of an alternative term, and because the reader has become accustomed to it from Nancy K. Baker's translation of Koch's *Versuch einer Anleitung zur Composition*. My sense is that Marpurg uses the term as a kind of brief pause.

6. By *Secundenaccord*, Marpurg means the chord containing the second and fourth degrees above the written bass, or in modern terminology, a third inversion seventh chord. See the Notes to the Reader.

7. Here a *Sextenaccord* is equivalent to a first inversion triad in modern terminology. An *ellipsis* is a term which describes the omission of a word or words necessary for the complete grammatical construction of a sentence, but which is not required for the understanding of it. Presumably Marpurg means here that if the bass note e is left out, the sense of the full cadence will still be understood.

8. The progressions included in this category of *Quasischlüße* consist of half cadences and deceptive cadences, as well as types of dominant to tonic cadences, where diminished seventh chords are sometimes substituted for the dominant chord and the dominant and tonic chords are often in inversion. Although in a sense these progressions could be called *Cadenzen,* Marpurg chooses not to use this term. I have therefore opted for the more literal translation of "quasi-closes."

9. I use the term full stop here in order to preserve Marpurg's use of the term *period* to describe the rhetorical unit of the sentence.

10. The rhetorical figure *aposiopesis* is the breaking off of a sentence with the sense incomplete.

# Selected Bibliography

The following list is by no means a complete record of all the works that have been consulted in the present very broad historical and interdisciplinary study. The bibliography represents only those writings which I feel have contributed significantly to the formation of my ideas and the substance of this work, and it is intended as a convenience for historians, theorists, and performers who would wish to pursue the subject of eighteenth-century musical punctuation and its philological origins. I originally considered making a distinction between primary and secondary sources, but abandoned the idea since many of them serve double functions: as commentaries on historical punctuation practices, and also as primary sources representing contemporary usage.

Agawu, V. Kofi. *Playing with Signs: A Semiotic Interpretation of Classic Music.* Princeton, NJ: Princeton University Press, 1991.

Alexanian, Diran. *Traité théorique et pratique du violoncelle: Theoretical and Practical Treatise of the Violoncello.* Preface by Pablo Casals; English version by Frederick Fairbanks; description of the violoncello by Caressa et Français. Paris, A. Z. Mathot, 1922.

Allen, W. S. "On Quantity and Quantitative Verse." In *In Honour of Daniel Jones: Papers Contributed on the Occasion of the Eightieth Birthday,* edited by David Ambercrombie, 3–15. London: Longmans, 1964.

Allihn, Ingeborg. "Die *Pièces caractèristiques* des C. P. E. Bach: Ein Modell für Gesprächskultur in der zweiten Hälfte des 18. Jahrhunderts." In *Carl Philipp Emanuel Bach: Musik für Europa,* edited by Hans Günter Ottenberg, 94–107. Frankfurt: Die Konzerthalle, 1998.

Anonymous. *A Treatise of Stops, Points, or Pauses.* London, 1680. Facsimile edition. English Linguistics, 1500–1800: A Collection of Facsimile Reprints. Menston, UK: Scolar Press, 1968.

Apfel, Ernst. "Ein Meneutt bei Johann Mattheson." *Die Musikforschung* 3 (1976): 295–99.

Austin, Gilbert. *Chironomia, or A Treatise on Rhetorical Delivery: Comprehending Many Precepts, both Ancient and Modern, for the Proper Regulation of the Voice, the Countenance, and Gesture.* London, 1806.

Bach, Carl Philipp Emanuel. *Briefe und Dokumente: Kritische Gesamtausgabe.* Edited by Ernst Suchalla. 2 vols. Göttingen: Vandenhoeck & Ruprecht, 1994.

———. *Sei sonate per cembalo: Che all'Augusta Maestà di Federico II, rè di Prussia D.D.D. l'autore.* Nuremberg, 1742. Facsimile edition, New York: Performers' Facsimiles, 1986.

Bach, Carl Philipp Emanuel. *Versuch über die wahre Art, das Clavier zu spielen.* Facsimile of the first edition, Berlin 1753 and 1762. Edited by Lothar Hoffmann-Erbrecht. Leipzig: Breitkopf and Härtel, 1957. Translated and edited by William J. Mitchell as *Essay on the True Art of Playing Keyboard Instruments.* New York: Norton, 1949.

Bach, Johann Sebastian. *Neue Ausgabe sämtlicher Werke.* Kassel: Bärenreiter, 1954–.

———. *Neue Ausgabe sämtlicher Werke: Kritischer Bericht.* Kassel: Bärenreiter, 1955–.

Bacon, Francis. *The Twoo Bookes of Francis Bacon: Of the Proficience and Aduancement of Learning, diuine and humane.* London: Henrie Tomes, 1605. Also available online at http://wwwlib.umi.com/eebo/image/611/.

Badura-Skoda, Paul. "A Tie Is a Tie Is a Tie: Reflections on Beethoven's Pairs of Tied Notes." *Early Music* 16, no. 1 (1988): 83–88.

Baillot, Pierre Marie François de Sales. *L'art du violon: Nouvelle méthode.* Paris: Dépôt central de la musique, 1835. Translated and edited by Louise Goldberg as *The Art of the Violin.* Evanston, IL: Northwestern University Press, 1991.

Baillot, Pierre Marie François de Sales, et al. *Méthode de violoncelle et de basse d'accompagnement.* Paris: Magasin de musique du Conservatoire royal, 1800.

Baker, Nicholson. "The History of Punctuation." In *The Size of Thoughts: Essays and Other Lumber.* New York: Random House, 1996, 70–88.

Barnett, Dene, with Jeanette Massy-Westropp. *The Art of Gesture: The Practices and Principles of 18th Century Acting.* Heidelberg: Carl Winter Universitätsverlag, 1987.

Barth, George. *The Pianist as Orator: Beethoven and the Transformation of Keyboard Style.* Ithaca, NY: Cornell University Press, 1992.

Batteux, Charles. *A Course of the Belles Lettres, or The Principles of Literature: Translated from the French of the Abbot Batteux, . . . By Mr. Miller; In four volumes.* London, 1761; originally published Paris, 1753. http://galenet.galegroup.com/servlet/ECCO.

Bean, Judith Mattson "Conversation as Rhetoric in Margaret Fuller's *Woman in the Nineteenth Century.*" In *In Her Own Voice: Nineteenth-Century American Women Essayists,* edited by Sherry Lee Linkon, 27–40. New York and London: Garland, 1997.

Beer, Johann. *Musikalische Diskurse.* Nürnberg, 1729. Facsimile edition, with an afterword by Heinz Krause-Graumnitz. Leipzig: VEB Deutscher Verlag für Musik, 1982.

Beethoven, Ludwig van. *Werke.* Edited by Beethoven-Archiv, Bonn, under the direction of Joseph Schmidt-Görg. Munich: G. Henle, 1961–.

Beghin, Tom. "Forkel and Haydn: A Rhetorical Framework for the Analysis of Sonata Hob. XVI:42 (D)." DMA thesis, Cornell University, 1996.

Bemetzrieder, Anton. *General Instructions in Music, Containing Precepts and Examples in Every Branch of the Science.* London: printed and sold by the author, 1785.

———. *Traité de musique: Concernant les tons, les harmonies, les accords et le discours musical.* Paris: Chez Onfroy, Libraire . . . , 1776.

Berg, Darrell M. "C. P. E. Bach's Character Pieces and His Friendship Circle." In *C. P. E. Bach Studies,* edited by Stephen L. Clark, 1–32. Oxford: Oxford University Press, 1988.

Berger, Karol. "The First-Movement Punctuation Form in Mozart's Piano Concertos." In *Mozart's Piano Concertos: Text, Context, Interpretation,* edited by Neal Zaslaw, 239–59. Ann Arbor: University of Michigan Press, 1996.

———. "The Form of Chopin's Ballade, Op. 23." *19th-Century Music* 20 (1996): 46–71.

Bernstein, Leonard. *The Unanswered Question: Six Talks at Harvard.* Cambridge, MA: Harvard University Press, 1976.

Bilson, Malcolm. *Knowing the Score.* DVD. Cornell University Press, 2005.

Bizzell, Patricia, and Bruce Herzberg. *The Rhetorical Tradition: Readings from Classical Times to the Present.* 2nd ed. Boston: Bedford/St. Martin's, 2001.

Blainville, Charles Henri de. *L'esprit de l'art musicale, ou, Réflexions sur la musique et ses différentes parties.* Geneva, 1754. Facsimile edition, Geneva: Minkoff, 1974.

———. *Histoire générale, critique et philologique de la musique.* Geneva, 1767. Facsimile edition, Geneva: Minkoff, 1972.

Blair, Hugh, *Lectures on Rhetoric and Belles Lettres, in Three Volumes.* Dublin, 1783. http://galenet.galegroup.com/servelet/ECCO.

Blavet, Michel. *Sonate, Op. 2, no. 2: La Vibray; Pour flûte traversière et basse continue.* Paris: Dumont, 1732. Facsimile edition, Courlay: Éditions J. M. Fuzeau, 1992.

Boccherini, Luigi. *Six string quartets, op. 32 (Gérard 201–206).* Edited by Mark W. Knoll. The Early String Quartet 2. 2 vols. Ann Arbor, MI: Steglein, 2003.

Bolton, Thomas. *A Treatise on Singing, Containing Anatomical Observations by John Hunter on the Management and Delivery of the Voice.* 2nd ed. London, 1812.

Bonds, Mark Evan. *Wordless Rhetoric: Musical Form and the Metaphor of Oration.* Cambridge, MA: Harvard University Press, 1991.

Bouhours, Dominique. *La manière de bien penser dans les ouvrages d'esprit.* Paris, 1687.

Boyden, David D. *The History of Violin Playing from Its Origins to 1761: And Its Relationship to the Violin and Violin Music.* Oxford: Clarendon, 1990.

Brahms, Johannes, and Joseph Joachim. *Johannes Brahms im Briefwechsel mit Joseph Joachim.* Edited by Andreas Moser. 2 vols. Tutzing: Hans Schneider, 1974.

Brainard, Ingrid. "The Speaking Body: Gaspero Angiolini's *Rhétorique Muette* and the *Ballet d'Action* in the Eighteenth Century." In *Critica musica: Essays in Honor of Paul Brainard,* edited by John Knowles, 15–56. Amsterdam: Gordon and Breach, 1999.

Broadhead, Glenn J. "A Bibliography of the Rhetoric of Conversation in England, 1660–1800." *Rhetoric Society Quarterly* 10 (1980): 43–48.

Brown, John. *Letters upon the Poetry and Music of the Italian Opera: Addressed to a Friend.* Edinburgh: Bell and Bradfute, 1789.

Budday, Wolfgang. *Grundlagen musikalischer Formen der Wiener Klassik.* Kassel: Bärenreiter, 1983.

Buffier, Claude. *Grammaire françoise sur un plan nouveau pour en rendre les principes plus clairs & la pratique plus aisée: Contenant divers traités sur la nature de la grammaire en général.* Paris: Nicolas Le Clerc, 1709. Translated as *A French Grammar on a New Plan, Translated into English.* London, 1734. http://galenet.galegroup.com/servlet/ECCO.

Burke, Peter. *The Art of Conversation.* Ithaca, NY: Cornell University Press, 1993.

Burney, Charles. *A General History of Music, from the Earliest Ages to the Present Period: To Which Is Prefixed, A Dissertation on the Music of the Ancients.* 4 vols. London, 1776–89. http://galenet.galegroup.com/servlet/ECCO.

Burney, Fanny. *Evelina, or The History of a Young Lady's Entrance into the World.* 3rd ed. London: T. Lowndes, 1779.

Butler, Charles. *The Principles of Musik in Singing and Setting.* London: John Haviland, 1636. Facsimile edition, New York: Da Capo, 1970.

Butler, Gregory. "The Fantasia as Musical Image." *Musical Quarterly* 60 (1974): 602–15.

———. "Fugue and Rhetoric." *Journal of Music Theory* 21, no. 2 (1977): 49–109.

Butterworth, Trevor. "Two Countries Separated by a Semicolon." *The Financial Times Weekend Edition*, September 17, 2005.

Callcott, John Wall. *A Musical Grammar*. Boston: West & Blake and Manning & Loring, 1810.

Cambini, Giuseppe Maria. *Nouvelle méthode théorique et pratique pour le violon, divisée en 3 parties*. Paris, ca. 1795. Facsimile edition, Geneva: Minkoff, 1972. Translated by Elisabeth Le Guin; http://epub.library.ucla.edu/leguin/boccherini/contents.htm

Campbell, George. *The Philosophy of Rhetoric*. Edited by Lloyd F. Bitzer. Carbondale: Southern Illinois University Press, 1988.

Cannon, Beekman C. *Johann Mattheson: Spectator in Music*. New Haven, CT: Yale University Press, 1947.

Cavalieri, Emilio de'. *Rapresentatione di anima, et di corpo*. Rome, 1600. Facsimile edition, Farnborough, UK: Gregg Press, 1967.

Charlton, David. "Instrumental Recitative: A Study in Morphology and Context, 1700–1808." In *Comparative Criticism: A Yearbook*, edited by E. S. Schafer, 149–68. London: Cambridge University Press, 1982.

Choron, Alexandre and Lafage, J. Adrien. *Nouveau manuel complet de musique vocale et instrumentale, ou, Encyclopédie musicale*. 6 vols. in 11. Paris: Roret, 1836–39.

Citron, Marcia J. *Gender and the Musical Canon*. Cambridge and New York: Cambridge University Press, 1993.

Clark, Jane. "Les Folies françoises." *Early Music* 8, no. 2 (1980): 163–69.

Conley, Thomas M. *Rhetoric in the European Tradition*. Chicago: University of Chicago Press, 1990.

Constable, John. *Reflections upon the Accuracy of Style*. London: Henry Lintot, 1731. http://galenet.galegroup.com/servelet/ECCO.

Cope, Kevin L., ed. *Compendious Conversations: The Method of Dialogue in the Early Enlightenment*. Frankfurt am Main and New York: P. Lang, 1992.

Corri, Domenico. *A Select Collection of the Most Admired Songs, Duets, &c*. 4 vols. *Domenico Corri's Treatises on Singing: A Four-Volume Anthology*. (1779–1795). Edited with introductions by Richard Maunder. New York: Garland, 1993.

Couperin, François. *Quatrième livre de pièces de clavecin*. Paris, 1730. Facsimile edition, New York: Broude Bros., 1973.

———. *Troisième livre de pièces de clavecin*. Paris, 1722. Facsimile edition, Courlay: Éditions J. M. Fuzeau, 1988.

Cram, David. "Seventeenth-Century Punctuation Theory: Butler's Philosophical Analysis and Wilkins' Philosophical Critique." *Folia Linguistica Historica* 8 (1989): 310–11.

Crystal, David. *Language and the Internet*. Cambridge: Cambridge University Press, 2001.

Daube, Johann Friedrich. *Anleitung zur Erfindung der Melodie und ihrer Fortsetzung*. Vienna: Christian Gottlob Täubel, 1797–98.

Dean, Winton. "The Performance of Recitative in Late Baroque Opera." *Music and Letters* 58 (1977): 389–402.

Diderot, Denis, and Jean le Rond d'Alembert. *Encyclopédie, ou Dictionnaire raisonné des sciences, des arts et des métiers, par une société de gens de lettres.* 17 vols. Paris, 1751–57 (vols. 1–7) and 1765 (vols. 8–17). Translated as *The Encyclopedia of Diderot and d'Alembert: A Collaborative Translation Project.* Project directors Dena Goodman, Jennifer Popiel, Brian Skib. http://name.umdl.umich.edu/did2222.0000.362.

Donawerth, Jane. *Rhetorical Theory by Women before 1900: An Anthology.* Lanham, MD: Rowman & Littlefield, 2002.

Donington, Robert. *The Interpretation of Early Music.* New York: St. Martin's Press, 1974.

Downes, Edward O. D. "*Secco* Recitative in Early Classical Opera Seria (1720–80)." *Journal of the American Musicological Society* 14 (1961): 50–69.

Dupont, Pierre Bonaventure. *Principes de violon par demandes et par réponce.* Paris: Boivin, 1740 (original ed. 1718).

Edgeworth, Maria, and Richard Lovell Edgeworth. *Practical Education.* 2 vols. London: J. Johnson, 1798. http://galenet.galegroup.com/servlet/ECCO.

*Encyclopedia of the Enlightenment.* Edited by Alan Charles Kors. New York: Oxford University Press, 2002. Also available through Oxford Reference Online.

Fénelon, François de Salignac de la Mothe. *Dialogues on Eloquence.* Translated by Wilbur Samuel Howell. Princeton, NJ: Princeton University Press, 1951.

Fielding, Henry. "An Essay on Conversation." In *Miscellanies, In Three Volumes.* London, 1743. http://galenet.galegroup.com/servlet/ECCO.

Fischer, Jacob. *Erläuterungen zur Interpunktions-Ausgabe: (Jacob Fischers Neuausgabe klassischer Tonwerke).* Berlin-Lichterfelde: Schlesingerische Buch- & Musikhandlung, 1926.

Forkel, Johann Nikolaus. *Allgemeine Geschichte der Musik.* Vol. 1. Leipzig, 1788. Facsimile edition, Graz: Akademische Druck- u. Verlagsanstalt, 1967. Translation and commentary and glossary of eighteenth-century terms by Doris Bosworth Powers as "Johann Nikolaus Forkel's Philosophy of Music in the Einleitung to Volume One of His *Allgemeine Geschichte der Musik* (1788): A Translation and Commentary with a Glossary of Eighteenth-Century Terms." PhD diss., University of North Carolina at Chapel Hill, 1995.

————. *Musikalische-Kritische Bibliothek.* Facsimile of Gotha edition, 1778–79, Hildesheim: Georg Olms, 1964.

Forschner, Hermann. *Instrumentalmusik Joseph Haydns aus der Sicht Heinrich Christoph Kochs.* Munich: Emil Katzbichler, 1984.

Foster, John. *An Essay on the Different Nature of Accent and Quantity, with Their Use in the Pronunciation of the English, Latin, and Greek Languages; Containing an Account of the Ancient Tones, and a Defence of the Present System of Greek Accentual Marks, against the Objections of Isaac Vossius, Henninius, Sarpedonius, Dr. G. and Others.* Eton, 1762. http://www.galenet.galegroup.com/servlet/ECCO.

Framery, Nicolas Étienne. *Encyclopédie méthodique: Musique.* 2 vols. Paris: chez Panckoucke, 1791–1818.

*Funk and Wagnalls Standard Dictionary.* New York: Harper and Row, 1983.

Fux, Johann Joseph. *Gradus ad Parnassum.* Vienna, 1725. Facsimile edition, New York: Broude, 1966. Translated by Joel Lester in *Between Modes and Keys,* 104–9. New York: Pendragon, 1989.

Gallini, Giovanni-Andrea. *A Treatise on the Art of Dancing.* London, 1762. http://galenet.galegroup.com/servelet/ECCO.

Gerwen, Rob van. "On Exemplary Art as the Symbol of Morality: Making Sense of Kant's Ideal of Beauty." In *Kant und die Berliner Aufklärung: Akten des IX Kant Kongresses,* 5 vols., 3:553–62. Berlin and New York: Walter de Gruyter, 2001.

Garcia, Manuel. *École de Garcia: Traité complet de l'art du chant; en deux parties.* Part 2. Paris: Author, 1847. Facsimile edition, Geneva: Minkoff, 1985. Collation and translation of 1847 and 1872 eds., edited by Donald V. Paschke as *A Complete Treatise on the Art of Singing.* 2 vols. New York: Da Capo, 1972.

Geminiani, Francesco. *The Art of Playing on the Violin.* London, 1751. Facsimile edition, London: Oxford University Press, 1951.

Georgia, Jennifer. "The Joys of Social Intercourse: Men, Women, and Conversation in the Eighteenth Century." In Cope, *Compendious Conversations,* 249–56.

Gigli, Girolamo. *Regole per la Toscana Favella.* Lucca: Salvatore e Giandomenico Marescandoli, 1734.

Girault-Duvivier, Ch. P. *Grammaire des grammaires.* Brussels: Meline, 1851.

Goethe, Johann Wolfgang von. *Briefwechsel zwischen Goethe und Zelter in den Jahren 1799 bis 1832.* Leipzig: P. Reclam, 1902.

Goodman, Dena. "Seriousness of Purpose: Salonnieres, Philosophes, and the Shaping of the Eighteenth-Century Salon." *Proceedings of the Annual Meeting of the Western Society for French History* 15 (1988): 111–21.

Gottsched, Johann Christoph. *Kern der deutschen Sprachkunst aus der ausführlichen Sprachkunst.* Leipzig: Bernhard Christoph Breitkopf, 1754.

Grétry, André. *Mémoires, ou Essais sur la musique.* 3 vols. Paris, 1789, 1797.

*Grove Music Online.* Edited by Laura Macy. http://www.grovemusic.com.

Gunn, John. *Forty Favorite Scotch Airs: Adapted for a Violin, German Flute or Violoncello, with the Phrases Marked and Proper Fingering for the Latter Instrument.* London: Preston, 1795.

———. *The Theory and Practice of Fingering the Violoncello, Containing Rules and Progressive Lessons for Attaining the Knowledge & Command of the Whole Compass of the Instrument.* London, 1793. Photo-reprint of 1793 edition in Charles Douglas Graves. "The Theoretical and Practical Method for Cello by Michel Corrette: Translation, Commmentary, and Comparison with Seven Other Eighteenth-Century Cello Methods." PhD diss., Michigan State University, 1971.

Gurlitt, Wilibald. "Musik und Rhetorik: Hinweise auf ihre geschichtliche Grundlageneinheit." In *Musikgeschichte und Gegenwart,* edited by Hans Heinrich Eggebrecht, 2 vols., 1:62–81. Beihefte zum Archiv für Musikwissenschaft. Wiesbaden: Franz Steiner, 1966.

Gutknecht, Dieter. "Performance Practice of Recitative Secco in the First Half of the Eighteenth Century." *Early Music* 33 (2005): 473–94.

Habeneck, François Antoine. *Méthode théorique et pratique de violon.* Paris: Canaux, 1840. Facsimile edition in *Violon: Les grandes méthodes romantiques de violon,* vol. 4, edited by Nicolas Fromageot. Courlay: Éditions J. M. Fuzeau, 2001.

Händel, G. F. *Elf Sonaten für Flöte und Basso continuo.* Edited by Hans-Peter Schmitz with a new edition by Terence Best. *Hallische Händel-Ausgabe.* Series IV, 3. Kassel: Bärenreiter, 1995.

Hanning, Barbara R. "Conversation and Musical Style in the Late Eighteenth-Century Parisian Salon." *Eighteenth-Century Studies* 22 (1989): 512–28.

Hansell, Sven. "The Cadence in 18th-Century Recitative." *Musical Quarterly* 54 (1968): 228–48.

Harris, Roy. Review of *Pause and Effect*, by M. B. Parkes. *Language Sciences* 16 (1994): 333–35.

Harris-Warrick, Rebecca. "The Phrase Structure of Lully's Dance Music." In *Lully Studies*, edited by John Hajdu Heyer, 32–56. Cambridge: Cambridge University Press, 2000.

———. "The Tempo of French Baroque Dances: Evidence from 18th-Century Metronome Devices." *Society of Dance History Scholars* 5 (1982): 14–23.

Harris-Warrick, Rebecca, and Carol G. Marsh. *Musical Theatre at the Court of Louis XIV: "Le mariage de la grosse Cathos."* Cambridge: Cambridge University Press, 1994.

Harrison, Bernard. *Haydn's Keyboard Music: Studies in Performance Practice.* Oxford: Clarendon, 1997.

Haydn, Joseph. *30 berühmte Quartett für 2 Violinen, Viola und Violoncello.* Edited by Andreas Moser and Hugo Dechert. Frankfurt: C. F. Peters, 1918.

———. *30 Celebrated Quartets for Two Violins, Viola and Cello.* Edited by Reinhold Jockisch. New York: International Music Company, 1972.

———. *Gesammelte Briefe und Aufzeichnungen.* From the collection of H. C. Robbins Landon. Edited by Dénes Bartha. Kassel: Bärenreiter, 1965.

———. *Werke/Joseph Haydn.* Edited by Joseph Haydn-Institut, Köln, under the direction of Georg Feder. Munich: G. Henle, 1958–.

———. *Zwei Streichquartette, op. 77, 1779.* Autograph facsimile with remarks by László Somfai. Budapest: Editio Musica, 1980.

Head, Matthew. "If the Pretty Little Hand Won't Stretch: Music for the Fair Sex in Eighteenth-Century Germany." *Journal of the American Musicological Society* 52 (1999): 203–54.

———. "Like Beauty Spots on the Face of a Man: Gender in Eighteenth-Century North-German Discourse on Genre." *Journal of Musicology* 13 (1995): 143–67.

Heinichen, Johann David. *Der Generalbass in der Komposition.* Dresden, 1728. Facsimile edition, Hildesheim: Georg Olms Verlag, 1969.

Hepokoski, James, and Warren Darcy. "The Medial Caesura and Its Role in the Eighteenth-Century Sonata Exposition." *Music Theory Spectrum* 19 (1997): 115–54.

Hiller, Johann Adam. *Anweisung zum musikalisch-zierlichen Gesange, mit hinlänglichen Exempeln erläutert.* Leipzig, 1780. Facsimile edition, Leipzig: Peters, 1976.

Höchli, Stefan. *Zur Geschichte der Interpunktion im Deutschen: Eine kritische Darstellung der Lehrschriften von der zweiten Hälfte des 15. Jahrhunderts bis zum Ende des 18. Jahrhunderts.* Berlin: de Gruyter, 1981.

Hofmann, Josef. *Piano Questions Answered: A Little Book of Direct Answers to Two Hundred and Fifty Questions Asked by Piano Students.* New York: Doubleday, Page & Co., 1909.

Hogwood, Christopher. "In Defense of the Minuet and Trio." *Early Music* 30 (2002): 236–51.

Honan, Park. "Eighteenth and Nineteenth Century English Punctuation Theory." *English Studies* 41 (1960): 92–102.

Hotteterre, Jacques. *Principes de la flute traversiere ou flute d'Allemagne, de la flute a bec ou flute douce, et du haut-bois.* Paris, 1720 and 1761. Facsimile edition, Geneva: Minkoff, 1973.

Howell, Wilbur Samuel. *Eighteenth-Century British Logic and Rhetoric.* Princeton, NJ: Princeton University Press, 1971.

Hufton, Olwen H. *The Prospect Before Her: A History of Women in Western Europe.* New York: Alfred Knopf, Distributed by Random House, 1996.

Hume, David. *Essays, Moral and Political.* 2 vols. Edinburgh: A. Kincaid, 1742. http://galenet.galegroup.com/servelet/ECCO.

Jones, William. *A Treatise on the Art of Music, in Which the Elements of Harmony and Air Are Practically Considered, and Illustrated by an Hundred and Fifty Examples in Notes, Many of Them Taken from the Best Authors: The Whole Being Intended as a Course of Lectures, Preparatory to the Practice of Thorough-Bass and Musical Composition.* Colchester: W. Keymer, 1784.

Keefe, Simon P. "Koch's Commentary on the Late Eighteenth-Century Concerto: Dialogue, Drama and Solo/Orchestra Relations." *Music and Letters* 79 (1998): 368–85.

———. *Mozart's Piano Concertos: Dramatic Dialogue in the Age of Enlightenment.* Woodbridge, UK, and Rochester, NY: Boydell Press, 2001.

Keiser, Reinhard. *La forza della virtù.* Facsimile edition, New York: Garland, 1986.

Keller, Hermann. *Phrasierung und Artikulation.* Kassel: Bärenreiter, 1955. Translated by Leigh Gerdine as *Phrasing and Articulation: A Contribution to a Rhetoric of Music, with 152 Musical Examples.* London: Barrie and Rockliff, 1966.

Kirkendale, Ursula. "The Source for Bach's *Musical Offering*: The *Institutio gloria* of Quintilian." *Journal of the American Musicological Society* 33 (1980): 88–141.

Kirnberger, Johann Philipp. *Der allezeit fertige Polonoisen und Menuettencomponist.* Berlin: G. L. Winter, 1757.

———. *Die Kunst des reinen Satzes in der Musik.* 2 vols. Berlin and Königsberg, 1776–79. (Vol. 1 first published in 1771 in Berlin by Christian Friedrich Voss.) Facsimile edition, Hildesheim: Georg Olms, 1968. Translation of 1st edition, vols. 1 and 2 (1771–76) by David Beach and Jurgen Thym with an introduction by David Beach as *The Art of Strict Musical Composition,* New Haven, CT: Yale University Press, 1982.

Kitchener, William. *Observations on Vocal Music.* London: Hurst, 1821.

Knigge, Adolf Freiherr von. *Practical Philosophy of Social Life, or The Art of Conversing with Men, in Two Volumes.* London, 1784. http://galenet.galegroup.com/servlet/ECCO.

Knouse, Nola Reed. "Joseph Riepel and the Emerging Theory of Form in the Eighteenth Century." *Current Musicology* 41 (1986): 47–62.

Koch, Heinrich Christoph. *Musikalisches Lexikon, welches die theoretische und praktische Tonkunst, encyclopädisch bearbeitet, alle alten und neuen Kunstwörter erklärt, und die alten und neuen Instrumente beschrieben, enthält.* Frankfurt, 1802. Facsimile edition, Hildesheim: Georg Olms, 1964.

———. *Versuch einer Anleitung zur Composition.* Vols. 2 and 3, 1787–93. Facsimile edition, 3 vols. Hildesheim: Georg Olms, 1969. Translated with an introduction by Nancy K. Baker as *Introductory Essay on Composition: The Mechanical Rules of Melody. Sections 3 and 4.* New Haven, CT: Yale University Press, 1983.

Kors, Alan, ed. *Encyclopedia of the Enlightenment.* 4 vols. Oxford and New York: Oxford University Press, 2002.

Lamy, Bernard. *The Art of Speaking: Written in French by Messieurs du Port Royal; In Pursuance of a Former Treatise, Entitled, The Art of Thinking. Rendered in English.* London: W. Taylor and H. Clements, 1708. http://galenet.galegroup.com/servelet/ECCO.

Le Blanc, Hubert. *Défense de la basse de viole contre les entreprises du violon et les prétensions du violoncelle.* Amsterdam: Pierre Mortier, 1740. Facsimile edition, Geneva: Minkoff, 1975.

Le Faucher, Michel. *The Art of Speaking in Publick, or An Essay on the Action of an Orator, as to His Pronunciation and Gesture.* 2nd ed. London, 1727. http://galenet.galegroup.com/servlet/ECCO.

Le Guin, Elisabeth. *Boccherini's Body: An Essay in Carnal Musicology.* Berkeley: University of California Press, 2006.

———. " 'One Says That One Weeps, but One Does Not Weep': *Sensible,* Grotesque, and Mechanical Embodiments in Boccherini's Chamber Music." *Journal of the American Musicological Society* 55 (2002): 207–54.

Lennard, John. *But I Digress: The Exploitation of Parentheses in English Printed Verse.* Oxford: Clarendon, 1991.

Lester, Joel. *Compositional Theory in the Eighteenth Century.* Cambridge, MA: Harvard University Press, 1992.

Lippman, Edward. *A History of Western Musical Aesthetics.* Lincoln: University of Nebraska Press, 1992.

Little, Meredith Ellis, and Natalie Jenne. *Dance and the Music of J. S. Bach.* Bloomington: Indiana University Press, 1991.

Löhlein, Georg Simon. *Clavier-Schule oder kurze und gründliche Anweisung zur Melodie und Harmonie: Durchgehends mit practischen Beispielen erkläret.* Leipzig: Waisenhaus- und Frommannischen Buchhandlung, 1765. Translated by Dora Jean Wilson as "Georg Simon Löhlein's *Klavierschule.*" PhD diss., University of Southern California, 1979.

Lowth, Robert. *A Short Introduction to English Grammar.* London, 1762. Facsimile edition. English Linguistics, 1500–1800: A Collection of Facsimile Reprints. Menston, UK: Scolar Press, 1967. Also available online at http://www.galenet.galegroup.com/servlet/ECCO.

Lussy, Mathis. *Traité de l'expression musicale: Accents, nuances et mouvements dans la musique vocale et instrumentale.* Paris: Heugel, 1874. At head of title: Médaille de mérite à l'Exposition universelle de Vienne, 1873. Translation of 4th edition (1882) by M. E. von Glehn as *Musical Expression, Accents, Nuances, and Tempo, in Vocal and Instrumental Music.* London: Novello, 1884.

Mace, Thomas. *Musick's Monument.* London, 1676. Facsimile edition, 2 vols., Paris: Éditions du centre national de la recherche scientifique, 1958–66.

Malcolm, Alexander. *A Treatise of Musick, Speculative, Practical, and Historical.* Edinburgh, 1721. Facsimile edition, New York: Da Capo, 1970.

Mancini, Giambattista. *Pensieri, e riflessioni pratiche sopra il canto figurato.* Vienna: Nella stamparia di Ghelen, 1774. The Editions of 1774 and 1777 Compared, Translated and Edited by Edward V. Foreman as *Practical Reflections on Figured Singing.* Minneapolis: Pro Musica Press, 1996.

Manfredini, Vincenzo. *Regole armoniche: O sieno precetti ragionati per apprender la musica* Venezia: Presso Adolfo Cesare, 1797.

Mann, Alfred. *The Study of Fugue.* New York: Dover, 1987.

Marpurg, Friedrich Wilhelm. *Anleitung zur Musik überhaupt und zur Singkunst besonders.* Berlin, 1763. Facsimile edition, Leipzig: Zentralantiquariat der deutschen demokratishen Republik, 1975.

———. *Clavierstücke mit einem practischen Unterricht für Anfänger und Geübter.* 3 vols. Berlin: Haude und Spener, 1762–63.

———. *Kritische Briefe über die Tonkunst.* 3 vols. Berlin: W. F. Birstiel, 1759–64. Facsimile edition, 2 vols., Hildesheim: Georg Olms, 1974.

———. *Principes du clavecin.* Berlin: Haude et Spener, 1756. Facsimile edition, Geneva: Minkoff, 1974. Translated by Elizabeth Loretta Hays as "F. W. Marpurg's *Anleitung zum Clavierspielen* (Berlin, 1755) *and Principes du clavecin* (Berlin, 1756): Translation and Commentary." PhD diss., Stanford University, 1977.

Martinn, Jacob-Joseph-Balthasar. *Méthode élémentaire pour le violon, contenant les principes de la musique, la manière de tenir le violon, toutes les gammes, en 24 leçons, six airs variés et six duos.* Paris: Frey, ca. 1810.

Mason, John. *An Essay on Elocution, or, Pronunciation.* London, 1748. Facsimile edition. English Linguistics, 1500–1800: A Collection of Facsimile Reprints. Menston, UK: Scolar Press, 1968.

———. *An Essay on the Power of Numbers.* London, 1749. Facsimile edition. English Linguistics, 1500–1800: A Collection of Facsimile Reprints. Menston, UK: Scolar Press, 1967.

Masson, Charles. *Nouveau traité des règles pour la composition de la musique.* Paris, 1699. Facsimile edition, New York: Da Capo, 1967.

Mattheson, Johann. *Kern melodischer Wißenschafft.* Hamburg, 1737. Facsimile edition, Hildesheim: Georg Olms, 1976.

———. *Der vollkommene Capellmeister.* Hamburg: Herold, 1739. Facsimile edition, Kassel: Bärenreiter, 1954. Translated by Ernest C. Harriss as *Johann Mattheson's "Der vollkommene Capellmeister": A Revised Translation with Critical Commentary.* Ann Arbor, MI: UMI, 1981.

Meude-Monpas, J. J. O. de. *Dictionnaire de musique: Dans lequel on simplifie les expressions et les définitions mathématiques et physiques qui ont rapport à cet art; Avec des remarques impartiales sur les poëtes lyriques, les versificateurs, les compositeurs, acteurs, executants, etc., etc.* Paris: Knapen, 1787. Facsimile edition, New York: AMS, 1978.

Miehling, Klaus. "Das Tempo bei Mozart." In *Mozart-Jahrbuch.* 625–32. Salzburg: Internationalen Mozart-Kongreß, 1991.

Mizler von Kolof, Lorenz Christoph. *Neu Eröffnete musikalische Bibliothek.* 4 vols. Leipzig, 1739–54. Facsimile edition, 3 vols., Hilversum: Frits Knuf, 1966.

Momigny, Jérôme-Joseph de. *Cours complet d'harmonie et de composition, d'après une théorie nouvelle et générale de la musique: Basée sur des principes incontestables, puisés dans la nature, d'accord avec tous les bons ouvrages—practiques, anciens et modernes, et mis, par leur clarté, à la portée de tout le monde.* 3 vols. in 2. Paris: Momigny, 1803–5.

Monboddo, Lord James Burnet. *Of the Origin and Progress of Language.* Vol. 2. Edinburgh, 1774. http://www.galenet.galegroup.com/servlet/ECCO.

Moore, John Weeks. *Complete Encyclopædia of Music: Elementary, Technical, Historical, Biographical, Vocal, and Instrumental.* Boston: J. P. Jewett, 1854.

More, Hannah. *Essays on Various Subjects, Principally Designed for Young Ladies.* London, 1777. http://galenet.galegroup.com/servlet/ECCO.

Morley, Thomas. *A Plaine and Easie Introduction to Practicall Musicke.* London: P. Short, 1597. Facsimile edition, London: Oxford University Press, 1937.

Morrow, Mary Sue. *German Music Criticism in the Late Eighteenth Century.* Cambridge: Cambridge University Press, 1997.

Mozart, Leopold. *Briefe und Aufzeichnungen, Gesamtausgabe.* Edited by the Internationalen Stiftung Mozarteum, Salzburg. Collected and explained by Wilhelm A. Bauer and Otto Erich Deutsch. 7 vols. Kassel and New York: Bärenreiter, 1962–75.

Mozart, Leopold. *Versuch einer gründlichen Violinschule.* Augsburg, 1756. Facsimile edition, Frankfurt am Main: H. L. Grahl, 1956. Translated by Editha Knocker as *A Treatise on the Fundamental Principles of Violin Playing.* London: Oxford University Press, 1985.

Mozart, Wolfgang Amadeus. *The Letters of Mozart and His Family.* Edited by Emily Anderson. 2nd ed. 2 vols. London: Macmillan, and New York: St. Martin's Press, 1966.

———. *Neue Ausgabe sämtlicher Werke.* Edited by the Internationalen Stiftung Mozarteum Salzburg. Kassel: Bärenreiter, 1955–.

Muffat, Georg. *Florilegium: Für Streichinstrumente, in Partitur mit unterlegtem Clavierauszug.* Edited by Heinrich Rietsch. Denkmäler der Tonkunst in Österreich 4. Vienna: Artaria, 1894–1895. Translated by David K. Wilson as *Georg Muffat on Performance Practice,* Bloomington: Indiana University Press, 2001.

Mylne, Vivienne. "The Punctuation of Dialogue in Eighteenth-Century French and English Fiction." *Library: A Quarterly Journal of Bibliography* 1 (1979): 43–61.

Nehrling, Hans. "Die antiken Versfüße, ihre Problematic und Überliefung bei Johann Mattheson." In *Musik als Text: Bericht über den Internationalen Kongress der Gesellschaft für Musikforschung, Freiburg im Breisgau, 1993,* 2 vols. 2:34–37. Kassel: Bärenreiter, 1998.

Neumann, Frederick. "The Appoggiatura in Mozart's Recitative." *Journal of the American Musicological Society* 35 (1982): 115–37.

———. "How Fast Should Classical Minuets Be Played?" *Historical Performance* 4, no. 1 (1991): 3–13.

*The New Grove Dictionary of Music and Musicians.* 2nd ed. Edited by Stanley Sadie and John Tyrrell. 29 vols. London: Macmillan, 2001.

*The New Princeton Encyclopedia of Poetry and Poetics.* Co-edited by Alex Preminger and T. V. F. Brogan; associate editors Frank J. Warnke, O. B. Hardison, Jr., and Earl Miner. Princeton, NJ: Princeton University Press, 1993. http://lion.chadwyck.com/lion_ref_ref/search.

Niedt, Friederich Erhardt. *Musicalischer Handleitung.* Parts II and III. 2nd ed. Hamburg, 1721 and 1717. Facsimile edition, Buren, Netherlands: Frits Knuf, 1976. Translated by Pamela L. Poulin and Irmgard C. Taylor with an introduction by Pamela Poulin as *The Musical Guide.* Oxford: Clarendon; New York: Oxford University Press, 1989.

Oleskiewicz, Mary. "Quantz and the Flute at Dresden: His Instruments, His Repertory, and Their Significance for the *Versuch* and the Bach Circle." PhD diss., Duke University, 1998.

Ong, Walter J. *Ramus, Method, and the Decay of Dialogue.* Cambridge, MA: Harvard University Press, 1983.

*The Oxford Companion to English Literature.* 5th ed. Edited by Margaret Drabble. Oxford: Oxford University Press, 1985.

Parkes, M. B. *Pause and Effect: An Introduction to the History of Punctuation in the West.* Berkeley: University of California Press, 1993.

Petrobelli, Pierluigi. "The School of Tartini in Germany and Its Influence." *Analecta musicologica Int.* 5 (1968): 1–17.

Quantz, Johann Joachim. *Essai d'une méthode pour apprendre à jouer de la flûte traversière.* Berlin: Chrétien Frédéric Voss, 1752. Facsimile edition, Paris: Aug. Zurfluh, 1975.

————. *Versuch einer anweisung die flöte traversiere zu spielen: Mit verschiedenen, zur beförderung des guten geschmackes in der praktischen musik dienlichen anmerkungen begleitet, und mit exempeln erläutert.* Berlin, J. F. Voss, 1752. Translated by Edward R. Reilly as *On Playing the Flute.* New York: Schirmer, 1985.

Quintilian. *De institutione oratoria.* Translated by Selby Watson as *Institutes of Oratory, or Education of an Orator.* 2 vols. London: H. G. Bohm, 1856. http://honeyl.public.iastate.edu/quintilian/index.html

Raessler, Daniel M. "London's Dancing Dogs, or, the Other Pianoforte School." *Early Keyboard Journal* 13 (1995): 81–105.

Rameau, Jean-Philippe. *Traité de l'harmonie reduite à ses principes naturels.* (Paris, 1722). Translated with an introduction and notes by Philip Gosset as *Treatise on Harmony.* New York: Dover, 1971.

Rameau, Pierre. *Le maître à danser: Qui enseigne la manière de faire tous les différens pas de danse dans toute la régularité de l'art, & de conduire les bras à chaque pas.* Paris: J. Villette, 1725.

Ramus, Petrus. *Arguments in Rhetoric against Quintilian: Translation and Text of Peter Ramus's Rhetoricae distinctiones in Quintilianum (1549).* Translated by Carole Newlands, with an introduction by James J. Murphy. DeKalb: Northern Illinois University Press, 1986.

Ranum, Patricia M. "L'hémiole chantée: Quelques réflexions sur les 'réflexions' de Herbert Schneider," *Revue de musicologie* 79 (1993): 227–62.

Ratner, Leonard. *Classic Music: Expression, Form, and Style.* New York: Schirmer, 1980.

————. "Eighteenth-Century Theories of Musical Period Structure." *Musical Quarterly* 42 (1956): 439–54.

Reicha, Antoine. *Traité de haute composition musicale.* 2 vols. Paris: Zetter & cie., 1824–25.

————. *Traité de mélodie, abstraction faite de ses rapports avec l'harmonie, suivi d'un supplément sur l'art d'accompagner la mélodie par l'harmonie, lorsque la première doit être prédominante le tout appuyé sur les meilleurs modéles mélodiques.* 2 vols. Paris, 1814. Translated by Peter M. Landey as *Treatise on Melody.* Hillsdale, NY: Pendragon Press, 2000.

Rempel, Ursula. "Women and Music: Ornament of the Profession?" In *French Women and the Age of Enlightenment,* edited by Samia I. Spencer, 170–80. Bloomington: Indiana University Press, 1984.

Riemann, Hugo. *Musikalische Dynamik und Agogik: Lehrbuch der musikalischen Phrasirung auf Grund einer Revision der Lehre von der musikalischen Metrikund Rhythmik.* Hamburg: D. Rahter, 1884.

Riemann, Hugo. *Musik-Lexikon: Theorie und Geschichte der Musik, die Tonkünstler alter und neuer Zeit mit Angabe ihrer Werke, nebst einer vollständiger Instrumentenkunde.* Leipzig: Verlag des Bibliographischen Instituts, 1882. Also the following editions: 3rd ed., 1887; 4th ed, 1894; 5th ed., 1900, and 7th ed., 1909, all published in Leipzig by M. Hesse. Translation by J. S. Shedlock as *Dictionary of Music* in several editions from 1893 to 1908, all by Augener in London.

———. *Vademecum der Phrasierung.* Leipzig: Max Hesse, 1900.

Riemann, Hugo, and Carl Fuchs. *A Practical Guide to the Art of Phrasing: An Exposition of the Views Determining the Position of the Phrasing Marks by Means of a Complete Analysis of Classical and Romantic Compositions.* New York: Schirmer, 1890.

Riepel, Joseph. *Anfangsgründe zur musicalishen Setzkunst: Nicht zwar nach alt-mathematischer Einbildungs-Art der Zirkel-Harmonisten, sondern durchgehends mit sichtbaren Exempeln abgefasset.* 5 vols. Regensburg: E. F. Baders, 1752–86. Reprint, Vol. 1 of Riepel, *Sämtliche Schriften zur Musiktheorie*, edited by Thomas Emmerig. 2 vols. Vienna: Böhlau, 1996.

Riggs, Robert. "Mozart's Notation of Staccato Articulation: A New Appraisal." *Journal of Musicology* 15 (1997): 230–77.

Robertson, Joseph. *An Essay on Punctuation.* London, 1785. Facsimile edition. English Linguistics, 1500–1800: A Collection of Facsimile Reprints. Menston, UK: Scolar Press, 1969.

Robinson, Paul A. *Opera, Sex, and Other Vital Matters.* Chicago: University of Chicago Press, 2002.

Rollin, Charles. *The Method of Teaching and Studying the Belles Lettres, or an Introduction to Languages, Poetry, Rhetoric, History, Moral Philosophy, Physicks, &c., Translated from the French, In Four Volumes.* London: A. Bettesworth and C. Hitch, 1734. http://galenet.galegroup.com/servlet/ECCO.

Rosenblum, Sandra. *Performance Practices in Classic Piano Music: Their Principles and Applications.* Bloomington: Indiana University Press, 1988.

Rosow, Lois. "French Baroque Recitative as an Expression of Tragic Declamation." *Early Music* 11 (1983): 468–79.

Rousseau, Jean-Jacques. *Dictionnaire de musique.* 2 vols. Amsterdam, M. M. Rey, 1768. Translated by William Waring as *A Complete Dictionary of Music: Consisting of a Copious Explanation of All Words Necessary to a True Knowledge and Understanding of Music*, 2nd ed. London: J. Murray, 1779; http://galenet.galegroup.com/servlet/ECCO.

———. *Écrits sur la musique.* In *Oeuvres complètes de J. J. Rousseau.* With historical notes by G. Petitain. Paris: Chez Lefèvre, 1859.

Russell, Tilden A. "Minuet Form and Phraseology in *Recueils* and Manuscript Tunebooks." *Journal of Musicology* 17 (1999): 386–419.

Saenger, Paul Henry. *Space between Words: The Origins of Silent Reading.* Stanford, CA: Stanford University Press, 1997.

Saint-Lambert, Michel de. *Les principes du clavecin.* Paris, 1702. Facsimile edition, Geneva: Minkoff, 1974.

Schenker, Heinrich. "Abolish the Phrasing Slur." In *Masterwork in Music.* Vol. 1 (*1925*), edited and translated by William Drabkin, 20–30. Cambridge: Cambridge University Press, 1994.

Schneider, Herbert. "Structures métriques du menuet au XVIIe siècle." *Revue de Musicologie* 78 (1992): 27–65.

Schuback, Jacob. *Von der musicalischen Declamation.* Göttingen: Vandenhoecks Wittwe, 1775.

Schubart, Christian Friedrich Daniel. *Ideen zu einer Ästhetik der Tonkunst.* Edited by Ludwig Schubart. Vienna: J. V. Degen, 1806.

Schulenberg, David. "Commentary on Channan Willner, 'More on Handel and the Hemiola.'" *Music Theory Online* 2, no. 5 (1996). http://www.societymusictheory.org/.

Schütz, Heinrich. *Der Beckersche Psalter.* 1628. Vol. 40 of the *Neue Ausgabe sämtlicher Werke.* Kassel: Bärenreiter, 1988.

Schwartz, Judith L., and Schlundt, Christena L. *French Court Dance and Dance Music: A Guide to Primary Source Writings, 1643–1789.* Stuyvesant, NY: Pendragon Press, 1987.

Scott, John T. *Essay on the Origin of Languages and Writings Related to Music.* Vol. 7 of *The Collected Writings of Rousseau.* Hanover, NH: University Press of New England, 1998. Also available online at http://www.netlibrary.com.

Sechter, Simon. *Die Grundsätze der musikalischen Komposition.* 3 vols. Leipzig: Breitkopf und Härtel, 1853–54. Translated by James Chenevert as "Simon Sechter's *The Principles of Musical Composition*: A Translation of and Commentary on Selected Chapters." PhD diss., University of Wisconsin, Madison, 1989.

Seifert, Herbert. "Das Instrumentalrezitativ vom Barock bis zur Wiener Klassik." In *De Ratione in Musica: Festschrift Erich Schenk*, edited by Theophil Antonicek, Rudolf Flotzinger, and Othmar Wessely, 103–16. Kassel: Bärenreiter, 1975.

Sheridan, Thomas. *A Course of Lectures on Elocution: Together with Two Dissertations on Language; and Some Other Tracts Relative to Those Subjects.* London, 1762. http://galenet.galegroup.com/servlet/ECCO.

Simpson, Christopher. *A Compendium of Practical Musick in Five Parts: Teaching, by a New and Easie Method.* London, 1667.

Sisman, Elaine. "Small and Expanded Forms: Koch's Model and Haydn's Music." *Musical Quarterly* 68 (1982): 444–75.

Spiess, Meinradus. *Tractatus musicus compositorio-practicus.* Augsburg: Lotter, 1745.

Sprat, Thomas. *The History of the Royal-Society of London for the Improving of Natural Knowledge.* London: J. Martyn and J. Allestry, 1667.

Staël-Holstein, Madame the Baroness de. *Germany.* Edited by O. W. Wight. Boston and New York: Houghton, Miflin and Co., 1859. Available online at http://www.hti.umich.edu.

Steele, Joshua. *Prosodia rationalis, or An Essay towards Establishing the Melody and Measure of Speech, to Be Expressed and Perpetuated by Peculiar Symbols.* London, 1775.

Stowell, Robin. *Violin Technique and Performance Practice in the Late Eighteenth and Early Nineteenth Centuries.* Cambridge: Cambridge University Press, 1985.

Strunk, William, Jr., and E. B White. *The Elements of Style.* 3rd ed. New York: Macmillan, 1979.

Sulzer, Johann Georg. *Aesthetics and the Art of Musical Composition in the German Enlightenment: Selected Writings of Johann Georg Sulzer and Heinrich Christoph Koch.* Edited by Nancy Kovaleff Baker and Thomas Christensen. Cambridge and New York: Cambridge University Press, 1995.

———. *Allgemeine Theorie der schönen Künste in einzeln, nach alphabetischer Ordnung der Kunstwörter aufeinanderfolgenden, Artikeln abgehandelt.* Leipzig, 1771–74. 2nd ed., 5 vols. Leipzig, 1792. Facsimile edition, 5 vols., Hildesheim: Georg Olms, 1967–70.

Tartini, Giuseppe. *Traité des agréments de la musique: Abhandlung über die Verzierungen in der Musik. Treatise on Ornaments in Music.* Introduction by Erwin R. Jacobi with a facsimile of the Italian text. Celle: H. Moeck, 1961.

Telemann, Georg Philipp. *Essercizii musici, overo, Dodeci soli et dodeci trii à diversi stromenti.* Hamburg: Presso dell'Autore, 1739–40. Facsimile edition, New York: Performers' Facsimiles, 1996.

———. *Fortsetzung des harmonischen Gottesdienstes: A Series of Sacred Cantatas for Seventy-two Sundays and Holy Days throughout the Year: For One Voice, Two Instruments, and Basso Continuo.* 6 vols. Hamburg, 1731–32. Edited by Jeanne Swack. Albany, CA: PRB Productions, 1996.

———. *Harmonischer Gottes-Dienst.* Vol. 1. 1725. Facsimile edition, presented by Susi Möhlmeier and Frédérique Thouvenot. Courlay: Éditions J. M. Fuzeau, 2002.

———. *Singe-, Spiel- und Generalbaß-Übungen.* Hamburg, 1733. Facsimile edition, Leipzig: Zentralantiquariat der DDR, 1983.

Thom, Eitelfriedrich, and Frieder Zschoch. 1993. *Tanz und Musik im ausgehenden 17. und 18. Jahrhundert: Konferenzbericht der XIX. Wissenschaftlichen Arbeitstagung, Michaelstein, 13. bis 16. Juni 1991.* Michaelstein/Blankenburg: Institut für Aufführungspraxis, 1993.

Toft, Robert. "Action and Singing in Late 18th- and Early 19th-Century England." *Performance Practice Review* 9 (1996): 146–62.

———. "The Expressive Pause: Punctuation, Rests, and Breathing in England 1770–1850." *Performance Practice Review* 7 (1994): 199–232.

———. *Heart to Heart: Expressive Singing in England, 1780–1830.* Oxford and New York: Oxford University Press, 2000.

Tosi, Pier Francesco. *Observations on the Florid Song.* 1723. Translated by Mr. Galliard and edited with additional notes by Michael Pilkington. London: Stainer and Bell, 1987.

Treitler, Leo. "The Beginnings of Music-Writing in the West: Historical and Semiotic Aspects." *Language and Communication* 9 (1989): 193–211.

Truss, Lynne. *Eats, Shoots and Leaves: The Zero Tolerance Approach to Punctuation.* London: Profile Books, 2003.

Türk, Daniel Gottlob. *Klavierschule, oder Anweisung zum Klavierspielen für Lehrer und Lernende.* Leipzig and Halle, 1789. Facsimile edition, Kassel: Bärenreiter, 1962. Translated with an introduction by Raymond H. Haggh as *School of Clavier Playing by Donald Gottlob Türk.* Lincoln: University of Nebraska Press, 1982.

Unger, Hans-Heinrich. *Die Beziehungen zwischen Music und Rhetorik im 16.–18. Jahrhundert.* Hildesheim: Georg Olms, 1969.

Varloot, Jean. "Diderot du dialogue à la dramaturgie: L'invention de la ponctuation au XVIIIe siècle." *Langue française* 45 (1980): 41–49.

Vial, Stephanie D. "Take Pause: Musical Punctuation in the Eighteenth Century." DMA thesis, Cornell University, 2000.

Vickers, Brian. "Figures of Rhetoric/Figures of Music?" *Rhetorica* 2 (1984): 1–44.

———. *In Defense of Rhetoric.* Oxford: Clarendon, 1988.

———. Review of *The Pianist as Orator: Beethoven and the Transformation of Keyboard Style,* by George Barth. *Rhetorica* 13 (1995): 98–101.

Walker, John. *The Academic Speaker; or, A Selection of Parliamentary Debates, Orations, Odes, Scenes, and Speeches, from the Best Writers.* Dublin, 1796. http://galenet.galegroup.com/servlet/ECCO.

———. *Elements of Elocution.* 2 vols. London, 1781. Facsimile edition. English Linguistics, 1500–1800: A Collection of Facsimile Reprints. Menston, UK: Scolar Press, 1969. http://galenet.galegroup.com/servlet/ECCO.

———. *The Melody of Speaking Delineated; or, Elocution Taught Like Music, by Visible Sings.* London, 1787. http://galenet.galegroup.com/servelet/ECCO.

———. *A Rhetorical Grammar, or Course of Lessons in Elocution.* London, 1785. Facsimile edition. English Linguistics, 1500–1800: A Collection of Facsimile Reprints. Menston, UK: Scolar Press, 1971. http://galenet.galegroup.com/servlet/ECCO. Walther, Johann Gottfried. *Musikalisches Lexikon.* Leipzig: W. Deer, 1732.

Watt, Thomas. *Grammar Made Easy.* Edinburgh, 1704. Facsimile edition. English Linguistics, 1500–1800: A Collection of Facsimile Reprints. Menston, UK: Scolar Press, 1972.

Webster, James. *Haydn's "Farewell" Symphony and the Idea of Classical Style: Through-Composition and Cyclic Integration in His Instrumental Music.* Cambridge and New York: Cambridge University Press, 1991.

———. "The Triumph of Variability: Haydn's Articulation Markings in the Autograph of Sonata No. 49 in E flat." In *Haydn, Mozart, and Beethoven: Studies in the Music of the Classical Period,* edited by Sieghard Brandenburg, 33–64. Oxford: Clarendon, 1998.

Webster, Noah. *A Philosophical and Practical Grammar of the English Language.* New Haven, CT: Oliver Steele, 1807.

Westphal, Rudolph. *Allgemeine Theorie der musicalischen Rhythmik seit J. S. Bach.* Leipzig: Breitkopf and Härtel, 1880.

Wheelock, Gretchen. *Haydn's Ingenious Jesting with Art: Contexts of Musical Wit and Humor.* New York: Schirmer Books; Toronto: Maxwell Macmillan Canada; New York: Maxwell Macmillan International, 1992.

———. "Marriage à la Mode: Haydn's Instrumental Works 'Englished' for Voice and Piano." *Journal of Musicology* 8 (1990): 357–97.

Wiedeburg, Michael Johann Friedrich. *Der sich selbst informirende Clavierspieler.* 3 vols. Halle and Leipzig: Verlag der Buchhandlung des Waisenhauses, 1765–75.

Wiehmayer, Theodor. *Musikalische Rhythmik und Metrik.* Magdeburg: Heinrichsofen, 1917.

———. *Neue instructive Ausgabe.* [New Instructive Editions of Works by Bach, Haydn, Mozart, Beethoven, Clementi, Schumann, Schubert and Others.] Magdeburg, Germany: Heinrichshofen's Verlag: ca. 1910–31.

Will, Richard. "When God Met the Sinner, and Other Dramatic Confrontations in Eighteenth-Century Instrumental Music," *Music and Letters* 78 (1997): 175–209.

Willner, Channan. "The Two-Length Bar Revisited: Händel and the Hemiola." *Göttinger Händel-Beiträge* 4 (1991): 208–31.

Wolf, Ernst Wilhelm. "Vorbericht als eine Anleitung zum guten Vortrag beim Clavierspielen." Preface to *Eine Sonatine, Vier affectvolle Sonaten und ein dreyzehnmal variirtes Thema.* Leipzig: Breitkopf, 1785; photo-facsimile included in master's thesis by Ellen Singleton Ligon, Cornell University, 1969. Translated by Christopher Hogwood as "A Supplement to C. P. E. Bach's *Versuch*: E. W. Wolf's *Anleitung* of 1785." In *C. P. E. Bach Studies*, edited by Stephen L. Clark, 133–57. Oxford: Clarendon Press; New York: Oxford University Press, 1988.

Wolf, Georg Friedrich. *Kurzgefasstes musikalishes Lexicon.* 2nd ed. Halle: J. C. Hendel, 1792.

Wolff, Christoph. "Defining Genius: Early Reflections of J. S. Bach's Self-Image." *Proceedings of the American Philosophical Society* 145 (2001): 474–81.

Zarlino, Gioseffo. *Le istitutioni harmoniche.* Venice, 1558. Facsimile edition, New York: Broude, 1965. Part III translated by Guy A. Marco and Claude V. Palisca as *The Art of Counterpoint.* New Haven, CT: Yale University Press, 1968.

# Index

Page references in italics refer to illustrations

accents (language): in classical rhetoric,
77; grammatical/rhetorical rules of,
110; in verse, 154
accents, musical, 76; agogic, 228, 322n80;
external, 110, 303n51; grammatical,
229; in minuets, 228; rhetorical, 229;
types of, 72; written, 140
acting manuals, eighteenth-century, 47
adagio style: affect of, 156; *versus* allegro,
125; slurs in, 130
*aera* (money), 157, 311n21
affect, musical: of arioso, 161; Baroque,
167; cheerful, 166; and composition
type, 167; despair, 158–59; of fantasias,
169; gesture in, 231; implicit
conventions in, 186–87; intense, 166; of
Mattheson's minuet, 207; in Mozart,
175; in musical punctuation, 107, 148,
150–76; in prose and verse, 167; of
recitative, 180, 197–98; serious, 166; in
slurs, 140; of sonatas, 167–68; in
Telemann, 197, 199
Agawu, Kofi: on musical semiotics, 14, 26;
on topics, 311n11
Albrechtsberger, Johann Georg, 219
Alexanian, Diran, 123
Algarotti, Francesco, 117
allegro style, *versus* adagio, 125
allemandes, 204–5
Allen, W. S., 296n71
Allihn, Ingeborg, 297n85
Anderson, Emily, 299n124
Angiolini, Gasparo, 67
antiquity: punctuation in, 34–36, 45,
285n17; reading in, 35, 36; word
separation in, 35–36, 285n20
Apfel, Ernst: on Mattheson's minuet, 206,
221–22, 228, 323n81

aposiopesis (rhetoric), 253, 324n10
appoggiatura: overuse of, 187; in
recitative, 186, 198; in vocal music, 185
arias: and dance melodies, 157; etymology
of, 157; parentheses in, 195; and
recitative, 162
arioso style, 180; affect of, 161; cadences
in, 233; in fantasias, 169;
masculine/feminine endings in, 234;
obbligato, 161; pauses in, 253; rests in,
313n61
arrangement (rhetoric), 33, 39, 40
articulation (language): anatomical usage
of, 122, 304n8; seventeenth-century,
305n11
articulation, musical: in bowing, 122–23,
305nn13–15; connective, 144;
definitions of, 121; and *détaché*, 123;
etymology of, 122; expressive function
of, 144, 148, 149; of figures, 135; five
perfect, 106, *106*; German, 306n20;
Haydn's, *136*, 136–41, *141*,
308nn65–66, 309n77; of instrumental
music, 123; legato as, 124; Leopold
Mozart on, 125, 126; modern function
of, 149; nineteenth-century, 306n19; of
periods, *136*, 136–39; of phrases, 121,
148, 308n62; *versus* punctuation,
121–49; rests in, 125; signs of, 123;
*silence d'*, 132, 134; slurs and, 121–24,
128–41, 147; staccato as, 124; in
stringed instruments, 121; symbols as,
123, 149; variants in, 149; vocal, 123
*articulus* (rhetoric), 305n11, 305n14
artifice, musical, 61
asterisks, in minuets, 227, 228, 320n26
Auenbrugger, Marianna and Katherina,
88

Humanists: on rhetoric, 38–39; use of punctuation, 39
Hume, David, 313n69; on women's conversation, 55
hypermeter, 302n46

iambs, 74, 76; in caesuras, 249; in minuets, 223, 223–24, 225, 226, 227, 228
incises, musical: incomplete, 111, 130; Mozart's use of, 128, 128, 130–31, 152; in recitative, 183, 236–37, 245, 254–55; and rests, 127–28
instrumental music: articulation of, 123; dialogue in, 82–83; eighteenth-century attitudes toward, 25; expressive aspects of, 25; extramusical associations of, 25, 283n31; geometric progression of, 156; linguistic analogies for, 14, 26; melody in, 204; parentheses in, 317n37; prose and verse structures of, 157; recitative, 181, 196–202, 318n42; relationship to vocal music, 25; semantic capabilities of, 87; topics of, 176; variety in eighteenth century, 26
Internet, punctuation use on, 6, 9, 58
interpuncts, Latin, 35, 36
invention (rhetoric), 33, 39, 40, 287n67

Jacobi, Erwin R., 306n26
Jenne, Natalie, 144, 147, 229
Joachim, Joseph, 133–34, 139
Jones, William: on musical dialogue, 83–86

Kant, Immanuel: on genius, 291n2
Keefe, Simon, 82, 83
Keiser, Reinhard: La forza della virtù minuet, 226, 226
Keller, Hermann, 301n12; on articulation, 124, 137; on fermata, 115; on rests, 100–101, 105, 106; on symbols, 117
keyboard music: customary touch in, 126, 126; gestures in, 68, 69; phrase divisions in, 113, 113, 151; slurs in, 139
Kirnberger, Johann Philipp, 297n84; on cadence, 90, 302n43; on fugues, 316n6; on harmonic progression, 107; on meter, 314n83; on minuets, 205–6. Works: Der allezeit fertige Polonoisen- und Menuettencomponist, 205; Die Kunst des reinen Satzes in der Musik, 28, 283n42
Kitchiner, William M. D., 104
Knigge, Adolf: Über den Umgang mit Menschen, 52; on women's

conversation, 55–56
knowledge: communication of, 42; production of, 33
Koch, Heinrich Christoph: on caesura, 131; on commas, 307n33; on concertos, 83; on declamation, 180; on gavottes, 310n4; on genius, 60, 291n2, 292n3; on incises, 111; incomplete phrases of, 98, 300n2; linguistic analogies of, 15–18, 27–28, 283n39; on melody, 107; on meter, 24, 72, 74, 145, 225; on minuets, 206, 207, 210–14, 211, 218, 219, 229; on monologue, 81; on musical dialogue, 82; and notation improvement, 301n16; on parentheses, 317n37; on pauses, 60, 61, 65; on phrases, 21–22, 99, 131; phrasing symbols of, 114; on portrayal of emotion, 167; on punctuation, 93, 102, 203, 301n4; on recitative, 180; on rests, 98–100, 102, 107, 127; on rhythm, 74, 124; on semicolons, 213; on sonatas, 311n5; on subject and predicate, 17, 112, 303n48; use of signs, 114, 228; Versuch einer Anleitung zur Composition, 16–18, 17, 60, 91, 98, 206, 210–14, 301n4, 323n5
Krohn, Caspal Daniel: Kleine Sonaten, 87
Kuhnau, Johann: Biblical Sonatas, 25
Kusser, Johann Sigismund, 216

Lafage, Adrien, 312n30
Lamy, Bernard: Art de parler, 43
Landon, H. C. Robbins, 314n77
language: deep structure of, 26; flexibility of, 155; musical concepts in, 15, 282n14; music notation and, 101; performed, 47; role in knowledge production, 33; Scholastics' concept of, 39; of science, 40–43; scientific study of, 73; sociopolitical factors in, 43–44; verse-like structures of, 23
language-music analogies: Grétry's, 9; Koch's, 15–18, 27–28, 283n39; Leopold Mozart's, 13, 14; for melody, 14; for meter, 23; for punctuation, 9–10, 13–31, 32, 60, 89, 90, 92, 171, 180–81, 227; for rests, 60, 90; for rhythm, 23
Latin language, metrical patterns of, 77
Le Blanc, Hubert, 157–58
Le Faucher, Michel: The Art of Speaking in Publick, 47

Handel's use of, 21, 23; in harmonic
progressions, 107; in Mozart, 21, 22; in
phrases, 98–100, 131; in recitative, 163,
165, 182–83; suppression of, 118, 118;
vocal, 104; voice in, 231; written and
unwritten, 7–8
Peacham, Henry, 305n11
performance, communication in, 231
*Peri Epideiktikon*, 310n2
periodicity, musical, 72–73, 92, 111, 180
periods (language): Cicero's use of, 35;
duration of, 46; of gesture, 48; musical
equivalent of, 102; Quintilian on,
34–35, 36, 37, 40, 71
periods, musical: articulation of, *136*,
136–39; cadence of, 184, *184;* in dance
form, 73; in dialogue, 79; of gesture,
48, 67–68; interior divisions of, xvi; in
melody, 180; in minuets, 211–14, 219,
227; Mozart's, *153;* punctuation of, 65,
134; in recitative, 182, 183–85, 189–90,
193, 199, 316n15, 317n26; sense units
in, 102; Telemann's, 199, 200–201
persuasion, in rhetoric, 40
*petit maîtres* (fops), 63, 292n14
Petrobelli, Pierluigi, 306n26
Pfannenberg, Johann Gottfried, 49
Philidor, André, *l'aîné: Le mariage de la
grosse Cathos*, 225, 226
philosophy: Cartesian, 41–42; in musical
dialogue, 82; Natural, 43
phrase divisions, musical: in dance music,
204; in keyboard music, 113, *113*, 151;
of minuets, 145; punctuation of, 93, 97,
98–120; slurs as, 116; symbols for,
112–17
phrases, musical: accents in, 112;
articulation of, 121, 148, 308n62;
beginnings of, 93, 112, *112*, 303n51;
binding of notes across, 147; caesuras
in, 131; completeness of, 21–22;
execution of, 91–92, 93, 300n131,
308n62; formation of, 97; Haydn's,
308n65; incommunicable aspects of,
304n68; incomplete, *98;* length of,
283n41; meter and, 92; pauses in,
98–100, 131; prose and verse, 312n30;
punctuation in, 93, 97, 98–120; rests in,
64, *64*, 97; space between, 141;
staccato, 307n33; strong and weak beats
in, 110–11; subject and predicate in,
*16*, 16–17, 21, 99, *99*, 112, 303n48;
torn, 111, *111;* upbeat formations of,

118; without rests, 65, *65*
Piani, Giovanni Antonio: articulation of,
122
pianos, changes in, 91. *See also* keyboard
music
Pinsky, Robert, 1
Plato, dialogues of, 289n106
Pledge of Allegiance, 4; authorship of,
279n12; during Civil Rights Movement,
2; gestures accompanying, 4, 5, 48,
280n19; modifications to, 2–3, 5;
pauses in, 1–3, 7, 8; political aspects of,
2, 3–4; punctuation of, 2, 4, 5, 37, 39,
97; rhetorical structure of, 4
poetry, and melody, 157
pointing theory. *See* punctuation
*polonaise*, 204, 318n8
Port-Royalists, French, 42, 43
printing, impact on punctuation, 3, 38–40
pronunciation (rhetoric), 287n67
prose (language): harmonious, 155–56,
157; structures of, 154, 155; subject
matter of, 179
prose, musical, 157–58; harmonic, 201;
recitative as, 158; rests in, 175; speech
in, 179; subject matter of, 179; verse
properties of, 202
prose and verse, 158, 160
prose and verse (language), 154, 155–56,
159
prose and verse, musical, 156, 159, 180;
affect in, 167; composing in, 312n30; in
instrumental music, 157; in vocal music,
157
prosody: ancient and modern, 76;
application to music, 78; eighteenth-
century concepts of, 78
psychology, behavioral, 41
punctuation (language): and accentuation,
90; in antiquity, 34–36, 45, 285n17;
Carolingian, 115; Cicero's use of, 35;
correctness in, 56–59; declamatory, 3;
development of, 98; Diderot on, 45,
289n110; eighteenth-century, 5–6, 61,
285n25; in eighteenth-century novels,
53; in eighteenth-century rhetoric, 27; in
electronic communication, 6, 9, 58; in
Elocution, 45, 46–47, 98; flexibility in,
57–58; German, 27; grammatical aspects
of, 5, 36–37, 71, 187, 291n142;
handbooks on, 28; historical discussions
of, 2; Humanists' use of, 39; impact of
printing on, 3, 38–40; imperfection of,

# Eastman Studies in Music